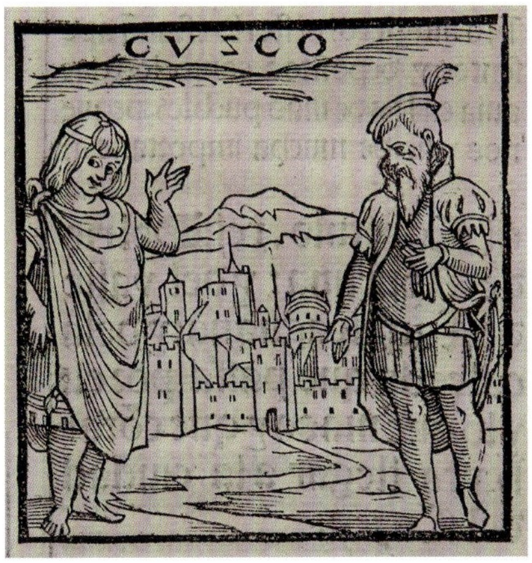
CVZCO

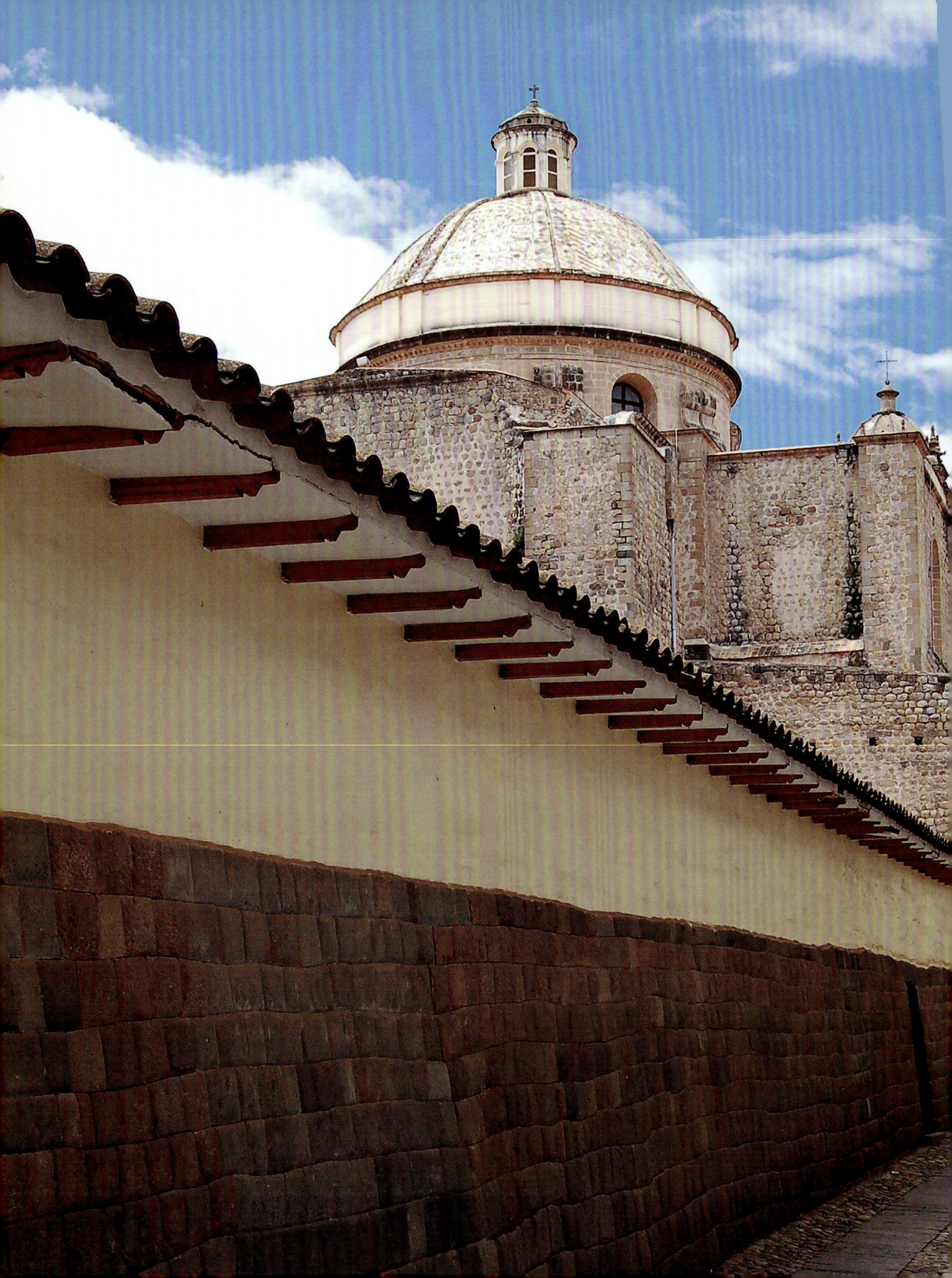

CUZCO

Incas, Spaniards, and the Making of a Colonial City

Michael J. Schreffler

Yale University Press
New Haven and London

First published by Yale University Press 2020
302 Temple Street, P. O. Box 209040, New Haven CT 06520-9040
47 Bedford Square, London WC1B 3DP
yalebooks.com | yalebooks.co.uk

ISBN 978-0-300-21811-4 HB
Library of Congress Control Number: 2020931944
10 9 8 7 6 5 4 3 2 1
2024 2023 2022 2021 2020

Designed by Catherine Bankhurst
Printed in China

Front cover: Artist unknown, *Cuzco during the Earthquake of 1650*, after 1650. Oil on canvas, 33.4 × 46.2 cm. Church of El Triunfo, Cuzco. Photograph by Raúl Montero Quispe.

Back cover: Calle Loreto, Cuzco. Photograph by Andy Krakovski.

Half-title page: Woodcut image of Cuzco, in Pedro de Cieza de León, *Parte primera de la Crónica del Perú* (Seville: Martín de Montesdoca, 1553), fol. 107v. Woodcut, ink on paper. Newberry Library, Chicago.

Frontispiece: Calle Loreto, Cuzco. Photograph by Jesús Escobar.

Bibliography: Coat of arms of Diego Rodríguez de Figueroa, 1540. Ink and pigment on paper. Archivo General de Indias, Seville.

Published with the support of The Institute for Scholarship in the Liberal Arts, College of Arts and Letters, University of Notre Dame.

FSC www.fsc.org MIX Paper from responsible sources FSC® C008047

Contents

Acknowledgments

Many generous institutions, colleagues, and friends have supported my work on this project. Funding for travel, research, and writing was provided by an Ailsa Mellon Bruce Fellowship at the Center for Advanced Study in the Visual Arts, National Gallery of Art, Washington, DC; a National Endowment for the Humanities Fellowship at the Newberry Library, Chicago; a Mendel Fellowship at the Lilly Library, Indiana University, Bloomington; the Program for Cultural Cooperation between Spain's Ministry of Education and United States' Universities; VCUarts; and the Institute for Scholarship in the Liberal Arts, College of Arts and Letters, University of Notre Dame. I am deeply grateful for their support. For their incisive questions, thoughtful suggestions, and kindhearted encouragement, I thank Rolena Adorno, Donato Amado, Brian Bauer, Sheila Blair, Jonathan Bloom, Elizabeth Boone, Claudia Brittenham, Derek Burdette, Alejandro Cañeque, Carolyn Dean, Diane Dillon, Miguel Falomir, Roman Flores, Karen Graubart, Danny Greene, Laura Gutiérrez Arbulu, Patrick Hajovsky, Aaron Hyman, Janna Israel, Barbara Johnston, Richard Kagan, Elizabeth Kuon, Evonne Levy, Peter Lukehart, Gillian Malpass, Emily McKnight, Margaret Meserve, Barbara Mundy, Stella Nair, Patricia Marroquin Norby, Mike Panbehchi, Joanne Pillsbury, Joanne Rappaport, Matthew Restall, and Amara Solari. I am especially indebted to Javier Tapia, with whom I first traveled to Cuzco; to the anonymous reviewers and Mark Eastment, Julie Hrischeva, and Sophie Neve of Yale University Press; to Marianne Fisher, for her skillful copy-editing and insightful queries; to my family; and to Tom Cummins, whose support has been boundless. I could not have completed the project without the steadfast guidance, insightful feedback, and perceptive advice of Jesús Escobar, to whom I dedicate this book.

Note on the Text

Quechua, the language of the Inca, was first rendered in alphabetic text by sixteenth-century Spaniards, who tried to capture the sounds of words they heard using their own spelling conventions. From that time forward, the way Quechua words have appeared in script and print has varied significantly. For example, the name of the city that is the subject of this book may be spelled in several ways, including Cuzco, Cusco, Qosqo, and Qusqu. Since one of the themes of this book is the instrumentality of writing in the broader changes that occurred in early colonial Peru, I follow Buchanan 1996 and Domínguez Faura 2015a in using modernized spellings of Quechua words as they were first rendered in sixteenth-century sources, such as Betanzos 1551–57. Quechua words are set in italic and are glossed in the text the first time they appear.

In its original usage, "Inca" ("Ynga") meant something like "ruler," but over time it has come to refer to a culture that flourished in Andean South America in the fifteenth and early sixteenth centuries. It is in that broader sense that I use the term in this book. All translations of primary sources are mine. In direct quotations, I translate "India" and "Indio" with the cognate "Indian," and "negra" and "negro" with "black." In my own references to the indigenous people of the Andes, I follow recent Anglophone scholarship on colonial Latin America in using the term "native" as an adjective. I occasionally use "native" as a noun in connection with a place name to describe a person born or living in that place.

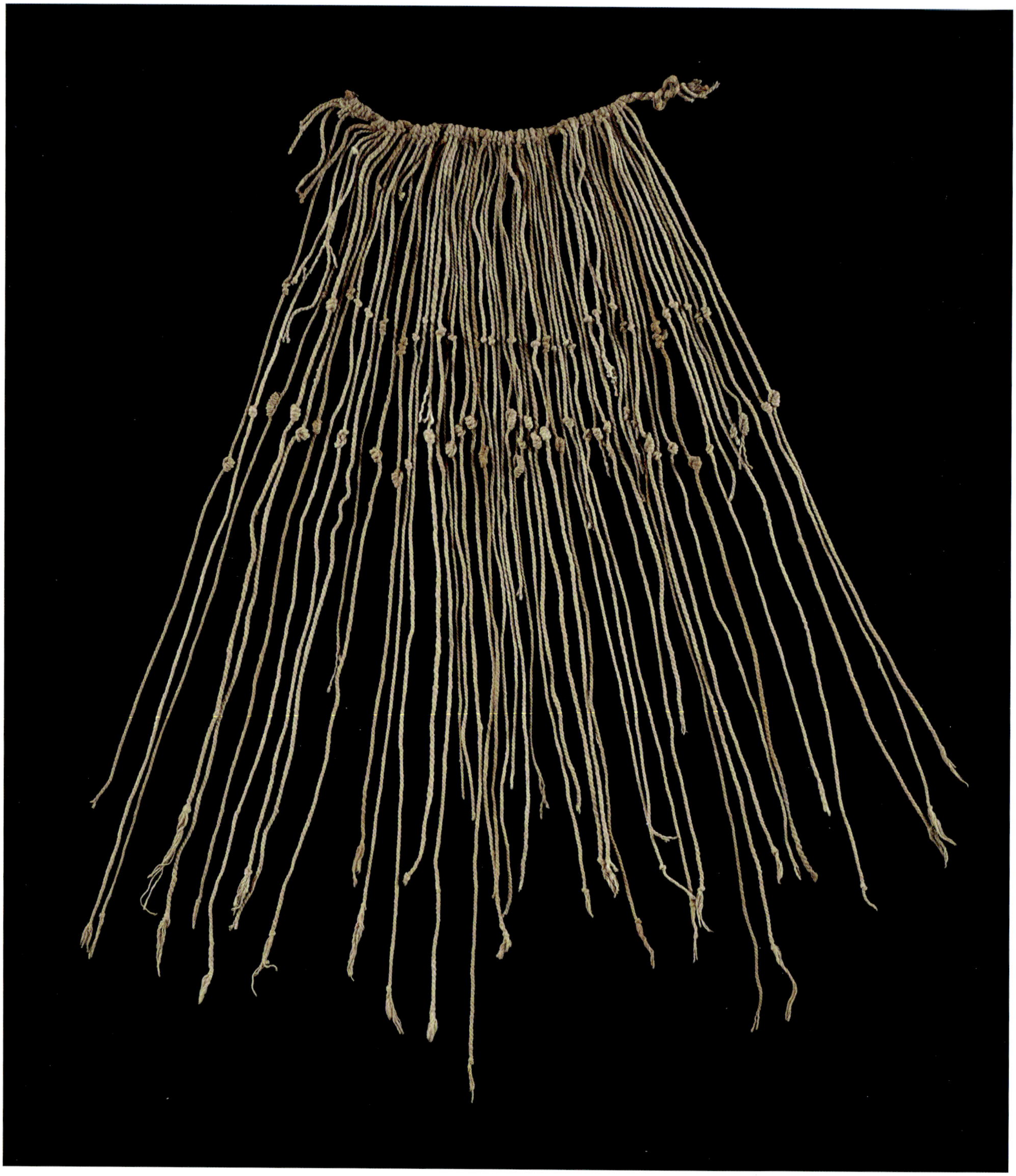

Introduction

In Search of Early Colonial Cuzco

In June 1950, the popular American magazine *Life* published a notice under the disquieting headline "Tremor in Peru Shatters Hemisphere's Oldest City." Cuzco, the ancient capital of the Inca Empire, had been struck by a powerful earthquake that claimed the lives of scores of its residents and rendered more than half its buildings uninhabitable.[1] A report filed in 1951 by the art historian George Kubler, head of the UNESCO recovery mission, noted that some of the most severe damage was inflicted on the city's seventeenth- and eighteenth-century churches, those erected in the wake of the Spanish invasion, conquest, and occupation of Peru. The church of the Dominican Order, known as Santo Domingo, was hit particularly hard: Kubler estimated some 2,800 tons of masonry had fallen from its tower alone.[2] The rear wall of the sanctuary and its external balcony, which were built atop a curving stone wall constructed by Inca masons in the fifteenth century as part of a temple dedicated to the Sun, had crumbled in ruin. Eliot Elisofon, a photographer for *Life*, captured some of this damage on film, and his image of Santo Domingo centers squarely on the intact Inca wall, a stately survival amidst the debris of the colonial church it had borne for centuries (fig. 0.1).

(*facing page*) See figure 0.8.

In the years following the earthquake, Santo Domingo's sanctuary and external balcony were rebuilt to restore the appearance of the structure that had taken shape over nearly three centuries of Spanish colonial rule (fig. 0.2). The result is one of the most evocative buildings in Cuzco. The dark polished stone of the Inca wall, its horizontality, and its bulky curvature contrast with the rougher, mortared masonry of the church, whose Solomonic (twisting) columns and arches spring from their pedestals to support latticework screens in dark wood. The bold distinctions between materials, techniques, and styles at Santo Domingo and throughout the historic core of Cuzco are visually arresting, and anyone who sees them cannot help but wonder what the city would have looked like in the past and how it came to appear as it does today.[3]

The composition of Santo Domingo's exterior sanctuary wall is the product of centuries of political, cultural, and seismic upheaval and, in turn, extensive campaigns of reconstruction, restoration, and modification. Among the most decisive eras in this history was the first half of the sixteenth century, when the Inca imperial capital, the domain of its powerful rulers, was remade into a Spanish colonial city. The changes wrought in Cuzco in the 1530s, 1540s, and 1550s are the main subject of this book. A close look at the events of those years provides insights into the history of an important Andean city in the earliest phase of Spanish colonial rule and, more broadly, underscores the centrality of architecture, writing, and ritual to the Spanish

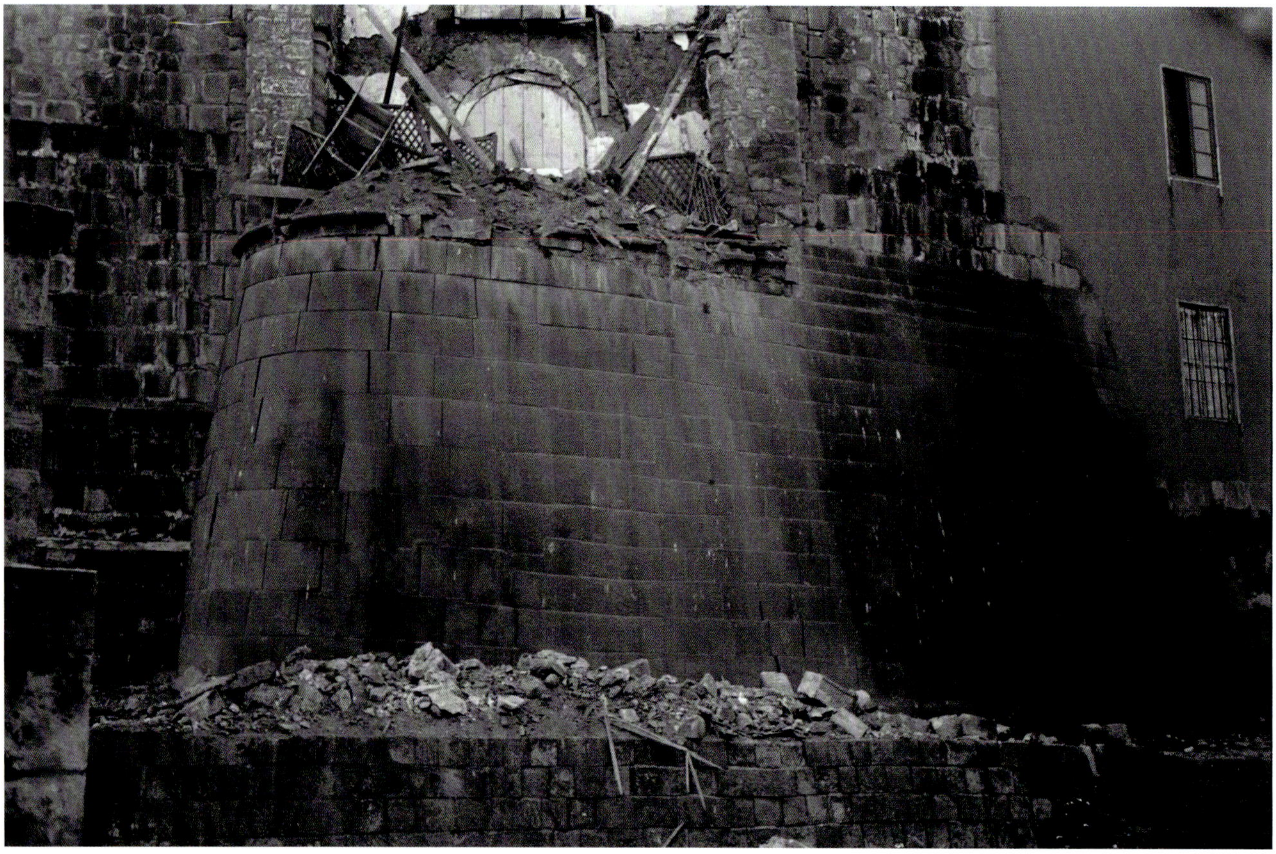

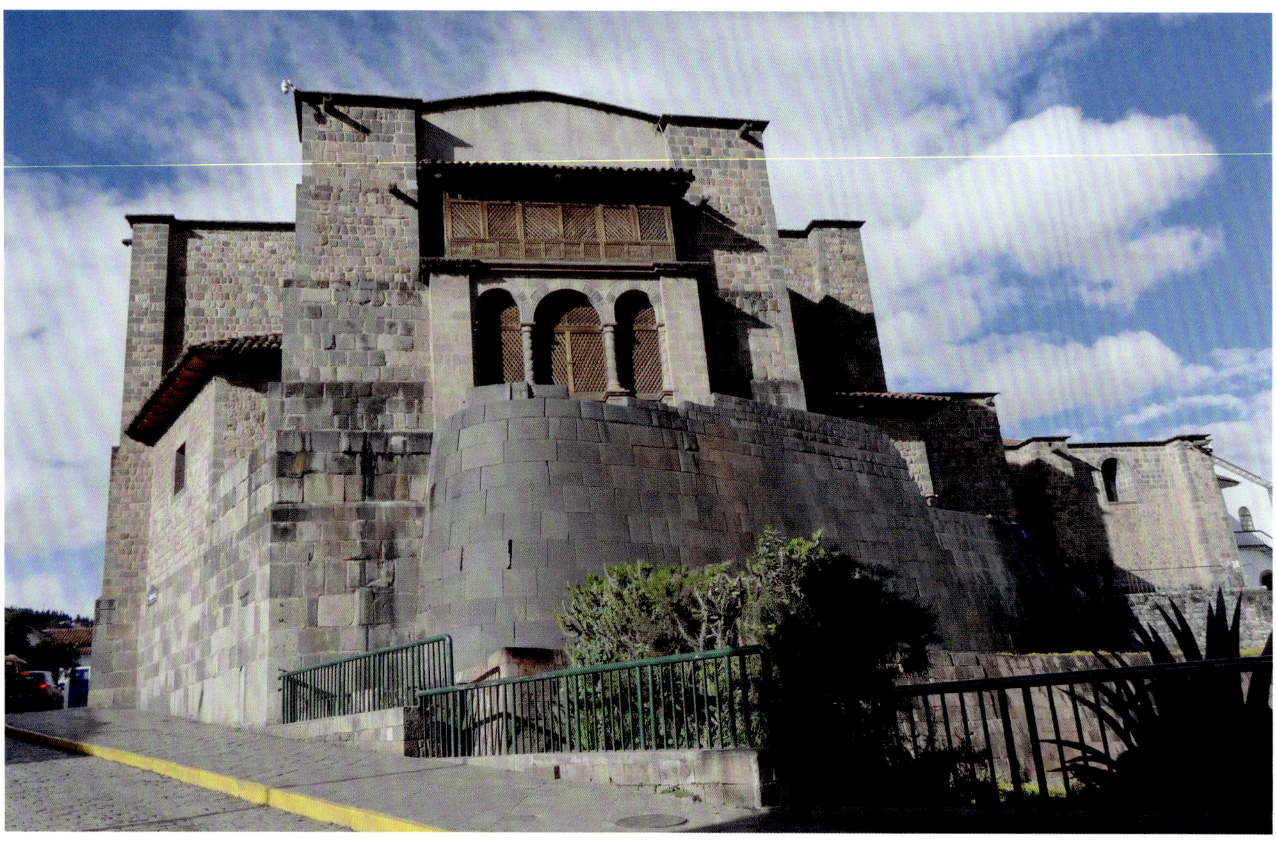

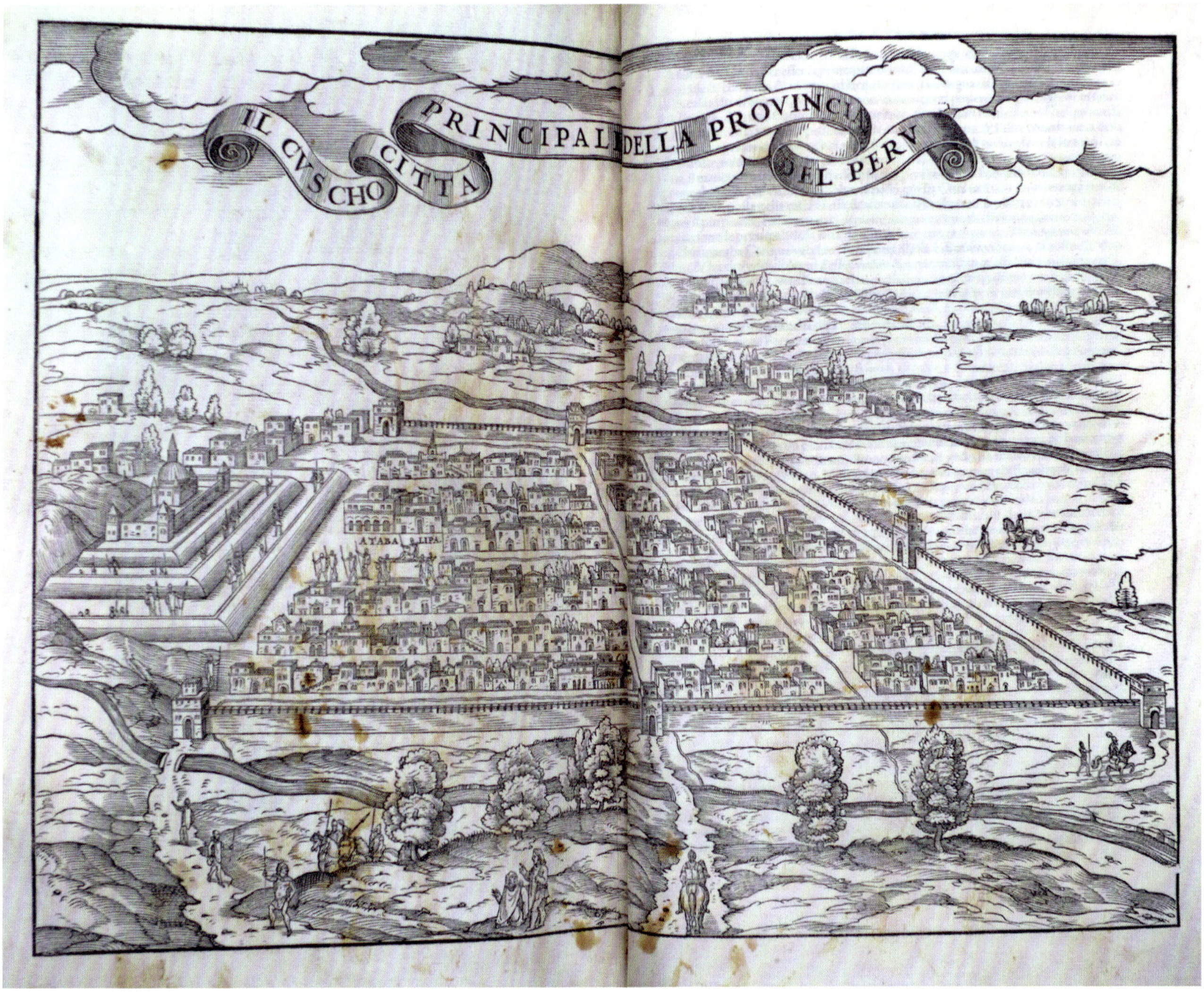

FIG. 0.1 (*facing page, top*) Eliot Elisofon, photograph showing earthquake damage to the church of Santo Domingo, Cuzco, 1950. The curved Inca wall that was incorporated into the Christian church is clearly visible in the center of the image.

FIG. 0.2 (*facing page, bottom*) The southwest façade and balcony of the church of Santo Domingo, Cuzco. Restored after the earthquake of 1950, the church juxtaposes Inca stonework with forms of European architecture characteristic of the 16th through 18th centuries.

FIG. 0.3 (*above*) Giacomo Gastaldi, "Il Cuscho, città principale della provincia del Peru," in Giovanni Battista Ramusio, *Terzo volume delle navigationi et viaggi* (Venice: Giunti, 1556). Woodcut, ink on paper, 30.1 × 35.5 cm. Field Museum Library, Chicago. This is the earliest extant image of Cuzco to depict its plan and buildings, though the depiction is largely imaginary.

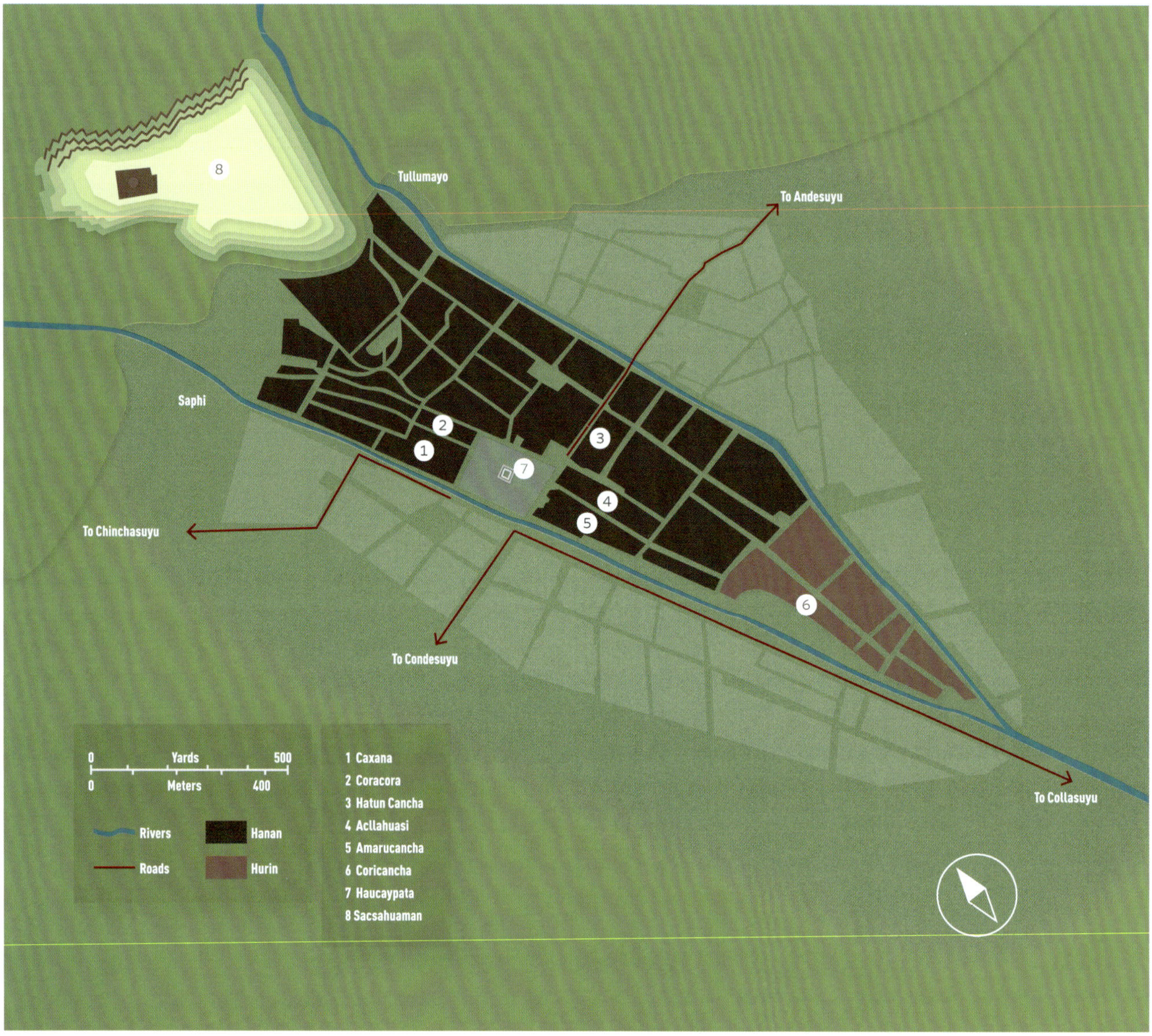

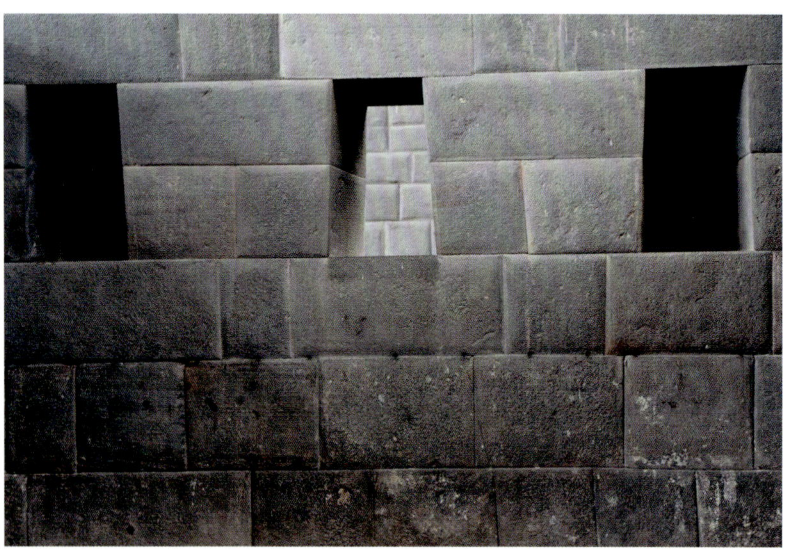

MAP 1 (*above*) Plan of Inca Cuzco showing the city's main arteries and compounds, and the division into *hanan* (upper) and *hurin* (lower) regions; the highest ground is that occupied by Sacsahuaman to the north.

FIG. 0.4 (*left*) An Inca wall in the cloister of the monastery of Santo Domingo, Cuzco. The mortarless stonework and trapezoidal windows and niches are typical features of Inca architecture.

Crown's sweeping project of invasion, occupation, and territorial transformation in the Americas. This study both sheds light on the ways in which local conditions in the Andes shaped the design and appearance of the Spanish colonial city, and illuminates the lure and limitations of the sixteenth-century texts and images that provide glimpses into this fascinating period of change.

Among the challenges in undertaking this project is the nature of the primary historical sources. In the parallel case of Mexico City—the former capital of the Aztec Empire, on whose foundations a Spanish colonial city was built in the sixteenth century—native scribes worked within pre-Columbian traditions to produce maps and pictorial manuscripts in the first decades of colonial rule. Those sources, together with early printed books and reports written by Spaniards, provide windows onto the city and its environs from multiple perspectives.[4] In contrast, there are no early visual representations of Cuzco made by either native Andeans or Spaniards who actually saw the city. The first extant view purporting to depict the city's plan and its buildings dates to 1556 and presents Cuzco as a walled city (fig. 0.3). Made by Giacomo Gastaldi (*c.* 1500–1566), an Italian artist who had never been to Cuzco, it appeared as an illustration in a collection of sixteenth-century travel accounts published in Venice.[5] Gastaldi's imaginative print would be modified and reprinted countless times in the sixteenth century and beyond, but it bears little resemblance to the Inca capital as understood by historians today.

Archaeological research, however, has provided a wealth of data on the plan of Cuzco and the design of its buildings in the time of the Inca. The Peruvian scholars Luis Valcárcel and Luis Pardo and the North American archaeologist John Rowe were among the first to conduct surveys and undertake excavation and restoration projects in the early twentieth century. More recent research has built upon that early work to envision Inca Cuzco as a densely built settlement situated between two canalized rivers, the Saphi and Tullumayo, descending from the adjacent hilltop site called Sacsahuaman (map 1).[6] Estimates vary, but the scale of its infrastructure and available resources suggest it may have housed a population of 15,000–20,000, with 100,000 or more inhabiting its environs.[7] It is often claimed that Cuzco was designed in the shape of a feline, with Sacsahuaman constituting its head and the area between the rivers forming its body, but it is more likely that the city came to be regarded that way only later, in the era of Spanish colonial rule.[8]

The inter-riverine core of Inca Cuzco consisted of a number of large stone compounds surrounded by perimeter walls, some of them serving as expansive palaces for Inca rulers and their kin. The streams converged near another walled compound, the House of the Sun, on whose foundations the church and monastery of Santo Domingo would later be built. Inca period walls restored in the monastery's cloister after the 1950 earthquake allow visitors today to examine at close range the mortarless stonework, canted walls, and trapezoidal doorways, windows, and niches that are characteristic of Inca architecture throughout the empire and which must have been present in many, or perhaps all, buildings in Inca Cuzco (fig. 0.4).

Archaeological studies of the appearance and plan of the city under Spanish rule are fewer than those focusing on the Inca settlement.[9] The colonial architecture visible in Cuzco today dates primarily to the period after 1650, when an earlier but similarly devastating earthquake destroyed many of the city's churches, monasteries, and convents (fig. 0.5). Of colonial period domestic architecture, Kubler noted in his UNESCO report of 1951 that the surviving structures dated largely to the seventeenth and eighteenth centuries. A handful of trapezoidal doorways of Inca construction adapted for use in colonial dwellings, however, remained standing. Among them is the one at calle Choquechaca 339, where a double-jamb doorway characteristic of Inca royal architecture is surrounded by courses of fine ashlar masonry (fig. 0.6). Today, it serves as the entrance to a hotel.

In other cases, colonial period portals are adorned with classicizing ornament and heraldic symbols. Among the best and earliest surviving examples is the doorway of the house built for the family of Juan de Salas Valdés (d. 1585), an early and illustrious Spanish resident of the city (fig. 0.7). Flanked by engaged fluted columns and ornamented jambs, and topped with a lintel bearing portrait busts and, above them, a coat of arms, this portal stands in contrast to the more restrained one at Choquechaca 339. While the Inca doorway's receding trapezoids gesture toward that which lies beyond them, the Salas Valdés portal is a barrier whose projecting ornaments signal a family's embrace of classical architectural forms and the elite social identity associated with them.[10]

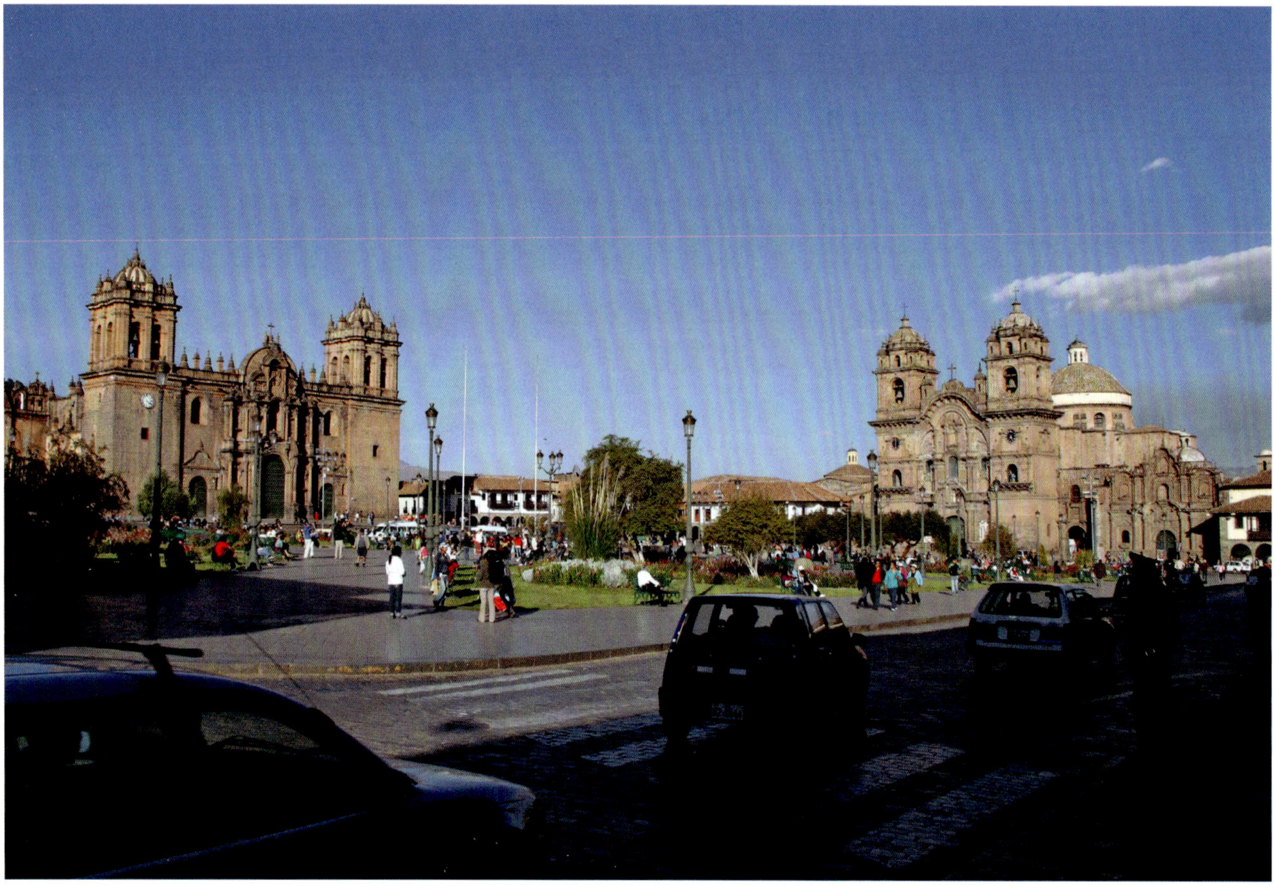

FIG. 0.5 The Plaza de Armas, Cuzco—the modern city's central plaza—with the cathedral (*left*) and the church of La Compañía (*right*). Like many of Cuzco's buildings, both were completed in the second half of the 17th century.

The archaeological record documents the transformation of Inca Cuzco into Spanish Cuzco as a sequence of material remains on a timeline spanning the fifteenth and sixteenth centuries, but more vivid accounts of change are recorded in texts from the early colonial period. These include the first *relaciones* (reports) written by Spaniards who accompanied the conquistador Francisco Pizarro (*c.* 1478–1541) through the Andes, legal documents produced by early colonial scribes, and more comprehensive histories—in print and manuscript form—of the Inca and the conquest of Peru. Some of these texts were produced by and for the agents of Spanish governance, and others emerged from the oral histories of native Andean elites; some were intended by their authors to have a wide readership, and others recorded the affairs of individuals or small groups.[11]

Previous scholarship has employed these textual sources in connection with the evidence of surviving Inca and colonial buildings to tell the story of change in sixteenth-century Cuzco in a variety of ways. In John Hemming's comprehensive *Conquest of the Incas*, Cuzco is but one of many settings for a series of conflicts spanning four decades in the sixteenth century. Hemming synthesizes colonial period texts to refine the traditional conquest narrative, focusing, he says, on "contacts between the two races" rather than the material conditions and instruments of change, a focus of this book.[12] A very different kind of study is Harold Wethey's *Colonial Architecture and Sculpture in Peru*, which includes a lengthy and detailed survey of Cuzco's built environment in the era of Spanish governance. Drawing from the evidence of documents and extant works of architecture, Wethey does not focus on the

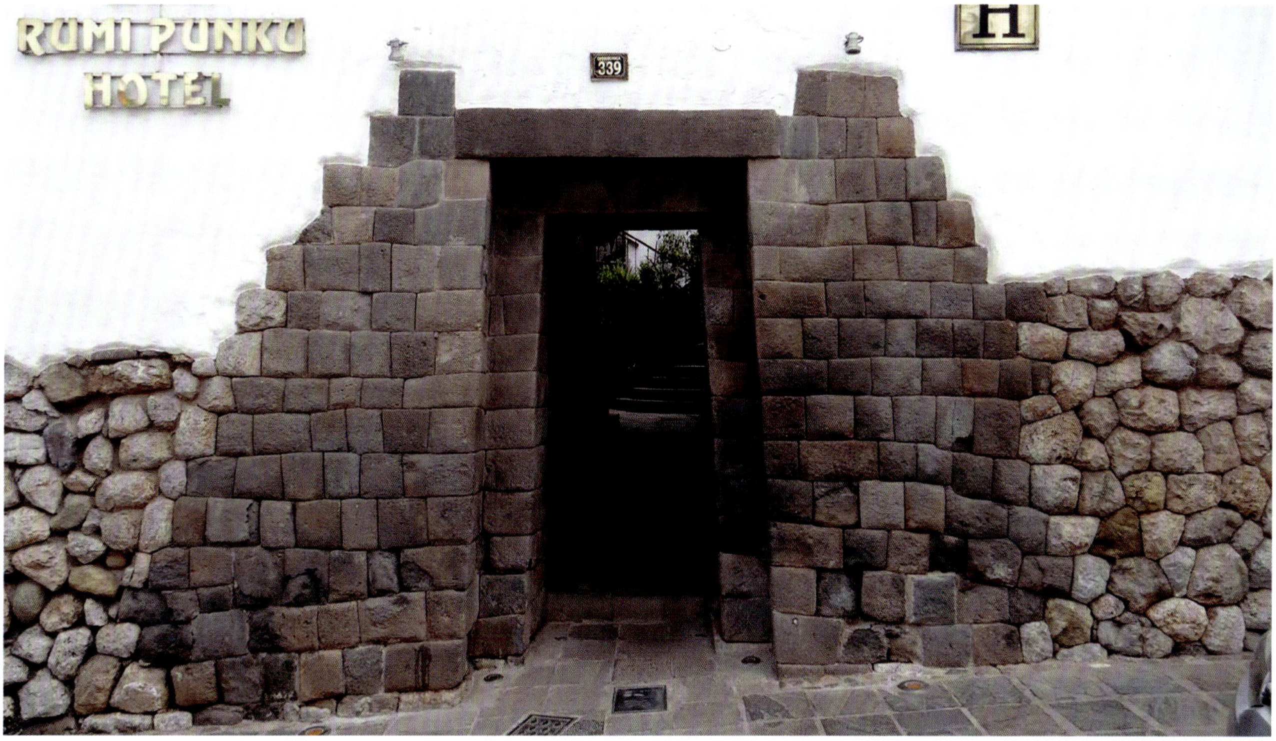

FIG. 0.6 (*above*) The entrance to calle Choquechaca 339, Cuzco. The double-jamb trapezoidal doorway is characteristic of Inca royal architecture.

FIG. 0.7 (*right*) The entrance to San Agustin 400, house of the Salas Valdés family, Cuzco, late 16th century. The classicizing and heraldic ornamentation contrasts with the flatter surfaces of Inca architecture.

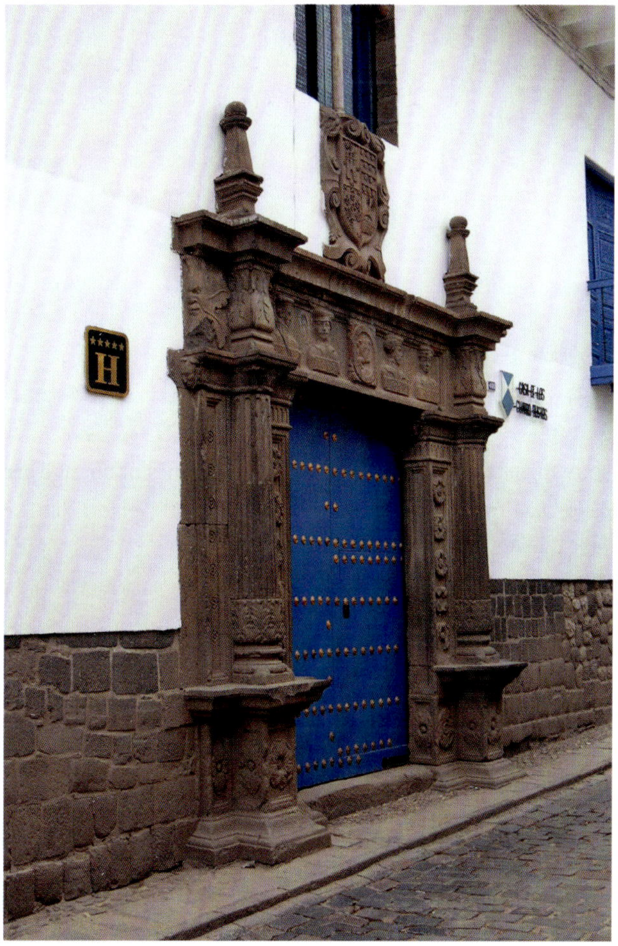

period considered in this book but, rather, on construction after the 1650 earthquake, the period in which, he says, "the full Baroque arrives in Peru."[13] Graciela María Viñuales's *El espacio urbano en el Cusco colonial* takes a more wide-ranging approach to the city, examining "symbolic structures" such as parishes and guilds, processional routes, local customs, and religious architecture, several examples of which she considers in detail and whose construction histories she traces into the eighteenth century. Inca practices and symbols, she argues, persisted alongside the city's Baroque sensibility, constructing a civic identity that is the synthesis of two cultures.[14]

In its focus on the sixteenth century, this book is aligned more closely with Valerie Fraser's *Architecture of Conquest* than it is with the work of Wethey or Viñuales. In a broad survey of the early colonial architecture of Andean South America, Fraser draws from a handful of surviving church portals and an array of sixteenth-century texts to argue that, for the Spanish, classical forms and ideals—and, more specifically, the gridiron city plan and the arch—were instrumental in the colonization and conversion of native peoples.[15] This book shares Fraser's interest in the nexus of architecture and governance, but it focuses on change in one city and examines the first decades of Spanish colonial rule, the prelude to the era of the classical forms she studies. Indeed, as James Lockhart, Gonzalo Lamana, and others have noted, the period considered in this book is a distinct phase in colonial Andean history, one in which the first generation of Spaniards held the positions of greatest power, and one characterized by a spirit of improvisation, experimentation, and transition.[16]

One way to tell the story of change in early colonial Cuzco would be to synthesize the sixteenth-century texts, identifying instances of consonance and dissonance between them, considering their correlation with the archaeological record, and exercising trained judgment to distill from them a history of the city that makes a claim to objectivity—a claim, that is, to have identified a singular early colonial reality. Lost in such an account, however, would be the voices of people who experienced the city at first hand, and whose writings record distinct mental images drawn from their sensory perceptions and shaped by memory, desire, and reason.[17] This book brings the sixteenth-century authors and the visions they conjure to the foreground, embracing an expanded definition of the image and positioning its analysis at the nexus of art history—understood here to include the history of architecture—and literary history. In so doing, the contradictions and idiosyncrasies in the primary sources come to be seen not as liabilities but rather as evidence of the multiple ways in which an ethnically, linguistically, and confessionally diverse host of historical actors conceived of the city and their places in it.

This book is not, however, simply a study of the representation of Cuzco in which "representation" is conceived as a phenomenon distinct from the actual transformation of the city in the first half of the sixteenth century. As Henri Lefebvre famously proposed, social space is a social product, and the representation of space in words and images is instrumental in its production.[18] The authors of texts in early colonial Spanish America, too, believed in the capacity of the written word and the vehicles for its dissemination—among them, books and documents—to bring about change, an effect that resonates not only with Lefebvre's work but also with interdisciplinary research emphasizing the agency of objects across space and time more broadly.[19] At the same time, the contents of early colonial books, pamphlets, and documents reveal other inanimate agents of change. Richly descriptive passages show how the performance of rituals and the introduction of a new ensemble of objects, images, and materials contributed to the production of a Spanish colonial city even before any major construction projects were undertaken.[20]

The prologue to this tale of the transformation of Inca Cuzco into Spanish Cuzco is that of an ancient Andean settlement's rise to prominence as the sacred center of the Inca Empire. Archaeological studies attest to the site's occupation in pre-Inca times, at least as early as the Killke period (1000–1400 AD).[21] The construction of the place that would become Inca Cuzco began sometime in the fifteenth century, and data pertaining to that process may have been recorded on *quipus*, assemblages of knotted cords made of cotton and camelid fibers whose mode of recordkeeping remains incompletely understood (fig. 0.8). The story of the Inca capital's construction would be recorded in ink on paper only later, in the first decades of Spanish colonial rule. Among the earliest sources to tell that story is the *Suma y narración de los Incas* (*Summary and Narrative*

FIG. 0.8 A *quipu*, 15th–16th century. Cotton, 70 × 53 cm. British Museum, London. The Inca recorded data on these fibrous devices. Variables such as the length and color of cords and the shapes and spacing of knots carried meaning.

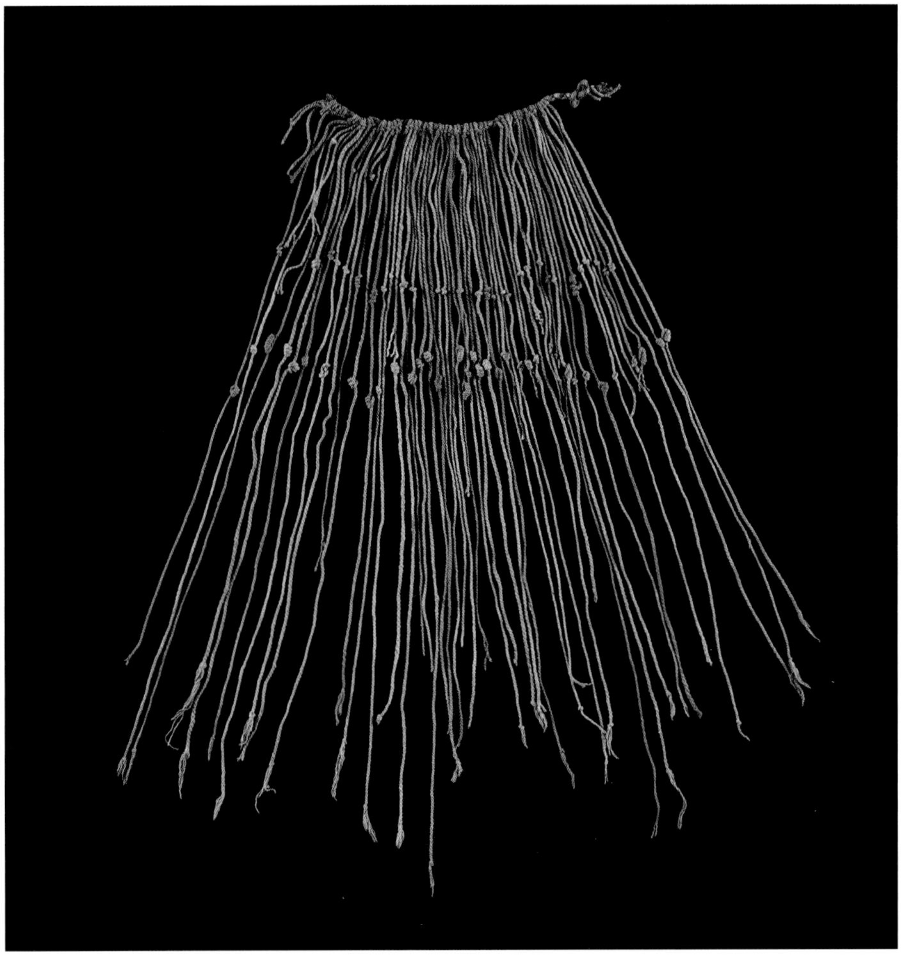

of the Incas), composed by Juan de Betanzos (*c.* 1519–76) in 1551.[22] Betanzos, a Spaniard, had learned Quechua, a language spoken throughout the Inca Empire, and that skill facilitated his compilation and translation of oral histories from native Andeans.

Betanzos's account of the construction of Cuzco, the subject of Chapter 1, underscores the settlement's prominent place in the history of the Inca. Conceived as the conceptual center of their empire and embedded in a sacred landscape, it did not take its now recognizable shape, he writes, until the reign of the ninth ruler, Pachacuti (d. 1471 or 1472), who ordered and oversaw its renovation and expansion. The stone-built environment of Cuzco would accommodate the Inca king, the mummies of his predecessors, members of the royal families and provincial administrators, and a host of servants. As described to Betanzos by his native informants, who could only imagine its appearance in the distant past, Inca Cuzco was more akin to a ceremonial center or palatine city than it was to an early modern one like Paris or Constantinople.[23] It served as the setting for an array of ritual practices, many of which took place in specially equipped architectural settings and involved participants from throughout the empire. At its height, that empire—which the Inca called Tahuantinsuyu (Realm of Four Parts)—may have contained as many as 13 million people.[24] From north to south, it spanned more than 3,000 km (1,864 mi.) (map 2).

In this early period, the buildings and spaces of Cuzco were closely associated with the Inca kings, who held the title Sapa Inca (Supreme Ruler). In the first decades of the sixteenth century, however, Cuzco's status as a conceptual center and the primary architectural expression of

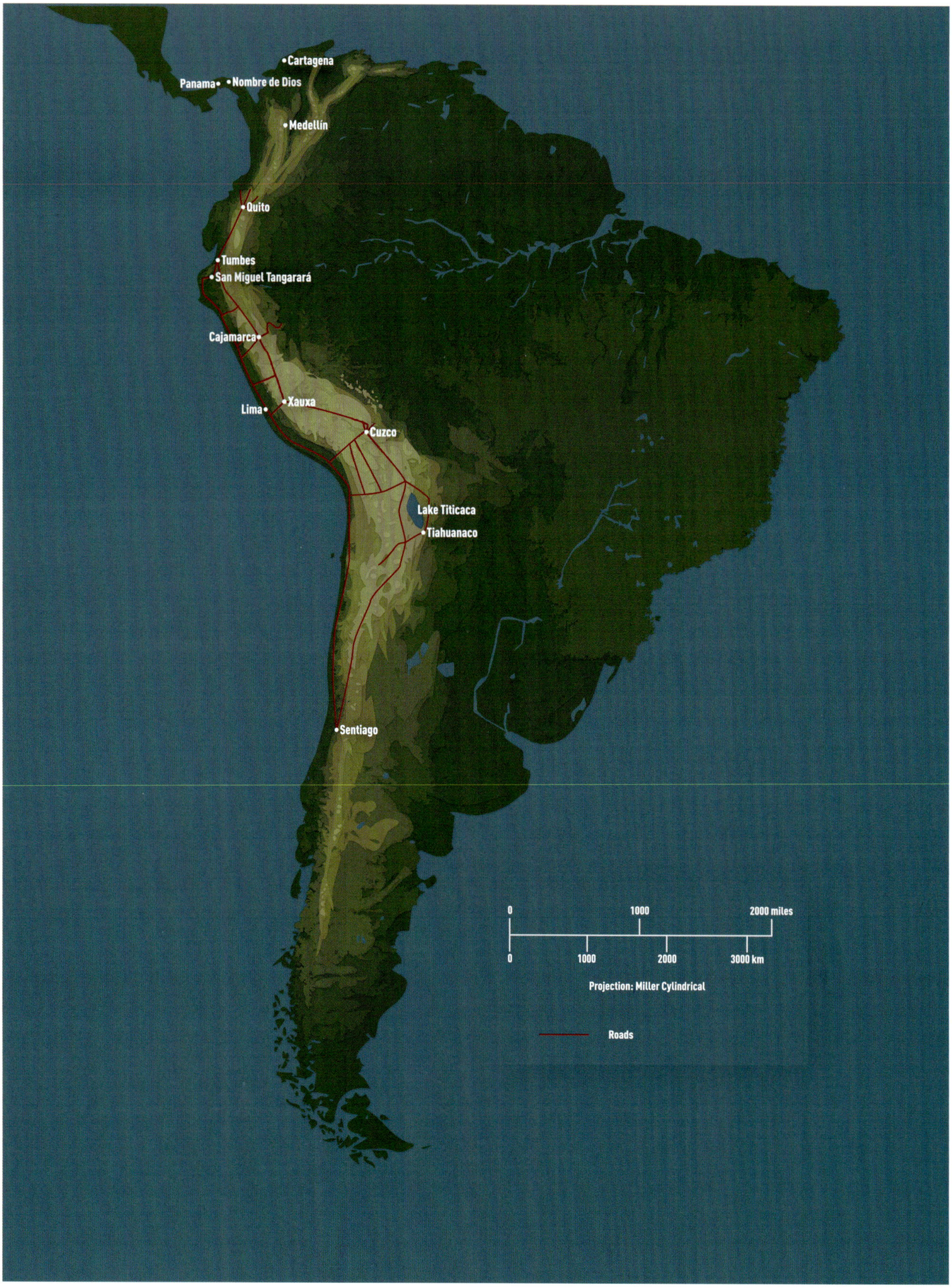
Cartagena
Panama
Nombre de Dios
Medellín
Quito
Tumbes
San Miguel Tangarará
Cajamarca
Xauxa
Lima
Cuzco
Lake Titicaca
Tiahuanaco
Sentiago
0
1000
2000 miles
0
1000
2000
3000 km
Projection: Miller Cylindrical
Roads

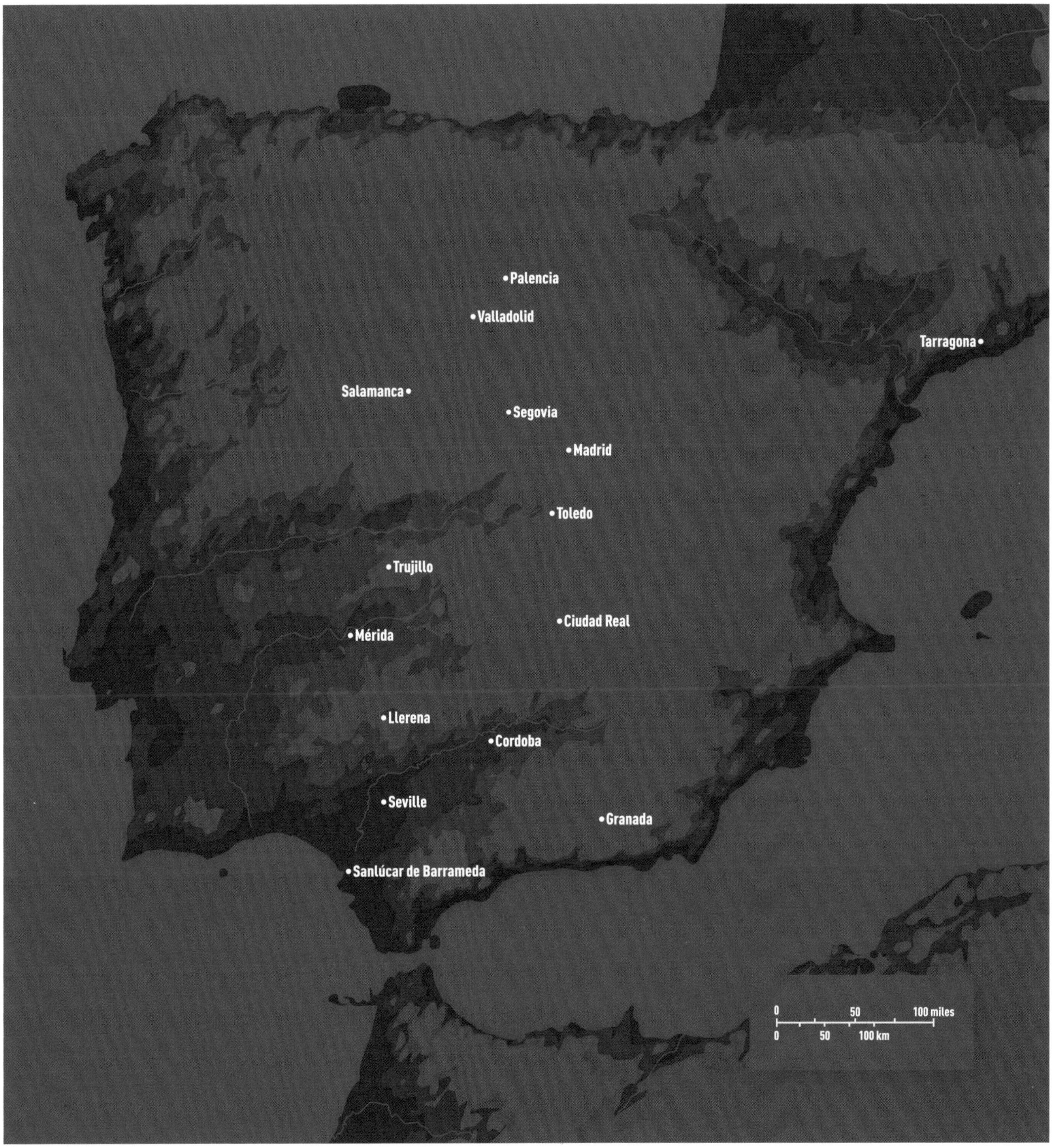

MAP 2 ***(facing page)*** South America, showing roads and cities mentioned in the text. At its greatest extent, the Inca Empire stretched from Cuzco northward beyond Quito, in today's Ecuador; southward beyond Santiago, Chile; and from the shores of the Pacific to the edges of the Amazon jungle.

MAP 3 ***(above)*** The Iberian Peninsula, showing cities mentioned in the text.

dynastic history and cultural metaphysics faced formidable challenges. The death of the Sapa Inca known as Huayna Capac (d. 1525) brought about protracted disputes over the succession between two of his sons, Atahualpa (*c.* 1500–33) and Huascar (*c.* 1491–1533). Struggle for control of Tahuantinsuyu eventually led to Huascar's execution at the hands of loyalists of Atahualpa. This state of affairs was complicated by incursions into the lands of the Inca by Francisco Pizarro, a Spaniard from Trujillo, Extremadura, and a band of fortune seekers—most of them also Spaniards (map 3). Departing from Panama in 1531, Pizarro and his cohort explored the northern coast and river valleys of South America and eventually made their way into the Andes, where they established strategic alliances with native communities, captured Atahualpa at the highland settlement of Cajamarca, and collected an enormous ransom in gold and silver before killing him in July 1533.

It was in this period that the Spanish first heard stories about Cuzco. Among them were those of Cristóbal de Mena (b. 1502) and Francisco de Xerez (b. 1497), both of whom had accompanied Pizarro on the first stages of the invasion and conquest of Peru. Neither Mena nor Xerez would ever see the capital of the Inca Empire in person, but their reports, explored here in Chapter 2, document the construction of rich mental images of a city of great importance and even greater wealth, the walls, floors, and roofs of its buildings plated in gold. This vision of Cuzco would not prove to be entirely accurate, but its invocation in the reports of Mena and Xerez points to the ways in which the dreams and desires of the Spaniards in Peru shaped their expectations of what they would find there. Indeed, even before Pizarro and his company set foot in Cuzco they had come to conceive of the city as a source of prodigious wealth and a crucial node in an expanding transatlantic system of trade and commerce.

Led by Pizarro, to whom the Crown had granted the title Governor of the Kingdom of Peru, the Spanish and their native allies, servants, and slaves entered Cuzco in November 1533. Four months later, Pizarro performed the civic ritual known as the Act of Foundation, the ceremony that brought the colonial city into being even though in appearance Inca Cuzco was altered only slightly. The ceremony centered on spoken proclamations recorded in a document penned by Pizarro's secretary, Pedro Sancho. That text, the centerpiece of Chapter 3, contains the earliest descriptive passages on Cuzco's design and appearance written by a Spaniard who personally saw it. However, it is more than just a representation of the city at that key moment in its history. Pizarro and his compatriots understood the document and the deeds it recorded as the means of assigning new names, functions, and values to existing buildings and spaces and, thus, as an instrument in the transformation of Inca Cuzco into Spanish Cuzco.

Following the Act of Foundation, Pizarro left Cuzco to consolidate his rule and establish other cities, among them Ciudad de los Reyes (City of the Kings), also known as Lima, which was founded in January 1535. Local governance in Cuzco was enacted by the *cabildo* (city council), and the actions of the councilors are documented by their official scribes in the minutes of their meetings, known collectively as the Acts of the Cabildo. The first book of the *cabildo*'s Acts, the key primary source for Chapter 4, spans the first year of the Spanish colonial city's existence. Among the measures recorded are the institution of civic ordinances related to buildings and streets, the ritualized assignment of housing lots to Spanish men, and the production of a now lost plan of the city. The text is the artifact of the *cabildo*'s reordering of the city, although rather than documenting radical change, it underscores the ways in which the material conditions of Inca Cuzco thwarted the ideal city plan envisaged by the Spanish colonial authorities.

The legitimacy of Spanish colonial Cuzco, with its plaza, church, city council, and houses for Spanish settlers interwoven into the fabric of Inca Cuzco, would be challenged vigorously by native forces aligned with another of Huayna Capac's sons, Manco Inca (1516–44), in a year-long siege launched in 1536. The story of this conflict is recorded in several early colonial texts, among them a report composed by the Spaniard Diego de Silva y Guzmán (d. 1576), a participant in the defense of Cuzco in 1536–37. His account, completed in 1539, guides the examination of this episode in Chapter 5. It highlights contested buildings and spaces in early colonial Cuzco, chief among them the hilltop "fortress" of Sacsahuaman and the city's main plaza. In effect, his text remakes Cuzco into a fortress city like those in which he and his contemporaries had lived on the other side of the Atlantic, and where some of them had participated in campaigns of territorial expansion under Charles V (1500–58), the Holy Roman Emperor and king of Spain. Counterpoints to Silva's version of the story include that of Betanzos and, decades later, that of one of Manco's sons, Titu Cusi Yupanqui (*c.* 1530–71), who persisted in regarding Cuzco as the center of a still intact Tahuantinsuyu rather than as one of many settlements founded by the Spaniards on the periphery of Charles V's expanding empire.

The Siege of Cuzco devastated the city's buildings and streets and ushered in a decade of political instability. A recent arrival to the Americas, Pedro de Cieza de León (*c.* 1520–54), would document the events of this period in his *Crónica del Perú* (*Chronicle of Peru*), drawing on contemporaneous documents to which he had access and the testimony of Spanish and native Andean participants and eyewitnesses. His accounts of battles between rival factions of Spaniards in the late 1530s and 1540s—the "civil wars" of colonial Peru—describe a context of shifting alliances in which a string of men vied for the right to govern. Chapter 6 considers the events of this period from the viewpoint of Cuzco and through the writings of Cieza de León, which reveal details about Cuzco's infrastructure, while also attesting to the emergence of a new spatial order and civic hierarchy in Peru as Lima, the coastal City of the Kings, supplanted Cuzco as the seat of governance.

Cuzco, however, would not fade into obscurity. The 1540s and 1550s—the focus of Chapter 7—saw the first major interventions into the plan of Inca Cuzco; civic records from that period document the new structures rising from the foundations of Inca Cuzco as well as the narratives and iconographies that imbued buildings and spaces with new ideas and values. The memories of Inca Garcilaso de la Vega (1539–1616), born in Cuzco to a native Andean mother and a Spanish father, provide a counterpoint to the official documents from this era, revealing some of the conflicts and bonds that set the stage for centuries of inventive cultural production in the ancient capital of the Inca.

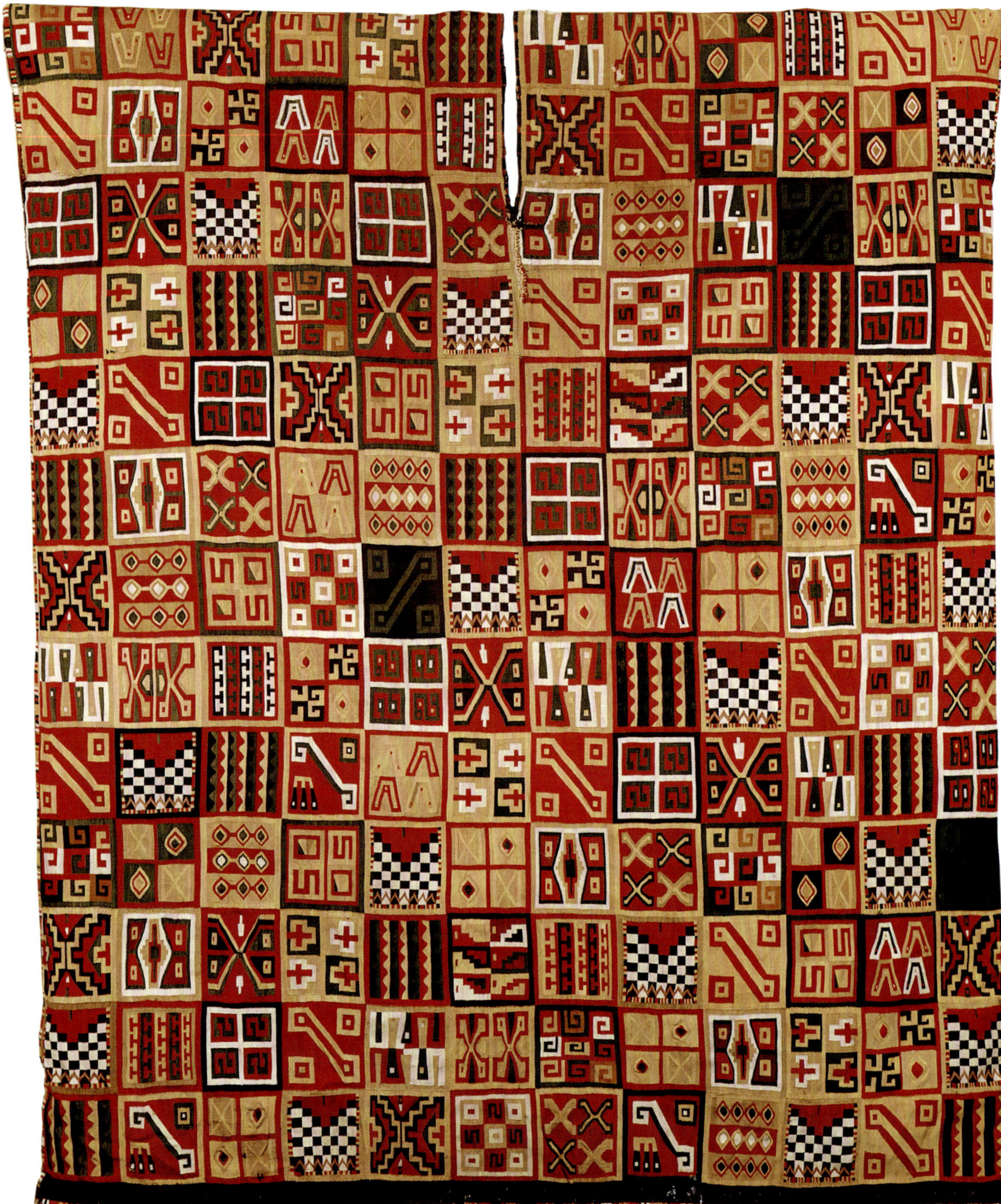

CHAPTER 1

Imagining Inca Cuzco

Juan de Betanzos, Angelina Yupanqui, and the Origin of a Sacred Center

Sometime around 1520, an Inca princess was born in Cuzco. Her mother was a noblewoman named Tocto, a Quechua word likening her to a supple conduit coursing with a life force. The sixteenth-century Spanish friar Domingo de Santo Tomás translated the term in his Quechua dictionary as "sprouting tree stem," and the Jesuit priest Diego González Holguín glossed it several decades later as "soft feathers of birds . . . whose quills are full of blood or fat."[1] The princess's father was Yamque Yupanqui, a relative and confidant of Huayna Capac (Young King), who was then the supreme ruler of the realms of the Inca. When he learned of the girl's birth, Huayna Capac bestowed a great honor upon her, designating her the future wife of his son Atahualpa, who then was probably in his teens. One year after making this decision, he presided over a ceremony on the festival plaza of Cuzco in which the city's noblemen and women cut the girl's hair and offered her extravagant gifts. As part of the ritual, Huayna Capac gave her a name that rendered her, like her mother, a conduit of sorts: Cuxirimay, "speaks good fortune."[2]

This story of Cuxirimay's birth and naming is recorded in the *Suma y narración de los Incas* (hereafter, *Suma y narración*), a text composed in Cuzco around 1551, nearly two decades after the first Spaniards had settled there. Its author was Juan de Betanzos, whose surname suggests a connection with the town of Betanzos, Galicia, in the northwestern part of the Iberian Peninsula. The details of his biography, however, remain frustratingly murky. He left Spain around 1533 as a young teenager, and upon arriving in the Americas, made the arduous journey southward to Lima, where he settled around 1536. His presence in Cuzco is first documented in 1543.[3]

Somewhere in the course of his journey, Betanzos learned Quechua. In the prologue to the *Suma y narración*, in which he addresses his patron, the Viceroy of Peru, Antonio de Mendoza (1495–1552), he reports that he spent six years writing a catechism and two vocabularies in that language, "one of terms, and the other of ideas, prayers, dialogues, and a confessional manual."[4] The acquisition of material for these works may have been among Betanzos's motivations for the journey. If he intended for them to circulate in print, though, his wish was never fulfilled. The original manuscripts in Betanzos's hand have not survived, but if they had, they would be the earliest known alphabetic texts composed in Quechua, predating the dictionaries by Santo Tomás and González Holguín by decades.

In or around 1544, the author of the elusive Quechua catechism and vocabularies married Cuxirimay, who was probably in her twenties. By then, she was no longer the "speaker of good fortune" as at some point in the previous decade she had been baptized and she was now known—to

(*facing page*) See figure 1.15.

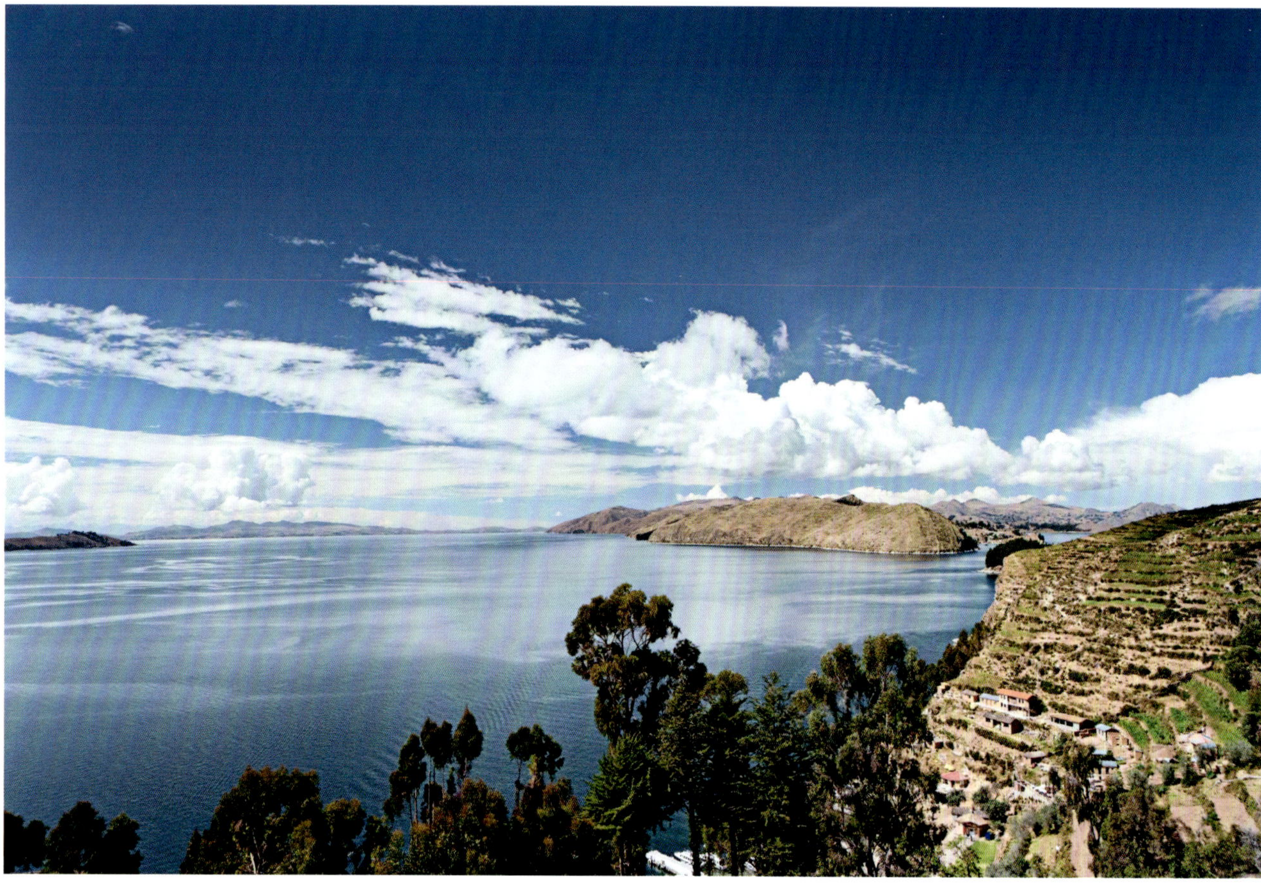

FIG. 1.1 Lake Titicaca. According to the Inca creation myth, the deity Contiti Viracocha emerged from this lake to create the sun, moon, stars, and the first human beings.

the Spanish, at least—as Angelina Yupanqui. It is fitting that she had abandoned her Quechua name, for by the time of her marriage to Betanzos she had experienced not good fortune but, instead, unimaginable tragedy. In 1532 or so, at the age of about ten, she had been taken from Cuzco into the northernmost provinces of the Inca Empire, where her marriage to Atahualpa was performed near Quito, the place of his birth. As her husband's principal wife, she accompanied him on his campaigns through the northern Andes as he consolidated his authority, often through the use of force. She was probably with him in Cajamarca, nearly 2,000 km (1,200 mi.) northwest of Cuzco, when he was taken prisoner and publicly executed by the Spanish in 1533. Following his death, Francisco Pizarro took Angelina as a sexual partner and fathered two children with her: Juan, who died in childhood; and Francisco, who went to Spain in 1551, around the time of the composition of the *Suma y narración*.[5]

Angelina's family name, Yupanqui, attested to her kinship with the Inca rulers, a lineage that included Atahualpa as well as his father, Huayna Capac. Her ancestry extended to their predecessors, and her high social rank in Cuzco afforded her access to a rich oral history. It is from that body of knowledge that Betanzos likely drew in compiling the *Suma y narración*. His informants, he wrote, were the elites of Cuzco—"not just one, but many, and of the oldest and most credible I found among these natives"—who conveyed their knowledge of Inca history to him in Quechua.[6] Chief among them must have been his wife, who had spent considerable periods of time in Cuzco both before and after the arrival of the Spanish in 1533. Her relatives in Cuzco also may have provided information, and Betanzos's earlier work in 1543 with *quipucamayocs*, the official keepers and readers of *quipus*, suggests they may have had a hand in the project as well.[7]

Betanzos was attentive to the form of the narratives conveyed to him, writing that, "in order to be a true and faithful translator, I must respect the style and construction of the speech of these natives."[8] His dedication to this principle is evident throughout the *Suma y narración*, its text evincing its origins in native oral history in a variety of ways. For example, he frequently uses the phrase "they say" to qualify his statements, and he incorporates his translation of many Quechua words and phrases into Spanish in the body of the text. In the story of Cuxirimay's birth, for instance, he writes that Huayna Capac selected the infant to be Atahualpa's *piuiguarme*, defining the term as "the legitimate and principal wife of his son Atahualpa."[9]

Emerging from the memories, imagination, and speech of Angelina Yupanqui and other Andeans, the *Suma y narración* is the earliest extant work on Inca history to rely so heavily on native informants. Read in parallel with the archaeological evidence, it constructs a remarkable vision of the architecture and plan of Inca Cuzco and reveals some of the ideas and values Angelina and her contemporaries associated with its buildings and spaces. A close reading of the *Suma y narración* reveals how at least some native perspectives on the Inca capital were rooted in a mythological narrative about the origins of the Inca and their history. At the same time, however, Betanzos's text now and again divulges the ways in which linguistic translation, authorial mediation, and the exigencies of the Spanish colonial present intervened in the telling of that story.

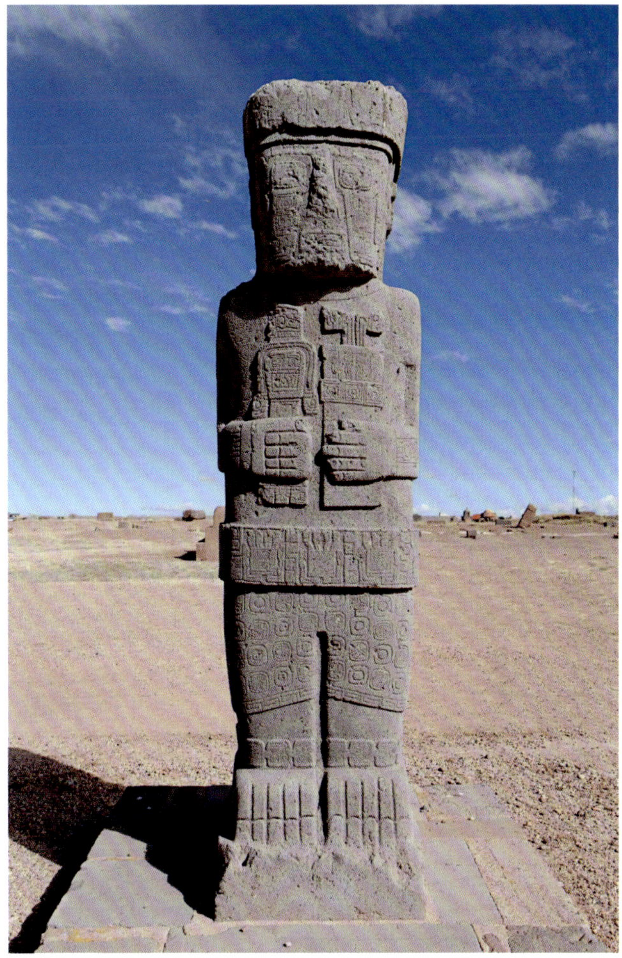

FIG. 1.2 The Ponce Monolith at Tiahuanaco, Bolivia, 1st century AD. Andesite, h. approx. 3 m. The figure holds ritual paraphernalia—a drinking vessel (left hand) and a snuff tray (right hand)—and probably stood in a temple courtyard.

The fate of the manuscript Betanzos composed in Cuzco in the 1550s remains unknown, but its contents are preserved in two early copies. An incomplete version dated to 1574, near the time of the author's death, is held in the library of the Royal Monastery of San Lorenzo at El Escorial. The circumstances of its acquisition have not been traced, but it was found there in the late nineteenth century and was published shortly thereafter by Marcos Jiménez de la Espada, a Spanish zoologist and the founder of the Geographic Society of Madrid.[10] It contains a history of the reigns and achievements of the first nine Inca rulers, beginning with Manco Capac, the founder of the dynasty, and ending with Yupanqui Pachacuti (d. 1471/72; hereafter, Pachacuti), the king credited with much of the construction of Cuzco.

A more complete sixteenth-century manuscript copy of the text was acquired in the 1980s by the Bartolomé March Foundation from the library of the duke of Medinaceli, a Spanish nobleman whose ancestors included royal officials who had served in the Americas and elsewhere in the Spanish Empire.[11] It is held today in the March Foundation's library in Palma de Mallorca and contains the chapters preserved in the Escorial manuscript as well as additional material on Pachacuti's successors. It also

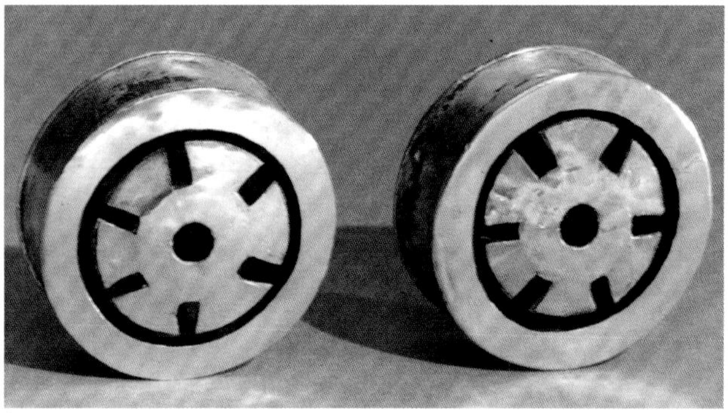

FIG. 1.3 Ear spools, late 15th to early 16th century. Gold and silver, 1.9 × 4.8 cm. Metropolitan Museum of Art, New York. Used to enlarge the earlobes as a sign of status, such spools were worn in the Andes long before the time of the Inca.

includes a second part, beginning with the struggle between Atahualpa and his brother Huascar for control of their father's realms, and ends with a chapter added several years later describing Betanzos's meeting with the viceroy of Peru in Lima in 1557.

Both sixteenth-century copies open with a prologue addressed to Viceroy Mendoza before recounting a myth of the origins of the Inca. Like so many other societal origin myths, it begins with the creation of the world. In ancient times, Betanzos writes, a deity called Contiti Viracocha emerged from a lake and created the sun, stars, moon, and the first human beings at a place called Tiahuanaco.[12] The lake from which the deity was said to have emerged is widely understood as being Lake Titicaca, the vast body of water situated between the modern nations of Peru and Bolivia at an altitude of 3,800 m (12,500 ft.) (fig. 1.1). The "Tiahuanaco" mentioned in the text can also be linked with a specific place: the ceremonial center and capital of a prehistoric state near the southeastern shore of the lake, whose monumental stone architecture was constructed in the course of the first millennium, long before the rise of the Inca Empire.[13]

At Tiahuanaco, Viracocha—whose name, Betanzos says, means "God, maker of the world"—created the first human beings out of stone and ordered them to settle in communities in the surrounding provinces.[14] This part of the story must have taken shape over the centuries in connection with direct and reported experience at the site of Tiahuanaco, where human figures carved in stone and erected in temple courtyards were among the most striking features of the built environment. An outsized figure preserved at Tiahuanaco today and known as the Ponce Monolith (fig. 1.2), so named for Carlos Ponce-Sanginés, the Bolivian archaeologist who uncovered it in the mid-twentieth century, is one of several anthropomorphic sculptures found there. It probably stood in ancient times in a sunken courtyard before being toppled, perhaps intentionally, at a later point in its history. Incised patterns on the figure's garments and headdress are similar to those found on textiles produced in the region in the first millennium, and the forms on its face may refer to paint or a mask. The figure holds ritual paraphernalia—a drinking vessel and a snuff tray—in its hands.[15]

Angelina and her kin may have conceived of such figures as the material remains of an ancient act of creation by Viracocha. Betanzos elaborates upon the origin story, writing that the creator deity ultimately formed several groups of people made of stone at Tiahuanaco, each led by their own chief, and ordered them to establish communities in particular places. The idea that humanity was born of stone underscores the mythological character of the story, but it also brings to the fore the primacy of that material to the Inca, and its embodiment for them of aspects of history, genealogy, and rulership.[16]

After he created the people made of stone and distributed them throughout the Andes, Viracocha traveled northward, stopping at the newly created settlements along the way and eventually arriving at the place that would become Cuzco. There, Betanzos writes, he appointed a chief named Alcaviçça as the local ruler and designated the area home to the people who would be called *orejones* ("big ears"), the male elites of Cuzco, whose large ornamental ear spools were markers of their status. Many examples of such ear spools from Andean cultures predating the Inca have been found by archaeologists, evidencing a long tradition in pre-Columbian South America of personal adornment focused on the ear. Few remain from the period of Inca rule, as the first Spaniards in the Andes looted and melted down many objects made of precious metals. A rare survival from the time of the Inca, though probably not from Cuzco, may be a pair of ear spools in the collection of the Metropolitan Museum of Art, New York (fig. 1.3).

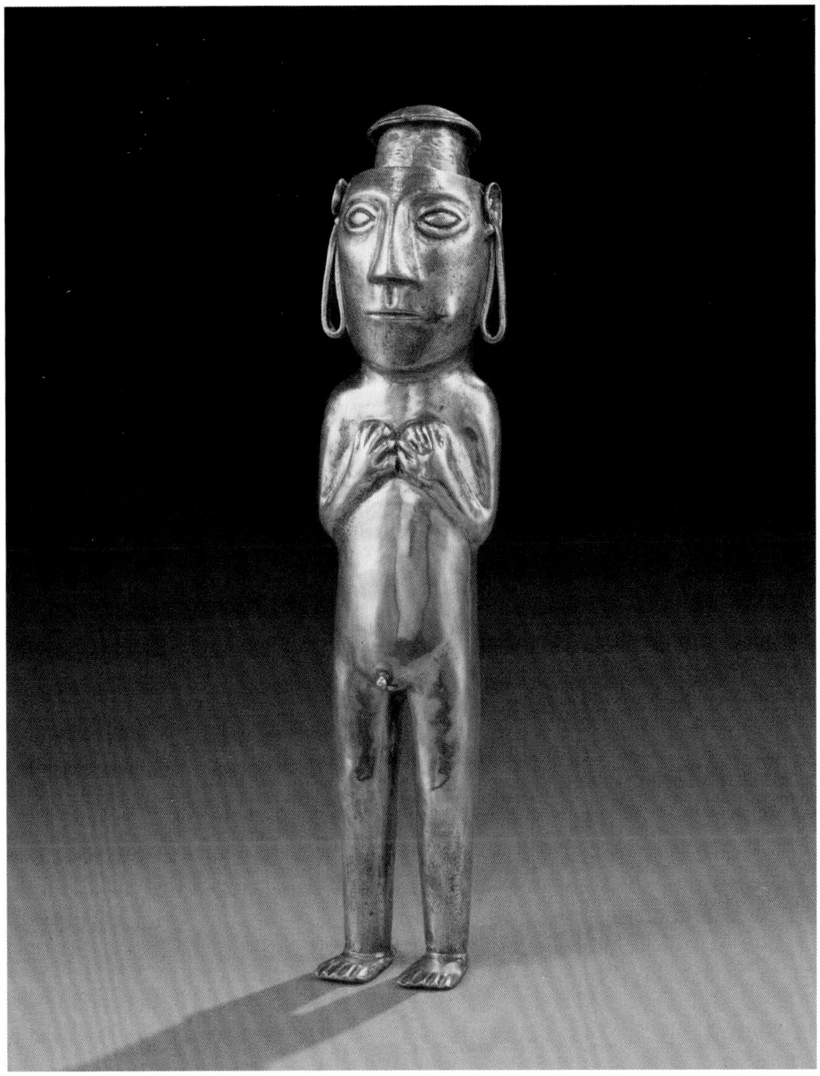

FIG. 1.4 Standing male figurine, 15th or early 16th century. Silver, h. 22.7 cm. Dumbarton Oaks Museum, Washington, DC. The greatly enlarged earlobes are a characteristic feature of such figures produced by the Inca.

Crafted in silver and gold, they are decorated with a radially symmetrical motif that at once emphasizes both the center and the circumference of the circular form, and which resembles the star-shaped mace heads of Inca weaponry as well as the six-pointed star motif appearing on textiles from coastal Peru. Nearly two inches in diameter, they could have been used only by a wearer with pierced and substantially extended earlobes—that is, with "big ears."

For elite Inca males, such treatment of the earlobes began at an early age. In a later chapter of the *Suma y narración*, Betanzos writes that the ritual of the first haircutting, which was performed when an elite male infant was one year old, also involved the naming of the child and the piercing of his ears. Such boys would later be initiated as warriors and dressed in an ensemble of fine goods including large gold earplugs. The symbolic importance of ear piercings is evident in the design of Inca figurines in which pierced and stretched earlobes are striking details in otherwise spare representations of the human form. In these hollow statues, made of hammered sheets of gold, silver, and metal alloys, the hanging earlobes are executed as simple looped wires (fig. 1.4). The emphasis on the ear in personal adornment as well as in artistic representation among the Inca underscores the importance of that organ in the acquisition of knowledge passed down through oral tradition, like that conveyed to Angelina Yupanqui and her

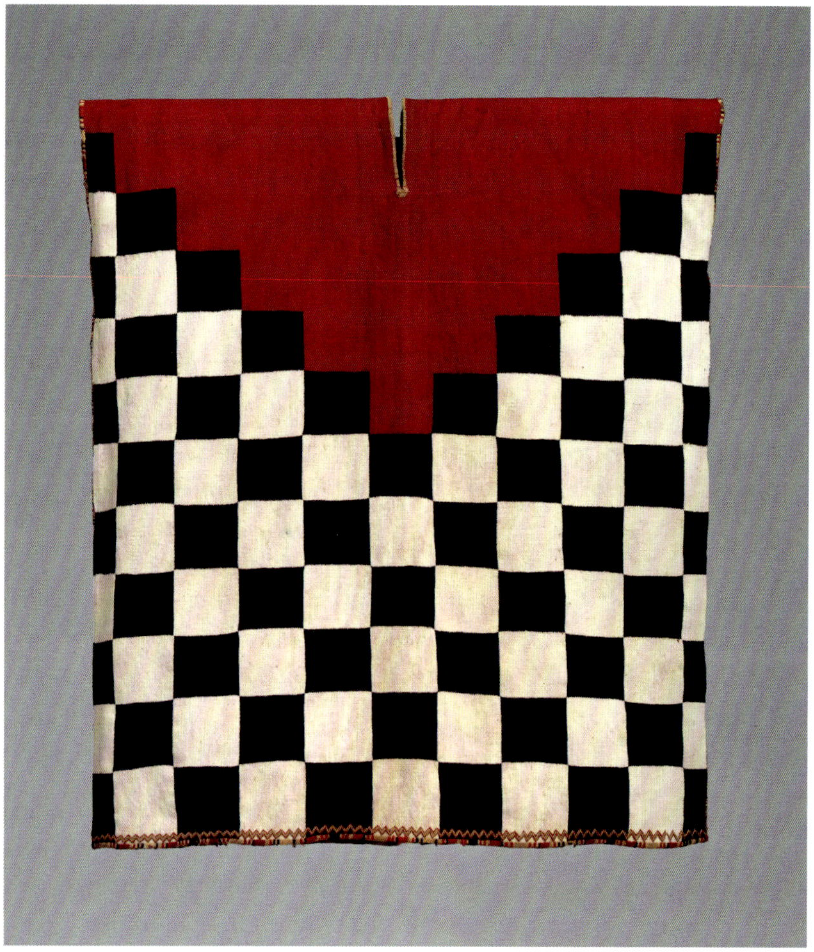

FIG. 1.5 (*left*) An Inca *uncu* (tunic) bearing a black-and-white checkerboard pattern with a red yoke, 16th century. Camelid fiber, 87 × 76.5 cm. Metropolitan Museum of Art, New York. This pattern is one of several standard designs for tunics worn by Inca men.

FIG. 1.6 (*facing page*) An Inca *uncu* bearing the "Inca key" pattern and horizontal stripes, 15th–16th century. Cotton and camelid fiber, 85.1 × 76.2 cm. Cleveland Museum of Art, Cleveland, OH.

contemporaries and recorded in the *Suma y narración*.[17] But Betanzos's reference to the *orejones* also shows that a sixteenth-century understanding of ancient Cuzco included its association with people: a group of men whose identity was marked in part by ear piercing and the use of large ear spools made of metal.

Betanzos continues with his recounting of the origin myth, writing that in ancient times Cuzco was an unremarkable village set on marshy land with only about thirty houses, which he describes as "small, made of straw, and very ruined."[18] Its water, he notes, flowed from springs in the sierra that swelled into streams as they passed through Cuzco and saturated its terrain. The inhabitants of the swampy village governed by Alcavicça, Betanzos writes, called their settlement "Cuzco." "As to what this name means," he continues, "nothing more can be said except that it was named this way long ago."[19] Linguists have proposed alternative interpretations of the toponym: Rodolfo Cerrón-Palomino identifies it as a term with roots in Aymara rather than Quechua and glosses it as "falcon."[20] It was this swampy village, Betanzos notes, that the founders of the royal Inca dynasty, Manco Capac and his sister-wife Mama Ocllo, chose as the place where they would build a settlement and live. The originary couple was believed to have emerged in the distant past with three other sibling couples, not from Lake Titicaca, as Viracocha had done, but from a cave at (or near) a place called Pacarictambo, which Betanzos translates as "house of creation."[21] The toponym is also that of a town some 32 km (20 mi.) south of Cuzco, and rock outcroppings and caves in its vicinity have been linked since at least the sixteenth century to the geographic features mentioned in the origin myth.[22]

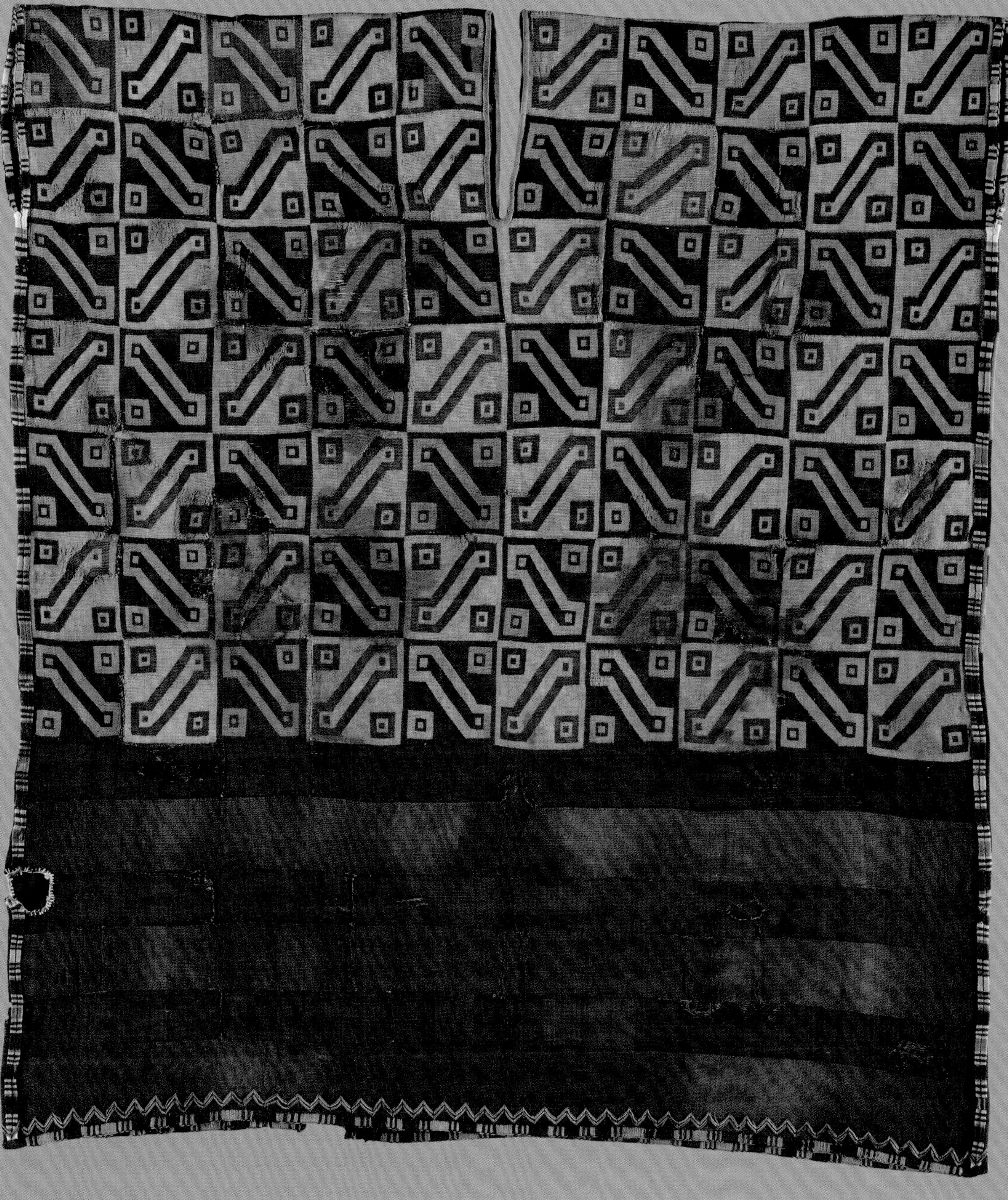

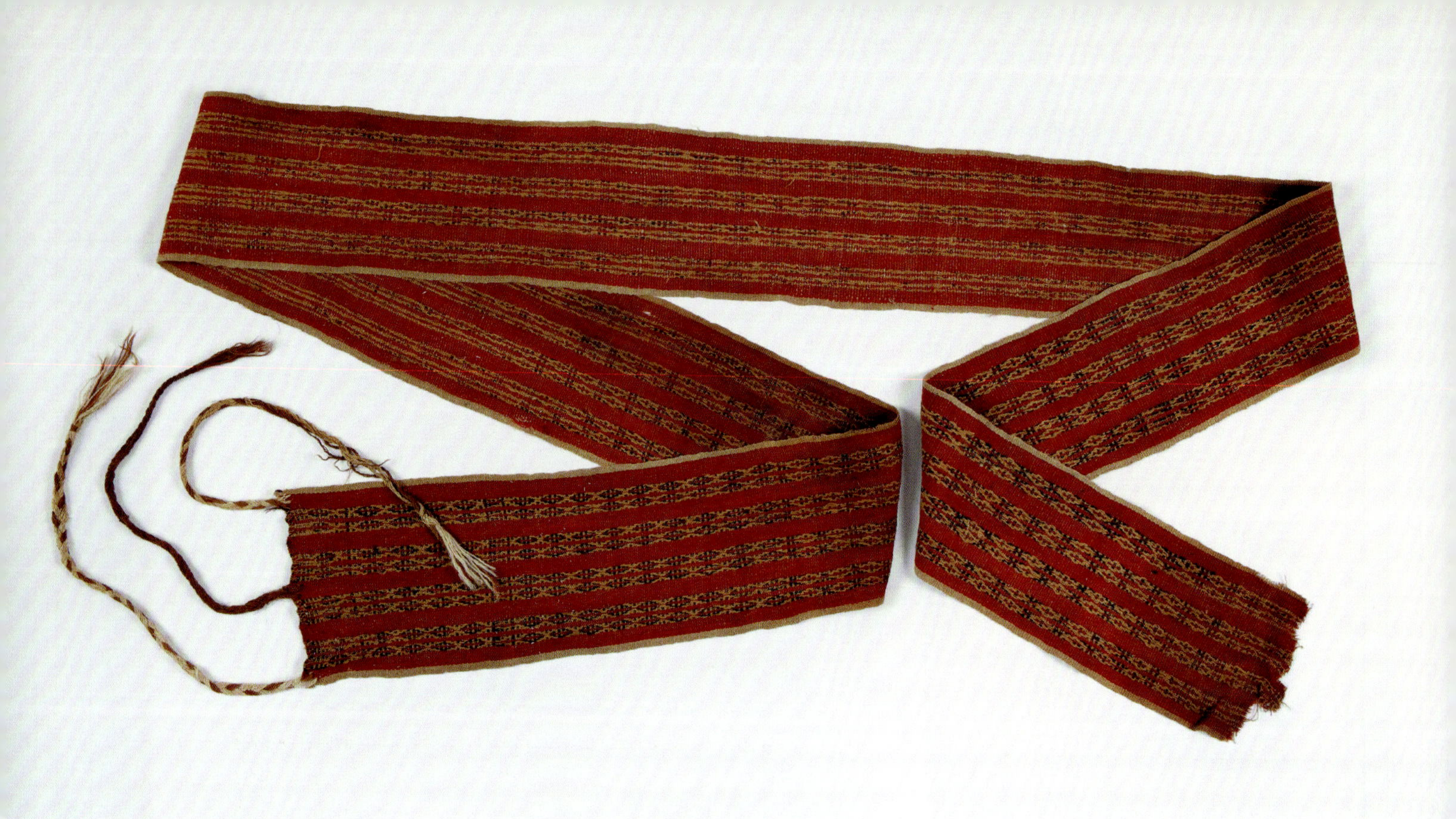

FIG. 1.7 An Inca *chumbi* (sash) with banded *tocapu* pattern, 15th–16th century. Camelid fiber, 257 × 13 cm. Fowler Museum at UCLA, Los Angeles. Such richly woven items were worn by women of high status in the Inca and colonial periods.

The narrative recited to Betanzos cannot be verified in its entirety by archaeological or other data, and it differs in some of its details from other recorded versions of the story.[23] What is most significant about the myth for Cuzco's later history is its assertion that the first Inca ruler and his sister-wife selected an unassuming wetland village as the place around which a kingdom would take shape. Narrative—here in the form of mytho-history—comes to be seen as an instrumental force in the legitimization of Cuzco as the sacred center of the Inca Empire. The myth also ascribes a number of highly symbolic acts to Manco Capac and Mama Ocllo, the first of which was the construction of a house and the planting of maize seeds they had brought from Pacarictambo, near the place where the streams that would come to be known as Saphi and Tullumayo converged. In addition to explaining the origin of Cuzco, the myth also provides an origin story for the Inca temple of the Sun, as the structure was understood to have been built on the site of the mythological couple's house.

The transformation of Alcavicça's modest village involved digging, planting, and building, but it also entailed the originary couple's introduction of an ensemble of objects and materials they had brought from Pacarictambo. Chief among them was their clothing, which is described as being of the highest quality. Manco and the other men, Betanzos writes, wore garments of fine wool woven with thin threads of gold, and around their necks they carried bags—also made of finely woven wool with gold threads—containing slingshots.[24]

The article of clothing Betanzos and Angelina Yupanqui would have imagined Manco Capac to have worn was a tunic, known in Quechua as an *uncu*, worn by elite Inca men in the fifteenth and sixteenth centuries and by their descendants in the colonial period. Surviving examples of these garments reveal how they were designed and produced. Finely woven with threads of cotton, camelid fibers, or a combination of the two, the *uncu* was a knee-length shirt formed of one or more rectangular lengths of fabric with openings for the wearer's neck and arms. The necklines and side seams of fine tunics were typically embroidered, and the bodies of the garments were woven with standardized geometric patterns that continued to be used, with some modifications, in the colonial period.[25]

Among the standard *uncu* patterns are at least two based on the form of a grid. In one of them, a field of alternating black and white squares is topped with a stepped yoke in red covering the wearer's chest and shoulders (fig. 1.5). The other is the one Rowe called "the Inca key checkerboard"—a name that references its faint formal affinity with the "Greek key" or "meander" design (fig. 1.6). Like the tunic designed with black and white squares, the "Inca key" tunic features two contiguous but differently patterned sectors, one used on the upper part of the garment and the other on its bottom third. The gridded patterns on these tunics resonate with a description from a report by Pizarro's secretary, Francisco de Xerez, who writes that a group of Inca men he saw in 1533 were dressed "in a livery of different colors, like squares on a chess board."[26]

Manco Capac and his male relatives were not the only ones to have brought exquisite garments into Cuzco, for Mama Ocllo and her female companions did so, too. They were dressed, Betanzos writes, "very richly in mantles and sashes they call *chumbis*, well made with gold thread and with very fine gold fasteners, some of which were pins two palms in length, which they call *topos*."[27] Here, the author's attention to vocabulary and translation again comes to the fore, as he introduces Quechua sartorial terminology into the Spanish-language narrative. The *chumbi*, he notes, was like a sash worn around the waist. It was used to secure a larger piece of cloth around a woman's body, thus creating a kind of belted wrap dress. Betanzos later describes a particular *chumbi* in his account of the Inca ruler Pachacuti's acceptance of his principal wife, writing that her relatives presented her to him "dressed in garments finely woven with gold and fine wool" including "a sash woven of fine wool and gold." On her sash, he notes, "there were many and diverse pictures," perhaps a reference to the geometric patterns called *tocapu* that adorned the finest of these garments, and which are preserved on some surviving examples (fig. 1.7).[28]

Betanzos's account asserts that in addition to bringing fine clothing to Cuzco, Mama Ocllo and her contemporaries also brought a rich assemblage of household goods, including "pots and small pitchers and plates and bowls and drinking vessels all made of fine gold."[29] Other colonial period accounts attest to the continued use of such objects at the time of Pizarro's invasion of the Inca Empire, but almost nothing of the range of gold vessels used in Cuzco has survived. Examples from elsewhere in the empire, however, may hint at the appearance of those used in the capital. A pair of small drinking vessels in the collection of the Art Institute of Chicago, made of an alloy of gold and copper (fig. 1.8), have a shape that calls to mind the step-bordered yoke of the black-and-white checkerboard tunic (see fig. 1.5) as well as the agricultural terraces that covered mountainsides throughout the realms of the Inca (fig. 1.9). Surviving vessels made of wood, called *queros*, also provide an idea of the design and, possibly, the geometric patterning of those made of precious metals—known as *aquillas*—in the time of the Inca (fig. 1.10).[30]

An important implication of this part of the origin myth conveyed in the *Suma y narración* is that the fine textiles and golden vessels brought to Cuzco marked the high status of the ancestral founding couple and contrasted with the clothing and everyday goods of the thirty households of lower status that had made up the village of Alcavicça until then. Indeed, Betanzos's informants imagined the transformation of the Cuzco of Alcavicça into the Cuzco of Manco Capac, Mama Ocllo, and the *orejones* as a process involving modification of the landscape through the planting of corn, the construction of a house, and the introduction of a new material and visual culture born of the deft manipulation of cloth, metal, and stone.

Following the story of the originary couple's establishment of their home in Cuzco, Betanzos jumps ahead, skipping several generations of rulers and recounting events in the reign of Pachacuti (r. 1438–71/72), whom he regards as the ninth Inca ruler. Pachacuti's name, Betanzos notes, means "change in time," and indeed the physical changes he is said to have made to Cuzco in the fifteenth century signaled the beginning of a new era.[31] Among his accomplishments was the construction of Cuzco's first monumental structure, a "House for the Sun, in which would be placed a statue to whom, in place of the Sun, [the people of Cuzco] could worship and make sacrifices."[32]

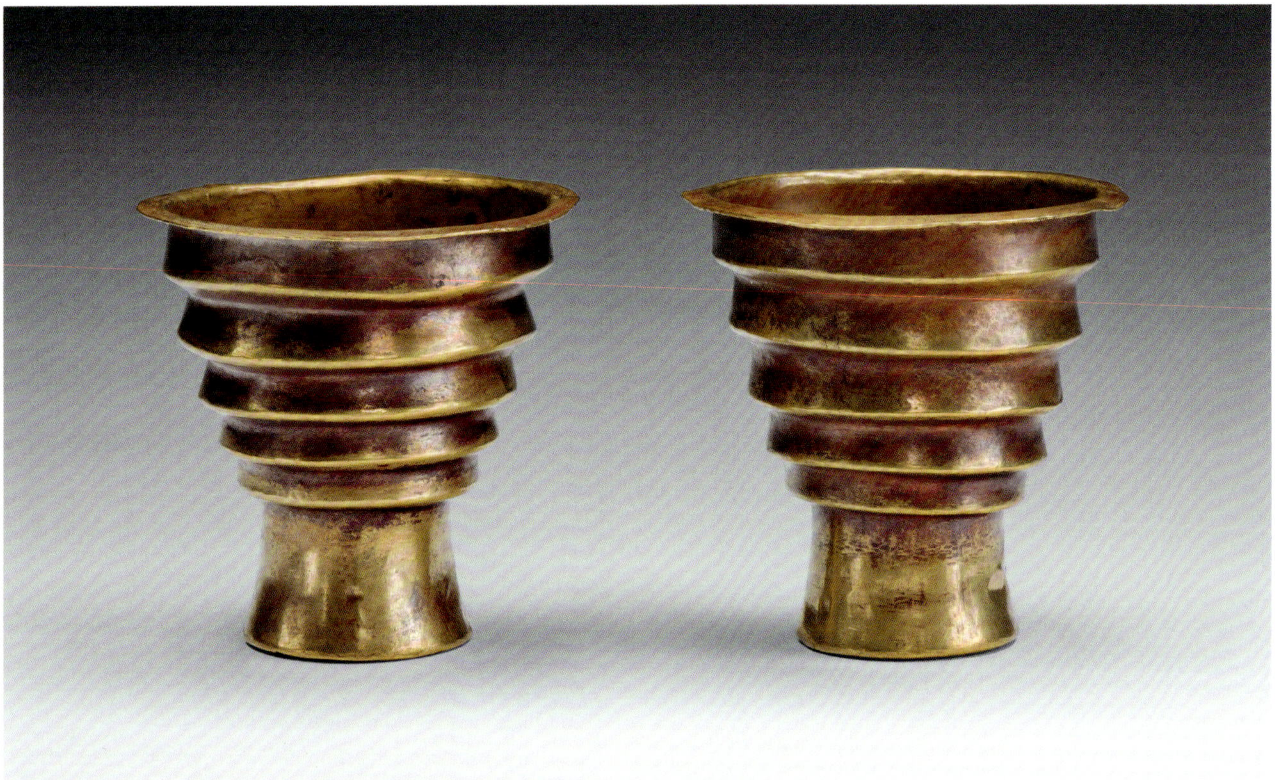

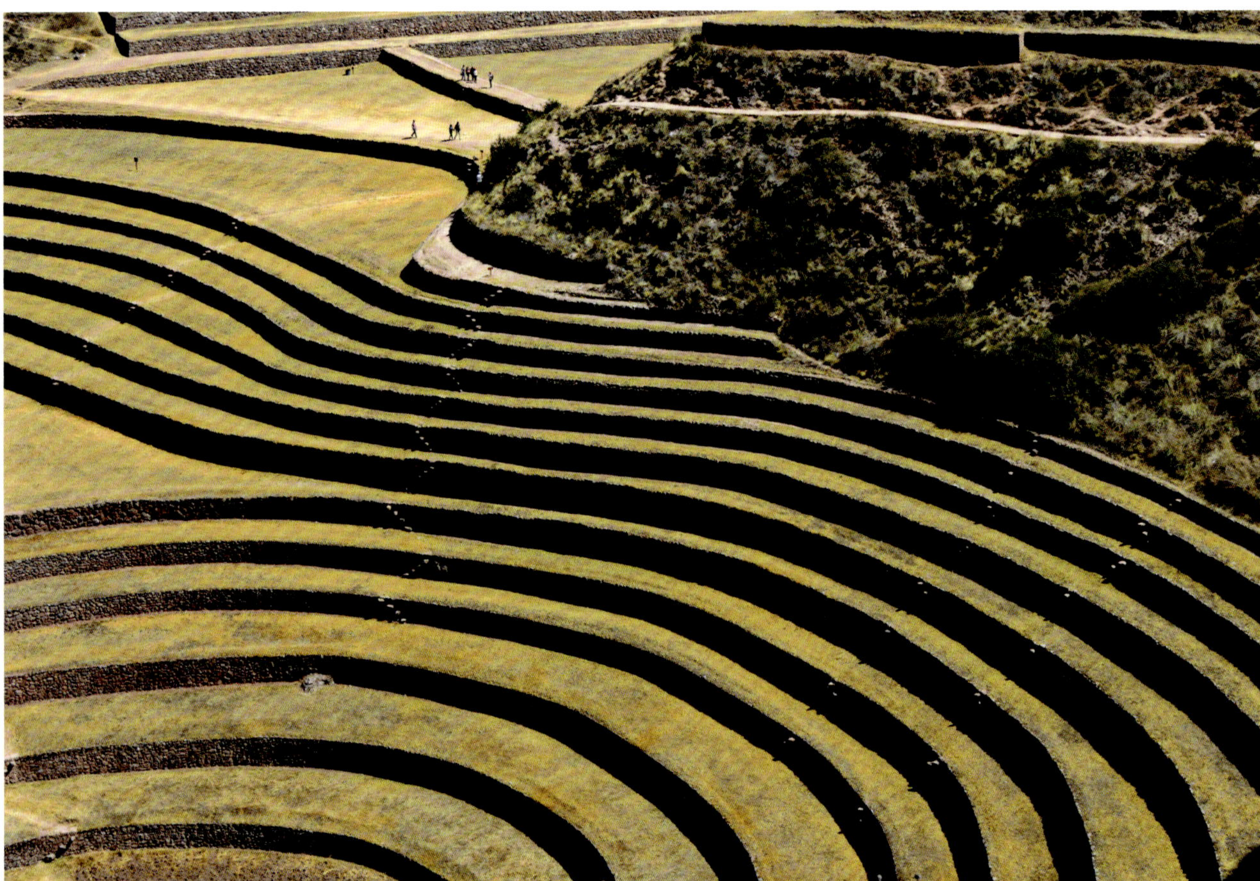

FIG. 1.8 (*facing page, top*) A pair of *aquillas* (metal drinking vessels) with stepped decoration reminiscent of other elements of Inca material culture, 15th–16th century. Gold and copper alloy, h. 7 cm. Art Institute of Chicago.

FIG. 1.9 (*facing page, bottom*) Terraces at Moray, northwest of Cuzco, 15th–16th century. Maize grown on terraces like these was used to make *chicha*, a fermented beverage consumed in pairs of vessels made of precious metals or wood.

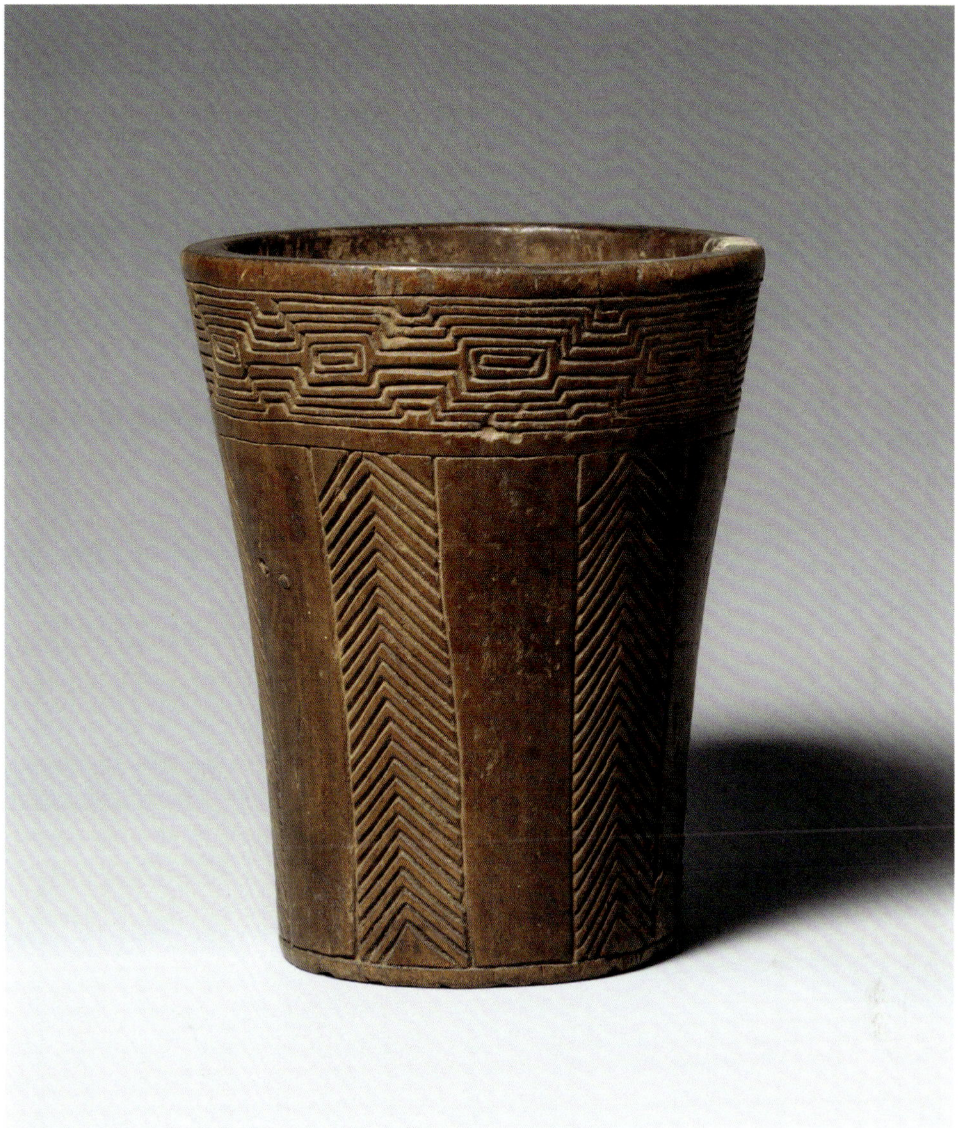

FIG. 1.10 (*right*) A *quero* (wooden drinking vessel) with characteristic geometric decoration, 15th–16th century. Wood, h. 17.8 cm. Metropolitan Museum of Art, New York. This cup would originally have been one of a pair.

The decision to begin the improvement of the city with a "House for the Sun," Betanzos writes, was driven by a supernatural event. In a story echoing that of Constantine and the Battle of the Milvian Bridge in late antiquity, the Inca king is said to have had a vision of Viracocha, who appeared to him in a guise that was bright like the sun. The vision occurred just before a victory he secured against the Chanca, an enemy state to the northwest of Cuzco. The sun like Viracocha spoke to Pachacuti, referring to him as his child and telling him to have no fear. To honor the deity, Pachacuti resolved to build a temple dedicated to the Sun, an act with a counterpart in Constantine's construction of a triumphal arch in the wake of his fourth-century victory.[33]

This passage in the *Suma y narración* speaks to the complex genealogies in early colonial texts, their engagement with European history, and the perplexing origins of mythic narratives more generally. But more importantly, it also reveals the history and symbolism of the House of the Sun as Angelina Yupanqui and her native contemporaries understood it. Its construction, they believed, was the act of Pachacuti, whose devotion to the Sun was rooted in an ancient origin story as well as in a supernatural vision he had experienced in battle. In sum, the narrative of the construction of the House of the Sun as recorded by Betanzos asserts a close relationship between the Inca king and the solar deity. This close relationship was central to Inca cosmology: the Sapa Inca was regarded as the son of the Sun, a living conduit to the supernatural who was different from, and superior to, the people he governed.

Pachacuti, Betanzos writes, was deeply involved in the design and construction of the House of the Sun. He selected for its site the place where the mythical Manco Capac and Mama Ocllo were imagined to have built their house and planted maize in the distant past. He determined its plan, measuring it and laying it out himself, and traveled to a quarry where he chose stones for the workers to cut on site. After the stone blocks were carved, workers transported them to Cuzco. Pachacuti supervised the work together with the lords of Cuzco, and it was finished, Betanzos writes, in a short time.[34]

Evidence from quarries in the environs of Cuzco supports the account of stone-carving techniques in the *Suma y narración* and other sixteenth-century sources. Most surviving Inca walls in Cuzco are built with blocks of andesite, a volcanic rock that abounds in nearby quarries such as those at Rumiqolqa, 32 km (20 mi.) to the southeast of the former Inca capital. The rock was cut on site at the quarry, using hammer-stones of varying sizes and metal chisels, before being transported by conscripted workers whose efforts were undertaken as tribute or tax paid by the provinces to the Inca state. Among the tools used to move the blocks from the quarry to the construction site were ropes made from the fibers of local vegetation and animal materials. The final shape and fit of the blocks were refined through a process of trial and error on site. These practices continued after the Spanish occupation of Cuzco, and Betanzos and his informants must have been familiar with them through direct experience.[35]

When construction of the House of the Sun was completed, Betanzos writes, Pachacuti appointed 500 virgin women and 200 young men to live there as servants to the deity, together with an elderly man who would serve as a caretaker. Ten days later, the temple was inaugurated with great fanfare. Llamas and alpacas were beheaded, and their bodies drained of blood before being cast into a large bonfire together with finely woven textiles, maize, and coca leaves. In a chilling ritual known as *capacocha*, a term Betanzos translates as "solemn sacrifice," specially selected young boys and girls from throughout the empire were richly dressed and adorned before being buried alive in the chamber that would house the image of the deity. The appearance of the chamber itself was modified: lines were painted on its walls using the blood of the sacrificed alpacas. The blood was also used to draw lines on the faces of the caretaker and servants of the Sun, as well as on those of everyone who came into the temple to throw offerings into the bonfire.[36] In this account, using animal blood to anoint a symbolic architectural space as well as the faces of individuals who participated in that space's inauguration visibly marked a community and linked it conceptually to its ruler, a deity, and a building, namely the sacred stone walls of the House of the Sun.

The bloodstained chamber, Betanzos writes, housed the temple's primary cult object: a solid gold image of the Sun in the size and shape of a one-year-old child, dressed in sandals of gold and a tunic woven from fine wool and golden threads.[37] Anthropomorphic images were a substantial part of the Inca's visual culture, as evidenced by the figurines in gold, silver, and other materials found buried as offerings throughout their lands (fig. 1.11). The image of the Sun, if it truly existed as Betanzos describes it, may have resembled those figurines, though constructed on a larger scale. In addition to being dressed in a tunic and sandals, the statue was said to have worn the *mascaypacha*, the red wool fringe or tassel that hung from a headband onto the wearer's forehead as part of the insignia of Inca kingship.

Betanzos's informants conceived of the House of the Sun as an architectural statement on the supremacy of the solar deity and as an affirmation of that deity's link to the Inca king. The relationship was rooted in events that were believed to have taken place in the past—in the time of Manco Capac and Mama Ocllo, and that of Pachacuti—and they were reinforced through elements of ornamentation such as the *mascaypacha*, worn by both the Sapa Inca and the image of the Sun, as well as through ritual practice. Betanzos writes, for example, that Pachacuti would regularly make burnt offerings of alpacas to the deity, and when he was in the chamber, no one else could enter. Such a vision of the ruler and the sacred image sharing a space to which access was highly restricted reinforced in spatial terms the close conceptual link between the two.

FIG. 1.11 Standing male figurine, 15th to early 16th century. Gold and silver alloy, h. 6.2 cm. Metropolitan Museum of Art, New York. The Inca buried such anthropomorphic figures as offerings.

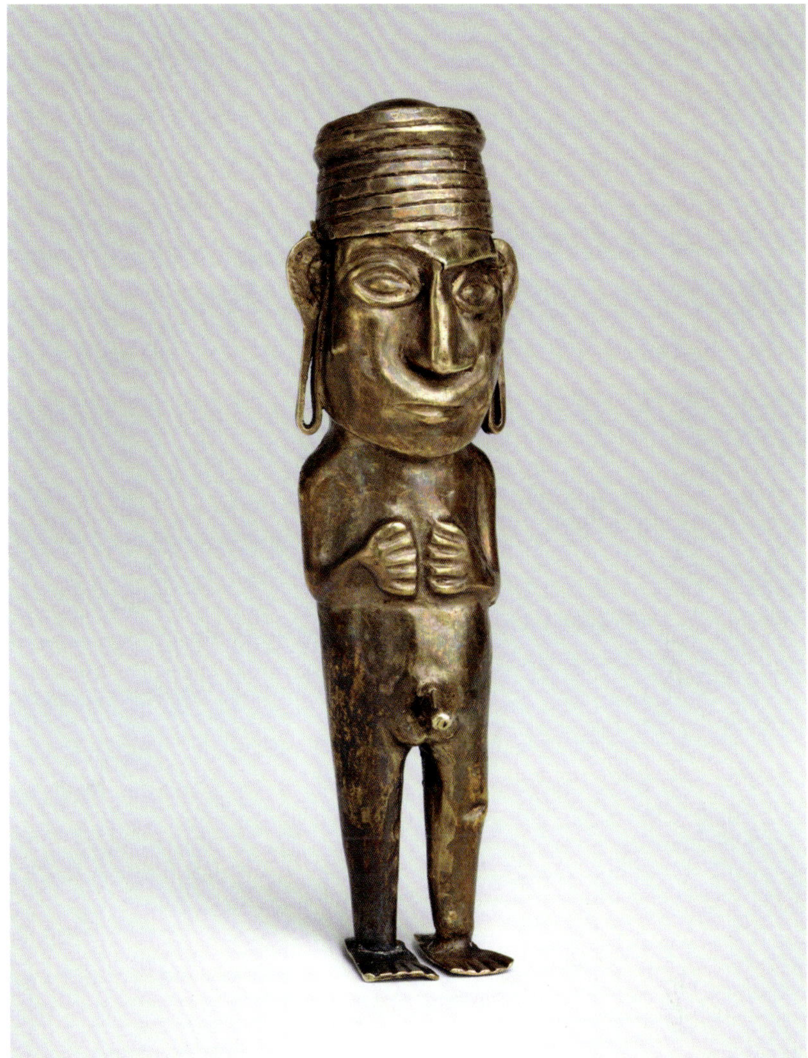

Angelina Yupanqui was not present at the inauguration of the House of the Sun; nor were Betanzos or any of his other informants. Some of the latter, however, may have been alive during the last years of Pachacuti's rule: a person born at the end of his reign (*c.* 1472) would have been around eighty years of age in the early 1550s, when the *Suma and narración* was composed. The account of the construction of the House of the Sun and the ceremonial recognition of its completion, however, like the story of the arrival of Manco Capac and Mama Ocllo to the same site, was rooted in oral history passed down to Angelina and her relatives. They may not have witnessed the events they described, but they would have been familiar with the House of the Sun and its ornamentation and, as elites in Cuzco, they likely would have witnessed ceremonies similar to those they described. It is in this way that oral history may have been embellished by the experiences and imaginations of both the informants and the author in the mid-sixteenth-century present to produce a vivid (but invented) rendering of events occurring in the distant past.

To students and scholars of Inca architecture as well as to modern tourists in Cuzco, the House of the Sun is known as Coricancha ("Compound of Gold"), a Quechua word that Betanzos does not use but which appears in chronicles composed later in the sixteenth century. Archaeological study at Coricancha has unearthed

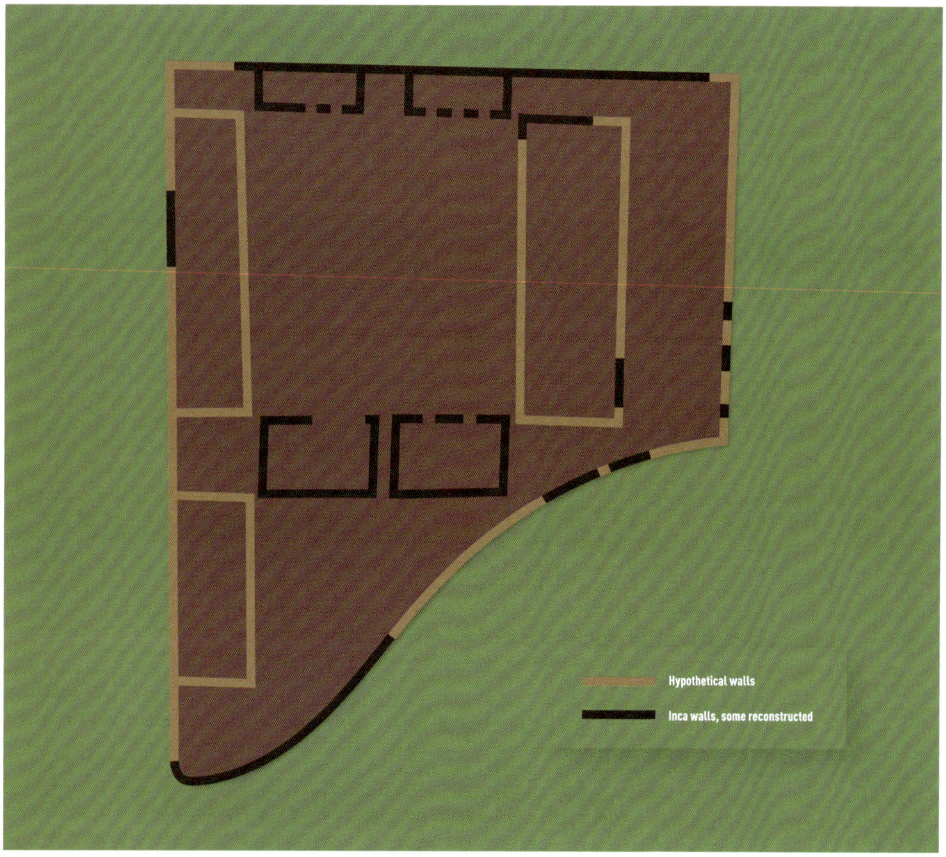

FIG. 1.12 (*left*) Plan of the House of the Sun (Coricancha), the great temple complex in Cuzco, showing existing and supposed walls.

FIG. 1.13 (*facing page*) The main cloister at the monastery of Santo Domingo, Cuzco, 16th century and later; it was originally a patio within the House of the Sun.

pre-Inca materials, suggesting that the site on which the temple was built had some importance in an earlier period. Examination of surviving Inca walls and foundations shows that the structure had grown over time from a building like the one described in the *Suma y narración* into an irregularly shaped walled compound with a patio surrounded by four or more single-room structures (fig. 1.12). Andean specialists refer to this type of enclosed compound composed of single-room structures by the Quechua name *cancha*. It is a characteristic form of Inca architecture, one found in settlements throughout the empire.[38]

The patio in the House of the Sun was transformed for use as the main cloister of the monastery of Santo Domingo in the sixteenth century, and eventually that space would be rebuilt with galleries on two stories (fig. 1.13). Modern excavations in the cloister have uncovered the burnt remains of llamas, thus lending credence to Betanzos's claim that animal sacrifices were offered to the image of the Sun. Also found were a child's jawbone and a set of primary teeth together with small human and llama figurines made of gold, silver, bronze, and *Spondylus* shell. Metal *tupu* pins accompanied the jawbone, teeth, and the human figurines, suggesting that, like the anthropomorphic golden image of the Sun, these children and statuettes may have been buried dressed in textile tunics or shawls.[39] This same assemblage is found in connection with the practice of the *capacocha* ritual throughout the Inca Empire: sacrificed children were dressed in fine textiles and buried with small vessels and figurines clothed in similarly designed garments of high quality (fig. 1.14).[40]

The golden image of the Sun was installed in its chamber in the House of the Sun, where it rested upon a wooden seat covered with iridescent feathers. The caretaker of the Sun, Betanzos writes, prepared food and drink for it "as if the Sun were a person who ate and drank," and the Inca king and the lords of Cuzco made offerings to it.[41] A passage from the *Suma y narración* recounting how Huayna Capac conducted an inspection of the temple may be rooted

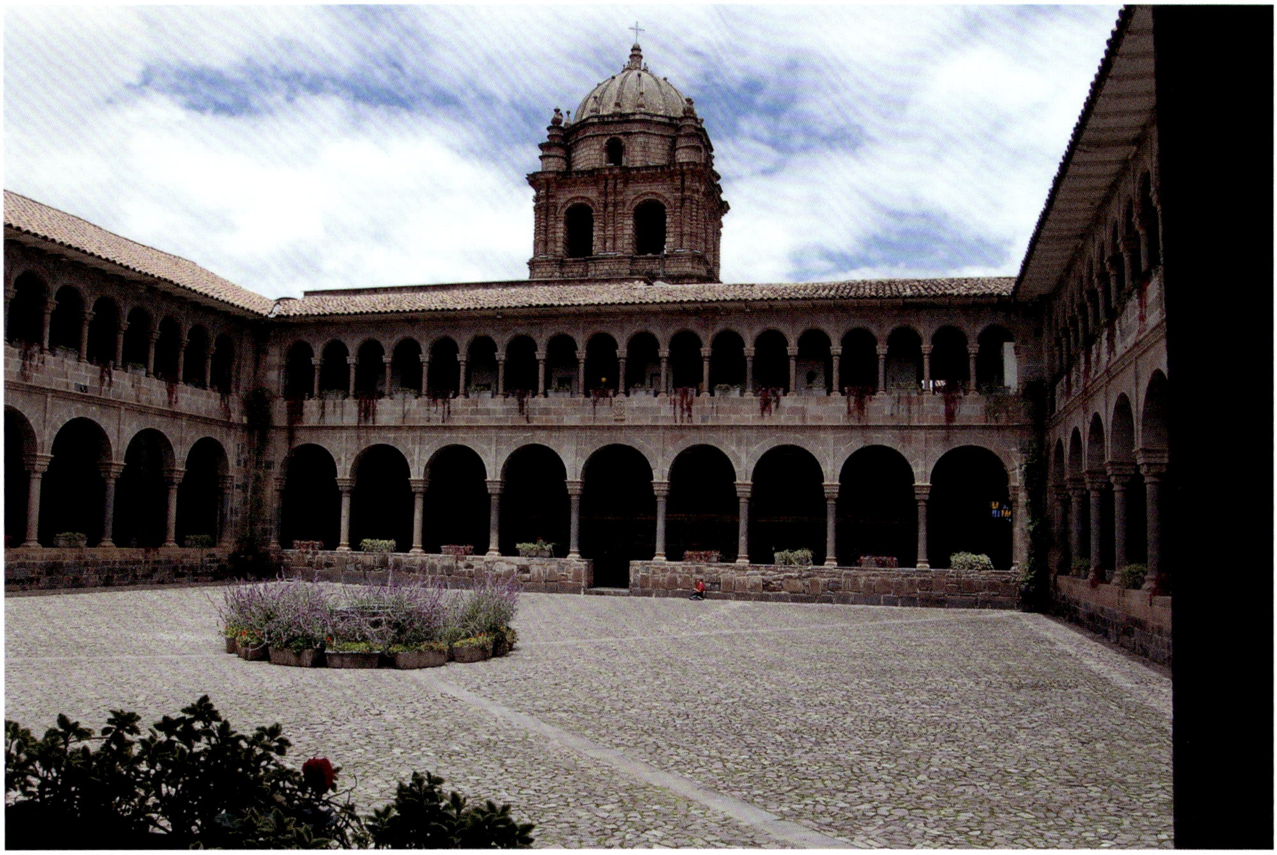

in the memories of Betanzos's informants concerning ritual practices, participants, and paraphernalia within the walls of the sacred compound during their own lifetimes:

> As he arrived at the door, [Huayna Capac] took off his shoes and holding his head somewhat low, he made his show of respect to the Sun. And then, before the image of the Sun, he himself lighted in a golden brazier a small bundle of firewood the servants of the Sun brought . . . and lighting fire he burned a lamb in it, sacrificing it to the Sun and beheading it alive first, and offering that blood that flowed out of the lamb to the Sun. When this was done, he left there, making his show of respect to the Sun, and entered inside the compound into a certain room where the caretaker of the Sun led him. The Inca entered with his cousin Yamque Yupanqui and the two lords who had been governors, and no one else went in. And in front of all of them, that lord caretaker of the Sun told the Inca about the things and riches of the Sun that were under his charge.[42]

This passage from the *Suma y narración* contends that when Huayna Capac entered the House of the Sun, three other men of high rank accompanied him—among them, Yamque Yupanqui, Angelina's father. To allow people of lower rank (*la gente común*) to show reverence to the solar deity, a second locus of worship was established. Betanzos says it was placed in the middle of Cuzco's festival plaza.

The large plaza at the core of Inca Cuzco was the setting for ceremonial feasting and an array of ritual acts, including those marking the accession and death of the rulers and the initiation of warriors drawn from the ranks of the Inca elite. It was also in that space, says Betanzos, that the ceremonial cutting of Cuxirimay's hair occurred on her first birthday.

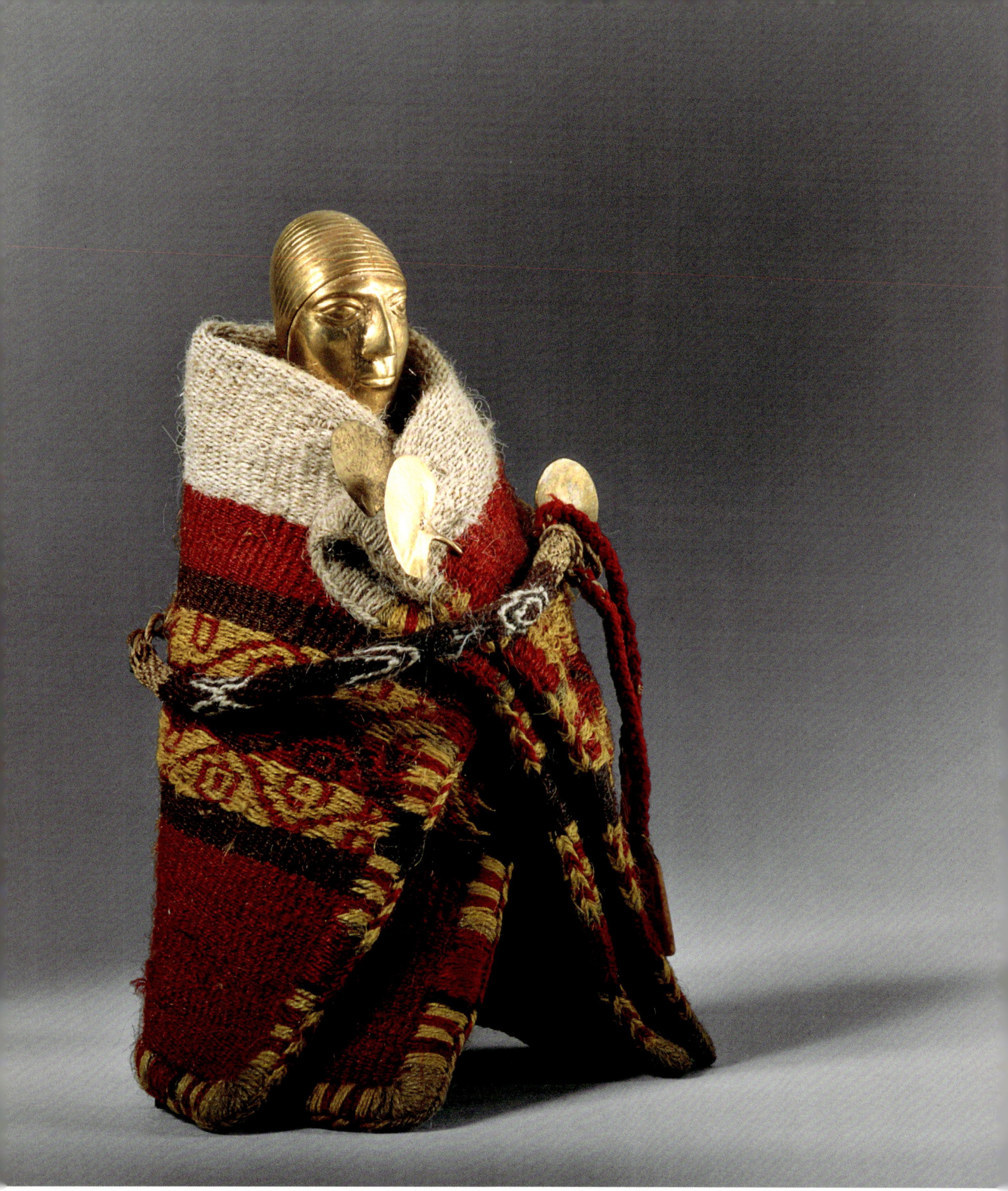

Known by the later sixteenth century as Haucaypata—a term González Holguín translates as "the plaza of Cuzco for festivals, rest, and drunkenness"—and situated on relatively level ground, it was bounded on its southwest side by the canalized Saphi, beyond which extended another large open space.[43] On its northwest side, a series of terraces ascended the mountainside and were cut through by another canalized stream, the Tullumayo.

In his recounting of the ritual of hair-cutting, Betanzos does not mention the presence of an object serving as a locus of solar worship in the plaza, but elsewhere in the text he does. The image of the Sun in the plaza, he writes, was a stone that was "carved like a sugarloaf, pointed on top, and covered with a band of gold."[44] Said to have been erected during the reign of Pachacuti near the time of the dedication of the House of the Sun, this stone monument to the deity was placed atop a hole into which devotees placed pieces of gold as offerings. The hole was covered, Betanzos writes, by a block of stone cut to serve as a base for the deity image. Around that platform, the people of Cuzco buried offerings to the Sun including figurines made of gold, "each one the length and thickness of one finger," arranged in groups to represent each of Cuzco's royal lineages. When the stone image of the Sun was set in place, the people of Cuzco sacrificed llamas and alpacas to it, just as the lords of Cuzco had done at the House of the Sun. This practice of making sacrifices in the festival plaza continued, the author notes, "from that time until the Spaniards entered the city of Cuzco"—that is, until 1533.[45]

The stone shaped like a sugarloaf no longer stands in the plaza of Cuzco, but analogues to that sacred object described by Betanzos may be the conical stones uncovered by archaeologists at a tiered platform at the site of Incapirca Waminan. Carved in andesite, two of the stones were fashioned with bases that would have enabled them to fit into a carved-stone socket. Similarly shaped stones have been found in excavations elsewhere in the Andes, thus suggesting that the form and shape of the stone described in the *Suma y narración* had a widespread use and symbolism.[46] Excavations at the center of the plaza undertaken in the 1990s, in connection with the maintenance of the nineteenth-century cast-iron fountain that stands there today, unearthed the remains of a diorite and limestone wall that may have served as an *ushnu*, a platform like the one at Incapirca Waminan that accommodated sacred conical stones.[47]

The study of the *ushnu* as a structural type among the Inca has revealed great variety in expressions of the form, but research has shown that extant *ushnus* share at least two features: a staircase providing access to the uppermost surface of the platform; and a hole, canal, fissure, or other means of access to the underground. According to Betanzos, the sugarloaf-shaped image of the Sun was positioned on a stone base; the remains of the stone structure uncovered near the center of the modern Plaza de Armas may thus represent the larger and more elaborate form the platform took in the years that followed its inauguration. An ensemble of objects associated with the ritual practice of the Inca was found buried nearby; it included pieces of decorated pottery, camelid bones, charcoal, and a set of miniature llama figurines made of gold, silver, and *Spondylus* shell.[48]

Betanzos relates the stories of the inauguration of the two sacred images of the Sun in a chapter entitled "How the Inca Yupanqui Made the House of the Sun and the Statue of the Sun."[49] The account emphasizes the interrelatedness of the House of the Sun and the festival plaza as settings for the installation of deity images and as the loci of ritual practices performed to honor that deity. One of the ways in which it does so is formal: Betanzos textually interweaves the stories of the origins of those spaces and the installation of their deity images. The chapter begins with the tale of the construction of the House of the Sun and the making of the anthropomorphic golden image of the Sun; it then shifts to a description of the stone monument in the plaza, before moving back and forth between the two sites once more. The complementarity of the two centers of worship is stressed in a variety of ways: one is an enclosed compound, the other is in an open space; access to one is

FIG. 1.14 (*facing page*) Female figurine dressed in a pinned mantle decorated with the "Inca key" pattern, such as were worn by Inca women, 15th or early 16th century. Gold and camelid fiber, h. 10 cm. Ethnologisches Museum, Berlin. The widespread distribution of these figurines in the Andes attests to their prevalence in ritual practice.

highly restricted, the other is open to a larger public; one of the cult objects is a naturalistic image, the other a geometric shape; one is made of gold, the other of stone.

These aspects of the text bring to the fore the duality, complementarity, and reciprocity that are characteristic of Andean metaphysics more broadly, presenting them as concepts through which Betanzos's informants understood the design and symbolism of Inca Cuzco. There and throughout the pre-Hispanic Andes, physical space and the people who occupied it were conceived in terms of two complementary parts known as *hanan* (upper) and *hurin* (lower). According to Betanzos, the definition of those sectors was part of the design and construction of the settlement. Pachacuti, he claims, ordered "three lords, his friends, to settle in the area from the House of the Sun down toward the confluence of the two rivers, and that the space where they built houses between the rivers and below it be called Hurin Cuzco, which means the low part of Cuzco."[50] Those three lords, the author notes, were related to Pachacuti, but their mothers were of low status, and thus their lineages and the sector of Cuzco in which they resided were of lower status than their more elevated complements.

With respect to Hanan Cuzco, Betanzos writes, "from the Houses of the Sun upward, with everything between the two rivers up to the hilltop . . . he [Pachacuti] gave and distributed to his closest relatives and descendants of his lineage."[51] This sociospatial arrangement was rooted in the complementarity of the two sectors of the city, but it also entailed a degree of asymmetry, with Hanan Cuzco having higher status and being more closely aligned with Pachacuti and his descendants. This conceptualization of space and its inhabitants in terms of "upper" and "lower" extended to the surrounding villages and, indeed, throughout the empire, and these sociospatial designations were central to the reciprocal relationships that structured activities of trade, labor, ritual practice, and other aspects of imperial administration.[52]

The visual culture of the Inca is replete with objects and images that gave form and shape to dyadic concepts like *hanan* and *hurin*. *Queros* and *aquillas* were made in pairs and used in ritual toasting and drinking to establish and maintain reciprocal relationships between individuals and social groups. The rectilinear geometric patterns on fine Inca textiles convey these concepts as well, but they do so in graphic form. For example, the repeating motif in the "Inca key" tunic features a diagonal line that divides a square space into two halves, each of which features a small square. The repetition of the motif on the tunics expresses duality and complementarity in other ways, too. Adjacent motifs are contraposed, differing from one another both in the disposition of the diagonal element and in the use of contrasting dark and light colors (see fig. 1.6).

The special character of the dual spaces designed as expressions of reverence for the Sun in Cuzco—the House of the Sun and the festival plaza—was made manifest through their status as centers of networks that spread from the Inca capital outward to the farthest reaches of the empire. The House of the Sun was conceived as the center of a network of sacred mountains, outcrops of rock, burials, and bodies of water that spread outward in all directions like the threads of a spider's web. The Inca called these sacred places *huacas*, a term Betanzos defines as "temple or idol."[53] Among the sacred objects and spaces in this network were some associated with the creation story told to Betanzos by his native informants: one was said to have been located at a spot where Viracocha had lit and then extinguished a great fire on his way to Cuzco; another was sited atop a mountain where he rested on that same journey.

The vast network of shrines of which these *huacas* were a part is described in other colonial period sources and is known as the *ceque* system. It consisted of more than 300 sacred objects and places conceived as points on forty-one imaginary lines emanating from the House of the Sun. The *huacas* are frequent points of reference in the *Suma y narración*, indicating that travel through the sacred landscape of the Inca Empire was understood by at least some Andean elites in relation to the location of those sacred objects and spaces. In the time of the Inca, the making of offerings to the *huacas* was an obligation imposed by the state and was intimately tied to official calendrics, demonstrating the degree to which the system fused the notions of space and time.[54]

The festival plaza, too, was the center of a network—an extensive system of roads that led from Cuzco into the four sectors of the empire. The sector called Chinchaysuyu was to the northwest, extending to the Pacific coast and reaching into the northern Andes beyond Quito. Andesuyu extended to the north and northeast of Cuzco, paralleling the course of Río Madre de Dios toward what is today the border between Bolivia and Brazil. Collasuyu, to the south and southeast, included the southern highlands of Bolivia, Chile, and Argentina, while Condesuyu, the smallest of the sectors in terms of area, extended to the southwest of Cuzco. Certain *tocapu* patterns on Inca tunics gave shape to this concept of Tahuantinsuyu as an entity composed of four parts. For example, a number of the repeating motifs on the spectacular tunic in the collection of Dumbarton Oaks (fig. 1.15) are quadripartite forms encapsulating the idea of the Inca Empire as "four parts in one" with great force and simplicity while simultaneously bearing witness to the production of the tunic through weaving, a process in which a grid of threads is the structure that gives shape to patterned cloth.

Ritual practice in Cuzco involved various forms of human activity taking place on both the festival plaza and the road system, thus reinforcing Cuzco's status as a center and amplifying its association with the Inca ruler. Betanzos provides several examples of this phenomenon, including the story of a six-day festival convened by Pachacuti to initiate the payment of taxes in the form of fine cloth. The lords of the provinces were called to Cuzco, where the festival plaza had been covered in grasses and decorated with branches full of flowers and birds. The lords of Cuzco, the provincial rulers, and the wives of those men engaged in ritual feasting, toasting and drinking, singing, dancing, and storytelling. At the end of six days, the provincial lords returned to their home settlements with instructions for the production of fine cloth. When the cloth had been produced, it was brought back to Cuzco, where it was kept in houses built for the storage of tribute goods. In this way, ritual and the tracing and retracing of steps on the extensive Inca road system facilitated imperial administration and economics. At the same time, this spatial practice sustained and intensified Cuzco's status as a center connected in multiple ways to settlements on its periphery.[55]

The account in the *Suma y narración* suggests that, for Angelina Yupanqui and Betanzos's other informants, the physical environment of Cuzco and an ensemble of finely crafted objects within it gave shape to Inca history, ritual practice, and metaphysics. For them, it was the center of a sacred landscape, having been built on the site where the mythic Manco Capac and Mama Ocllo were said to have founded the dynasty in the ancient past. Actual construction, they believed, was spearheaded by Pachacuti, and Cuzco housed two deity images conceived as links to the supernatural and, simultaneously, as reminders of the king's status as the son of the Sun. The division of the city into two complementary parts, *hanan* and *hurin*, rendered it a spatial model through which the intertwined narratives of history and kinship were understood. Finally, as the setting for an array of rituals through which the realms of the Inca were governed, Cuzco was—for Angelina and her kin—the center of the world. This view of Cuzco persisted into the 1550s, when Betanzos composed the *Suma y narración*, but it was a very different conception of the city and its infrastructure from that held by the Spanish fortune seekers, who learned of the existence of the Inca capital only in the early 1530s. It is to their visions of Cuzco that we now turn.

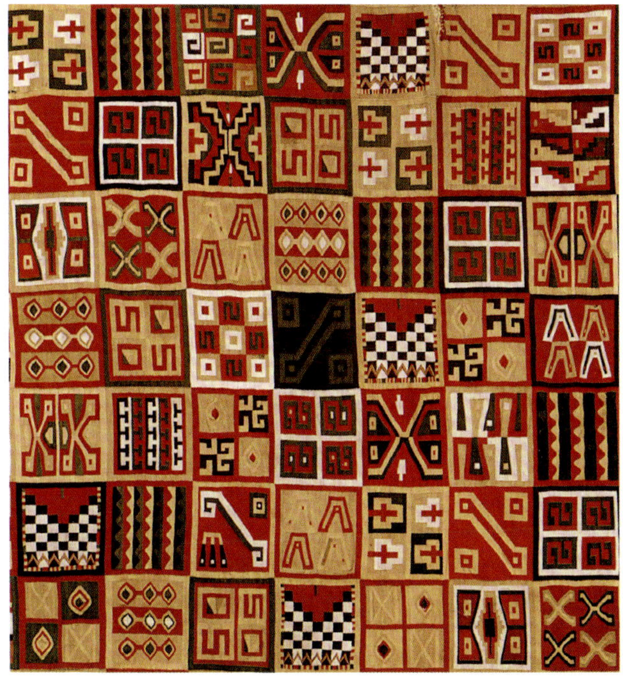

FIG. 1.15 Detail of an Inca *uncu* (tunic) decorated all over with *tocapu* patterns, 15th or early 16th century. Camelid fiber and cotton, 90.2 × 77.2 cm. Dumbarton Oaks Museum, Washington, DC. The spectacular patterning of quadripartite motifs reflects the Inca worldview of four parts in one, with the quadripartite whole embodied in the Sapa Inca, the tunic's likely wearer.

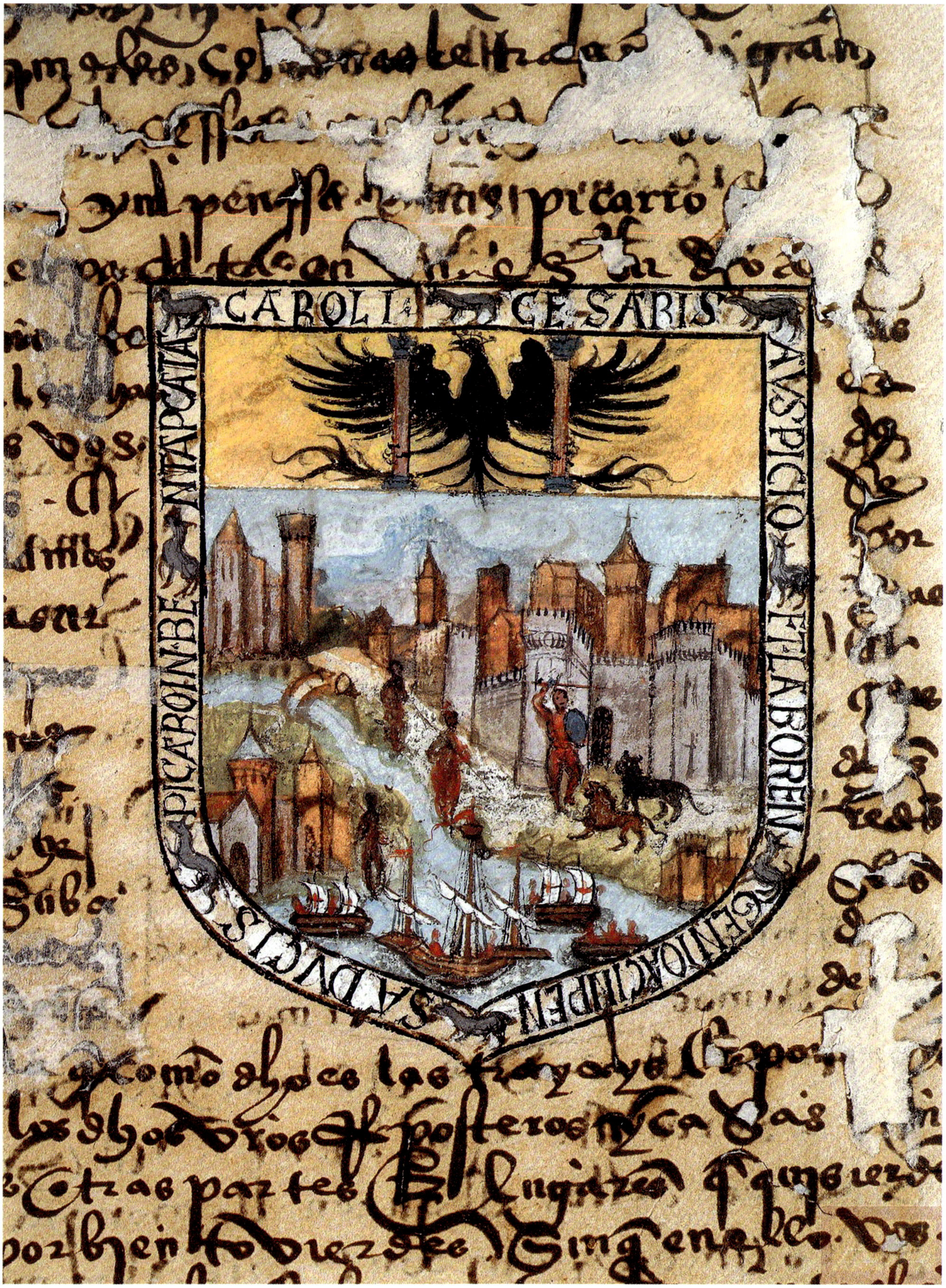
CAROLI CESARIS
AVSPICIO ET LABORE INGENIO AC IMPEN
SA DVCIS
PICARRO INBENTA ET PACATA

CHAPTER 2

Dreaming of Inca Cuzco

Cristóbal de Mena, Francisco de Xerez, and the Conquest of Peru

Sometime after the ceremony in which he cut Cuxirimay's hair on the festival terrace, Huayna Capac left Cuzco with a multitude of warriors—Betanzos says 50,000—bound for Quito, a royal administrative center 1,600 km (1,000 mi.) away in the northernmost reaches of the empire. The ruler and his cohort traveled on foot along the Chinchaysuyu road, which snaked its way northward through the Andes. The road was an impressive feat of design and construction; much of it was paved, some stretches were remarkably wide, and many parts survive intact today (fig. 2.1).[1] The king and his retinue stopped to rest at way stations along the route, and they arrived at their destination several months later. Inca Quito—like Inca Cuzco—was a densely built environment replete with temples, palaces, and festival halls to accommodate the Inca elite and their ritual practices. But unlike Cuzco, little of Inca Quito remains visible today, though foundations of Inca structures lie beneath many of its colonial period buildings.[2]

Huayna Capac would spend the next few years in Quito, at the end of which time he fell seriously ill. The illness, Betanzos writes, "took his reason and understanding and gave him a skin disease like leprosy that greatly weakened him."[3] Whether that disease was smallpox, which had caused the death of a great number of native people in Aztec Mexico since the 1520s, is a topic of debate.[4] Realizing he was near death, and after some equivocation, the ailing Sapa Inca named as his successor his son Huascar, who had remained in Cuzco. He died four days later, in 1525, and as was customary at an Inca ruler's death, the noblemen who were with him in Quito mummified his body. Betanzos describes the process in great detail:

> They had him opened and all his flesh taken out, preparing him so that he not be harmed and without breaking any bone. They prepared and cured him in the sun and the air, and after being dried and cured, they dressed him in prized clothing and placed him on a sumptuous litter well adorned with feathers and gold. And with the body now being this way, they sent him to Cuzco.[5]

Huayna Capac—now a richly garbed desiccated corpse—returned to the sacred center of his realms, tracing in reverse the path he had taken from Cuzco to Quito six years earlier. Dressed in fine clothing and placed on a platform decorated with feathers and gold, his affinity with the similarly dressed and adorned cult image in the House of the Sun was clear. His mummy bundle would now take its place among the most revered objects in the sacred center of the Inca Empire.

(facing page) See figure 2.3.

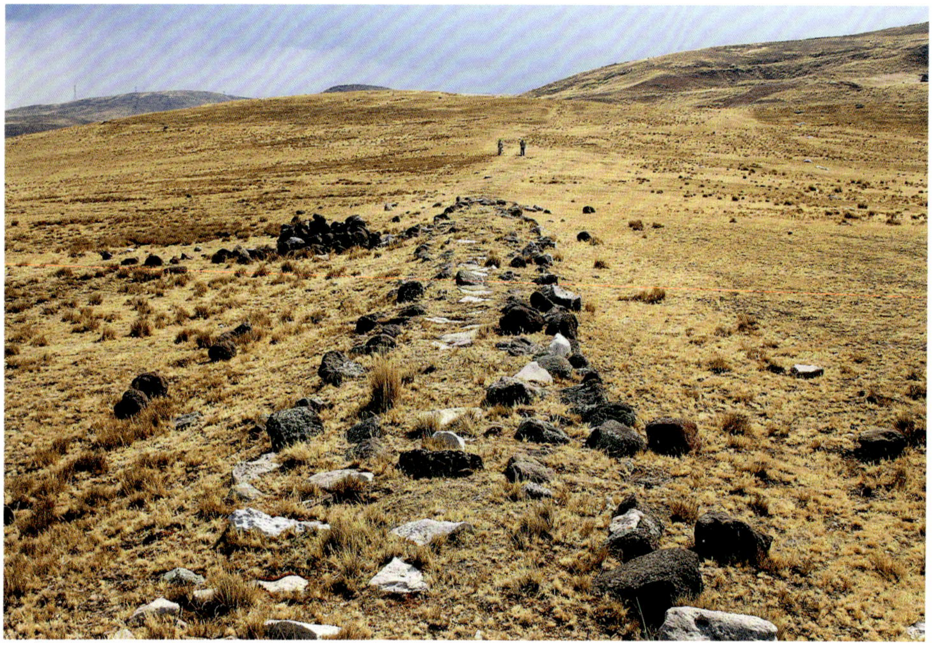

FIG. 2.1 A stretch of the Chinchaysuyu road southwest of Xauxa. Huayna Capac and his retinue came this way on their journey to Quito in *c.* 1520; just over a decade later, Francisco Pizarro and his company passed in the other direction on their way to Cuzco.

The death of Huayna Capac marked the end of a reign that had lasted for more than three decades, and like the deaths of kings in so many other places and times, it gave rise to a period of political unrest. According to Betanzos, neither Huascar nor his brother Atahualpa was considered a legitimate son of their father, and the death of the ruler intensified the enmity between the two potential heirs and the factions allied with them. The structure of the *Suma y narración* acknowledges the magnitude of this turn of events as they were remembered in the 1550s, for it is at this point in the narrative that a new section of the manuscript is signaled graphically with a second title page. "Here begins the story of the two sons of Huayna Capac, called Atahualpa and Huascar," Betanzos writes, "and of the wars and divisions there were between the two brothers over which of the two would be lord and would rule."[6]

The events of this period as recorded in the *Suma y narración* are strongly biased, favoring—as one might expect—Angelina's former husband, Atahualpa. Huascar, in turn, is presented as a heartless and paranoid drunkard. In one striking passage, Betanzos reports that Huascar ordered the flaying of one of Atahualpa's messengers, the latter's skin to be cured and used as the head of a war drum. On another occasion, he directed his underlings to decapitate Atahualpa so that he could drink from his skull. Betanzos recounts in detail the story of the expedition to find Atahualpa, behead him, and bring his head to Huascar, striking a tragicomic note in reporting that the leader of the mission was none other than Cuxirimay's brother, whose kinship with his sister is signaled by his name, Cuxi. Following Huascar's order, Cuxi and his troops departed from Cuzco, making their way northward on the Chinchaysuyu road, but they were captured by Atahualpa's forces before they were able to fulfill their mission. Atahualpa, the author writes, embraced his would-be assassin; the two joined forces against Huascar, and together they arranged for Cuxirimay, then just ten years old, to be brought to them from Cuzco. A passage in the *Suma y narración* provides a moving detail about her rescue: when the young girl was found in the Inca capital, she was crying, for she thought her brother had been killed. One cannot help but think that Angelina herself remembered the episode and recounted it to Betanzos decades later.[7]

In the wake of Cuxi's capture and the shift in his allegiance, Atahualpa came to consider himself the ascendant Inca ruler. To affirm his status, he embarked on a series of conquests in which he subjugated rebellious communities and consolidated his power in the northern provinces. In the town of Caranqui (near present-day Ibarra, Ecuador) he accepted the *mascaypacha* to mark his sovereignty over the realms of the Inca, and fulfilled his deceased father's wish that he take Cuxirimay as his principal wife.[8] After his investiture and marriage, he continued on his journey, moving southward through the Andes with Cuxirimay, his retainers, and his warriors. Sometime in the early 1530s, they were all in the highland settlement of Huamachuco, south of Cajamarca, when three messengers from the distant village of Tangarará, some 700 km (435 mi.) to the northwest and closer to the coast, arrived with remarkable news:

> Some white and bearded people have arrived in our town .... They have a kind of sheep on which they ride and travel, and they are very much larger than ours. These men are dressed so that no skin but their hands and face is seen. And of their face, only half of it is seen because the other half is covered with a beard. These men are fitted with a kind of belt over their garments and from it hang pieces of silver that look like those sticks that the women put in their warp threads to tighten what they are weaving.[9]

This, Betanzos writes, was the first time Atahualpa, Cuxirimay, and their retinue became aware of the existence of Francisco Pizarro and his company. The Tangarará messengers' description of them brings to the fore the dynamics of perception and translation in early colonial Peru. In a move that emphasizes the primacy of both cloth and metal in Inca visual and material culture, the daggers and swords carried by Pizarro's men are likened to weaving tools. Stressing the novelty of the horse to Quechua-speaking native Andeans, the messengers compared Pizarro's mounts to sheep (*ovejas*), referring to the llamas, alpacas, and other camelids native to the region.[10]

As Atahualpa and Cuxirimay were learning of the arrival of the "white and bearded people," those foreigners in the realms of the Inca were also using words and images to make sense of people, places, and things that seemed in some ways familiar to them, and, in other ways, quite alien. Their early experiences in the Andes are documented in accounts penned in the 1530s by Spaniards in Pizarro's company, and those writings, too, demonstrate the complexities of communication in an intercultural setting. Indeed, they provide a wholly different perspective on Inca Cuzco, its plan, its buildings, and their symbolism from that related to Betanzos by his native informants in the 1550s. These early sixteenth-century mental images of the city would be an operative force in the transformation of Inca Cuzco, recasting its infrastructure as a Spanish colonial settlement and repositioning it within a set of legendary narratives, a new system of governance, and a transatlantic economy based in precious metals.

"In February 1531, we boarded ship at the port of Panama, which is in Tierra Firme. We were two hundred and fifty men, eighty of them with horses, and we set sail with the very magnificent and brave nobleman Francisco Pizarro as captain." So begins *La conquista del Perú, llamada la nueva Castilla* (*The Conquest of Peru, called New Castile*; hereafter, *Conquista del Perú*), a fourteen-page booklet first published in the Seville printing shop of Bartolomé Pérez (active 1527–42) in April 1534 (fig. 2.2). Nowhere in the text does the name of its author appear, but the historian Raúl Porras Barrenenchea attributed it in the 1930s to Cristóbal de Mena, one of several experienced and literate captains in the company led by Pizarro. Mena hailed from the Spanish town of Ciudad Real, about 300 km (186 mi.) northeast of Seville (see map 3, p. 19), but as is the case with his contemporary Juan de Betanzos, little more about his early years has come to light. By 1528 he was an officeholder on the town council of Granada, Nicaragua, one of the earliest Spanish settlements on the American mainland, and as he notes in the opening line of the booklet, he participated in Pizarro's third expedition into Peru.[11]

For his part, Pizarro had arrived in the Americas in 1502, in the fleet of Nicolás de Ovando (1460–1511), the governor of Hispaniola, who, like the future conqueror of Peru, hailed from Extremadura. Pizarro rose through the ranks of conquistadors, leading expeditions on the Central American mainland before becoming one the closest and most trusted associates of Pedrarias Dávila (*c.* 1468–1531), the man appointed by King Ferdinand to explore and govern the lands around the Caribbean then known as Tierra Firme. Dávila appointed Pizarro to the municipal council of the town of Panama in 1519, and in the 1520s Pizarro led two exploratory expeditions in search of riches in Peru before returning temporarily to Spain in 1528. In July

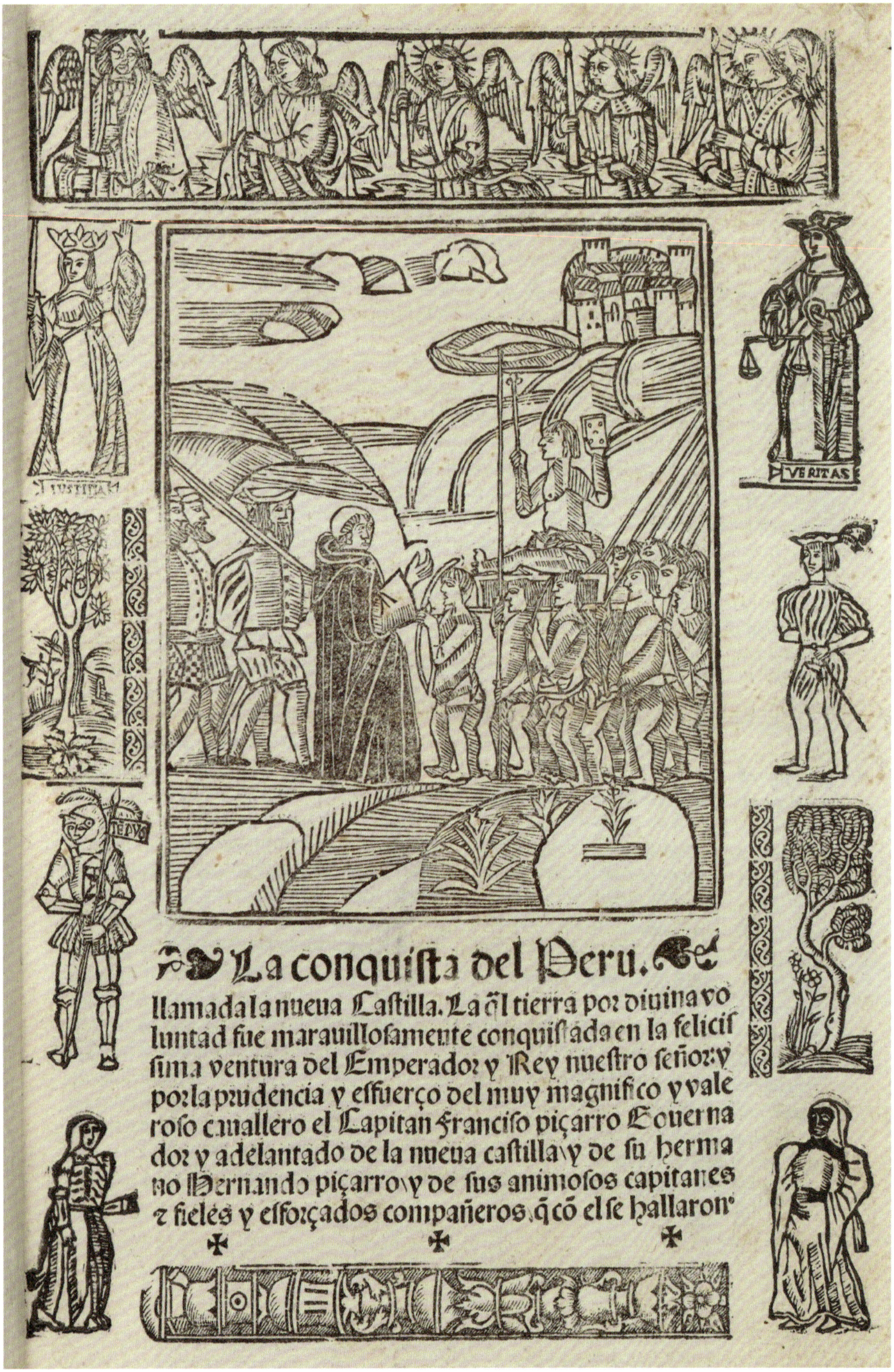

La conquista del Peru.

llamada la nueua Castilla. La q̃l tierra por diuina vo
luntad fue marauillosamente conquistada en la felicis
sima ventura del Emperador y Rey nuestro señor: y
por la prudencia y esfuerço del muy magnifico y vale
roso cauallero el Capitan Francisco piçarro Gouerna
dor y adelantado de la nueua castilla y de su herma
no Hernando piçarro y de sus animosos capitanes
z fieles y esforçados compañeros q̃ cõ el se hallaron.

FIG. 2.2 (*facing page*) Title page of Cristóbal de Mena, *La conquista del Perú* (Seville: Bartolomé Pérez, 1534). Ink on paper. New York Public Library, New York. The image shows a meeting between the Dominican friar Vicente de Valverde and Atahualpa, the Inca king, which took place in 1532.

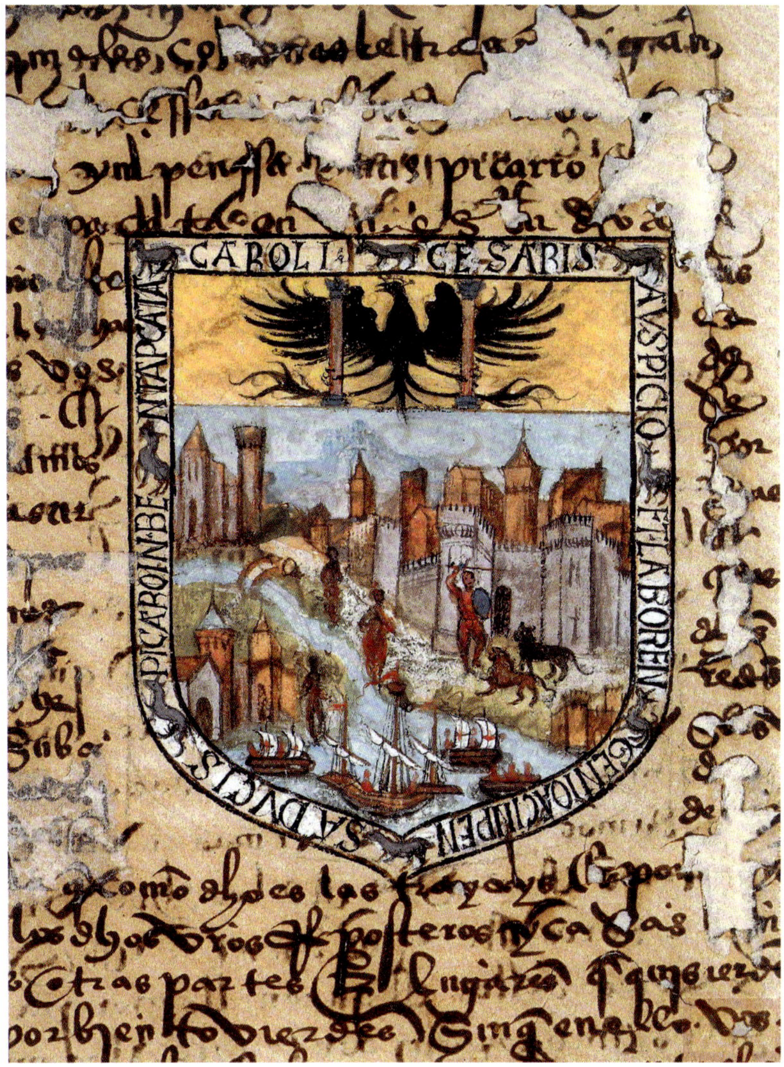

FIG. 2.3 (*right*) The coat of arms granted to Francisco Pizarro as expedition leader in 1529. Pigment and ink on paper. Archivo General de Indias, Seville. The walled city is not an accurate representation of Tumbes, but reflects the centrality of town-building to the Spanish Crown's conception of territorial expansion.

1529, at the Alcázar of Toledo, Empress Isabel of Portugal (1503–39), then acting as regent for the Holy Roman Emperor, Charles V, granted Pizarro the license for the conquest and settlement of the "land and province of Peru."[12]

It was also in Toledo in 1529 that the Crown granted Pizarro a coat of arms, its imagery colorfully proclaiming his status as a royally appointed expedition leader (fig. 2.3). The insignia of the Holy Roman Emperor—a crowned black eagle and two columns on a gold ground—appears atop a naturalistic representation of a walled city, identified in the accompanying text as Tumbes, near the coast in northern Peru. Two animals, described as a lion and tiger, face a man bearing a sword and a shield; beneath them, a body of water filled with sailing vessels flows between a number of other buildings and indistinct human figures. The text framing the imagery asserts that the patronage of Emperor Charles V made it possible for Pizarro to discover (*inventa*) new lands and pacify them.[13] The image constructs a visual narrative of travel by ship and the discovery and protection of territory, here presented as a walled city bearing no resemblance to Tumbes as it would have appeared in 1529, but reflecting instead the architectural and spatial unit of imperial expansion in the Americas.[14]

Pizarro's stay in Spain would come to an end in January 1530, when he departed for the Americas from the port of Sanlúcar de Barrameda—about 100 km (62 mi.) southwest

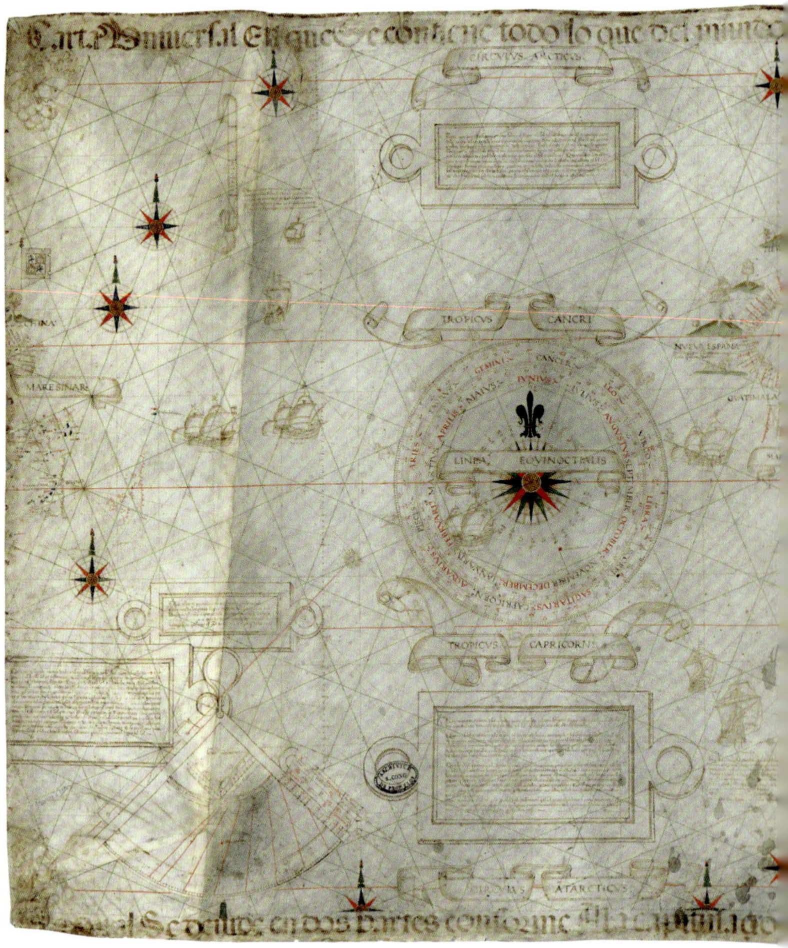

FIG. 2.4 Diogo Ribeiro (designer), *Carta universal* (Borg. Carte naut. III), 1529. Ink and pigment on vellum, 85 × 204 cm. Biblioteca Apostolica Vaticana, Vatican City. The map integrates South America into wider trade networks, and marks such key navigational features as rivers and ports.

of Seville—with a newly recruited company of men eager to participate in his third expedition into Peru. Among them were his brothers Hernando, Juan, and Gonzalo. Crossing the Atlantic and arriving several months later at the port of Nombre de Dios on the Isthmus of Panama, they joined Mena and a host of other fortune seekers setting sail southward early in 1531. Mena makes quick work of describing the company's progress in the first year, noting that not long after their departure they arrived at a native settlement he calls Coaque on the central coast of present-day Ecuador. There, he writes, they found some gold.

Mena's reference to that precious metal is the first of many in the *Conquista del Perú*, and other texts on the events of the 1530s in Peru, too, present the pursuit of wealth as the chief objective of Pizarro's company, far outweighing the acquisition of territory or religious conversion as a motivating factor. Earlier experiences in the Americas such as those of Christopher Columbus (1451–1506) and Hernán Cortés (1485–1547) had confirmed the presence of gold in the New World, and the expectation that the conquerors of Peru would find even more precious metals is made clear in the text of the license the empress granted to Pizarro in Toledo:

> In the first six years, from the gold that is taken from the mines, you shall pay us one tenth, and after those six years, you shall pay one ninth, and so on, the rate descending each year until arriving at one-fifth. But of the gold and other things that are had from ransom or cavalry raids, or any other way, you have to pay us one-fifth of all of that.[15]

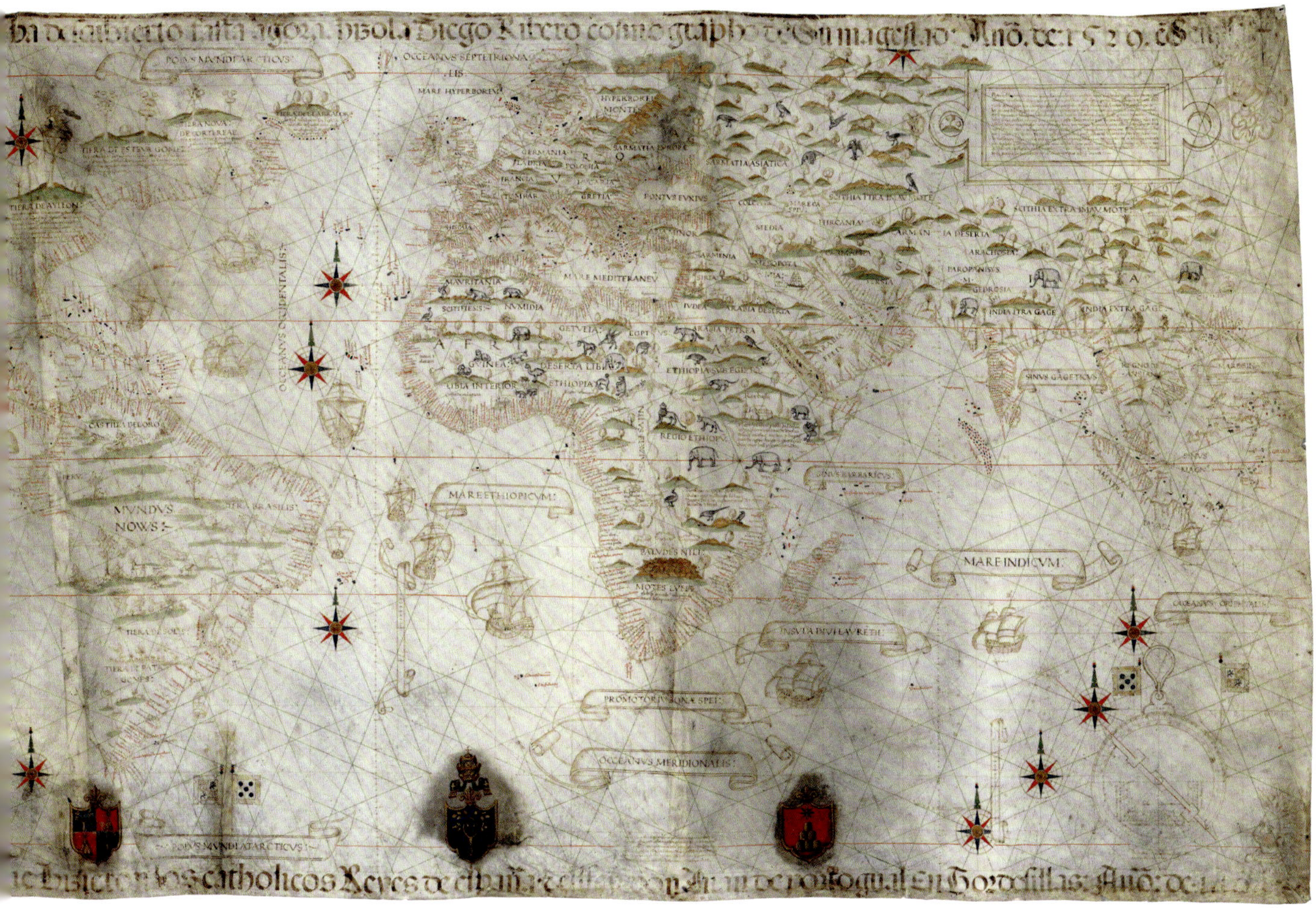

The payment of the royal fifth (*quinto real*) had its origins in the political economy of the medieval Islamic world, where it was imposed to fund caliphal projects and programs of social welfare. Centuries later, under Ferdinand and Isabella and their successors, the tax would continue to be levied on precious metals to fund imperial expansion around the Mediterranean that, in at least some cases, hinged on the defeat of Muslim armies.[16]

Mena does not specify the form of the gold he and the other participants in the expedition found in Coaque, but the context of the passage does not suggest it was acquired through mining. The upper central coast of Ecuador had been an important center for the production of objects made of gold and gold alloys since the Formative period (3500–600 BC), and jewelry made of those materials was worn by the area's inhabitants and buried in the tombs of the deceased long into the colonial era.[17] From Coaque, Mena writes, Pizarro's company continued southward to an island called Puná, off the coast of Ecuador near the port town of Guayaquil, where they stayed for four or five months before making their way to Tumbes, where they stayed for another two or three months.

Some of the men in Pizarro's cohort had been in Tumbes previously, having stopped there as part of an earlier expedition in the late 1520s. Among them was Pedro de Candía (*c.* 1494–1542), an experienced soldier of fortune whose name identifies him with his place of origin in Crete, then a colony of the Republic of Venice. The Cretan conquistador had a special familiarity with Tumbes: he had written a report describing it, accompanied by a now lost

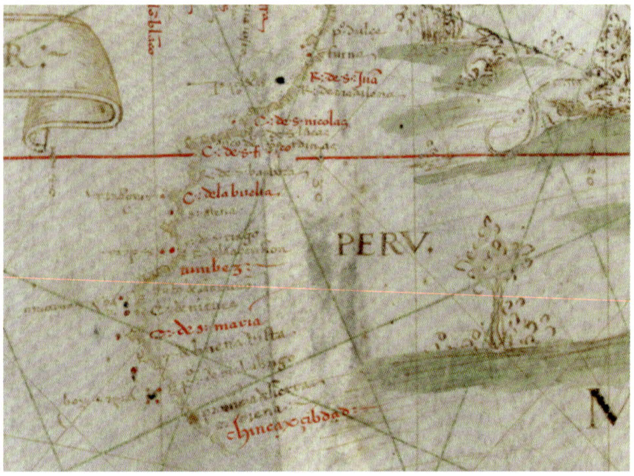

FIG. 2.5 Detail of figure 2.4, showing "Tumbes" marked in red on the coast to the left of "Peru."

image, both of which he carried to Spain when he traveled there with Pizarro in 1528. That picture may have been one of the points of reference for the designer of Pizarro's coat of arms. Candía's report also contributed to building the reputation of Tumbes: its name appears repeatedly in the conquest license issued to Pizarro by Empress Isabel, indicating that it was regarded as an important town in Peru. It takes on this same status in early maps of the Americas, such as the one designed by the royal cosmographer Diogo Ribeiro in 1529, on the eve of Charles V's coronation as Holy Roman Emperor, and concurrent with the issuing of the Pizarro coat of arms (figs 2.4, 2.5).[18] Its name written in red, Tumbes appears as one of a number of marked towns and rivers on the Pacific coast of Peru. The map demonstrates how representations of space—here in the form of words and visual imagery—facilitated the production of new configurations of territory in the early sixteenth century. In this vision of Peru, Cuzco does not exist, but port towns and rivers are marked with care in the interest of aiding navigation and, ultimately, the extraction of riches.

From Tumbes, Pizarro and his followers traveled inland to Tangarará, where they founded a settlement they called San Miguel, presumably named in honor of its foundation on or near the Archangel Michael's feast day in September. While there, Mena writes, "we received news of a great lord named Atahualpa, who was at war with his older brother, called Cuzco."[19] This passage has its counterpart in Betanzos's account of the events of this period: it is in Tangarará that Pizarro and his men learn of the existence of Atahualpa, Huascar, and the Inca polity itself, and it is the messengers from that same place who report to Atahualpa and Cuxirimay on the arrival of Pizarro. At the same time, Mena's use of the word "Cuzco" to refer to a person, Huascar, rather than a place, underscores once more the complexities of perception and translation in this early period of cultural encounter. As Susan Ramírez has noted, the term "Cuzco" was used consistently in this way in the earliest accounts of Spanish exploration in Peru, perhaps reflecting a concept of rulership in which both the ruler and the place in which he was present at any given time were regarded as "the Cuzco."[20] However, the use of the term as a name for the Sapa Inca quickly disappeared from the Spanish accounts, thus providing an example of the ways in which language was instrumental in fostering change in early colonial Peru. As its human referents died or were subjugated, Cuzco became simply a place.

After learning of the existence of the "great lord named Atahualpa," many of those in Pizarro's company began journeying southward into the Andes in search of him. Their first encounter with him occurred in Cajamarca in November 1532 and is pictured in the woodcut print adorning the title page of the *Conquista del Perú* (fig. 2.6). Sitting atop a litter borne by attendants, he holds a scepter in one hand and, in the other, a tome described in the accompanying text as "the book of our sacred law"—presumably a breviary or Bible—that had been given to him by the Dominican friar Vicente de Valverde (*c.* 1495–1541).[21] Valverde, a Spaniard from the town of Oropesa, just west of Toledo, had joined Pizarro three years earlier in Spain. Of the five other friars who accompanied him on his voyage to the Americas in January 1530, Valverde was the only one to reach Cajamarca.[22] The image shows him with a tonsured head and dressed in a dark, hooded robe as he gestures toward Atahualpa, whose clothing—nothing but a cloth around his waist—is not in keeping with habits of dress among the Inca. The image provides a jarring counterpoint to the descriptions of the distinctive tunics given by Betanzos, but at the same time hints at the kinds of garments worn by Spanish men in the early sixteenth century. The designer of the woodcut, who must

FIG. 2.6 Detail of title page of Cristóbal de Mena, *La conquista del Perú* (Seville: Bartolomé Pérez, 1534). Ink on paper. New York Public Library, New York. The depiction of the Inca (*right*) as almost naked indicates the designer's lack of knowledge about his subject, and his familiarity with stereotypical European images of the native people of the Americas.

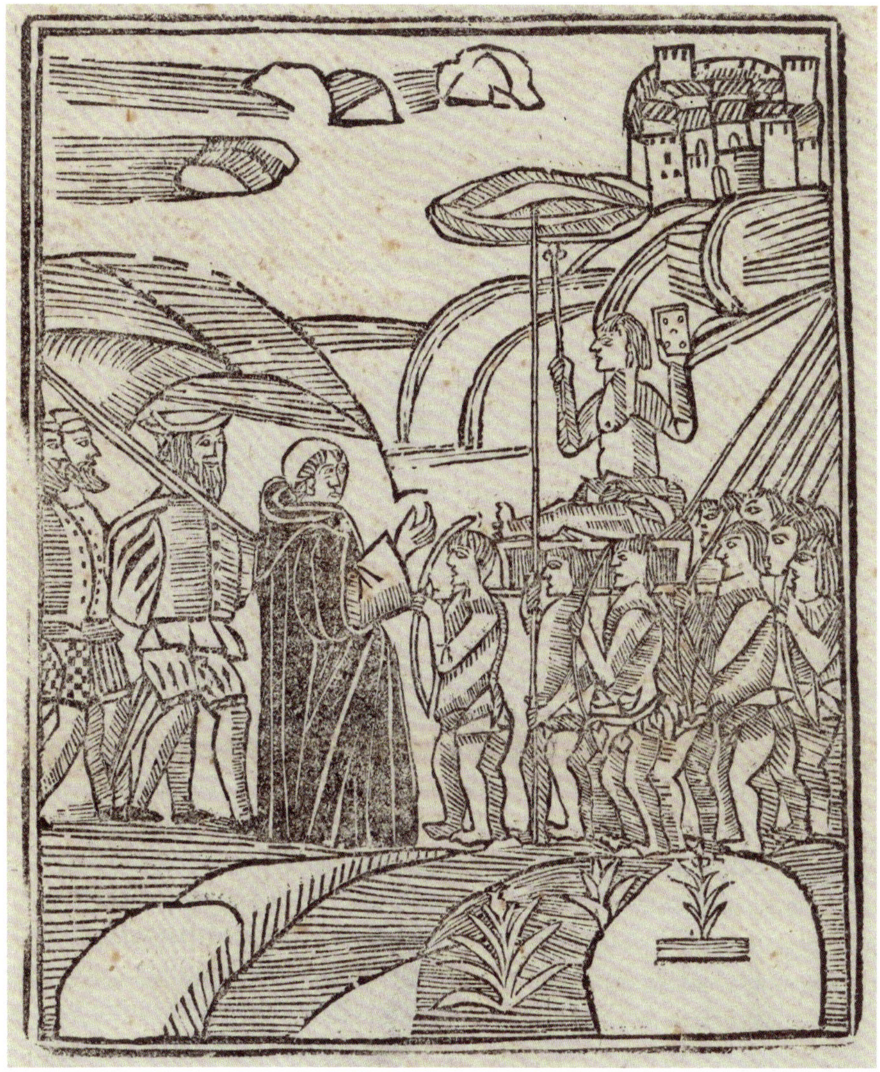

have been employed by the printing shop of Bartolomé Pérez in Seville, would have been familiar with the robes of friars and the doublets, knee-length breeches, and hats of men like those in Pizarro's cohort, but he would not have known through personal experience what kind of clothing an Inca king wore. Instead, he relied upon stereotypes of the inhabitants of the Americas as naked, or nearly so, and probably consulted other printed images of non-European peoples in devising his composition.[23]

Mena describes the encounter portrayed in the image in some detail. Valverde, after reading aloud from the breviary, offered it to Atahualpa, "thinking that he wanted to kiss it."[24] His reaction, however, signaled neither esteem nor even interest in the book: instead of kissing it, he threw it over the heads of his attendants and to the ground. That act, says Mena, precipitated the Spaniards' attack on Atahualpa's men and the imprisonment of Atahualpa himself.[25]

Mena's *Conquista del Perú* belongs to a genre of narratives known in the sixteenth-century Spanish-speaking world as *relaciones* (sing. *relación*). Works in this genre are characterized by their narration of events by an author who participated in them, and in that sense they are like memoirs or journals, texts similarly shaped by the writer's various recollections and desires. Mena's *relación* took its place in a genealogy of texts that included the "letters" of Hernán Cortés, the conqueror of Mexico, to the Holy Roman

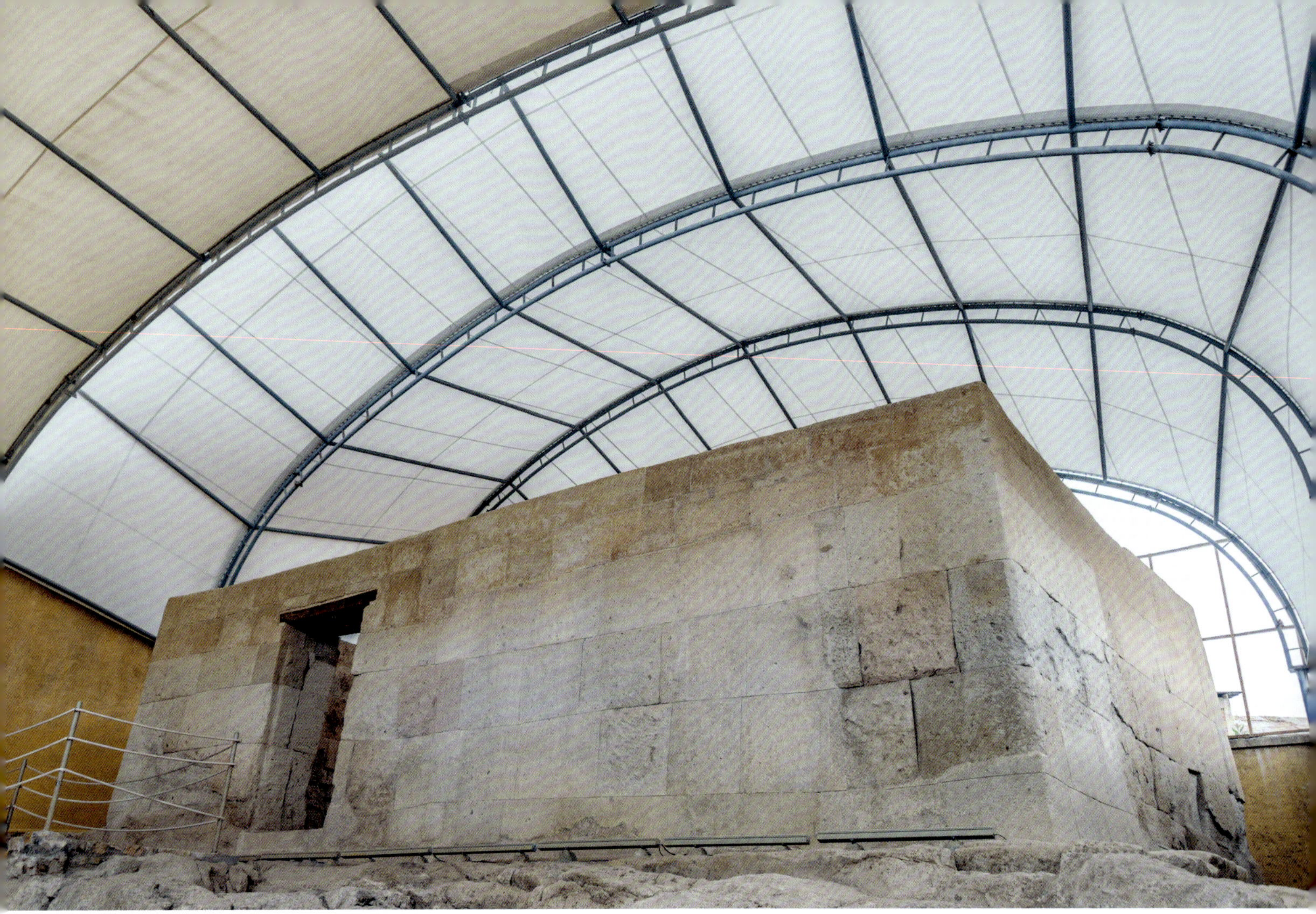

FIG. 2.7 Atahualpa's Ransom Room, Cajamarca, Peru, 15th–16th century. Approximately 12 × 8 m. Tradition has it that this is the room Atahualpa filled with gold from Cuzco in the hope of buying his freedom from the Spanish.

Emperor, as well as Pedro de Candía's report on Tumbes. In this genre of writing, the author typically stressed his status as a participant in the acts about which he wrote through frequent use of the first person, rich descriptions of people, places, and things, and outright claims of direct witnessing.[26]

The *relaciones* of Mena and his contemporary Francisco de Xerez provide the earliest printed descriptions of the Inca capital written by participants in the conquest of Peru. A close reading of those texts centering on their treatment of the architecture and urban form of Cuzco provides insight into the ways in which representation—here in the form of description—produced dreamlike visions of the Andean imperial capital that set the stage for its transformation into a Spanish colonial city even before Pizarro and his allies set foot there.

In Cajamarca, Pizarro and his men imprisoned Atahualpa and demanded he pay them a ransom in gold and silver. Here, Mena's narrative echoes earlier tales of the capture and confinement of other rivals to the Spanish Crown, such as that of the French king Francis I at the Battle of Pavia in 1525, or, a few years earlier, that of Moctezuma II, the ruler of Aztec Mexico. Atahualpa, Mena writes, agreed to pay the ransom, promising to fill a large room with gold and a walled area in the town's plaza with "silver cups"—a reference to the *aquillas* used in Inca ritual toasting and drinking. A one-room stone structure standing in Cajamarca today is popularly regarded as the "ransom room" the Inca king filled with gold, and although evidence supporting this association is scant, it is nonetheless an effective mnemonic device in the modern city, calling to mind events said to have occurred hundreds of years in the past and contributing to the maintenance of the city's identity as a key site in the history of Peru (fig. 2.7).

Mena writes that the imprisoned Inca ruler told Pizarro there were other places in his empire where the Spanish could find large quantities of gold and silver. He told the conquistador to send his men to those places, where they could "strip bare certain houses that were plated with gold."[27] Upon hearing this, Pizarro sent three men to find these gold-plated walls. Other sources identify them as Juan Zárate, a notary from Orduña, in the Basque country; Pedro Martín de Moguer, whose surname reveals his town of origin in Andalusia, 90 km (56 mi.) west of Seville; and Martín Bueno, also from Moguer.[28] They traveled first to Xauxa, a provincial administrative center where they obtained gold from one of Atahualpa's captains, before continuing onward to Cuzco, about 875 km (544 mi.) to the southeast. They made this journey, Mena says, with "many people who carried them in hammocks, and they were very well served," presumably by the "blacks and Indians of service" mentioned by Mena elsewhere in the text.[29] When they finally arrived in Cuzco, they met with one of Atahualpa's representatives—a captain named Quizquiz—who had led attacks on Huascar's loyalists. His name, Mena writes, "means barber in their language," a statement that might be taken as evidence of the author's having engaged with a native translator. González Holguín, however, translates the term differently, as *pajarito*—"a little bird."[30]

Captain Quizquiz, Mena writes, showed little respect to the three new arrivals in Cuzco, but nonetheless he directed them to the "quarters [*bohíos*] of the Sun in which [the Inca] worshipped," which were "plated with gold with some large plates on the side where the sun rises, and even more on the shady side, which had gold of lower quality."[31] Inside the compound, he claims, Pizarro's men found a great number of golden and gold-plated pitchers, a "platform [*silla*] of gold where they made their sacrifices that was so large that it weighed 19,000 pesos," and "a very large basin of gold." The basin, he notes, weighed more than 12,000 pesos.[32] Mena's references to the platform and basin call to mind the similar ritual paraphernalia Betanzos described as being set up in the plaza of Cuzco to house the sugarloaf-shaped deity image there. It is also noteworthy that Mena's descriptions include not only object types—a platform, a basin, cups—but also the weight of those objects. The inclusion of weight as a descriptor here points to one of the ways in which things made of gold and silver were assessed by those in Pizarro's company, their worth stemming not from their use value but from their exchange value, rendered numerically. A similar regard for precious metals is evident in the *Suma y narración*. For example, in a passage referring to the pins that fastened the mantles worn by Pachacuti's principal wife, Betanzos writes that each of them "would weigh two pounds in gold."[33]

References to buildings in Cuzco being made of gold also appear throughout the second *relación* on the conquest of Peru to appear in print. Entitled *Verdadera relación de la conquista del Perú* (*True Account of the Conquest of Peru*; hereafter, *Verdadera relación*), it was written by Francisco de Xerez and was printed in July 1534, just three months after the first appearance of Mena's *Conquista del Perú*. Xerez was a native of Seville who, in 1514, at the age of seventeen, sailed to the Americas in the fleet of Pedrarias Dávila. He would spend twenty years in the Americas, during which time he participated in all three of Pizarro's expeditions into Peru and served as official secretary to the conquistador.[34] The *Verdadera relación* records the events of this period, beginning with the ill-fated first expedition southward from Panama on November 14, 1524, and eventually recounting the events of the successful third expedition, the same one recorded by Mena. The links between the two *relaciones* extend even beyond their content, for the first edition of Xerez's account—also printed in Seville by Bartolomé Pérez—opened with the same image of Atahualpa and the Spaniards as had appeared as the frontispiece to Mena's *Conquista del Perú* (fig. 2.8).

The first description of the Inca capital in Xerez's text comes as a report provided by Hernando de Soto (*c.* 1496–1542), an experienced and high-ranking participant in the expedition, who, like so many of Pizarro's associates, hailed from Extremadura. Returning from an expedition he had led, he met with Pizarro at an

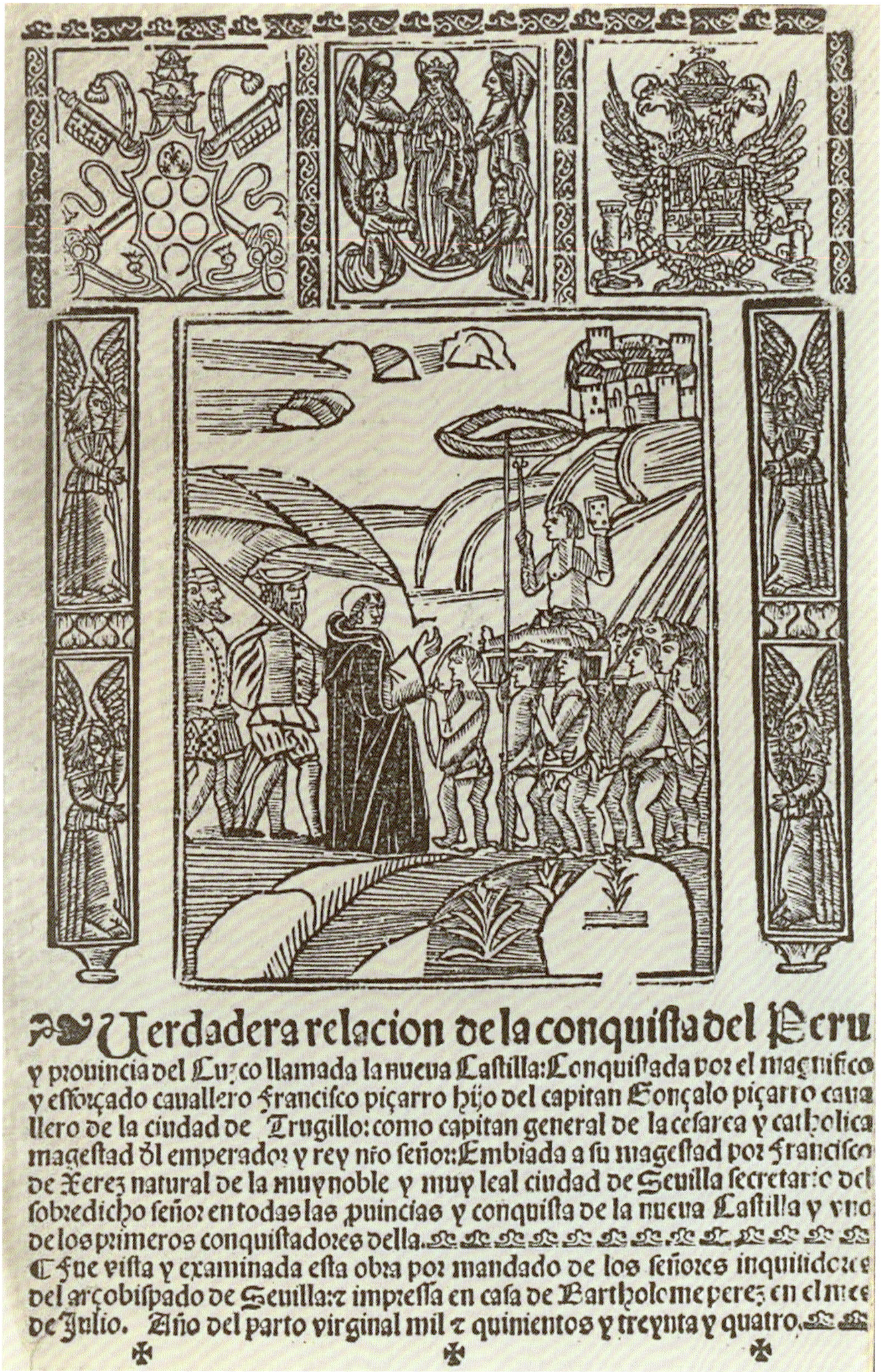

FIG. 2.8 Title page of Francisco de Xerez, *Verdadera relación de la conquista del Perú* (Seville: Casa de Bartolomé Pérez, 1534). Woodcut, ink on paper. John Carter Brown Library, Providence, RI. The image is the same as that used for Cristóbal de Mena's *La conquista del Perú* (fig. 2.2).

encampment in the Piura River valley in northern Peru and reported on an encounter he had with one of Atahualpa's captains, who had told him about Cuzco and its riches. The city, he said, was surrounded by a large wall, and in one of its buildings there was a room that housed the mummified body of Huayna Capac, its floor, walls, and roof plated in silver and gold. Moreover, there were "twenty other houses whose walls were plated with a thin sheet of gold on the inside and on the outside."[35] This fantastic vision of gilded architecture appears once again in Xerez's account of the events that followed the capture of Atahualpa in Cajamarca. Like Mena, he tells the story of the three men who traveled to Cuzco in search of gold for the king's ransom, writing that one of them—the notary Zárate—returned to Cajamarca in May 1533 and provided a description of the city:

> He said that the city of Cuzco is as large as has been said, and that it rests on a mountainside near the plain. The streets are very well arranged and paved with stone, and in the eight days they were there, they were not able to see all that there was. He said a house of Cuzco had gold plating.[36]

The image of Cuzco that takes shape in the *relaciones* of Mena and Xerez centers squarely on grandeur and wealth, the latter in the form of houses ornamented with gold and silver and containing things made of those materials. As Mena notes, the three men sent to Cuzco claimed that throughout the city "there was so much gold that it was marvelous."[37] The texts provide little other information about the city, and in that sense the gold-plated walls of Cuzco come to stand in for its entirety. This vision contrasts sharply with the one described by the informants of Betanzos, in which the city was conceived in terms of two signature spaces and symbolic centers—the House of the Sun and the festival plaza—and held value that was historical, political, and supernatural rather than strictly economic. Moreover, the description of the House of the Sun in the *Suma y narración* emphasizes its fine stonework rather than its adornment with gold plates, and the text refers to the use of precious metals in its construction on just two occasions. The first occurs in the description of a repair:

> At the time they were building it, as they were setting a certain stone, a piece about three fingers wide and long broke off the join, and [Pachacuti] ordered that some silver be melted there and poured into the stone.[38]

The second occurs in the author's account of the achievements of Pachacuti's successor, Topa Inca (r. 1471–93). Following the conquest of some provinces in Andesuyu, to the north and east of Cuzco, the ruler's forces returned to the capital city with the spoils of their war. From the gold they brought, Betanzos writes, Topa Inca ordered "a strip be made two and a half palms wide, and that it be thin, with the thickness that of a small tin plate." The strip was to fit around the House of the Sun, and it was installed there "on the exterior, from where the straw of the roof is to where the stonework of the house is."[39] It is possible that some of the author's informants would have been alive during the reign of Topa Inca, and it is likely that some of them would have seen the House of the Sun, presumably adorned with this strip of gold, before the arrival of Zárate, Moguer, and Bueno in Cuzco in the first months of 1533.

The descriptions of the House of the Sun in the accounts of Mena, Xerez, and Betanzos underscore its prominence in Cuzco. For the Inca, it was the most sacred shrine in all of the empire and, according to the origin story recorded by Betanzos, it was the first building constructed in the sacred center of Cuzco. For the Spanish, by contrast, its worth was more economic than symbolic. A reading of the descriptions of the compound in these texts, however, reveals significant differences. Mena and Xerez say that it had entire walls plated with gold, but Betanzos describes a structure adorned with only a thin golden cornice. It is this latter vision of the compound that is most widely accepted by scholars today, and modern reconstructions of the building typically include a gilded cornice. Physical evidence supporting the presence of such ornamentation are the protrusions and incisions atop some Inca walls at Santo Domingo that may have served in some way to secure plates of metal (fig. 2.9).[40] The decoration of the building with an ornamental strip of gold recalls Betanzos's description of the sugarloaf-shaped stone in the city's festival plaza, likewise adorned with a band of gold. Other parts of the House of the Sun may have been similarly ornamented: a trapezoidal niche in one of its surviving walls is carved with holes and ridges suggesting

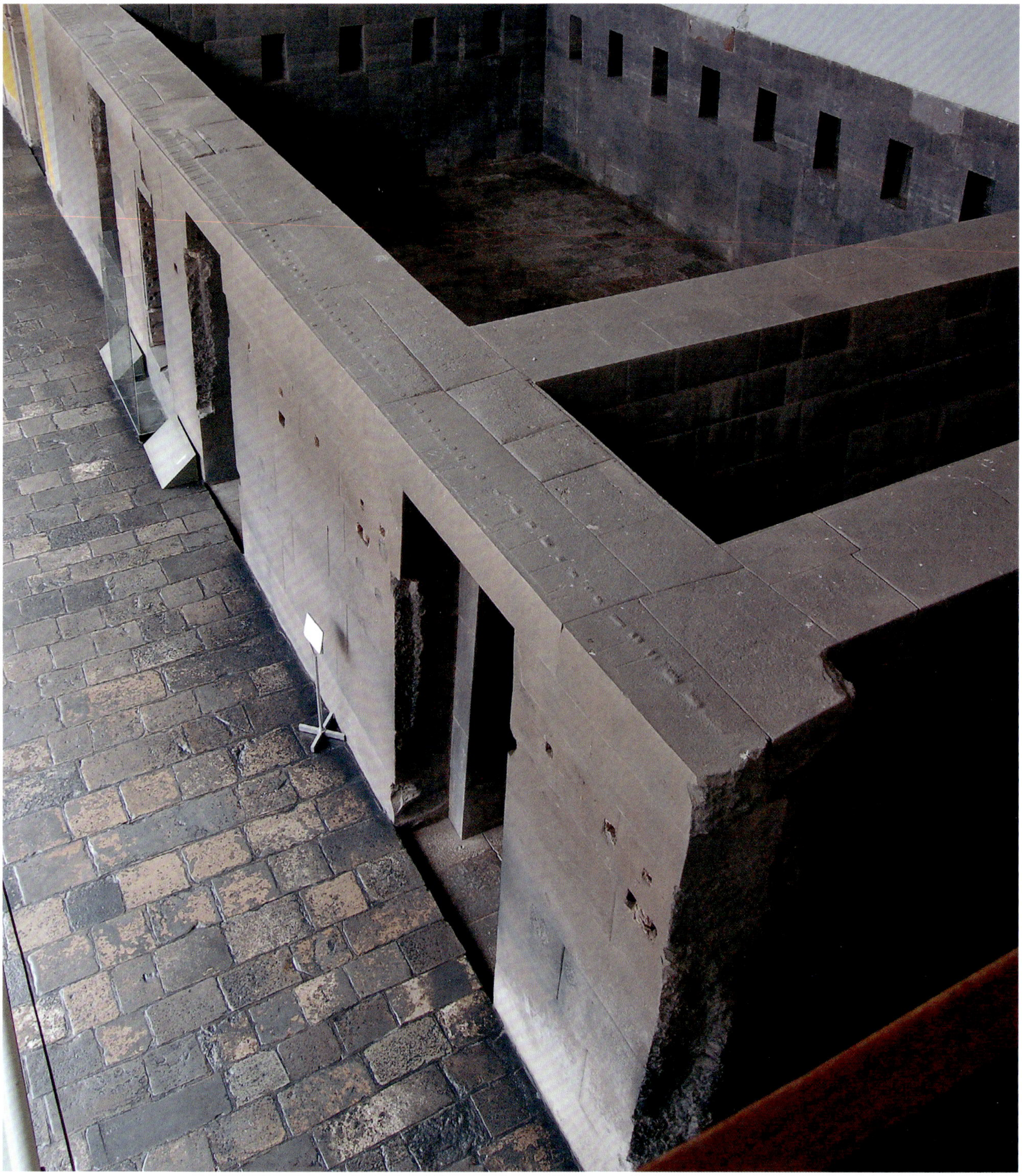

FIG. 2.9 Inca walls within the monastery of Santo Domingo, Cuzco, 15th–16th century. Like the sugarloaf-shaped stone image of the sun in the festival plaza of Inca Cuzco, some of the stone walls of the House of the Sun were adorned with a strip of gold attached to their uppermost courses.

that metal plaques or other forms of embellishment may have been affixed to it (fig. 2.10).

As this survey of the early *relaciones* makes clear, the descriptions by Mena and Xerez, in which buildings in Cuzco have entire walls, floors, and ceilings clad in precious metals, do not square with other colonial period sources or with physical evidence at the House of the Sun and other buildings in Cuzco. How, then, can these reports of gilded buildings be explained? The forces that gave rise to those early descriptions of Inca Cuzco become clearer when they are considered in light of precedents in the early literature on world travel, exploration, and conquest.

By the time Mena and Xerez were writing their *relaciones* on the conquest of Peru, the marvelous image of a building with floors, roofs, and walls of gold had long been in circulation. Early examples are found in Pliny the Elder's *Natural History*—composed in the first century and printed in multiple editions in the fifteenth and sixteenth centuries—in which he describes the Golden House of Nero, and in Marco Polo's *Description of the World* (also known as *Travels* and *Il milione*), composed in the late 1200s and circulated widely in print and manuscript copies in the following centuries. Polo (b. *c.* 1254), a Venetian said to have left his home in his teens and traveled to the Yuan Empire of Kublai Khan, may have spent nearly two decades of his life in East Asia before returning to Venice. His description of a palace on the island of Cipango (usually identified as Japan) emphasizes the use of precious metals as construction materials:

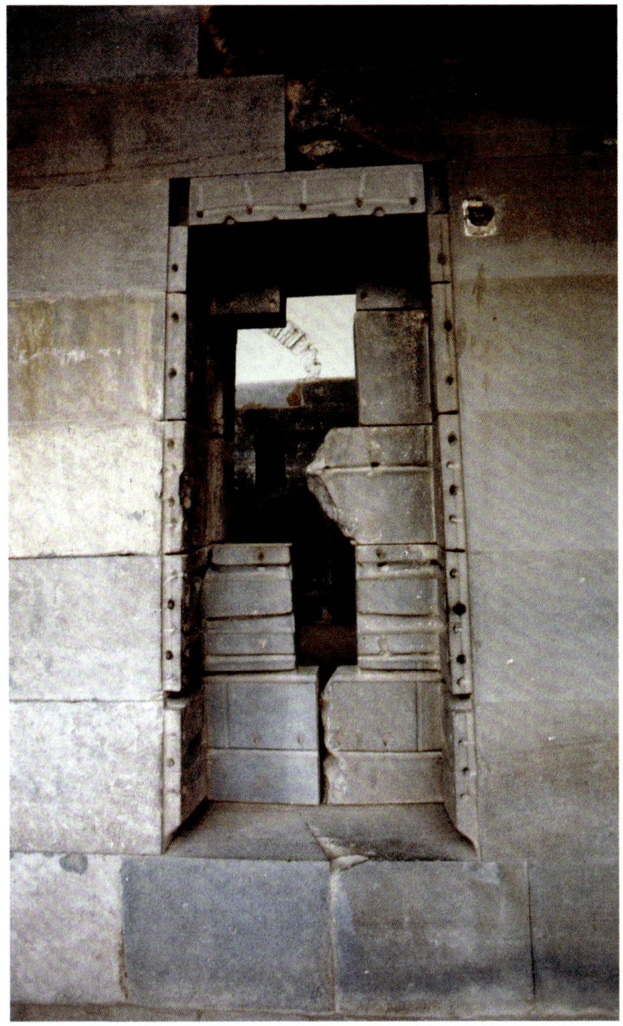

FIG. 2.10 Niche in an Inca wall in the monastery of Santo Domingo, Cuzco, 15th–16th century.

> The palace of the lord of the island is very large, and it is covered with gold, just as churches here are covered in lead. And all of the floors of the rooms are covered in gold to a height of two fingers; and all of the windows and walls and other things and also the halls are covered in gold, and its value cannot be told.[41]

Christopher Columbus was familiar with Marco Polo's writings and owned a copy of the *Description of the World*, its annotations suggesting his careful engagement with it. Polo's claims must have been very much on his mind in 1492 as he explored the Caribbean, where he hoped to find the island of Cipango and its golden palace. He refers to it in his *Diario* a number of times. In his entry for Saturday, October 13, he writes: "so as not to lose time, I want to go to see if I can come across the island of Cipango." By October 23, he thought he knew its location: "Today I want to set off for the island of Cuba, which I think must be Cipango, according to the signs that these people give of its grandeur and riches." The next day, he was even more certain: "By the signs that all of the Indians of these islands and those in my ships are giving me—as I don't understand their language—it is the island of Cipango, of which they tell marvelous things."[42]

Columbus did not find the palace of gold on the island of Cuba, but his hopes were raised again on December 24, when he met some native people on the island of Hispaniola (today, Haiti and the Dominican Republic) and asked them about the location of gold mines. "Among other places that they named where there was gold, they said Cipango, which they call Cibao, and there they affirm that there is a great quantity of gold."[43] Columbus would ultimately come to realize that the place the native people called Cibao was not the storied island of gold described by Marco Polo, and his failure to find it encouraged others to continue to imagine it, write about it, and look for it. In January 1513, Vasco Núñez de Balboa (1475–1519), who would later be among the first Spaniards to see the Pacific Ocean, wrote a letter to King Ferdinand claiming that in the province of Darien (Panama) there was a native chief named Davaive, who "has gold in great quantity in his house," and that to his house was brought all the gold found by those in the region. "This chief Davaive," he writes, "has a great foundry of gold in his house. He has 100 men who work the gold continually."[44] Even chroniclers who never had been to the Americas wrote of buildings made of (and containing) gold in this early era of Spanish exploration. Sometime between 1525 and 1528, Fernán Pérez de Oliva (*c.* 1494–1531) wrote in his *Historia de la invención de las Indias* of a native king on the island of Hispaniola who ruled over Cibao and was called, he said, "the Lord of the House of Gold." Pérez de Oliva's text was derived in part from Peter Martyr d'Anghiera's *De orbe novo* (1516), more commonly known as *Decades*, in which he, too, referred to this king: "Cacique Caunaboa, Lord of the House of Gold."[45]

The conviction that gold would be found throughout the Americas also surfaces in official communication from the Crown to the leaders of expeditions in the New World. More than a decade before the Empress Isabel issued the license to Pizarro for exploration in Peru, King Ferdinand signed his *Instrucción* to Pedrarias Dávila. In that document of August 1513, he appointed Dávila as captain general and governor of the territory known as Tierra Firme. Perhaps in response to the reports he had received from Balboa and others, however, he saw fit to rename the entire territory, writing that "now we order it to be called *Castilla Aurífera*" (Golden Castile). It would come to be more commonly called Castilla del Oro, and indeed, the region is labeled this way on Ribeiro's *Carta universal* (see fig. 2.5).[46]

The *relaciones* of Mena and Xerez show that the idea of palaces and temples made of gold continued to circulate in the literature of exploration and conquest in the 1530s. Key to the operation of the motif in all the cases cited is the portrayal of the building in question not as something the authors themselves have seen but instead as something they have heard about from others. Columbus, as noted above, believes he is near the island of Cipango because of the "signs" he is given by its native residents. References to buildings made of gold in the *relaciones* of Mena and Xerez are similarly mediated. In the *Conquista del Perú*, it is Atahualpa who first describes Cuzco to Pizarro in this way—presumably through the use of a translator—and it is Pizarro's envoys who later confirm the description upon their return to Cajamarca. In the *Verdadera relación*, Xerez presents Soto's description of Cuzco's golden buildings as information provided by a native Andean chief and, presumably, translated for him.

This early image of Cuzco as a city with walls plated in gold took shape as the conquistadors dreamed of riches and as the *relaciones* of Mena and Xerez circulated in print in 1534 and later. In this way, the built environment of Cuzco was set in the minds of Pizarro and his contemporaries as a highly desirable commodity: a city of gold for which adventurers had long been searching but which they had never found. Representation, here in the form of words on paper, signals that Mena, Xerez, and their contemporaries and readers mentally positioned Cuzco both within the larger space of an expanding Christian empire and, at the same time, as part of the spatial and economic order of early modern transatlantic capitalism.

The House of the Sun may have been adorned with a smaller amount of gold than Mena and Xerez believed, but it was ornamented in some way with that precious metal. Mena reports that Pizarro's envoys, after having been directed there by Captain Quizquiz, "decided to strip those quarters [of the Sun] with some copper bars." They did so, Mena writes, "without any help from Indians, because they [i.e., the Indians] did not want to help since it was the quarters of the Sun, saying that they would die."[47] The passage evokes the image of the men, presumably with the help of their servants, using metal tools to remove gold plates

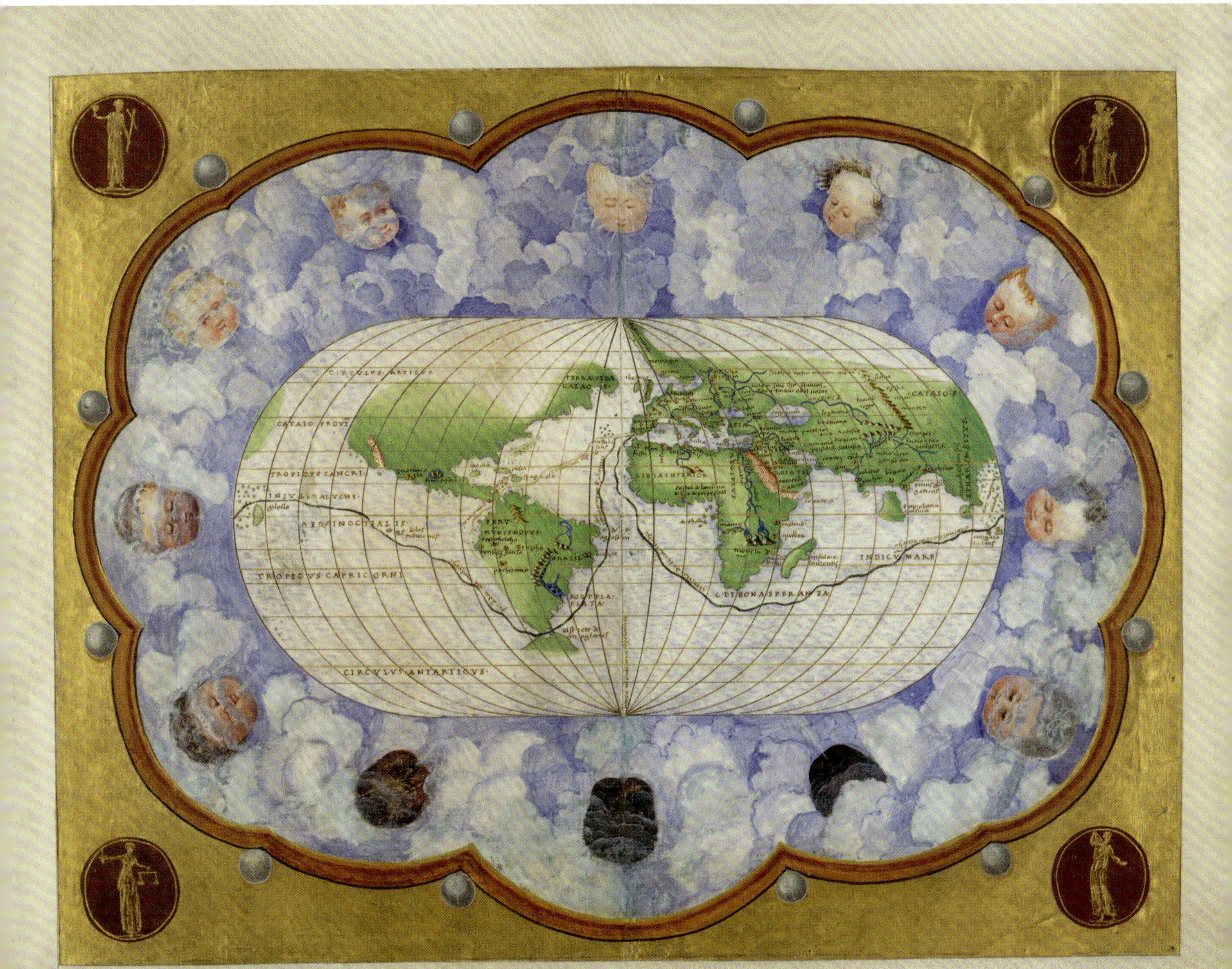

FIG. 2.11 Battista Agnese, world map, *c.* 1543–45. Ink, pigment, and gilt on vellum, 25.1 × 32.7 cm. John Carter Brown Library, Providence, RI. The map positions Spain near the center and stresses its control over networks of economic exchange.

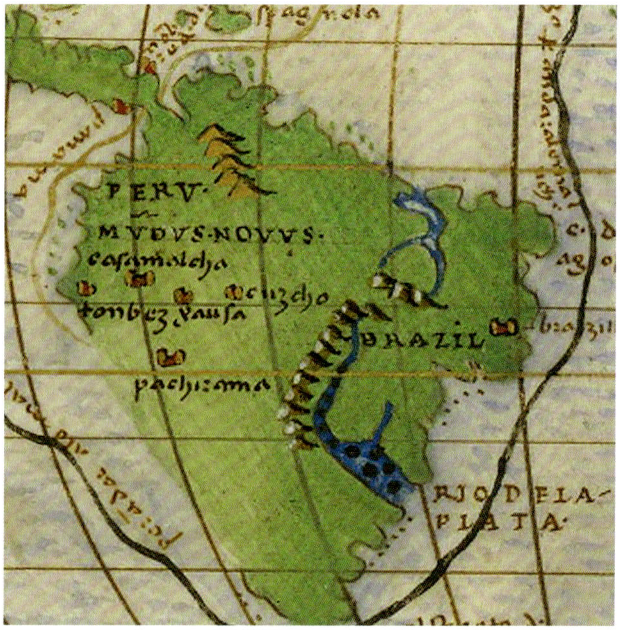

FIG. 2.12 Detail of figure 2.11, showing South America with key cities labeled.

affixed to the stone walls of the compound. At the same time, it emphasizes the different values these two opposing parties projected onto the building. For the Spanish, it was the House of the Sun's golden ornament that gave value to the structure, but for the native Andeans of the city the compound's symbolism was so great that its being plundered made them fear for their lives.[48] In other ways, though, Mena says the native inhabitants of Cuzco cooperated with the Spanish, gathering vessels (*cántaros*) of gold and offering them for the ransom of Atahualpa. Xerez, too, writes of the stripping of gold-plated buildings in Cuzco. From one of them, he claims, "they took off seven hundred plates, which together weighed five hundred pesos," and from another they took "a quantity of two hundred thousand pesos," though the latter was of poor quality.[49]

The Spaniards' servants and slaves carried the plates of gold, together with gold vessels and other valuable things—some of them made of silver—to Cajamarca. Xerez stresses the abundance of the precious metals taken from Cuzco, and he provides even greater detail about the haul. Two hundred loads of gold and twenty-five of silver, he says, arrived at Cajamarca on June 13, 1533, and another sixty loads of gold arrived later. "The largest part of all of this," he says, "was in plates, like the planks of wooden boxes, three or four *palmos* [25–30 in.] in length. This they took off the walls of the quarters (*bohíos*), and they had holes, so that it seems they were attached by nails." Pizarro ordered that these objects be melted down right away. "They made bars of it," Mena notes, "and these they distributed among the people."[50] Just as the ornament and contents of the House of the Sun were melted down and made into bars of gold and silver at Cajamarca, so the built environment of Cuzco was transformed on the pages of Mena's and Xerez's *relaciones* into a rich economic resource to be distributed to the conquistadors. The House of the Sun had become, for them, one of a number of legendary Houses of Gold, and the Cuzco of Betanzos's informants—the sacred and geographic center of an empire—was rendered a very different kind of place.

Xerez writes that the melting and distribution of the gold at Cajamarca was finished on the day of Santiago, July 25, 1533, and that the final quantity totaled 325,539 pesos. Lockhart's synthesis of other early sources on the event values the treasure in silver and gold at more than triple that amount, at 1.5 million pesos.[51] It was distributed among the men at Cajamarca proportionally by rank: Pizarro, his brothers Hernando and Juan, and Hernando de Soto received the largest shares of the haul. For his part, Mena was dissatisfied with the amount of gold he was allotted. "To many of those who earned it," he writes, "[Pizarro] gave less than what they deserved. And I say this because it was done this way with me."[52] It is perhaps in connection with this dissatisfaction that Mena was among the first group of Spaniards to return to Spain after the events at Cajamarca. Xerez, too, would return to Spain shortly after the distribution of gold, having broken his leg and being unable to continue the journey with Pizarro south through the Andes. Both men arrived in Seville in December 1533, and Mena's *Conquista del Perú* was printed just four months later.

It must have been during those four months that an artist associated with Pérez's printing shop conceived and executed the image that would appear as the frontispiece to the printed accounts of both Mena and Xerez, taking as its subject the encounter between Valverde and Atahualpa in Cajamarca, rather than the House of Gold in Cuzco or the distribution of its treasure (see figs 2.2, 2.8). On the pages of those booklets, Cuzco takes its place in a narrative of travel through the Andes in search of riches. Other early imagery, however, would position the sack of Cuzco and distribution of gold at Cajamarca within a different structure: that of a transatlantic economy centered on the Iberian Peninsula. Not long after the publication of the texts by Mena and Xerez, the Genoese cartographer Battista Agnese (*c.* 1500–1564) and his workshop in Venice began producing multiple versions of a luxury manuscript atlas including a map of the world.[53] An especially fine example is the one commissioned by Charles V in 1542 and held today in the collection of the John Carter Brown Library (fig. 2.11). It presents Seville near the center of the pictorial space and as a point of origin, the place at which lines marking maritime routes begin and, ultimately, end. One of those routes is drawn in gold and is labeled "por andar al Perú" ("to go to Peru"); it crosses the Atlantic and the Isthmus of Panama, terminating on the Pacific coast of South America. Inland towns are indicated by rectangular forms suggesting clusters of buildings painted in gold, among them Tumbes, Cajamarca, and Cuzco (fig. 2.12). On this map, Cuzco is not the center of the world, as Betanzos's informants would conceive of the city in the *Suma y narración*; instead, it is a distant city whose connection to a powerful center—the Spanish port of Seville—is rendered in terms of economic exchange.

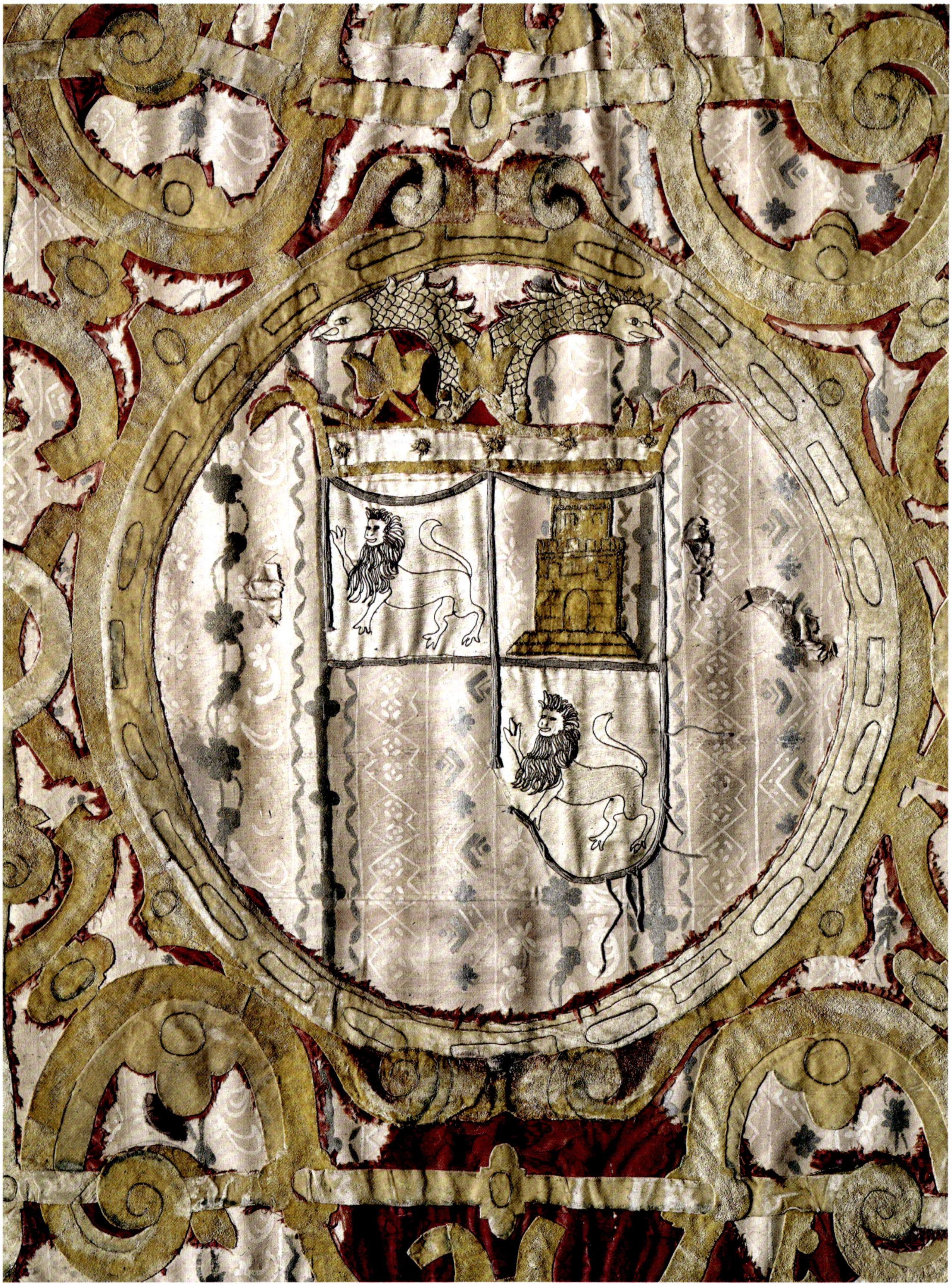

CHAPTER 3

Imagining Spanish Cuzco

Francisco Pizarro, Pedro Sancho, and the Act of Foundation

Among those receiving the smallest shares of gold at Cajamarca was Pedro Sancho, the man who would succeed Francisco de Xerez as Pizarro's secretary. Like his predecessor, Sancho, too, wrote a *relación* documenting the deeds of his compatriots in Peru. Signed and dated July 15, 1534, in Xauxa, his report would have a very different fate from those of Xerez and Cristóbal de Mena, which were printed and sold within months of their authors' arrivals in Seville. Sancho's *relación* would not appear in print until 1556, more than two decades after he composed it, and close in time to Betanzos's completion of the *Suma y narración*. And while the reports by Mena and Xerez were printed in their native Spanish, that of Sancho made its first appearance as an Italian translation forming part of a collection of twenty-four accounts of European exploration in the Americas. The compilation was edited by the Venetian humanist Giovanni Battista Ramusio (1485–1557) under the title *Navigationi et viaggi* (*Travels and Voyages*), and was published in Venice, which was then an important center for the collection, publication, and dissemination of texts on the Americas.[1]

The manuscript penned by Sancho in Xauxa has never been found, nor has any other version of the report predating the one published in Venice in 1556. Much of the author's biography, too, remains lost to time. His name does not appear in the catalog of passengers to the Indies, and he is not mentioned in the *relaciones* by Mena and Xerez. His place of birth is the subject of disagreement: some of his personal and professional associations in the Americas suggest he was born in or around Medina de Rioseco, near Valladolid, but other evidence indicates that his origins were farther to the northeast, in the town of Calahorra.[2]

Entitled *Relatione per sua maestá* (*Report for His Majesty*; hereafter, *Relatione*), Sancho's text spans twenty-nine pages in Ramusio's compilation. It opens in Cajamarca in 1533 with a description of the arrival of Atahualpa's ransom—"five hundred and some bars of gold removed from some walls of the houses of Cuzco"—and its melting and distribution to Pizarro's men.[3] The ransom was supposed to have bought Atahualpa his freedom, but that was not to be. The Spanish came to believe the Inca king, while in captivity, had secretly ordered an attack on his captors. As Betanzos tells the story, Atahualpa did indeed order an attack, but not on the Spanish. Instead, he sought the death of his brother Huascar, who was duly killed by Cuxirimay's brother Cuxi.[4] Nonetheless, Pizarro was convinced that Atahualpa posed a threat to his authority, and ordered his execution. Sancho describes Atahualpa's death by garroting in Cajamarca dispassionately, adding a

(*facing page*) Detail of figure 3.4.

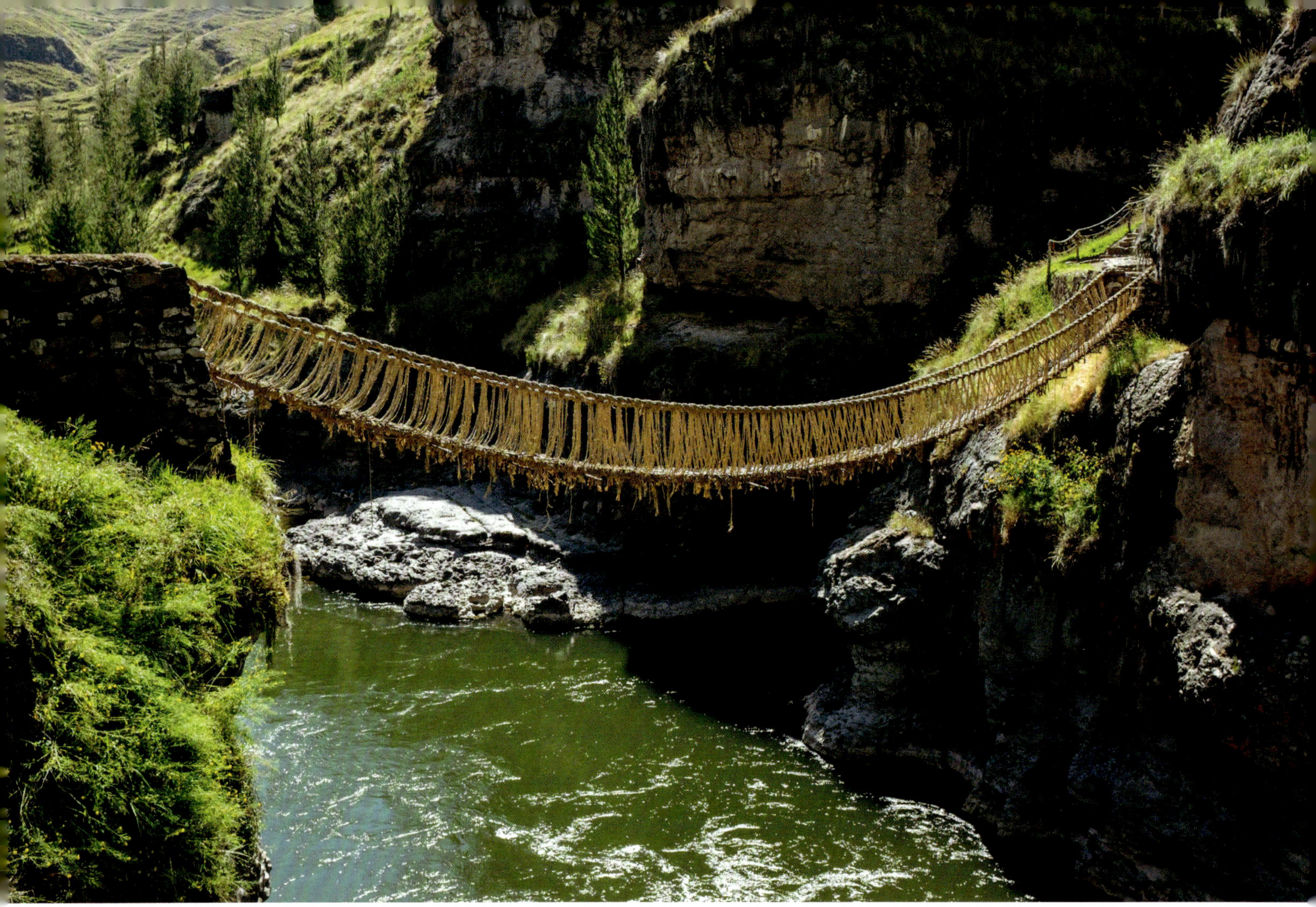

FIG. 3.1 Bridge over the Apurimac River, Peru. The techniques used for weaving such bridges are centuries old; Pedro Sancho describes encountering similar structures in the Andes in the 16th century.

grim detail that speaks to a desire that the act should serve as a warning: "that night, his body was left in the plaza so that everyone might be given news of his death."[5] A few days later, he writes, Pizarro and his band of newly rich followers left Cajamarca in search of other settlements to conquer and greater riches to acquire. Traveling with the company were native porters who carried their gold and other belongings. Cuxirimay probably accompanied them too, for it was around this time that Pizarro took her as a sexual partner.

The Pizarro party made its way southward on the Chinchaysuyu road from Cajamarca through the Andes, resting at way stations, crossing snow-covered mountain passes, and encountering periodic resistance from native adversaries. They eventually arrived at Xauxa, where Pizarro intended to found a town. According to Sancho, however, the foundation was not entirely successful. "There was not one of the Spaniards who would agree to stay there," he writes, noting that they were fearful of the presence of armed Andean warriors in the area.[6] In the end, a small number of Spaniards did, indeed, remain in Xauxa, but most of them continued on to Cuzco, where Governor Pizarro would successfully enact the foundation of a town.

The primary sources on the foundation of Cuzco provide insight into how towns were established in early

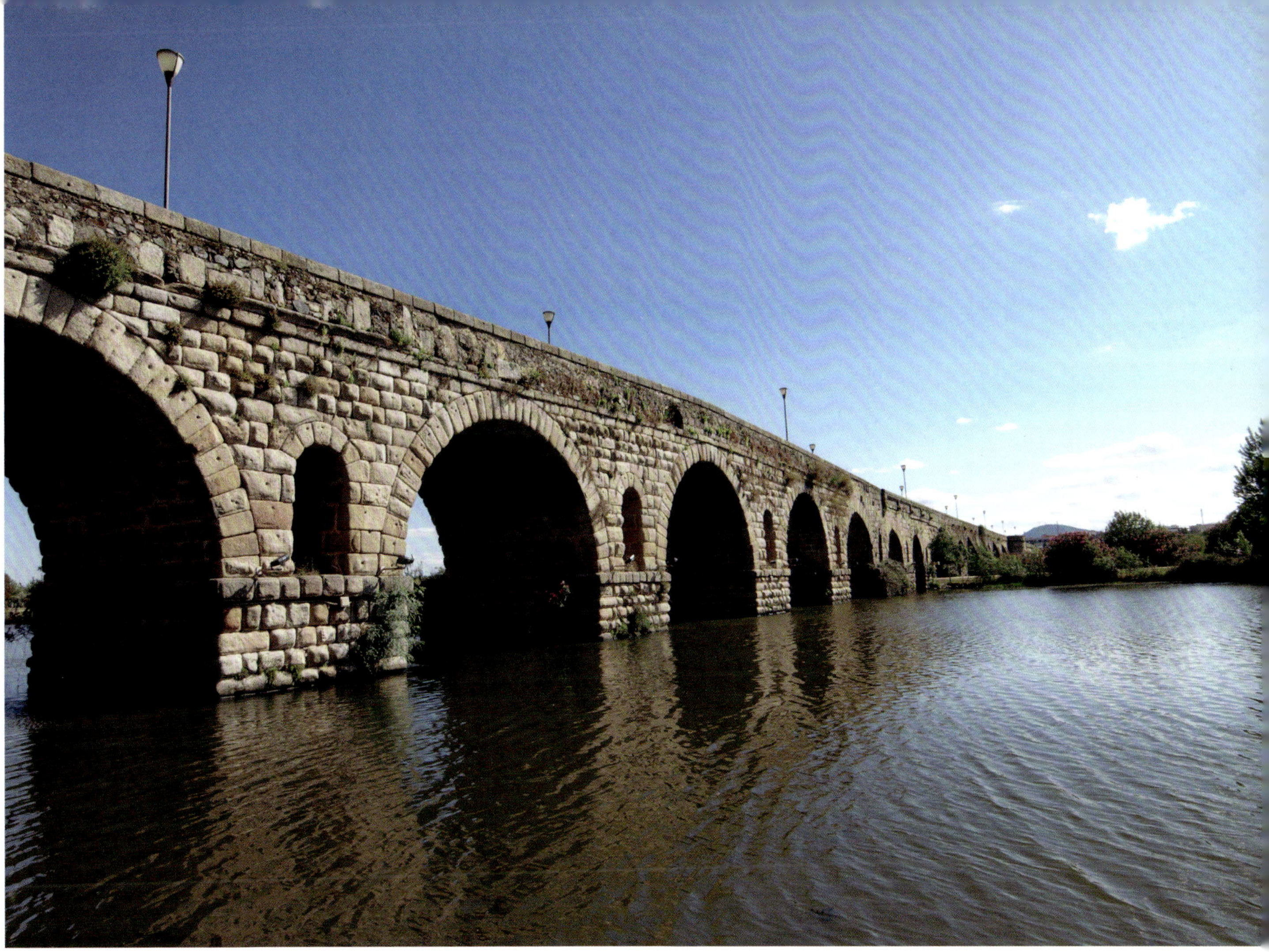

FIG. 3.2 Roman bridge over the Guadiana River, Mérida, Spain. The solid stonework of European bridges like this one contrasts strongly with the woven bridges early Spanish colonists found in Peru.

colonial Spanish America. At the same time, Cuzco is a special case. Unlike early colonial Mexico City, which was built on ruins in the aftermath of battles between Cortés's men and those of Moctezuma, Cuzco was still an intact built environment in 1533, when Pizarro and his followers arrived there. As Sancho's writings show, the transformation of the capital of the Inca Empire into a Spanish colonial city occurred, at first, not through construction but rather through ritual practice and the production of documents, both of which were understood by Sancho and his contemporaries as tools for the transformation of space. In Cuzco, that transformation would be initiated on the festival plaza, a place that native Andeans like Cuxirimay knew as a setting for other kinds of ritual, and which was steeped in Inca history and metaphysics. For Pizarro, Sancho, and the other Spanish settlers, however, Cuzco's value was to be found elsewhere, its impressive, stone-built environment encouraging them to imagine what it could become in the future.

As Sancho tells the story, one hundred men on horseback and thirty on foot made the journey from Xauxa to Cuzco. Together with their servants, slaves, and native allies, they traversed challenging terrain and crossed rivers on net-like bridges made of rope or woven branches—remarkable feats of Inca engineering that caught the author's attention. He describes their construction and the experience of crossing them in detail:

> If the river has rocky banks on both sides, they reinforce them with a large, high stone wall, and then they place four large poles of two palms or a little less across the river. And between them, in the form of trellises, they weave green branches two fingers thick, so that none is looser than the other, interlinked well. And on top of these they place branches across, in that the water below cannot be seen, and in that way, they make the floor of the bridge. And in the same way they weave a wall on the sides of the bridge, with these same greens, so that no one may fall into the water, of which there is no danger, although to those who are not practiced, crossing [the bridge] looks like a dangerous thing, for since the span is great, the bridge twists when a man passes over it, [and] one always goes downward to the midpoint, and then climbing until one has finished crossing to the other side.[7]

Bridges like this demonstrate the pervasiveness of weaving practices in all aspects of Inca culture, although here it is woven branches and reeds rather than camelid fibers that are of interest to the author. They continued to be used throughout the colonial period in Peru, but in more recent times most have been replaced by structures built from more permanent materials. An exception is a bridge crossing the Apurimac River south of Cuzco, whose design and construction square in many ways with the passage from the *Relatione*, evidencing the continuity of the practice over centuries (fig. 3.1).[8] Sancho's treatment of the bridge is one of the longest and most complete descriptions of a structure in his text, perhaps because there were such stark differences in materials and building techniques between the Inca bridges he saw in the Andes and those with which he would have been familiar in Spain. Among the latter must have been Roman bridges like the one in Mérida, Extremadura, where a long sequence of stone arches spans the Guadiana River (fig. 3.2).

As the expedition continued southward, Pizarro's company engaged in a series of skirmishes with bands of Andean adversaries. At one point, Sancho writes, Pizarro ordered the imprisonment of a native leader with the tongue-twisting name of Chilichuchima, a man previously considered an ally to the Spanish, but now regarded as a traitor. Arriving at a settlement called Xaquixahuana, north of Cuzco, Pizarro ordered that he be burned alive, an act that must have reminded all who saw it of the execution of Atahualpa some months earlier in Cajamarca. For Pizarro and the leaders of his company, killing the native chief in such a public and spectacular way was a warning to their adversaries of the punishment they could inflict. Similarly horrific executions would continue to be carried out in the decades to come in the enduring struggle for power in the Andes.

The expedition continued onward to Cuzco, and eventually Pizarro and his followers arrived there "without any other resistance or battle," says Sancho, "on Friday, at the hour of high mass, on the fifteenth day of the month of November of the year of the birth of our Savior and Redeemer Jesus Christ MDXXXIII."[9] Their approach was from the northwest, and they would have caught their first glimpse of the Inca capital from a hilltop occupied today by the modest adobe church of Santa Ana. From that vantage point, they would have seen Cuzco's numerous stone and adobe structures topped with thatched roofs in the valley below, and at least one of the towers of Sacsahuaman rising above the cliff to the north. Descending the hill and following the course of the canalized Saphi River to the southeast, they eventually arrived at Cuzco's great festival plaza—a large open space known today as the Plaza de Armas (fig. 3.3). It was there, says Sancho, that "Governor [Pizarro] made all of the Christians take accommodations in the quarters that were around the plaza of the city."[10] For Cuxirimay, who by now was called Angelina, the arrival must have been a bittersweet homecoming. These "quarters" in which the Spaniards were to stay were the palace compounds and festival halls of the Inca that had long served as the backdrop to ceremonies, among them Huayna Capac's cutting of her hair. The *Suma y narración*, to which we might look for a hint at her point of view, is brief and dispassionate in recounting Pizarro's entry into Cuzco, noting only that when he did so, he found his emissaries Hernando de Soto and Diego de Almagro (*c.* 1475–1538) there amassing gold and silver.[11]

Sancho's recounting of the company's arrival illustrates the instrumentality of language and writing in the

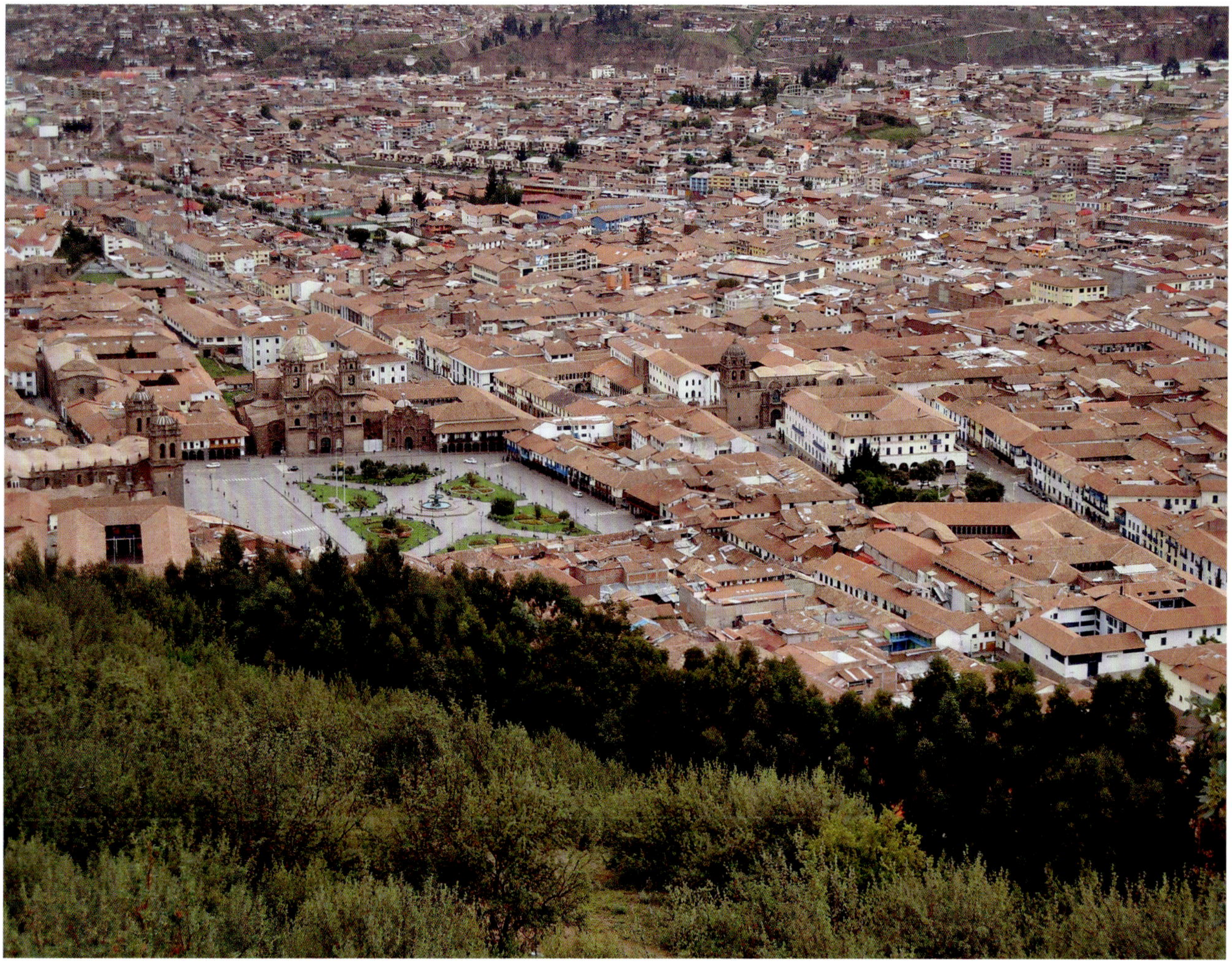

FIG. 3.3 The Plaza de Armas, Cuzco, viewed from the north. The site of Inca Cuzco's great festival plaza, the square remains a place of social interaction for tourists and residents alike.

transformation of Inca Cuzco into Spanish Cuzco. On the pages of his report, the Inca capital becomes a "city." For Sancho and his peers, this term referred to both a built environment and a well-governed citizenry, and it was in the public spaces of a city that the two came together. The Spanish must have imagined the Inca plaza as such a space, a counterpart to those constructed in Spain and the Americas as sites of civil interaction and good governance, and which were at once functional and symbolic.[12] Sancho's description of Cuzco thus demonstrates the ways in which his perception of the built environment, and the words he used to describe it, contributed to that environment's transformation. Equally significant were the political rituals that took place there in the first months of Spanish occupation.

Among the native Andeans who arrived in Cuzco with Pizarro and his company was Manco Inca (hereafter, Manco). Like Atahualpa and Huascar, he was one of Huayna Capac's sons. Pizarro recognized his noble genealogy, as did the native elites in Cuzco; indeed, a few weeks after his arrival there, Manco was the focus of an extraordinary ritual by which the native elites of Cuzco proclaimed him the Sapa Inca. The strategy of affirming the legitimacy of a native ruler as a means of solidifying an alliance was, by this time, a standard practice of the Spanish in the Americas. Following the death of Atahualpa at Cajamarca, for example, Pizarro acknowledged one of Atahualpa's half-brothers as the Inca king's successor. Sancho explains his aim in doing so thus:

> As [the native people] were accustomed for a long time to being in obedience to one Lord, and paying tribute to him, it would have caused great confusion if he [Pizarro] had not done so, for each of them would rebel under his authority, and it would be difficult to bring them into friendship with the Spaniards and into the obedience of His Majesty.[13]

As it turned out, this new king died during the subsequent journey to Cuzco, thus clearing the way for Manco to assume the title.

In his description of the ritual, Sancho writes that the native elites of Cuzco "gave [Manco] obedience in the plaza of that city following their custom, acknowledging him as their Lord."[14] To mark their recognition of his status as Atahualpa's successor, says Sancho, they presented him with a bundle of white feathers. The description of this ritual in the *Relatione* is brief, as it is in the *Suma y narración*, where Betanzos simply reports that the lords of Cuzco "performed their festivals and joyous ceremonies and fasts and sacrifices" to mark Manco's investiture.[15] He does not mention the white feathers, but he discusses them elsewhere in the text, noting that one of the laws put in place by Pachacuti stated that the men of his lineage were required to wear one or two hawk feathers on their heads. Other colonial period sources note that a cluster of white feathers from the wings of a bird of prey known as the *corequenque* hung on the ruler's forehead flanking the *mascaypacha* and symbolizing the sociospatial division of Cuzco and, more generally, the Inca Empire, into the two kinship groups of *hanan* and *hurin*.[16]

In his account of this ritual of accession, Sancho demonstrates no awareness of the symbolism of the white feathers, and his inclusion of the detail of their presentation to Manco may have to do with his own recognition of their similarity to the large plumes worn as markers of status on the helmets of European military leaders. But if the ritual of Manco's accession truly occurred as Sancho reports it, then the young native ruler and the indigenous noblemen would have understood the symbolism of the feathers perfectly well. More generally, the performance of the ritual on Cuzco's plaza, surrounded by the buildings associated with the Sapa Inca and his predecessors, reinforced the spatial and material dimensions of his authority both within the Inca capital and in its environs, even though the city was now occupied by Spanish Christians.

The performance of this ritual on the plaza demonstrates the symbolic flexibility of that space in the first weeks and months of the Spanish occupation. When the native elites of Cuzco presented Manco with white feathers, they were surrounded not only by the palace compounds of Inca Cuzco but also by the encampment of Pizarro's men, who had been ordered to set up tents in the plaza, keep their horses there, and watch for approaching enemies. Manco's investiture, then, may have been understood by the Spanish not so much as a challenge to Pizarro's authority but, rather, as an expression of alliance, albeit one that acknowledged differences in traditional conceptions of rulership. Through it, the lords of Cuzco joined the Spanish in their opposition to a common enemy—"those of Quito," as Sancho calls them.

The presentation of the white feathers to Manco and the recognition of his authority on the plaza preceded another solemn ceremony enacted in the very same place but involving a larger cast of characters and a different set of ritual paraphernalia. It occurred, Sancho says, on Christmas Day 1533, slightly more than a month after the Spaniards' arrival in Cuzco. Friar Valverde, he writes, said Mass, and then Pizarro walked onto the plaza, where a large group of men awaited him. Among them was Manco, who was seated, Sancho notes, on a stool and surrounded by a multitude of native chiefs and warriors, who sat on the ground. Among the Inca, the use of such a stool was a privilege reserved for the supreme ruler, the seat functioning, like the *ushnu*, to elevate him above all those in his presence.

Pizarro ordered that the Spanish, too, sit in the expansive space of the plaza as he prepared to deliver the *Requerimiento*, the text whose public reading was an obligation to the Crown and an essential step in the conquest

FIG. 3.4 Coat of arms from a royal standard, 16th century. Applied silk. Museo del Ejército, Toledo. The standard employs materials and imagery that would have been unfamiliar to native Andeans before the arrival of the Spanish, though the idea of communicating through textiles and symbols was well established in Inca culture.

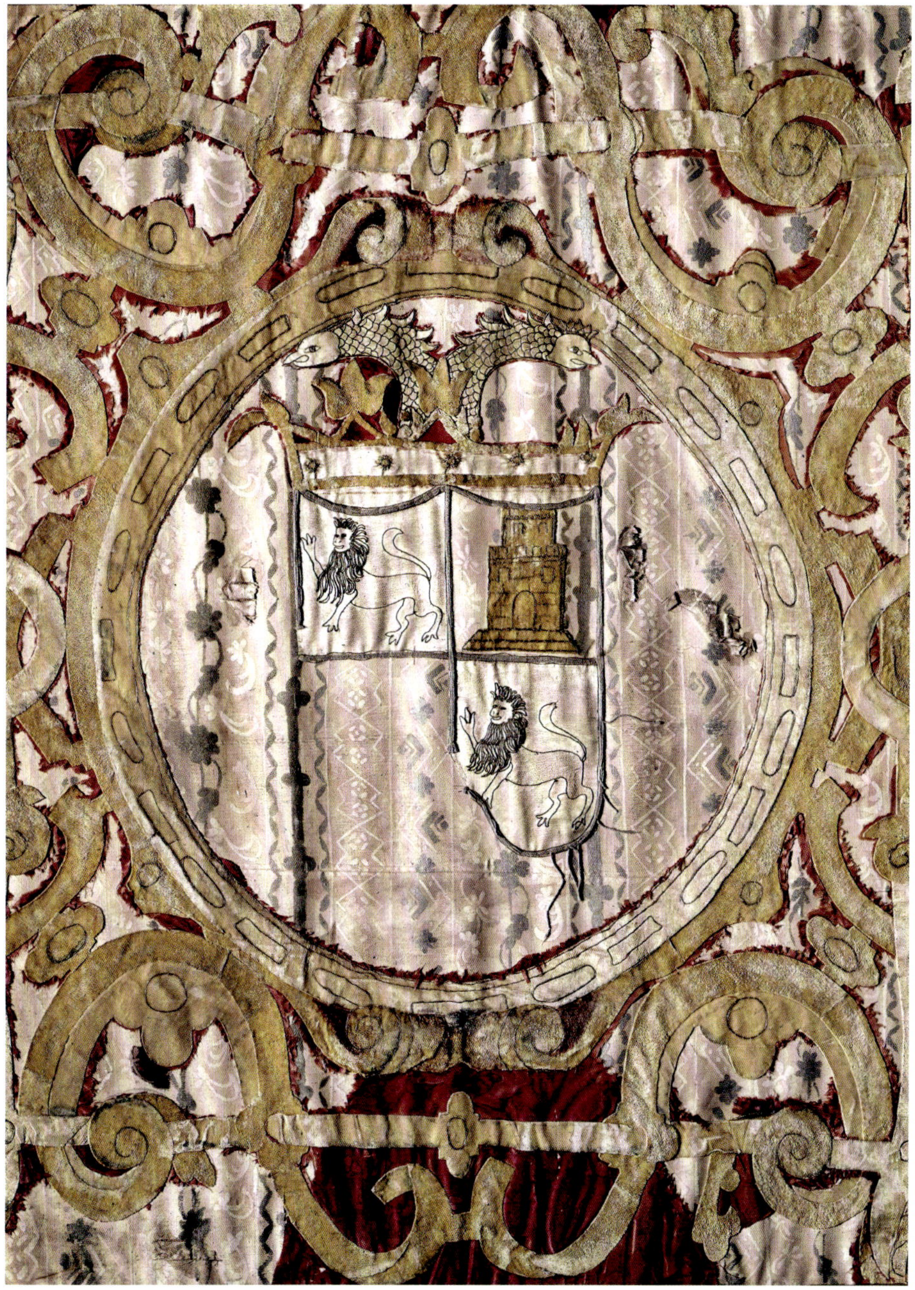

of territory. As Sancho recounts the story, it was he himself who read the text aloud as an interpreter translated it into Quechua for its intended audience.[17] Sancho does not record the text of the *Requerimiento*, but it would have been similar to that issued to Pizarro's longtime associate Pedrarias Dávila by King Ferdinand—then acting as regent for his daughter, Queen Juana—for use in the conquest of Castilla del Oro in 1513. The text is voiced in the first person, and its content indicates that it was directed to an audience of adult men. "I implore and require you," begins its key passage, "to recognize the Church as master and overseer of the world, and the Supreme Pontiff, called the Pope, in its name, and the King and Queen our lords in its place, as overseers and lords and kings of these islands and mainland." Those who agreed to these terms would be rewarded: "Your women, children, and property will be left to you free of obligation so that you shall do with them freely as you wish." The consequences of not complying were severe:

> With the aid of God, I will march in powerfully against you, and I will wage war against you on all sides and in all ways that I can, and I will subject you to the yoke and obedience of the Church and Their Highnesses, and I will take you and your women and children and I will make slaves of them, and as such I will sell and make use of them as His Highness orders, and I will take all of your property . . . and I assure you that the mounting deaths and damages shall be your fault, not that of His Highness, nor mine, nor that of these noblemen who come with me.[18]

Composed by the Spanish jurist Juan López de Palacios Rubios in 1512, the text emerges from the experience of medieval Iberia, where certain interpretations of Islamic law required that conquerors notify their foes of their intentions, including the demand of submission to Islam and the payment of a tax. In the Christian reconquest of the Iberian Peninsula, the kings of Castile appropriated this practice, which itself had come out of ancient Roman ritual. It was this complex of ideas and ritualized speech that informed the *Requerimiento* as it took shape in the early sixteenth century.[19] The reading of the decree, then, was itself an act whose form derived from intercultural, multiconfessional contact.

In Cuzco, on Christmas Day 1533, the ritual reading of this text entered into yet another system of cultural exchanges, this time with the native people of Andean Peru. Sancho reports that all of those present in the plaza of Cuzco complied in recognizing the authority of the Church, the Pope, and the Holy Roman Emperor, Charles V. A series of ceremonial acts marked the end of the ritual, including the raising of the royal standard and the sounding of trumpets. For the Spanish, these were familiar acts, familiar sounds, and familiar objects, but for the native Andeans, they were novelties. A sixteenth-century royal standard traditionally associated with Pizarro—its castles and lions depicted two-dimensionally on silk and surrounded by curvilinear ornamentation (fig. 3.4)—demonstrates some of the new materials and symbols the Spanish brought to Cuzco, where textiles such as tunics and sashes had borne other kinds of symbolic imagery, in the form of the *tocapu*, since time immemorial.

Other acts that were performed had to be left out of the *Relatione*, says Sancho, "to avoid prolixity." He does, however, provide details of one of them. Manco, he writes, "stood up, and with a vessel of gold, handed a drink to [Pizarro] and the Spaniards."[20] Here, the toasting and drinking so central to Inca ritual are inserted in the performance of a medieval Spanish act of invasion and occupation on the plaza of Cuzco, thus providing a new dimension to both practices and serving as an early example of the kinds of intercultural juxtaposition, combination, and attachment that would occur in Cuzco for years to come. The standard and other ritual paraphernalia of the Spanish, too, entered into the ensemble of objects and images in Cuzco, setting the stage for a range of appropriations and inventions that were iconographic rather than ceremonial.

It is difficult to know what to make of Sancho's account of the reading of the *Requerimiento* in Cuzco. Other sixteenth-century sources relate these events differently or, like Betanzos, do not mention them at all. Sancho's recording of this episode and his claim that it happened shortly after Manco's investiture might be taken as evidence of Pizarro's acumen: after allowing the native elites to recognize Manco as their ruler, he demanded and obtained their allegiance to another sovereign, Charles V. Whether or not Manco would have known the details of the agreement he made is debatable; at the same time, it could have been in his own interest to comply, thus allying himself with the Spanish. The passage in which Manco toasts Pizarro with a golden vessel is especially intriguing with regard to the native ruler's intentions. Among the Inca, ritual toasting and drinking marked momentous events and cast them in terms of exchange and reciprocity, ideas that would have informed the way Manco and his native contemporaries interpreted the ritual reading of the *Requerimiento*.[21] Did Sancho understand this, including the episode in his account as a way of demonstrating that Manco believed he was exchanging allegiance for protection?

The question of what really happened on the plaza of Cuzco in November and December 1533 cannot be answered with certainty, but what is clear is that Sancho's narration of these events reveals that for him—and, presumably, for Pizarro and his followers—the space was conceived as the site on which both native Andeans and Spaniards in Cuzco performed rituals of state. Surrounded by *cancha* compounds and massive agricultural terraces rising to Sacsahuaman, it had been the sacred site of ceremony for many decades, and its history was known to Manco and the native chiefs and warriors who, Sancho says, were with him there during the reading of the *Requerimiento*. The adaptability of the plaza would be demonstrated once more several months later, when Pizarro, Sancho, and the city's first Spanish settlers used it as a setting for the political ritual that would officially transform Inca Cuzco into a new and different kind of place.

On March 23, 1534, slightly more than four months after his arrival in Cuzco, Pizarro performed the Act of Foundation, the ritual through which the Spanish city came into being. The performance of this ritual was no ordinary occurrence; he previously had established only two other towns: San Miguel, in the Chira River valley of northern Peru, and Xauxa, though the latter foundation may not have been wholly successful. Xerez offers a summary of the process in his account of the foundation of San Miguel in his *Verdadera relación*, describing the company's arrival at the site and the determination of its suitability. Friar Valverde, he writes, played an important role in the process:

> [After] the area and the river banks were seen by the reverend father friar Vicente de Valverde, monk of the order of Santo Domingo, and by the officials of Your Majesties, the Governor [Pizarro], in accord with these people, as Your Majesties order, settled and founded a town in the name of Your Majesties. In this region and river valley are found the causes and qualities necessary in territory that is going to be settled by Spaniards, and the natives will be able to be of service without suffering too much fatigue, since it is the will of Your Majesties that their protection be respected.[22]

Both Xerez and Mena note that San Miguel was established on the site of an existing settlement called Tangarará. As often happened, and notwithstanding Valverde's inspection of the site, the settlers soon found it to be unsuitable and moved to a new location. The initial site of the San Miguel settlement thus remains the subject of some debate. It may have been at or near the northern Peruvian town in the Chira River valley that bears the name Tangarará today.[23]

By establishing towns in San Miguel, Xauxa, and, later, Cuzco, Pizarro was complying with a key component of the Spanish Crown's philosophy and practice of governance in the Americas. The early modern Spanish monarchy was conceived as a network of structurally similar towns on both sides of the Atlantic, and the foundation of towns in the Andes expanded that network into new territory. Isabella and Ferdinand's instruction to Nicolás de Ovando, issued from Granada in 1501, addressed this issue, ordering him to establish towns in places he selected and inspected, noting that Christians were not to live outside of those settlements and stipulating that he could build up to three fortresses. The only other works of architecture the ordinances mention are *casas de fundición*, smelting houses for the processing of gold, which were to be carefully guarded wherever they were established.[24]

References to the foundation of towns in the Americas also appear in King Ferdinand's *Instrucción* of 1513 to Pedrarias Dávila, which stipulates that towns should be set up on healthy sites with access to the sea and fertile land. The founder, the document specified, should apportion lots to the settlers, on which they could build houses, and the plan of the town should include a plaza and a church.[25] For his part, Pizarro would have become personally familiar with the foundation of towns during his first decade in the Americas. Dávila founded at least six towns in Castilla del Oro, among them Panama, established in 1519. Pizarro was not present for the performance of the Act of Foundation for that town, but he was appointed as one of its council members, a post that would provide him with the knowledge on which he would draw in the following decades.

Another of the towns Dávila founded was Natá, located to the southwest of Panama. A document recording its foundation ritual survives in a sixteenth-century copy held today in the Archivo de Indias, Seville, and that text—voiced in the first person—purports to be the ritual script Dávila used in the ceremony. Xerez, who had worked as a notary in Natá, may have had a hand in its production. As the earliest extant Act of Foundation for all of Spanish America, it provides insight into how the ritual was practiced during Pizarro's first years in the Americas, and offers a telling point of comparison with the Act of Foundation for Cuzco, recorded by Sancho more than a decade later.[26]

Like the *Requerimiento*, the Act of Foundation centered on the public reading of a text. Both the document and its oral dissemination were conceived as instruments through which governors established and ordered civic space. At the same time, the writing and reading of the Act brought into being new kinds of personhood in that space, providing participants and witnesses with new social identities as *vecinos* (residents) of the newly founded towns. Its form and contents drew from centuries-old Spanish laws and customs as well as from the terms of royal edicts and contracts for exploration in the Americas. A reading of the extant Acts of Foundation from the sixteenth-century Americas shows there is some consistency to their structure, but significant differences among them suggest that, unlike the *Requerimiento*, the text was not strictly codified. Rather, it seems that scribes like Sancho, together with the participants in the ritual, understood the defining structure of the script but, at the same time, had the freedom to adapt it as they saw fit.[27]

Sancho refers to the production and performance of the Act of Foundation for Cuzco in the *Relatione*:

> The Governor [Pizarro] ordered that a majority of the Spaniards he had with him should gather, and he performed an Act of Foundation and creation of the town, saying that he was settling it and founding it just as it is, and he took possession of it in the middle of the plaza. And as a sign of founding it and the start of building the town and colony, he performed certain ceremonies as included in the Act which was written up, which I, the scribe, read in a loud voice in the presence of all.[28]

The document to which Sancho refers has been lost, but an early copy of it is held today in the library of the Palacio Real in Madrid. It consists of nine quarto pages written in a sixteenth-century hand and concludes with the claim that it was "taken from the original" by a scribe named Simon de Alzate, who worked in that capacity in the Americas in the 1540s.[29]

The Act of Foundation for Cuzco is revealing on a number of levels. Its multiple references to the built environment in which the ritual took place contrast with the lack of such data in the document for Natá and are arguably the earliest known records of Cuzco's infrastructure composed by an eyewitness. But even apart from its utility as a source for the architecture and plan of the Inca capital, its inclusion of those details underscores the centrality of Cuzco's existing buildings and urban form to the way events unfolded in the first months of the Spanish colonial city's existence. At the same time, it demonstrates that for Pizarro, Sancho, and their contemporaries, the pronouncement of ritual phrases, the performance of ritual acts, and the composition of a document were among the tools necessary for the production of urban space.

As in the text from Natá, the Act of Foundation for Cuzco opens with the Trinitarian formula ("In the name of God the Father and Son and Holy Spirit") and an invocation. The Cuzco document differs from its Panamanian counterpart, however, in the considerable length of this section. In Natá, the opening prayer was a formality completed in just a few lines of text, but in the Cuzco document it fills three-quarters of a page and includes an excursus on the history of permanent settlements. All of the descendants of Adam and Eve, it proclaims, "built houses and homes where they lodged and lived, looked for the most suitable land they could find that produced fruit and gave them sustenance . . . and made laws with which the republic was ruled and was well governed."[30] These statements at the beginning of the document have no counterpart in the other surviving sixteenth-century Acts of Foundation, although they do reiterate certain passages in the writings of Francisco de Vitoria (*c.* 1483–1546), a Dominican friar and political theorist whose lecture *De potestate civili* (*On Civil Power*), delivered in Salamanca in 1528, also emphasizes the antiquity and necessity of civil society and the institution of the city.[31] In light of these correspondences, it seems likely that the highly literate and experienced Dominican Vicente de Valverde, whose role in the foundation ceremony in San Miguel is clear, was also instrumental in the foundation of Cuzco. Indeed, he may have had a hand in composing the document and, perhaps, might even have read this part of it aloud on Cuzco's festival plaza on March 23, 1534.

The primary message of this first section of the Act is that the foundation of Cuzco is part of a larger, universal Christian history dating back to the beginning of biblical time. In this sense, it echoes the rhetoric of the *Requerimiento*, which traces the idea of governance by high-ranking men (and their subjects' obedience to them) to the time of Adam and Eve. The opening lines of the Act of Foundation thus position the city of Spanish Cuzco within a new temporal order, placing it at the end of a long lineage of settlements extending back to the time of the Old Testament.

Following the invocation, the text shifts to the first person. "I, Francisco Pizarro," it begins, continuing with an expression of the conquistador's loyalty to the king, a proclamation of his status as governor, and a statement of his intention to establish "a town of Spaniards settled by Christians"—a turn of phrase also appearing in the document from Natá.[32] Following this is a reference to an inspection that assessed the suitability of Cuzco for settlement. Valverde, who had also been involved in the inspection at San Miguel, accompanied the royal accountant Antonio Navarro in taking stock of the site and its resources. Their findings are summarized in the Act of Foundation. Cuzco, the text boasts, was "sited in a valley that is fertile of sustenance, in between two rivers, near sources of good water and woodland for firewood, mountains and pastures to raise livestock, and rivers and ponds for fishing."[33] The Act of Foundation for Natá, too, indicates that the selected locale had "all of the qualities and provisions and necessary things to found and make a town, and to be able to maintain and sustain it."[34]

The text from Cuzco, however, moves beyond natural resources to note the city's array of fine buildings that would serve the Spanish well:

> [There are] storehouses and houses of lords and old buildings of stone that are abandoned and without owner or lord, where the Spanish that settle here could at little cost and without much work take wood and stone for the buildings of the town [such as] houses as well as the church and a wall of stone.[35]

The passage presents Cuzco as a built environment with great potential for use by the Spanish. The claim that "the Spanish that settle here could at little cost and without much work take wood and stone for the buildings of the town" looks to the future and expresses Cuzco's value differently from how Mena and Xerez did in their accounts of its houses made of gold. Those earlier texts cast Cuzco as a commodity whose precious materials were melted into fungible assets in the form of bars of gold, but the Act of Foundation presents it instead in terms of its use value, equating it with a quarry and a store of lumber to be used in the construction of a Spanish colonial city that existed only in its founders' imaginations.

The part of the text that follows the inspection and description of the site includes the Act's most compelling passages. It opens with a repetition of the Trinitarian formula, this time in Latin—"In nomine patrijs et filij et spiritus sancti, amen"—and continues with a series of proclamations in which the founders' belief in the transformative power of words and ritual acts is palpable. "The plaza of this town that I make," the governor's script declares, "shall be this one that was made by the natives, and the lots where the residents must build their houses shall be plotted and consigned around it."[36] The next lines are striking in their vivid evocation of Pizarro's engagement with the physical setting:

> Today, Monday the 23rd day of the month of March in the year of the birth of our savior Jesus Christ, 1534, on this *picota* that a few days ago I had made and placed in the middle of this plaza on the steps of stone that it has that are not finished being carved, with this dagger that I carry in my belt I carve something of them and cut and carve a knot of wood of the said *picota* . . . and I make all of the other acts of possession and formalities of the foundation of these works to which I am obligated and which I ought to do . . . designating the name of this said town that I have founded, the very noble and great city of Cuzco.[37]

The "steps of stone that are not finished being carved" to which the passage refers must have been the *ushnu*, the ceremonial platform whose remains lie beneath the modern plaza, near its fountain, and where in the time of the Inca the sugarloaf-shaped stone image of the Sun was displayed. The text indicates that prior to the performance of the ritual, Pizarro had ordered that a *picota*, a pillar made of wood, be erected on this platform. The erection of such a pillar may have been facilitated by the presence of a cavity atop the *ushnu* and leading into the earth beneath it, a feature of such platforms found throughout the Inca Empire.[38]

There are a number of precedents for the erection of a pillar or *stele* at the foundation of an architectural space in classical antiquity, among them the inscribed *stelae* and

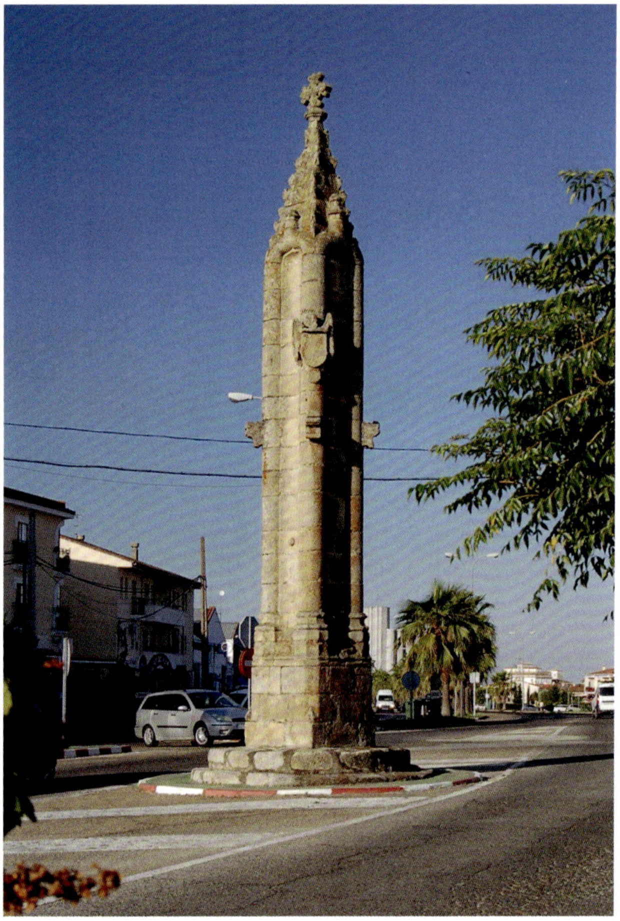

FIG. 3.5 *Picota* in Trujillo, Spain, 15th century. Spanish settlers erected *picotas*—columns that represent civic authority—in many colonial towns in Peru.

pillars of ancient Greek foundation ceremonies.[39] But the more direct point of reference for Pizarro, Sancho, and other Spaniards present at the Act of Foundation in Cuzco was their own experience on the Iberian Peninsula and in the Americas. In the sixteenth-century Spanish world, the *picota* (sometimes called the *rollo*) was a certain kind of pillar: a highly symbolic one associated with town governance and the exercise of justice in the form of corporal punishment. An early reference to its use appears in the thirteenth-century legal code known as the *Siete partidas* of Alfonso X, which asserts that judges can order criminals to be "put in disgrace"—presumably tied or chained—at the *picota*.[40] In the centuries that followed, *picotas* made of wood or stone were set up in towns throughout much of the Iberian Peninsula. In light of its function, the *picota*'s symbolism was clear: it marked the presence of a code of laws and their enforcement in the town in which it was erected.[41]

A number of *picotas* from the era of the conquest of Peru survive in Spain today, among them a highly ornamented one in Trujillo, Pizarro's birthplace, from the late fifteenth century (fig. 3.5). Constructed of stacked granite blocks, its four columns rise from bases in each corner of a stone platform. Its role as a symbol of both temporal and spiritual authority is evident in its decoration. One of the columns supports a sculpted eagle bearing the arms of Ferdinand and Isabella; crowning the structure is a pyramidal form topped with a cross; and projecting from its sides are protrusions presumably used for hanging the condemned.[42]

Pizarro, Sancho notes, used his dagger to scrape the steps of the *picota*'s stone platform and to carve a knot of wood out of the *picota* itself. Here, too, there are ancient and medieval Iberian precedents for the foundation of towns involving the ritual modification of the natural environment through acts such as plowing the earth and cutting the branches from trees. These practices were continued in early sixteenth-century Spain and the Americas. At the foundation of Frontera de Cáceres (Honduras), the scribe Francisco Cepero recorded that a certain Bartolomé de la Celada, identified as the royal accountant, performed the Act of Foundation by "cutting branches from the trees and pulling up the grass and digging into the earth with his hands." Similar practices occurred at the foundation of Trujillo (Honduras) on May 18, 1525, and at Santiago de los Caballeros (Guatemala) on November 22, 1527.[43]

Along with installing the *picota*, Pizarro proclaimed the city's name as "the very noble and great city of Cuzco." The name is accorded importance on the page of the written Act through distinctive graphic representation (fig. 3.6). Here the scribe may have been approximating the look of moveable type, or at least referring to the reproduction of text in the form of print, and the presentation of the city's name in this way sets the stage for its presentation in print decades later in Sancho's *Relatione* and on maps of the Americas. This section of the text concludes with Sancho's statement that, as he had the *Requerimiento*, he read the Act of Foundation "word for word" in the plaza of Cuzco in the presence of witnesses.

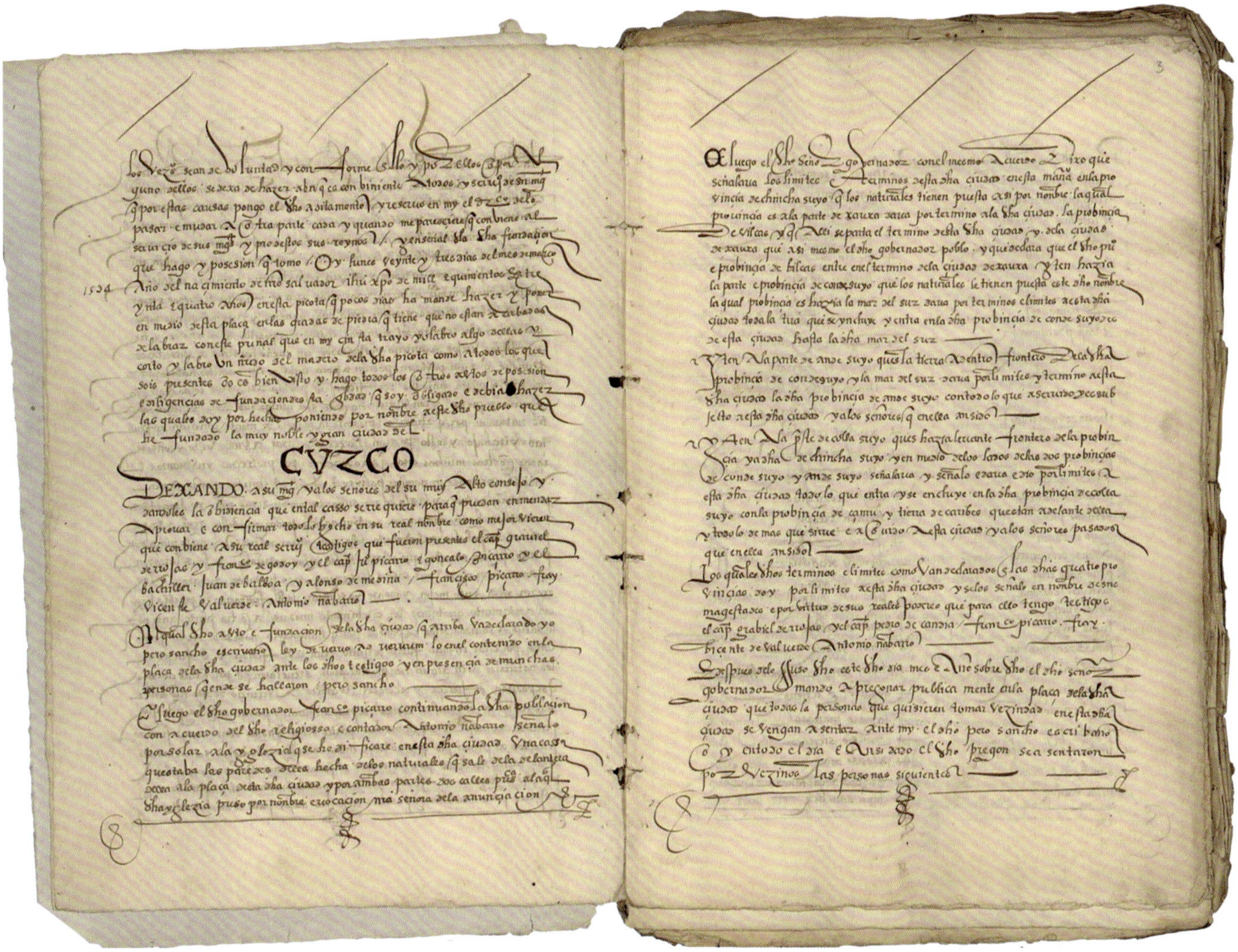

FIG. 3.6 The Act of Foundation of Cuzco, fols. 2v–3r, 1540s. Ink on paper. Real Biblioteca, Madrid. The text of this document was read aloud before witnesses in Cuzco's central plaza on March 23, 1534, officially founding the Spanish city.

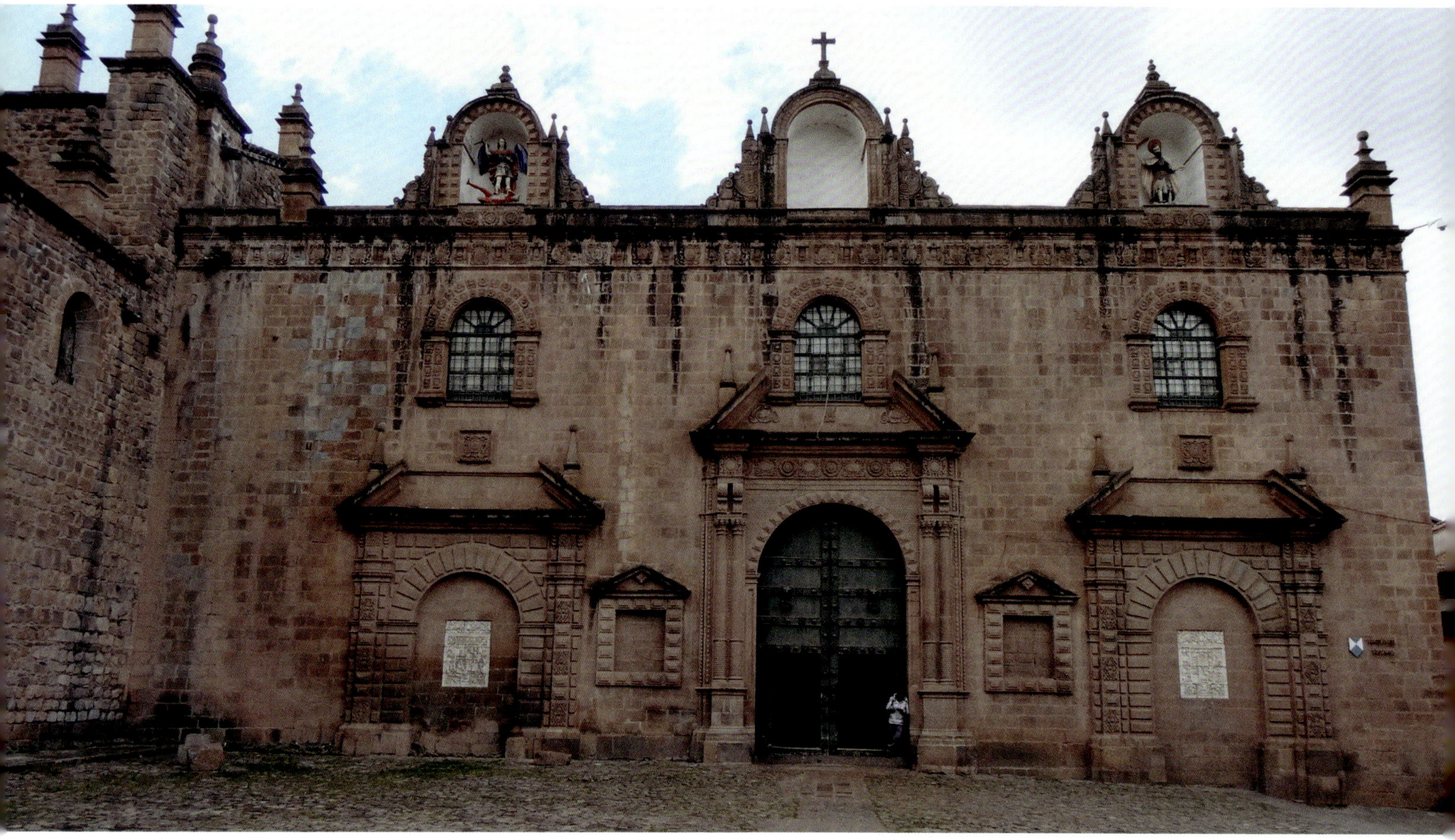

FIG. 3.7 The façade of the church of El Triunfo, Cuzco, late 17th century. This is the likely site of Cuzco's first Christian church, selected by Francisco Pizarro during the Act of Foundation in 1534.

The text then shifts to the third person, with Sancho recording the selection of the location for the city's church, an undertaking also documented in the Act of Foundation for Natá. In that earlier foundation, Pedrarias Dávila placed a wooden cross on a plot of land where the first church would be built. The Act of Foundation for Cuzco does not mention the placement of a cross but, instead, identifies an existing structure as the site of the church. Sancho writes:

> In agreement with the said priest [Valverde] and the accountant Antonio Navarro, he [Pizarro] designated for the plot of the church that will be built in this city a building whose walls were made by the natives and that opens out to the front of the plaza of this city and on both sides, two straight streets . . . He gave as the name of the said church Our Lady of the Annunciation.[44]

The text does not specify which of the buildings whose "walls were made by the natives" and faced onto the plaza Pizarro had selected, but documents produced several months later indicate it was a structure on the northeast side of the plaza on an elevated terrace. The site occupied by El Triunfo, one of two churches flanking the cathedral today, is probably that designated by Pizarro for a church in 1534 (fig. 3.7). Its façade dates to the seventeenth century, its three portals, three arched windows, and three niches above the cornice anticipating the three aisles in Cuzco's only church with a central plan.[45]

Perhaps more than in any other part of Pizarro's foundation of Cuzco, the passage on the selection of the Inca structure for the church renders architectural and spatial change as a rebirth, akin to the sacrament of baptism: through the uttering of words and the performance of a ritual act, a building made by the Inca becomes a church for Christian Spaniards. The pronouncement of the building's new identity, however, was only one dimension of its transformation. The dedication of the church to the Virgin of the Annunciation positioned it in a new temporal order, calling to mind narratives of the lives of the Virgin and Jesus Christ, and the calendar of the church, which celebrates the Feast of the Annunciation on March 25, two days after Pizarro performed the Act of Foundation.

At once a ritual and a document, the Act of Foundation was largely an act of the imagination that reconfigured the existing built environment of Inca Cuzco to create a Spanish colonial city. In an early modern rendition of the process known today as "adaptive reuse," the *ushnu* became a base for the *picota*, the symbol of civic authority; an existing hall-like structure became a church, the symbol of ecclesiastic authority; and the plaza became the site of a new ensemble of rituals and everyday practices. The text of the Act, however, conceals much more than it reveals. The House of the Sun, now stripped of its golden ornament and robbed of its contents, is never mentioned. This omission effectively repositions what Betanzos described as the most highly symbolic space in Cuzco, ignoring its centrality in the worldview of the Inca and moving it to the periphery of the Spanish city. The fate of the sugarloaf-shaped image of the Sun, too, remains unclear. Was it removed from its place in the plaza, or did it stand on the *ushnu* alongside the newly erected *picota*?

The whereabouts of Angelina Yupanqui, Manco, and other native Andeans at the time of the Act of Foundation is not revealed in the text, which, in fact, ignores the presence in Cuzco of all but the participants in the ritual. But regardless of whether or not they were on the plaza when Sancho read the document aloud, it is certain that they did not erase from their minds the symbolism of Cuzco's buildings and plan and the story of its foundation in ancient times by Manco Capac and Mama Ocllo on the site of the House of the Sun. In effect, the Act of Foundation gave rise to the phenomenon the literary historian Walter Mignolo has called "coexisting territorialities," in which the process of colonization introduces a regard for landscapes and towns that differs markedly from that of the colonized people occupying those spaces.[46] For his part, Pedro Sancho showed little awareness of the age-old conception of Cuzco's buildings and spaces that coexisted with the new one he was helping to produce in March 1534, and his writing on the city in the days and weeks that followed the Act of Foundation would contribute forcefully to its further transformation.

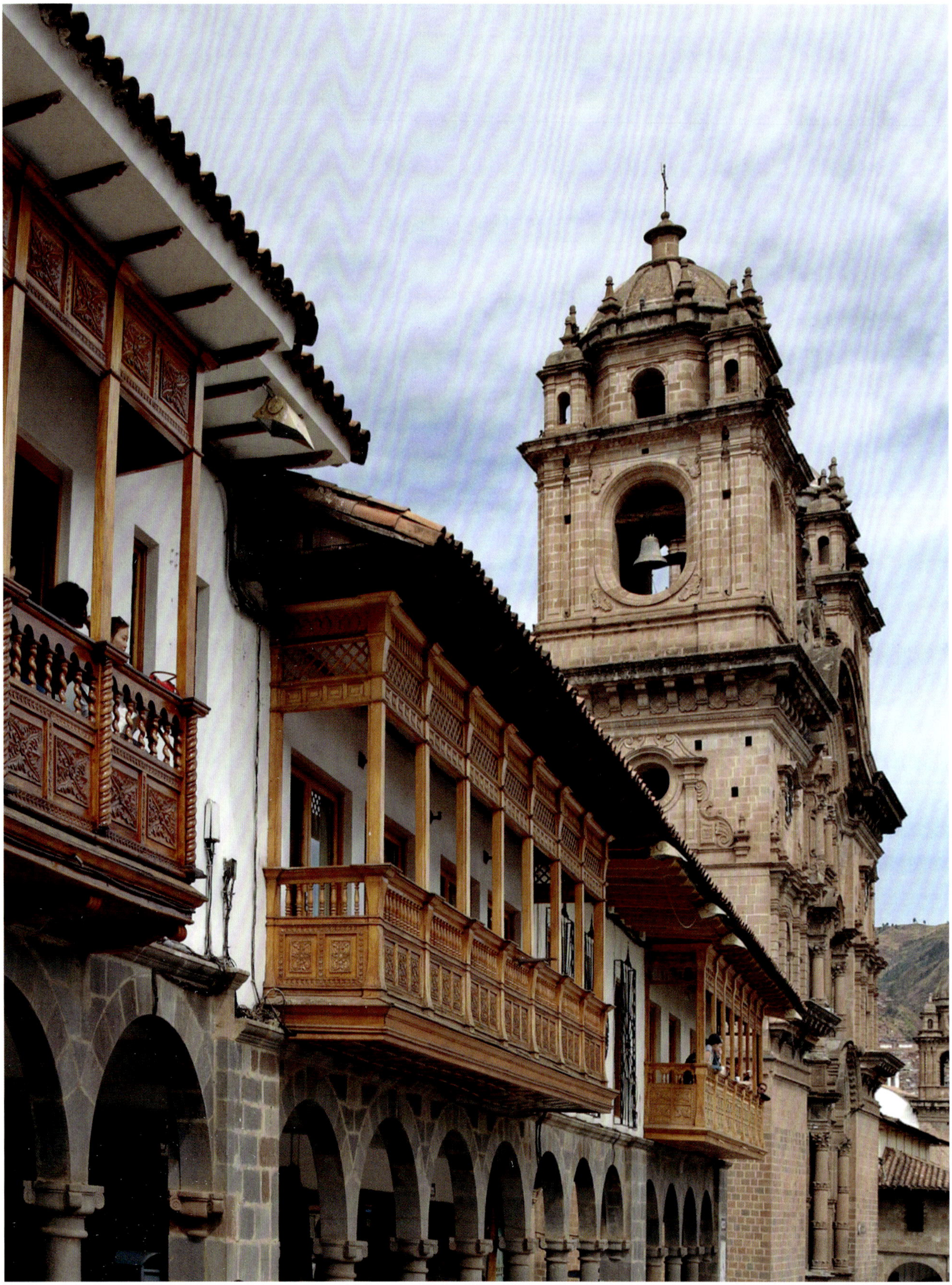

CHAPTER 4

Planning Spanish Cuzco

The City Council and the Distribution of Lots

The day after Pizarro performed the Act of Foundation, March 24, 1534, Pedro Sancho composed a register of Cuzco's eighty-seven new settlers, most of whom were Spaniards (fig. 4.1).[1] Topping it was Diego de Almagro, Pizarro's partner in the earliest expeditions southward from Panama in the 1520s, and the only man listed with the title *mariscal* (marshal). Almagro, however, would not reside in Cuzco, having embarked sometime earlier on a mission to pursue native adversaries in the northern Andes. Following his name were those of other men of high rank, including Pizarro's longtime associates Hernando de Soto and Pedro de Candía, and his brothers Juan and Gonzalo. At the bottom of the list were the names of men of lesser status, including Juan García, Cuzco's town crier. The register ultimately constructs a vision of the city not as a built environment but rather as a *civitas*: a society of citizens bound by a code of law.[2] In that sense, the list—with its hierarchical ordering of names neatly arranged in columns and framed by margins—might reasonably be considered the earliest surviving image of Spanish colonial Cuzco.

From Sancho's register, Pizarro selected those he would appoint to the *cabildo* (city council). For its two highest-ranking officials, known as *alcaldes*, he chose men with experience in town governance. One was Beltrán de Castro, who hailed from the town of Moya, about 270 km (168 mi.) east of Madrid, and had been in the Americas since the 1520s. He had previously held office on the council of the short-lived town of Bruselas, in what is today Costa Rica. The other was Pedro de Candía, who had written a *relación* describing Tumbes several years earlier. Pizarro also named eight lower-ranking officials called *regidores*: his brothers Juan and Gonzalo, Rodrigo Orgóñez, Pedro del Barco, Juan de Valdivieso, Gonzalo de los Nidos, Francisco Mexía, and Diego de Bazán. Of these ten appointees, only four—Candía, the two Pizarro brothers, and Valdivieso—had received shares of gold at Cajamarca. The others had joined Pizarro's cohort more recently, some of them having roamed the Andes under the leadership of Almagro.[3]

The appointments of these men to the offices of *alcalde* and *regidor* involved a ceremony, described by Sancho, in which they appeared before Pizarro, received their orders, and swore an oath of office. Pizarro's charge to the council members was formulaic, but his script is of interest with regard to the transformation of Inca Cuzco into Spanish Cuzco. Pizarro, Sancho writes:

> Gave them all complete power so that they would be able to exercise and practice the said offices of *alcaldes* and *regidores* in this said city and in each of its districts according to and in the manner in which they should . . . *and according to how the other* alcaldes *and*

(*facing page*) Detail of figure 4.4.

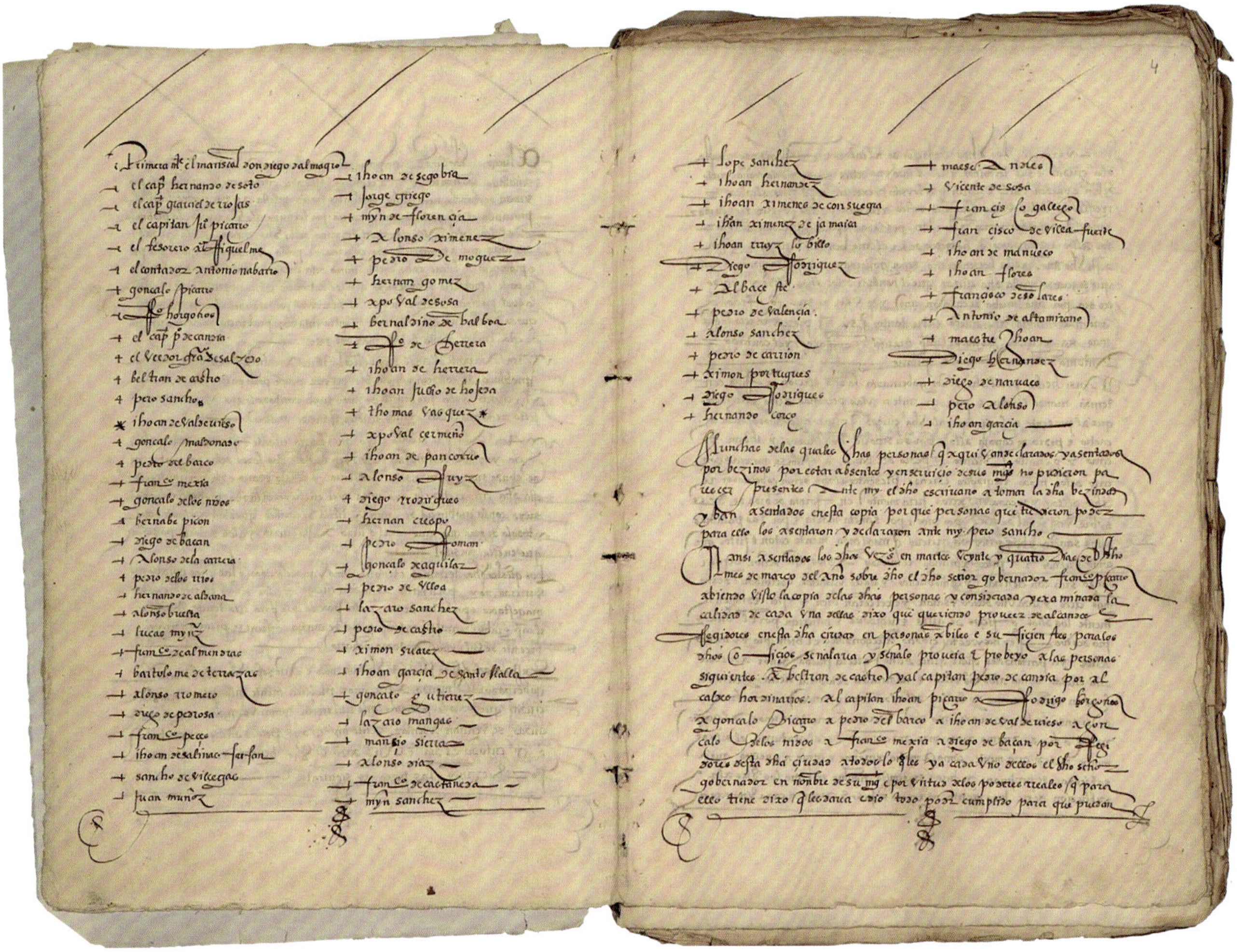

FIG. 4.1 The Act of Foundation of Cuzco, fols. 3v–4r, 1540s. Ink on paper. Real Biblioteca, Madrid. These pages list the names of the eighty-seven men who settled in Cuzco in 1534, starting with "el mariscal don Diego de Almagro."

> regidores *exercise and practice it in the towns and villages of these kingdoms and of the other neighboring ones that in the name of their majesties are settled.*[4]

This reference to the *alcaldes* and *regidores* in other towns, villages, and kingdoms underscores the roles of Pizarro and Sancho in the ongoing construction of a transatlantic political geography consisting of cities founded by royally appointed governors and ruled locally by *alcaldes* and *regidores*. Cuzco would now take its place among them.

The institution of the *cabildo*, with its two classes of councilors, had deep roots in medieval Iberian history and was a standard part of the foundation of Spanish colonial towns. In the Americas of the 1520s and 1530s, Spanish governors invariably formed *cabildos*, but the number of officials in any given settlement varied. In Cuzco, the complement of councilors—two *alcaldes* and eight *regidores*—was large, an indication that Pizarro envisioned it as a sizable and important city.[5] At the same time, making those appointments allowed him to distribute political favors widely and, in so doing, oblige his compatriots to reciprocate with loyalty.

A few days after appointing the city council, Pizarro returned to Xauxa, accompanied by a cohort including Manco and, presumably, Angelina Yupanqui. Sancho recounts the trek northward, noting that they reached their destination in April 1534. It was there, he writes, that Pizarro received word that native enemy troops had gathered just to their north, on the road to Cajamarca. He also received and read letters reporting on events in San Miguel and Cuzco. In recounting these episodes, Sancho crafts an image of Pizarro in which he is no longer the itinerant leader of a company of fortuneseekers making his way through the Andes but, instead, a governor who rules from a fixed location and who communicates closely with the towns under his command. The act of writing is central to this mode of governance, rendering his secretary a key figure in the administration of Spanish Peru.[6]

It was in Xauxa in 1534 that Sancho composed his *Relatione*, completing it in July of that year. Like other *relaciones* composed in sixteenth-century Spanish America, it includes descriptions of native settlements, focusing on their natural resources and architecture. His description of Cuzco, however, is far more detailed than any of his other descriptive passages, and its isolation as a distinct chapter in the text signals a shift from narration to ekphrasis and encomium. Its lyrical opening line sets a laudatory tone: "The city of Cuzco, being the primary place where the lords made their residence, is so great and so beautiful, and with so many buildings, that it would be worthy of being seen in Spain."[7]

Unlike his list of settlers, which presented Cuzco in terms of *civitas*, Sancho's description of the city focuses almost entirely on its buildings and plan. "The roads are made in cruciform, and very straight," he writes, adding that "all of them are paved, and in the middle of each one passes a conduit of water paved in stone." This geometric orderliness, he notes, extends to the plaza, which is "made in a square shape, and for the most part flat, and paved in small stones."[8] These passages can be read as visions of an ideal urban design, but they are also part of the earliest treatment of the Inca settlement written by a person who had spent a significant amount of time there. Sancho's description provides enticing details about a place whose appearance in the 1530s remains incompletely known even today, and thus it is an important source for the history of Cuzco's design and appearance. It is, however, also a source for other kinds of historical information. In its emphasis on certain details and its elision of others, it demonstrates how habits of perception and description facilitated the earliest stages of the transformation of Inca Cuzco into Spanish Cuzco. Sancho's vision of the city, however, contrasts in many ways with the one recorded by other eyewitnesses on the pages of a different kind of source: the minutes of the meetings of the nascent city council. Considered in relation to each other, the texts reveal the multiplicity of interests that influenced the city and its design in its first year of Spanish colonial rule.

Among the first buildings Sancho describes are the houses of Inca elites:

> [The city is] filled with the residences of lords since no poor people live in it, and all of the lords used to build their houses there, and all of the *caciques* [leaders] as well, because the *caciques* did not remain there constantly. Most of these houses are made of stone, and the others have half of the façade in stone. There are [also] many houses made of earth, and they are made with beautiful order.[9]

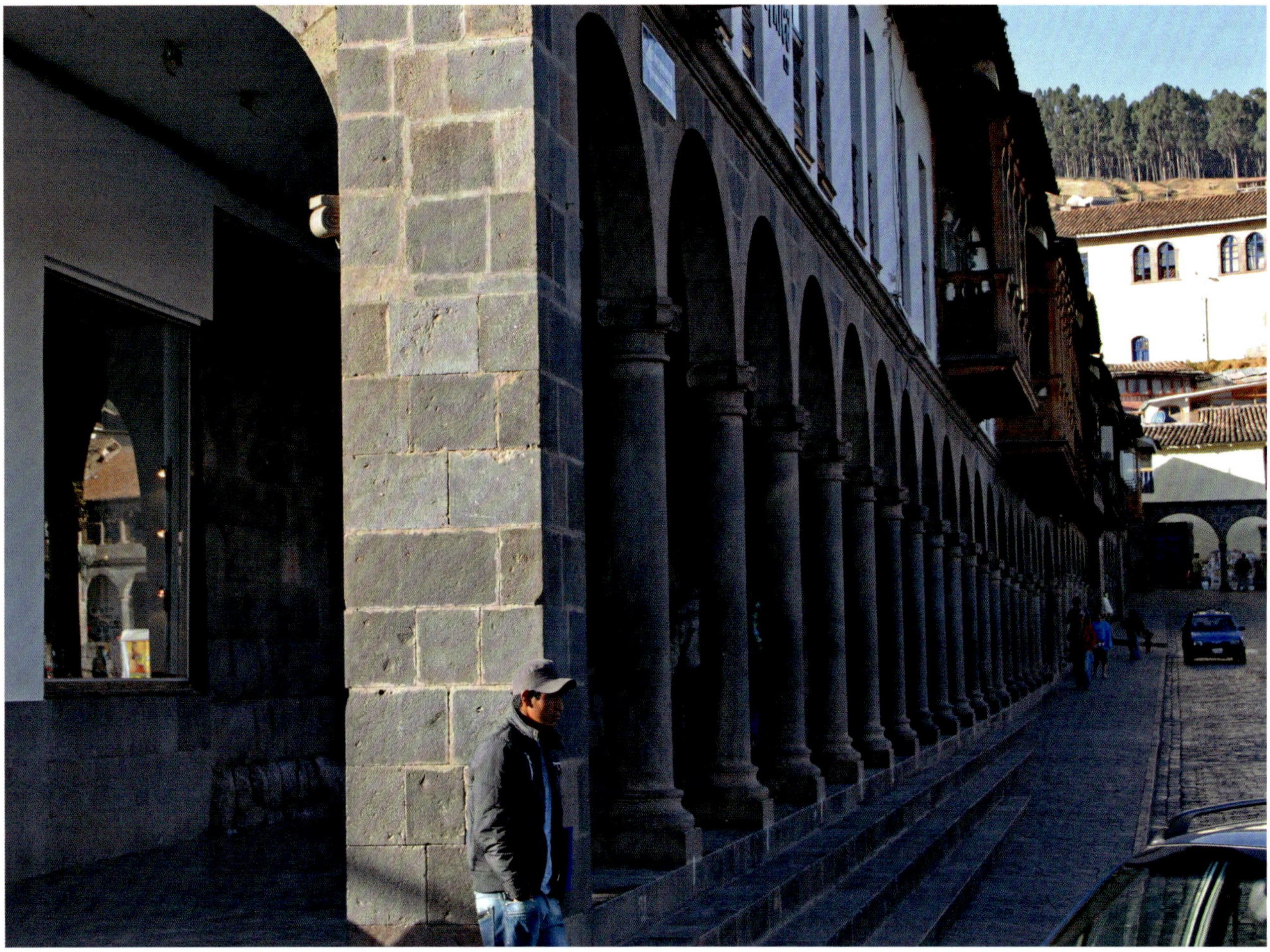

FIG. 4.2 Arcaded shops and restaurants on the site of Caxana, Huayna Capac's house in Cuzco. Some reconstructed Inca walls are visible to the right of the shop window on the left.

The most impressive of the four houses, Sancho writes, was that of Huayna Capac, the father of Manco, Atahualpa, and Huascar, and the illustrious ruler whose mummified corpse had been carried to Cuzco from Quito. Of particular note, he says, is the portal of that house, which was made of "red and white marble and of other colors."[10] Red and white marble are materials a sixteenth-century Spaniard like Sancho would have recognized, but they are not present in Inca royal architecture in Cuzco and its environs. Thus this curious passage raises questions about the words Sancho would have used to describe the portal, and about how Ramusio, who translated and published the account in mid-century Venice, might have rendered them. A reddish andesite, for example, was widely used in Cuzco, most notably at the House of the Sun, and there is evidence of the use of red pigment on the walls of high-prestige buildings elsewhere in the Inca Empire. In any case, the passage serves as a reminder that Inca Cuzco may not have been as monochromatic as its stone remains encourage us to imagine.[11] Moreover, Sancho's emphasis on the portal as an architectural element worthy of scrutiny might be seen as a habit of description rooted in his experience of Spain, where the portals to the houses of titled citizens were often adorned with symbolic imagery revealing the identity of their residents.

Sancho does not specify the location of Huayna Capac's house, but other colonial period texts identify it as an expansive *cancha* compound called Caxana, located on the northwest side of the plaza (for Caxana and other compounds mentioned in this section, see map 1, p. 12). The history of its construction remains unknown, but it may have been built during Huayna Capac's reign, at the end of the fifteenth century or the beginning of the sixteenth. Ethnohistorical sources and the remains of a few Inca-period walls on the site suggest that Caxana, like other compounds in Cuzco, included several interior patios and many rectangular single-room buildings, and that adjacent to it was a large festival hall.[12] Today, the site on which it stood is occupied by shops and restaurants fronted with an arcade and facing onto the Plaza de Armas (fig. 4.2).

Two of the other houses described by Sancho must have been those standing across the plaza, opposite Caxana. One is identified in early sources with the evocative name Amarucancha (Serpent Compound). It stood on the site currently occupied by La Compañía (the church of the Jesuit Order) and its related patios, and early sources associate it with both Huayna Capac and Huascar.[13] The remains of its enclosure wall can be seen today on calle Loreto, a narrow passage with walls built in courses of rectangular ashlars (fig. 4.3). On the north side of Amarucancha, and also fronting the plaza, was another compound, known as Hatun Cancha (Great Compound). This housed a number of festival halls, and either within its walls or adjacent to it was the compound known as the *acllahuasi*. Here lived the *acllacona*, the "Chosen Women," who worked under the supervision of expert craftswomen known as *mamacona* to weave fine cloth and who made *chicha*, a fermented beverage, in the service of the Sapa Inca.[14] The streets and buildings of colonial and modern Cuzco have largely obscured the space formerly occupied by this enormous complex, but significant portions of its walls, many of them built with trapezoidal niches, remain visible in the convent of Santa Catalina and in the shops, hotels, and restaurants in the area surrounding it (fig. 4.4).[15]

It is unclear which of the remaining structures on the plaza was the one Sancho regarded as the fourth of the houses of the lords. It may have been one of the buildings on the northeast side of the plaza, elevated above it on a terrace. Early sources and archaeological investigation indicate that the site accommodated a compound known as Ochullo, perhaps associated with Pachacuti, on or near the site currently occupied by the cathedral. To the west of Ochullo was another compound associated in some early sources with Atahualpa's brother-rival, Huascar.[16] The imprecision of Sancho's description and the fragmentary survival of Inca walls on that side of the plaza, however, present challenges to attempts at reconstruction.

In his description of the houses of the lords of Cuzco, Sancho mentions the name of only one ruler, Huayna Capac. He had been dead for nearly a decade by the time Sancho was writing, so the effect of the description of his house and, by extension, those of the unnamed lords is to present Inca Cuzco (falsely) as an abandoned city available for settlement by the Spanish. Sancho addresses the city's availability more directly in discussing his understanding of the laws of inheritance among the Inca: "Each past lord has here [in Cuzco] his house of tribute goods that were given him in his life, because no succeeding lord (so is the law among them) may after the death of the past lord come to it in the inheritance."[17] This passage may indicate the author's awareness of Inca customs of inheritance as related to him by a native informant, but it also echoes the rhetoric of the *Requerimiento*, which stressed that the property of a conquered people would be taken from them only if they did not comply with the demand for obedience to the Crown. In Cuzco, Sancho says, the buildings are abandoned, an important detail that he also notes in the Act of Foundation. The implication is that the "houses of the lords" and other buildings in Cuzco do not belong to anyone, and thus they can be taken freely.

When Pizarro and his followers first arrived in Cuzco, in November 1533, the highest-ranking men in the group took shelter in the palaces mentioned by Sancho. Pizarro himself occupied Caxana, or at least a part of it, and Angelina Yupanqui probably stayed there with him in the house that once belonged to the Sapa Inca who gave her the name Cuxirimay and arranged her marriage to his son Atahualpa. It was also in that compound that the *alcaldes* and *regidores* of the city council convened their first meeting, on March 25, 1534, just two days after the erection of the *picota* in the plaza of Spanish Cuzco.[18] Pizarro attended the meeting together with the two *alcaldes*, four of the eight *regidores*, and a scribe, Diego de Narváez. Narváez, who was probably in his twenties in 1534, had sailed to the Americas from Spain in 1526. His surname and social connections in the

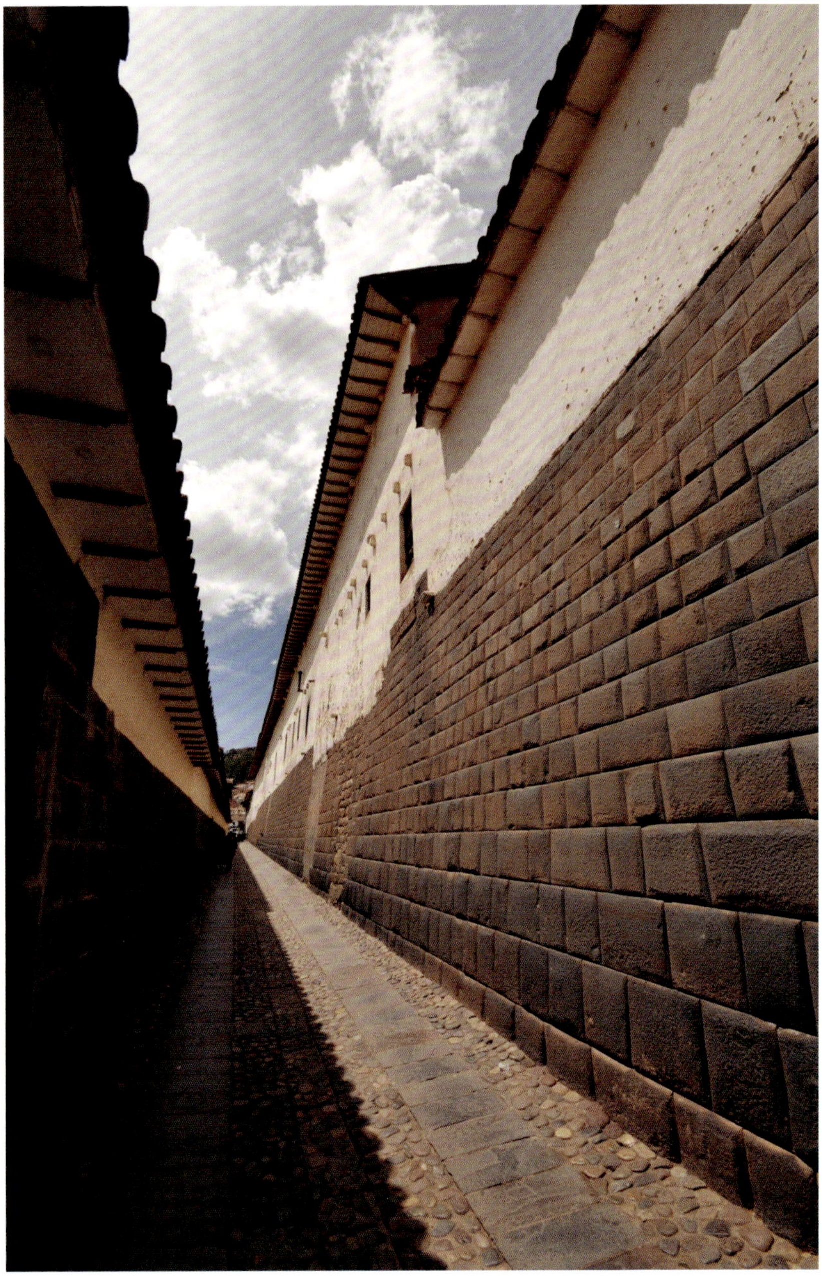

FIG. 4.3 (*left*) Calle Loreto, Cuzco. The wall on the right was once part of the Inca compound Amarucancha, which later became the residence of Hernando de Soto, the first lieutenant governor of Spanish Cuzco.

FIG. 4.4 (*facing page*) Arcades on the site of Hatun Cancha, one of Inca Cuzco's great compounds, which was later repurposed as housing for high-ranking Spanish settlers. Behind the arcade is the church of La Compañía, on the site of Amarucancha.

Americas suggest that he was from the region of Navarre, in northern Spain. He had been in Cajamarca with Pizarro during the time of Atahualpa's captivity, and had received a small share of the gold and silver distributed there. His name appears near the bottom of the list of settlers registered by Sancho, an indication of his relatively low social status or, at least, of the low esteem in which Sancho held him.[19]

The matters taken up by the council at their first meeting and in the days, months, and years that followed are documented in their official records, the Acts of the Cabildo, composed by Narváez and his successors. Several volumes of the sixteenth-century Acts are held in the Regional Archive in Cuzco, but the records of the first months of the council's activity in 1534 are in the collection of the Morgan Library in New York City. The library's

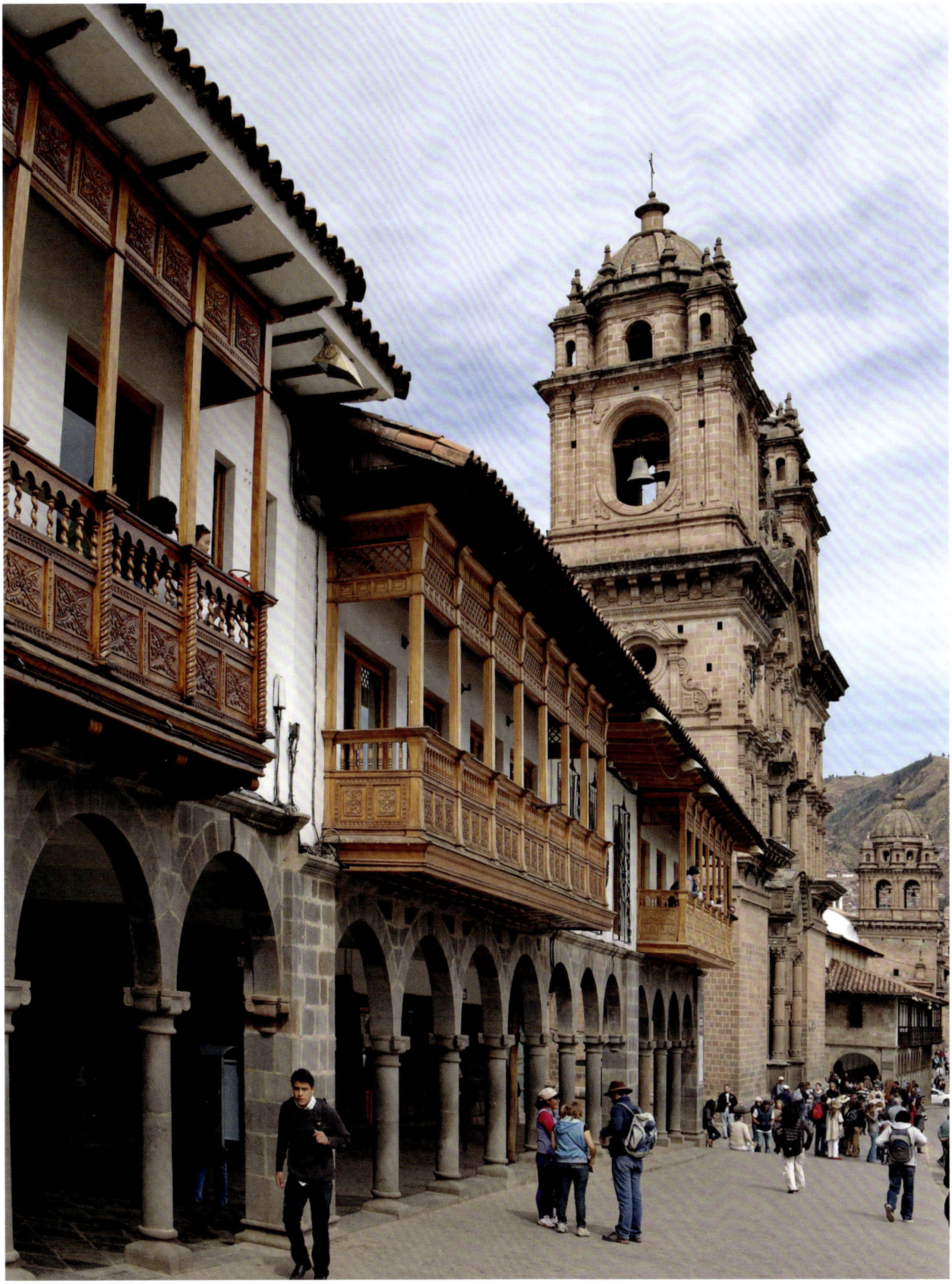

acquisition of the manuscript is not well documented, but anecdotal evidence contends that the archaeologist Adolph Bandelier, who spent a considerable amount of time in Peru in the 1890s, purchased it from a market vendor in Lima and then sold it to the acquisitive financier J. P. Morgan.[20]

The first order of business at the inaugural meeting was Pizarro's formal presentation of documents authorizing him to establish the city and govern it. These were the *provisiones reales* (royal provisions), in which the Crown designated him *gobernador* (governor), *adelantado* (frontier administrator), and *capitán general* (captain general). Issued in Toledo by the Empress Isabel in 1529, Pizarro's scribes or servants must have carried copies of them since that time. Narváez records reading these documents to the city councilors, who then took them in their hands, kissed them, and held them on their heads, saying they would comply with their contents.[21] The presentation of documents such as these occurred at city council meetings throughout the sixteenth-century Americas, and the record of the events at the meeting in Cuzco emphasizes the materiality of documents—the perception that they were objects to be read, circulated, and touched—as well as a belief in their agency.

The recognition of Pizarro's authority to govern in the name of the Crown took place in a building that Sancho and his contemporaries believed to have been the palace of an Inca ruler. In that sense, the symbolic architecture of the Inca gave a degree of legitimacy to the governor's authority, and its use by the city councilors intimated a transfer of power from the Sapa Inca to Pizarro. At the same time, the council's use of Caxana for this purpose further attests to the flexibility of the built environment of early colonial Cuzco, recalling how the plaza had been the setting for Manco's accession as well as the reading of the *Requerimiento* and the Act of Foundation.

The *cabildo* met again on the next day in a different location: "the house and residence of Hernando de Soto in a large hall."[22] This structure is later described as being in, or adjacent to, Amarucancha. The Acts do not explain why the *cabildo* changed its meeting place, but it may have been precipitated by Pizarro's impending departure from Cuzco for Xauxa and Soto's appointment to the role of lieutenant governor in his absence. At this meeting Pizarro presented a set of ordinances for the governance of the city. These would be the first of many such regulations issued in Spanish Cuzco, and, like those routinely imposed in other Spanish towns in the Americas, they defined and regulated the city's infrastructure as well as the behavior of its citizenry. This aim was articulated in the minutes of the meeting: Pizarro issued the ordinances, Narváez notes, "for the good of the land and its natives and of this city of Spaniards that will stay and reside here."[23]

The first ordinance addressed the symbolism of the city's architecture and noted a potential problem with the establishment of Spanish Cuzco in the built environment of Inca Cuzco:

> Since this city was founded in the same place and town that the natives had made . . . there are [already] many built and occupied houses of the lords who have been in this city. Since they are sumptuous houses and built for great lords, the natives and illustrious men and chiefs of the land who there are at present hold them in great esteem and veneration, and if they were rebuilt or removed by the Spanish who are to reside in this city and in the said houses, it could happen that the natives rebel.[24]

The passage points to the presence of significant numbers of native Andeans in the city and contradicts the claim made just three days earlier in the Act of Foundation that the Spanish would be able to use the existing structures as sources for stone and wood in constructing their own houses. Perhaps Angelina Yupanqui and her kin had told the city councilors something about the history of Cuzco and the respect with which native Andeans regarded its buildings. Destruction of an existing structure was now punishable by a fine of 500 pesos of gold, half to be paid to the Crown and half for public works in the city. A second ordinance, too, raised the specter of civil unrest, decreeing that in order to prevent a revolt, no Spanish resident of the city could demand gold, silver, or cloth from the native people of Cuzco. The punishment for doing so was a fine of 250 pesos of gold to be paid to the Crown and the same amount to be paid to the city.[25] The institution of these fines indicates an emerging recognition among at least some of the Spaniards in Cuzco that architecture, precious metals, and textiles held symbolic value for native Andeans, and that disrespectful acts such as the destruction or confiscation of those things could result in rebellion.

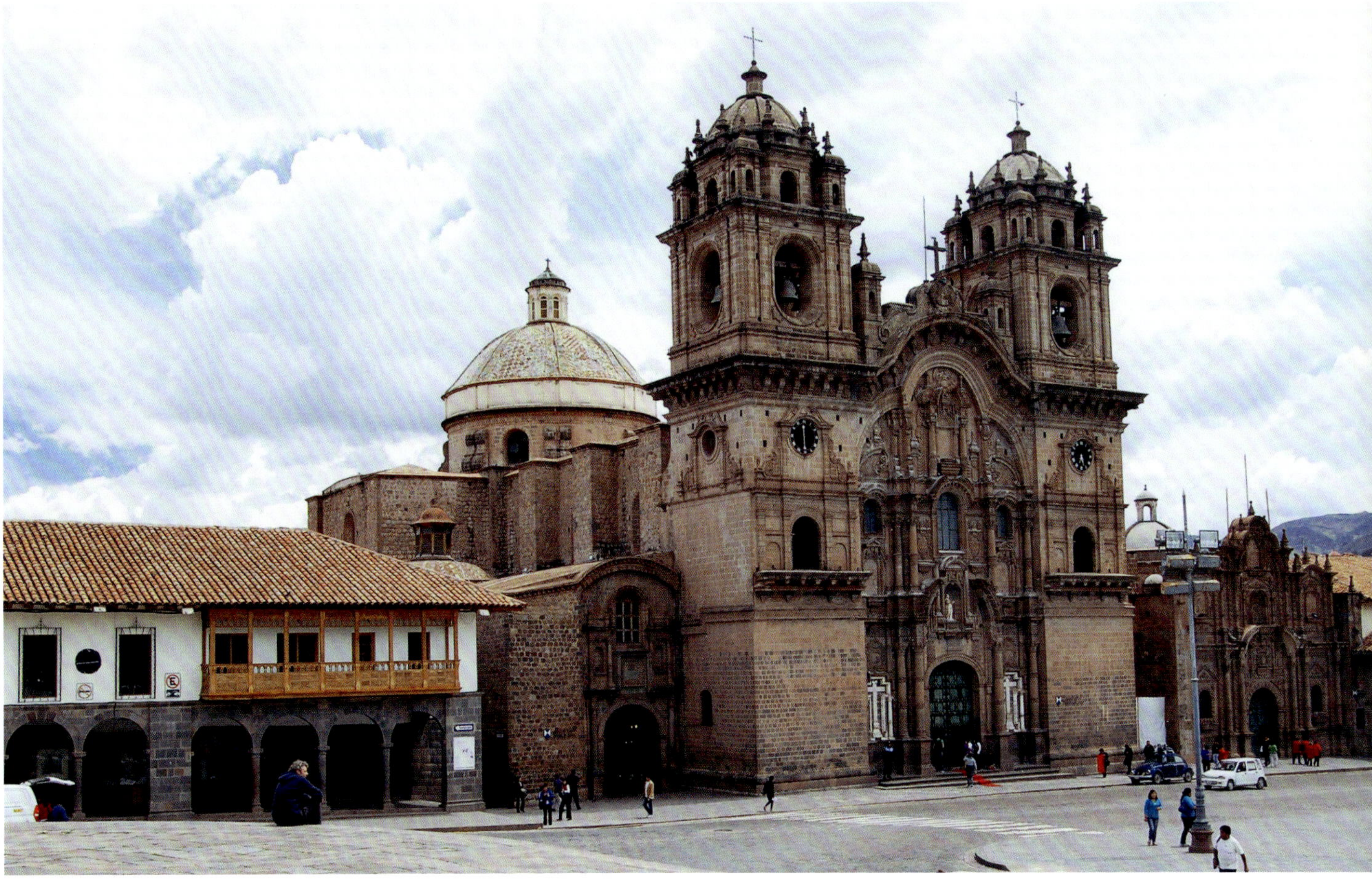

FIG. 4.5 The church of La Compañía, with the chapel of Our Lady of Loreto (*left*). The 17th-century chapel occupies the likely site of the first meetings of the *cabildo* (city council).

Narváez notes that the town crier, Juan García, read the ordinances aloud in the plaza on Sunday, March 29, at ten o'clock in the morning. Identified in legal documents as *negro*, García hailed from Extremadura and was also the Pizarro company's piper, a role often paired with that of town crier.[26] The ordinances he read differed somewhat from those presented to the *cabildo* days earlier, perhaps indicating that they had undergone revision or paraphrasing. Nonetheless, García's words emphasized the same anxieties about native Andeans as had been voiced to the councilors. "None of the said residents nor other persons," he announced, "may dare to enter in any of the houses or halls of native chiefs and leaders of this city of Cuzco . . . nor may they allow their Indian servants to enter in such halls." Moreover, "no one shall order their Indians to take firewood and straw from any hall or house of this said city nor from another neighboring town."[27] The punishment for violating this ordinance was severe: a native servant who took wood and straw from a house would be put to death, and his master would have to pay 100 pesos to the Crown and make a contribution in the name of the deceased to the hospital. García's public reading of the ordinances would have occurred in the vicinity of the *picota*, thus demonstrating that the plaza and its pillar of justice were linked to the exercise of civic authority in the form of capital punishment.

This passage is also noteworthy in that it contains the earliest reference to a hospital in Cuzco. The expectation that such an institution would be established is intimated in the royal provisions, which touch on salaries for a doctor and a druggist. A hospital is mentioned again in the record for Monday, May 30, 1534, on which day the civic officials allocated a quantity of silver for its support.[28] If an existing structure in Cuzco had been identified for that use, then its location is not revealed in the Act of Foundation. The intriguing but imprecise references to this early institution demonstrate one of several instances in which the Acts of the Cabildo, like the text by Sancho, can frustrate efforts to reconstruct the early city in detail.

The Acts for May 30 also record the civic officials allocating funding for the church, naming a certain Hernán Gómez *mayordomo* (steward) of that institution and giving him a quantity of silver, a ladle or aspergillum for holy water, two candlestick holders, and two cruets. The materials from which these objects were made are not specified, nor is their design or place of manufacture. Such objects, however, were routinely taken to the Americas from Spain, and the Crown sometimes provided funding for their purchase. For example, in a royal decree dated December 8, 1535, the Empress Isabel ordered that Friar Valverde—recently promoted to the rank of bishop of Cuzco—set up churches in the villages of Peru, filling them with liturgical objects sent from Spain.[29] The objects entrusted to Gómez, together with books, candles, and perhaps an altar table, might be understood, then, as the minimum requirements for outfitting a newly founded church in Spanish colonial America. The introduction of these objects into a structure built by the Inca demonstrates one of the ways in which ritual practice and its related paraphernalia contributed to the transformation of space in early colonial Cuzco. The ritual feasting that had taken place in the building appropriated for the church had been replaced by the rituals of the Mass and the administration of sacraments.

Two days later, on June 1, 1534, the councilors would designate a building for use as a meeting place. They had been convening in a hall in Amarucancha considered to be the property of Hernando de Soto, and the record for the meeting on that day reveals their intention to continue meeting nearby from that point onward. "There does not seem to be another building that is better suited nor on a better site in this city," Narváez writes, "than a building that is on this plaza at the corner of the Royal Street that goes to the Houses of the Sun, bordering Amarucancha on one side, and on the other side, the plaza, and on the other side the said Royal Street."[30] His description suggests the plot selected was that currently occupied by the chapel dedicated to Our Lady of Loreto and connected to La Compañía on its northeastern side (fig. 4.5). Like so many other buildings in the historic core of Cuzco, the chapel was built in the years after the earthquake of 1650. Its two-storied façade includes an arched portal flanked by engaged columns supporting a cornice bisected by a plaque bearing the date 1654. Documentary sources link its construction to the Flemish Jesuit priest Juan Bautista Egidiano and note that it functioned as a *capilla de indios* (Indian chapel).[31]

The council's early records do not indicate where most of Cuzco's eighty-seven Christian settlers and their servants were living in the weeks following the foundation ceremony, nor do they address where the native inhabitants were residing. It is clear only that Pizarro had taken Caxana, or at least part of it, and that Hernando de Soto was residing somewhere in Amarucancha. On October 25, 1534, however, the civic officials received Pizarro's order from Xauxa to designate housing lots for the Spanish citizens.[32] The assignment of lots (*solares*) was a standard part of the establishment of towns in Spanish America. It is mentioned in the license granted to Pizarro in July 1529, with the stipulation that "the residents and settlers [of a town] shall be given the lots and lands appropriate to their persons, according to what was done and is done on the island of Española."[33] The reference to Española (or Hispaniola) is telling: it was there that, in 1502, Nicolás de Ovando had founded Santo Domingo, a city that took shape over time as an irregular grid of streets. By the 1520s, it accommodated houses for the citizenry, a church, a town hall, and several plazas. As the license granted to Pizarro makes clear, the earlier foundation of settlements in the Caribbean had become a model for later foundations on the mainland.[34]

Pizarro would have known Santo Domingo and its design from his experience there three decades earlier, but his experiences of the 1520s with Pedrarias Dávila in Panama would have had an even greater impact on his understanding of Spanish colonial urbanism. The Crown's instructions to Dávila stated some key principles and practices for the founders of towns:

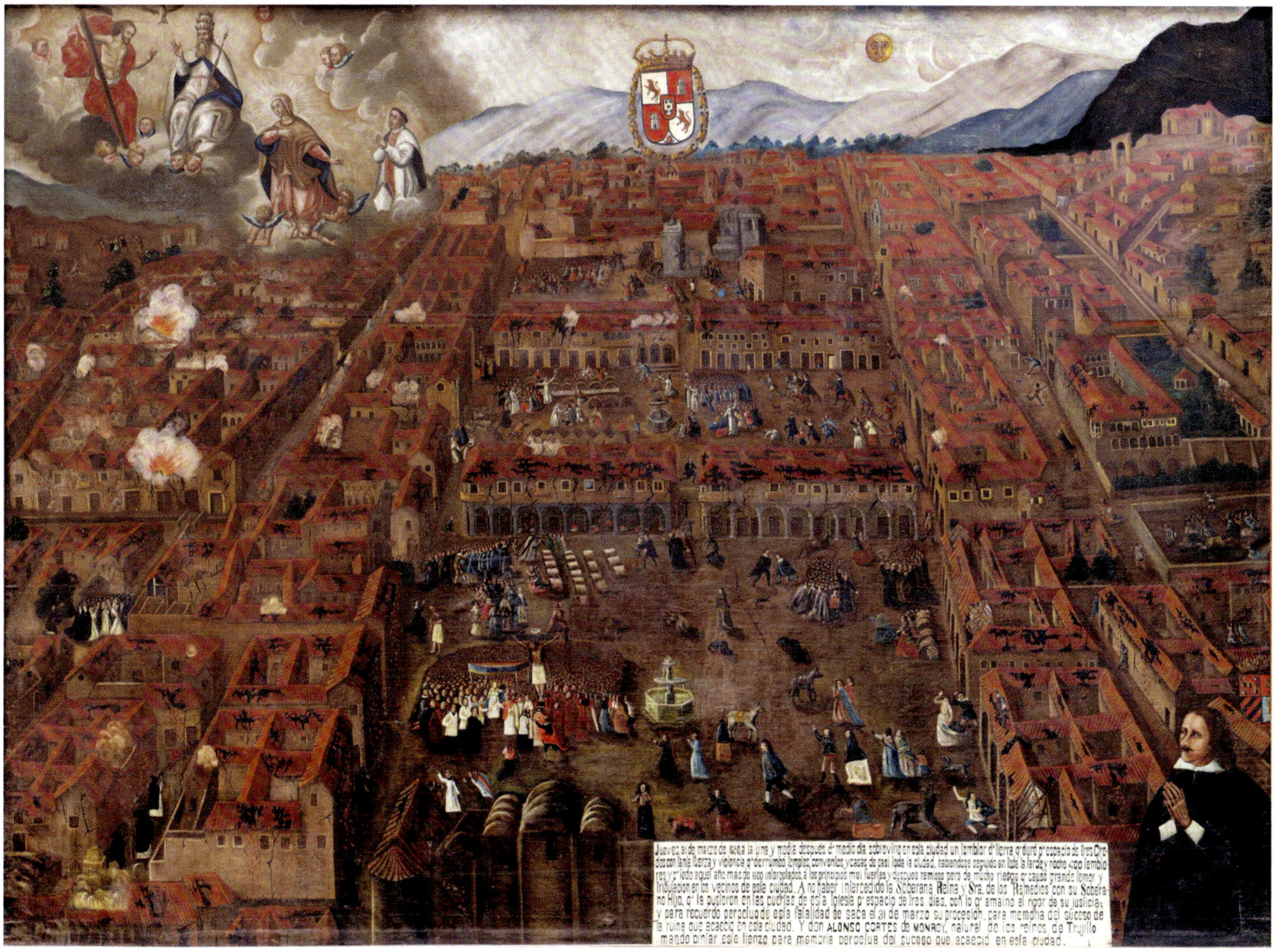

FIG. 4.6 Artist unknown, *Cuzco during the Earthquake of 1650*, after 1650. Oil on canvas, 33.4 × 46.2 cm. Church of El Triunfo, Cuzco. This large and detailed painting is a precious resource, as few images survive of Cuzco before this catastrophic earthquake.

> You must apportion lots in the place to make houses, and those lots have to be apportioned according to the qualities of the people, and they shall be from the beginning given in such order. In that way, when the lots are distributed, the town will appear to be ordered, as much in the place where you put the plaza, as in the place where the church is, and as in the order that the streets have. For in places newly made with order in the beginning, they remain ordered without any work or cost, and the others are never ordered.[35]

The passage insists upon the importance of planning and mentions a plaza and well-ordered houses and streets, precisely the elements Sancho emphasizes in his description of Cuzco.[36] This correspondence is not coincidental. As a scribe charged with reading and writing official documents, Sancho would have known of the principles articulated in official instructions, and he would have understood their equation of architectural and urban orderliness with social and political orderliness. His description of July 1534, with its reference to straight, paved streets, a rectilinear plaza, and stone houses of the lords, presents Cuzco as already well ordered. The recognition of these elements of a well-planned city might be seen—like his comment on the portal of Caxana—as one of the scribe's mental habits, a practice that guided his description.

Cuzco's orderliness would be enhanced by the distribution of housing lots "according to the quality of the people."

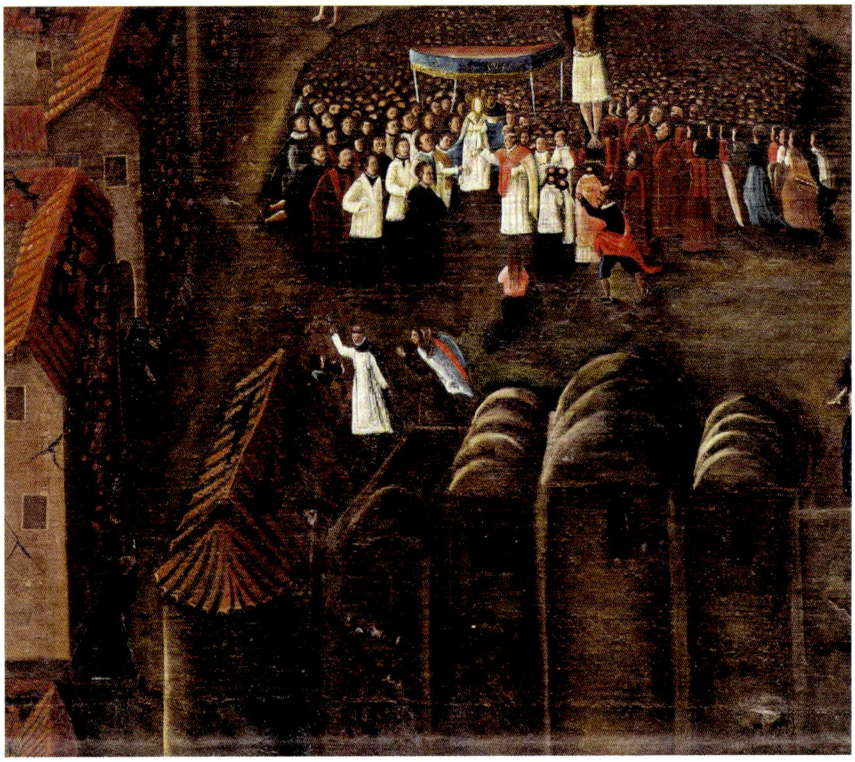

FIG. 4.7 Detail of figure 4.6, showing a building on the likely site of the first church in Cuzco (now occupied by the church of El Triunfo). The shape of the structure roofed with red tiles is consistent with an Inca hall adapted for Christian worship.

It was Soto, acting as Pizarro's lieutenant, who took charge of this task. Reiterating a point emphasized in the ordinances, he provided caveats that effectively doomed the project from the start. Spanish settlers, he said, could not build anything new on the lots assigned to them, nor could they remove any native peoples from the houses in which they were currently residing. This warning is perplexing with respect to the aim of providing property for the settlers, but it serves as another reminder of the presence of native Andeans in the core of the city, a fact suppressed or ignored in most of the early sources.

The actual distribution occurred four days later, on October 29, 1534, at a meeting led by Soto and attended by the councilors. After some discussion, they agreed that each of the assigned lots would measure 200 square feet. Like the Act of Foundation, the Distribution of Lots took the form of a political ritual entailing the production of a document. Soto began by designating a lot for the church, described in the text as being bounded on one side by the plaza, on another by the road that led to Collao (the Titicaca Plateau, presumably reached by exiting Cuzco on its eastern side), and on another by the houses of the *alcalde* Beltrán de Castro.[37] The description of these boundaries does not allow for precise identification of the lot's location, but other passages in the text indicate that it was in the vicinity of the building Pizarro had selected for the church earlier in the Act of Foundation. The assignment of this lot was accompanied by a change in the church's dedication: Soto refers to it as "Our Lady of the Immaculate Conception" rather than "Our Lady of the Annunciation," as Pizarro had called it. The reason for this change is not clear; perhaps it indicates that assigning additional property to the existing building was understood to establish a new institution.

As noted, tradition holds that the space assigned to the first church is that currently occupied by the church of El Triunfo (see fig. 3.7), but what the building looked like in 1534 can only be imagined. The earliest surviving visual image of the site lies in the bottom left of a painting depicting Cuzco during the earthquake of 1650 (figs 4.6, 4.7). It shows the northern end of a structure whose appearance is in keeping with that of a church adapted from an Inca

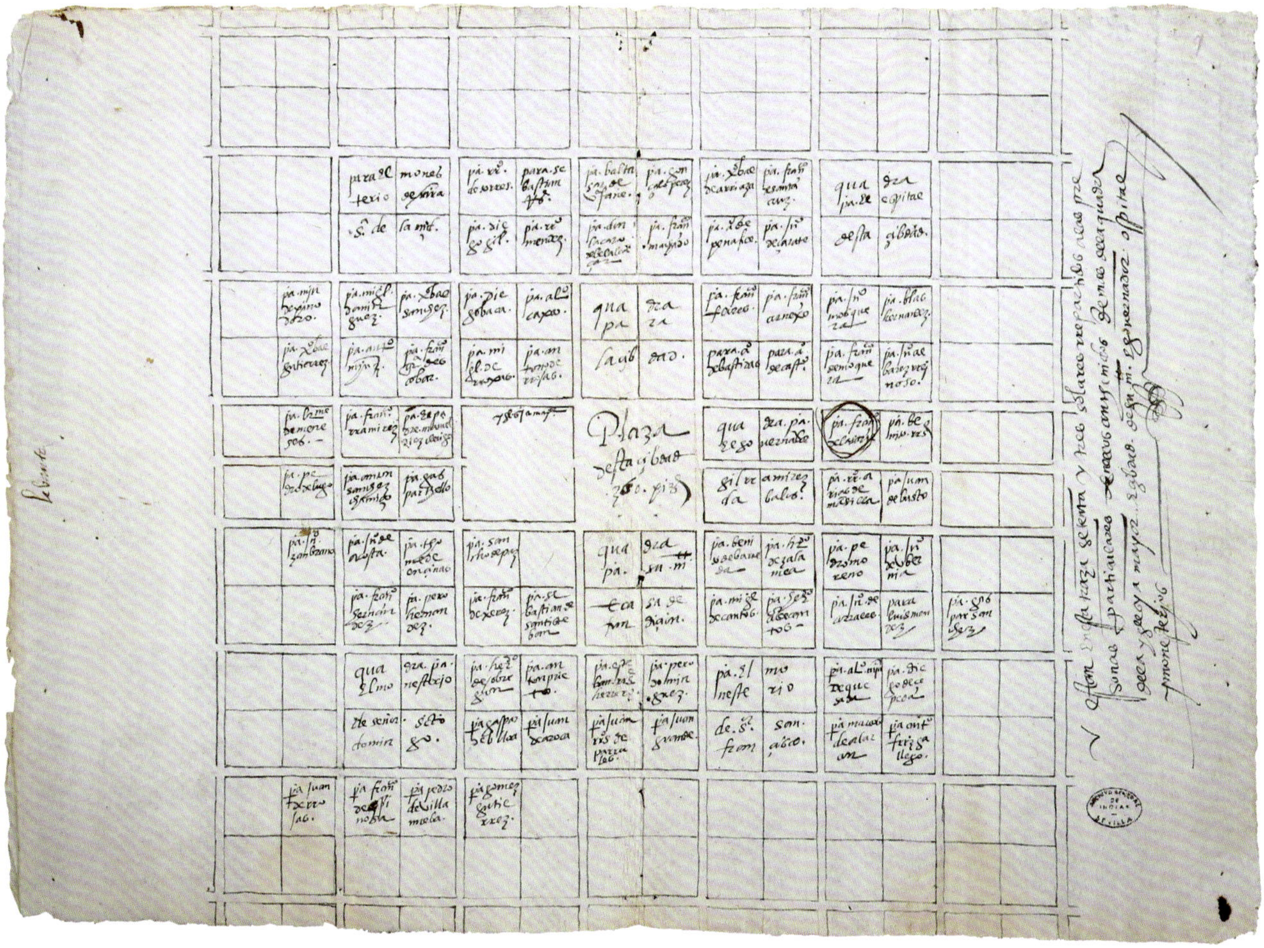

FIG. 4.8 The foundation plan of Baeza, Ecuador, 1559. Ink on paper, 31.5 × 43.7 cm. Archivo General de Indias, Seville. The plan shows a typical gridiron layout, with a central plaza (*plaza desta ciudad*) surrounded by four quadripartite lots labeled (*clockwise from top*): block for the city [council] (*quadra para la ciudad*); block for governor Gil Ramírez Dávalos (*quadra para el governador Gil Ramírez Dávalos*); block for His Majesty and foundry (*quadra para su m[ajestad] y casa de fundición*); and main church (*iglesia mayor*).

hall. Long and rectangular, it is topped with a red-tiled roof and includes a rounded apse, presumably added to the original structure.

The next lot Soto designated was for the city council, which would also be the site of a foundry. The fusion of these entities and activities into a single institution and architectural space underscores the continuing centrality of the acquisition and distribution of gold and silver to Spanish colonial expansion in the Americas. The council received a space "in the large hall [*galpón*] that is on the terrace [*andén*] above the plaza."[38] A reasonable interpretation of this passage is that the assigned location was in the vicinity of the church rather than in Amarucancha, where the *cabildo* had been meeting up to this point. Just as the building to be used as the church was adapted for its new use through its furnishings and the activities that took place within its walls, so the Inca structure that became the *cabildo*'s hall would be transformed through the ritual performed by Soto and through the introduction of paper, ink, chairs, and tables to its interior.

A telling precedent for the Distribution of Lots in Cuzco is the enactment of the same ritual in Natá. Dávila's Act of Foundation for that town notes that its streets were to be set up "in the order and manner they are marked and drawn on the plan I made of the said city and town."[39] The plan to which the text refers remains unknown, but it is thus described in the document:

> The streets and plazas of the said city shall be straight and in order and agreement. I made and founded the said town making each row [*hilera*] of those that appear in the said plaza four contiguous lots together, and the said islet [*isleta*] surrounded by public streets. And for each lot I assign one hundred paces which are two hundred feet square . . . and for the church and house of *cabildo* I assign two lots . . . and between the church and the *cabildo* a street in the middle, and for the public plaza I assign an entire islet of four lots.[40]

This is an early description of such a plan—perhaps the earliest one to survive—and the language used constructs the image of a grid formed by straight streets and rows of quadripartite plots of land, each quadrant measuring 200 square feet, arranged in rows.

This description of the now lost plan for Natá corresponds to one of the earliest Spanish American town plans to survive: that of Baeza, Ecuador, established in March 1559, in what is today the Napos province of Ecuador, by Gil Ramírez Dávalos, a native of the Iberian town of Baeza, and the man would be appointed governor of Quito (fig. 4.8). It centers on a plaza whose size is that of each of the quadripartite lots surrounding it, and those lots, in turn, are framed by streets. In Baeza, the church and the *cabildo* were awarded four lots each, as was the founder. This kind of plan would have been an important point of reference for Soto and the other officials in Cuzco who performed the Distribution of Lots.

After assigning lots for Cuzco's church and the *cabildo*, Soto distributed property to ninety-one men, most of them Spaniards (map 4). He recognized Pizarro's rank by giving him four lots in Caxana, the place he had chosen on his arrival in Cuzco. Pizarro was not present at this time, nor was Almagro, who received three lots in a compound the scribe calls "the houses of Huascar" ("las casas de Guaxacar"), a compound located to the northeast of Caxana not far from the church, on the first terrace above the plaza. In between the lots of Pizarro and those of Almagro were the two lots assigned to Gonzalo Pizarro. Juan Pizarro—one of the town's *regidores*—was awarded two lots "on his terraces" ("en los andenes del"), perhaps a space near the *cabildo*, church, and the houses of Huascar. Nearby was the lot assigned to the *alcalde* Beltrán de Castro, described in the text as being in the structure called Ochullo, probably in the vicinity of the present cathedral. Even though the record of this process does not allow for a precise reconstruction of the plan, the spatial order that begins to emerge is one in which the property of Almagro is flanked by that belonging to members of the Pizarro family, an arrangement positioning all of them at the top of the city's social hierarchy, and rendering the northwest side of the plaza as the site highest in rank.[41]

On the other side of the plaza, Soto designated two lots in Amarucancha for himself. The text refers to these lots as the place "where he [Soto] is now" ("do[nde] agora esta"), his residence as well as the place where the *cabildo* had been holding its meetings. It was perhaps in that space that the assignment of lots actually occurred. A number of officials were awarded lots in Hatun Cancha, among them the royal treasurer Alonso Riquelme, the *regidores* Francisco Mexía and Pedro del Barco, and the *alguacil mayor* (bailiff or sheriff). Other awards to officeholders were in the vicinity of the House of the Sun. The *regidor* Gonzalo de los Nidos was given a lot "in the meat market at the House of the Sun," a description that suggests the temple compound—or at least part of it—had been adapted to a new use. The lot awarded to the *regidor* Diego de Bazán was nearby.[42]

The locations of many of the other lots Soto assigned on that day are more difficult to place. Pedro de Candía's award is described vaguely as "two plots in the *corral* where he is now, in the part of it that he wants inside of it"; a certain Gonzalo Hernández, evidently a member of the clergy, was awarded a lot "in the *corral* where he is now." Similar language is used to describe the awards made to the *regidor* Juan de Valdivieso, the captain Gabriel de Rojas, and others.[43] In sum, the Distribution of Lots was done through the production of a document, but the document alone does not provide enough information to reconstruct all the assignments. Its intelligibility depended upon direct

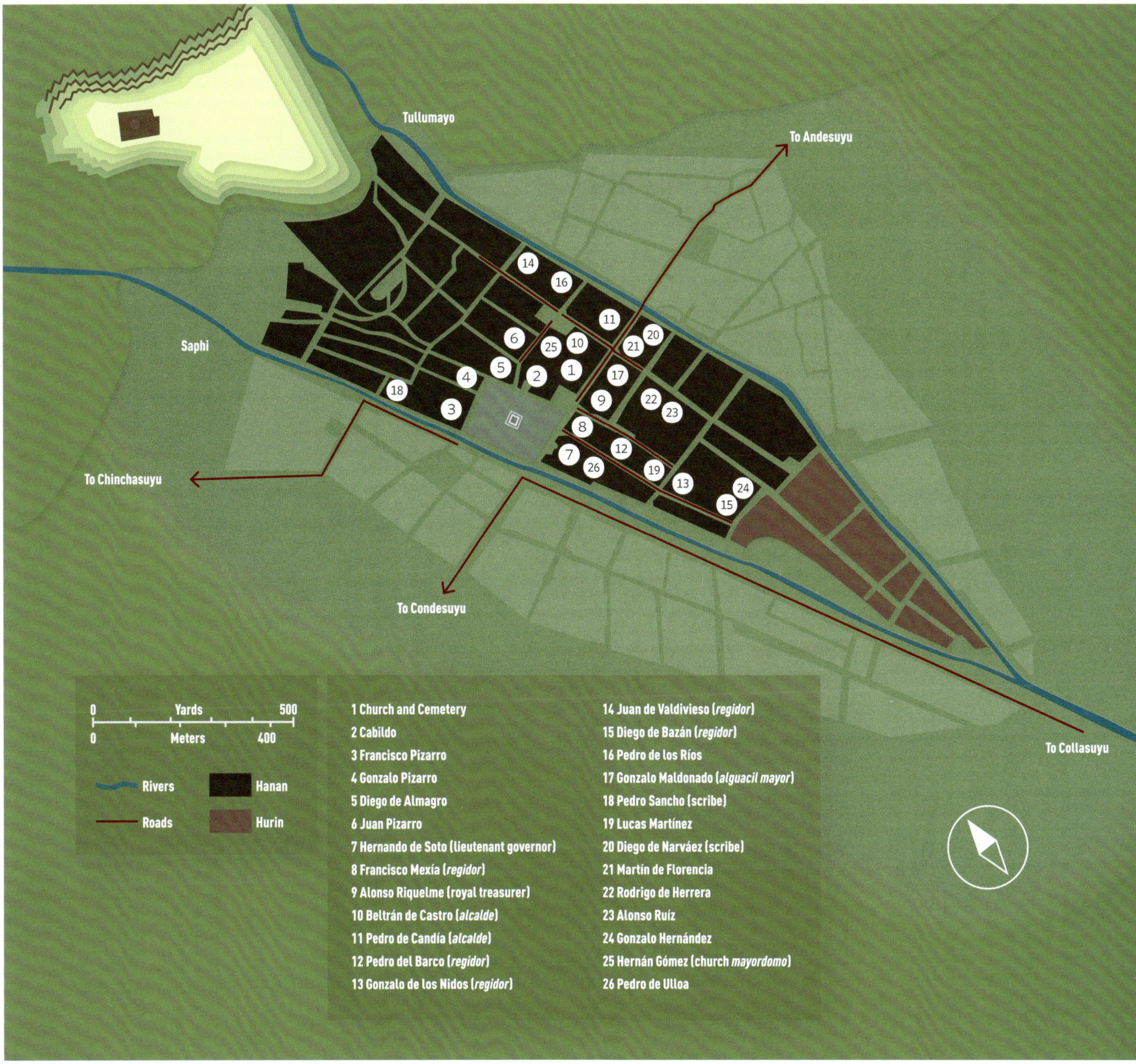

MAP 4 Plan of Spanish colonial Cuzco, showing the approximate locations of the lots distributed to Spanish settlers in 1534, with those of the highest status located nearest to the plaza. The locations marked 1, 3, 4, 5, 7, 8, and 18 can be deduced from the document of October 29, 1534. The others are based on inferences supported by that document and Garcilaso de la Vega's later description of the city and its residents in his *Primera parte de los comentarios reales de los Incas* (1609).

knowledge of Inca Cuzco's buildings and compounds and the details of their occupation by the first Spaniards to take lodging there. A drawn plan like the one produced in Baeza may have facilitated the process, as Soto and his colleagues could have made correlations between it and the buildings with which they were familiar. What is clear, however, is that the size of the property award was understood to be a sign of the recipient's status, and that properties fronting onto the plaza were reserved for those of high rank. Most of the men received one lot; those who received more than that were Pizarro (four lots), Almagro (three lots), Juan and Gonzalo Pizarro (two lots each), Hernando de Soto (two lots), Pedro de Candía (two lots), and Gabriel de Rojas (one and a half lots). Those whose lots faced onto the plaza were Francisco and Gonzalo Pizarro, Soto, and Mexía. The text also reveals other aspects of the logic of the distribution. Pizarro's scribe, Pedro Sancho, was awarded a lot directly behind that of his patron; Narváez, the *cabildo*'s scribe, had a lot in the vicinity of the *alcaldes* and *regidores*, and Hernán Gómez, the *mayordomo* of the church, was placed adjacent to the building for which he cared. The Distribution of Lots ultimately reinforces in spatial terms the social hierarchy and institutions of the Spanish colonial city through the strategic placement of its citizens, even as it seems to have left sectors of the city intact as the property of Andean elites.

In spite of its vagaries, the text presents an image of a grid of 200-square-foot lots taking shape in the place that had been the sacred center of the Inca Empire. The densely built environment of Cuzco, however, did not lend itself readily to this kind of uniformity. The magistrates acknowledged this problem in the record of their meeting:

> Most of the lots that are distributed have been built in this city that the native Indians had before now, so that there are many blocks, or *corrales*, that have more than the said 200 hundred feet that we have designated for a lot, and others have less, such that the said 200 hundred feet cannot be given all together in some lots without damage or harm to some residents and without other lots becoming damaged.[44]

To address the disjunction between the rigid geometry on which the assignment of lots was predicated and the actual disposition of structures in Cuzco, the *cabildo* proposed a solution: certain lots could make up in length what they lacked in width, and the city councilors would adjust them when necessary following an inspection.

The design of Inca Cuzco, with its numerous walled compounds, may have superficially seemed compatible with the gridiron plan, but in reality the two layouts—the rigid Spanish colonial grid and the looser plan of Inca Cuzco—were wholly incongruent. Moreover, the ordinances for Cuzco put in place by Pizarro prohibited the destruction or modification of existing buildings and the eviction of their indigenous residents, thus limiting the potential for changes in the spatial status quo. A passage in the text addressing this problem provides more detail on the native residents of Cuzco at this time:

> Since in many of the lots that are distributed among the residents in this city there are at present living and inhabiting them Indian women in service of the Sun [*mamacona*] and in service of the ancestral lords, and it could be that if they are cast out of their houses and places of dwelling, it may result in harm and unease for the natives, and they may rebel against their service to His Majesty [and] against the Spaniards who are in this city, we order and command that no resident nor any other person move, build, or destroy the quarters [*bohíos*] or the houses where the said mamaconas [*sic*] are and where native Indians were.[45]

This passage indicates that the *mamacona* were among the native Andeans who remained in Cuzco at this time. It is likely that at least some of the many lots assigned to Spanish settlers in Hatun Cancha encroached on their traditional space, the *acllahuasi*, thus necessitating this caveat in the *cabildo*'s minutes. When the city councilors reconvened more than a week later, on November 9, 1534, they drew up a plan of the city. If that plan has survived, its whereabouts are unknown. One wonders, though, if it would have resembled the gridiron plans for other Spanish towns founded and settled in the sixteenth-century Americas, such as that of Baeza, or if it had been adapted to accommodate the irregular design of Inca Cuzco.[46]

The insistence upon a gridiron plan even in the face of such an insurmountable obstacle as the densely built environment of Cuzco suggests that, for Soto and the other civic officials, there was no alternative. Indeed, other governors had used it in the foundation of towns since early in the century. The ubiquity of this plan has been the subject of research since the early twentieth century, when scholars sought to identify precedents for its use and the reasons for its adoption in sixteenth-century Spanish America. More recent scholarship has focused on its symbolism in the ordering of space and citizens and its role as an instrument of colonial domination.[47] Considered in the context of the broader practices of Spanish colonial administrators in early sixteenth-century Peru, however, a different view of the plan comes into focus. The assignment of lots occurred in a way similar to the distribution of gold at Cajamarca. There, Pizarro awarded his men a certain number of shares, or in some cases a fraction of a share, of the entire haul of gold, with men of highest rank receiving the largest quantity. Similarly, in the distribution of property in Cuzco, settlers were awarded a certain number of 200-square-foot lots. The number of plots received indicated a settler's status, or, in the terminology of the conquest license, his "quality." In effect, the ritual of the Distribution of Lots converted buildings and urban space in Cuzco into commodities like gold and silver. The palaces, temples, and festival halls of the sacred center of the Inca were transformed into private property for new settlers, just as the golden cups, bowls, and figurines of the Inca had been melted down and formed into ingots to be distributed and exchanged for other commodities.

The record of the Distribution of Lots in the Acts of the Cabildo evokes an image of the city that is very different from that which Pedro Sancho offers in the Act of Foundation and the *Relatione*, both penned just months earlier. Sancho's writings present it as largely deserted and available for occupation by the Spanish. In contrast, the *cabildo*'s minutes describe a city populated in part by native Andeans for whom the buildings of Cuzco held both functional and symbolic importance, and for whom the dismantling or even the modification of those structures would be disruptive in many ways. If the Act of the Foundation and Sancho's description emphasize the concept of the ideal city from the Crown's perspective, the *cabildo*'s minutes underscore the untidy details of urban design and property ownership faced by the multiethnic residents of Cuzco in the 1530s. This episode serves as a remarkable example of the agency of architecture, for even as Pizarro and the city councilors attempted to plan the city, the infrastructure of the sacred center of the Inca Empire resisted the imposition of the grid, the form that marked the presence of Spanish colonial rule throughout the sixteenth-century Americas.

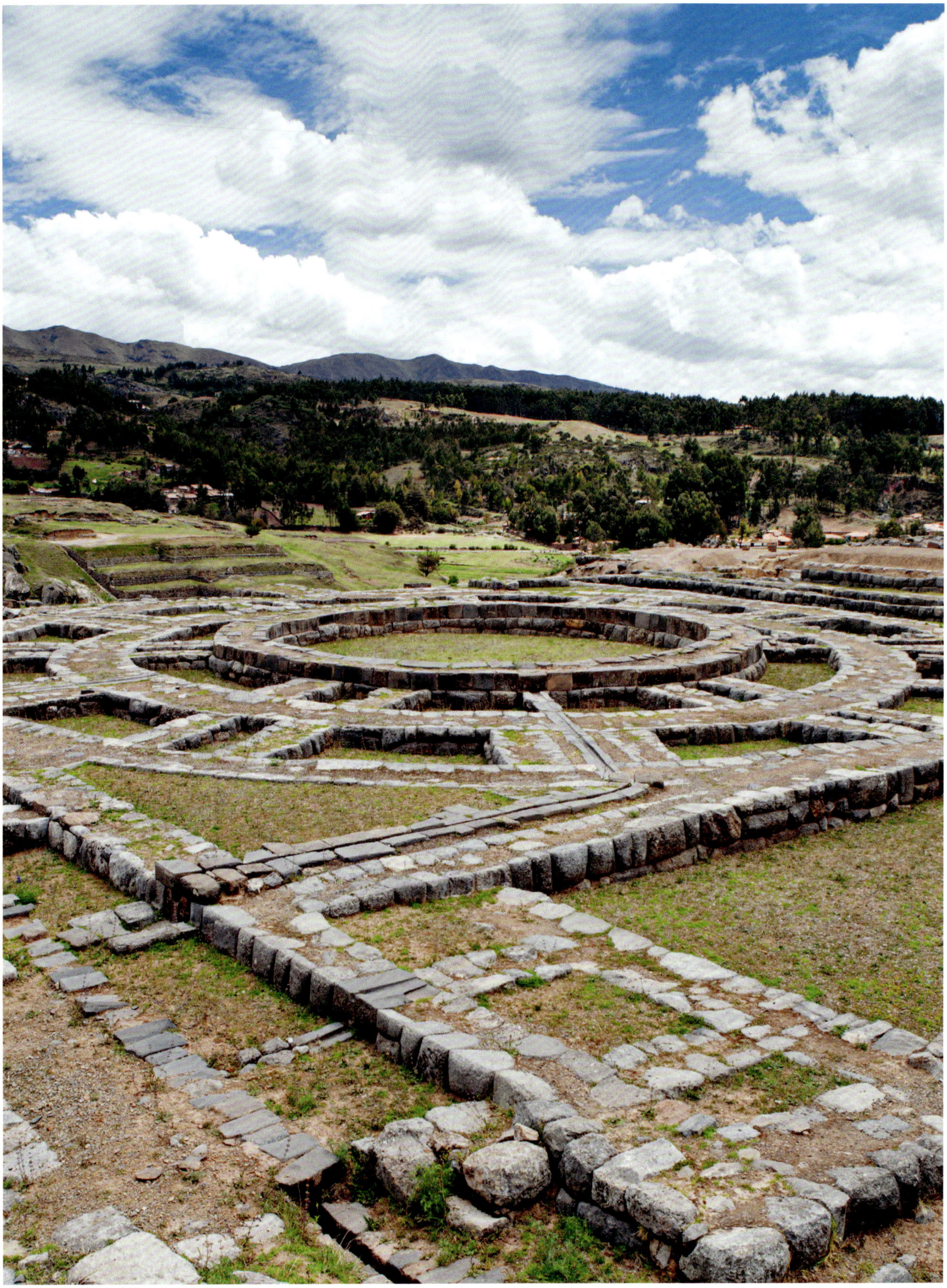

CHAPTER 5

Razing Spanish Cuzco

Manco Inca and the Siege of Cuzco

Through the ritual of the Distribution of Lots, the city councilors recast Inca Cuzco as a Spanish colonial city with a church, a city hall, and housing lots for Spanish settlers surrounding the plaza and filling the stone compounds leading to the House of the Sun. Sacsahuaman, however, is never mentioned in the text. The *cabildo*, it seems, regarded that hilltop complex as distinct from the zone they were reimagining—with some difficulty—as a grid of 200-square-foot lots. Pedro Sancho had a different view. For him, Sacsahuaman was a significant sector of the city, and his treatment of it consumes more than half of the description of Cuzco in his *Relatione*. "Over the hill toward the part of the city that is round and very rugged," he writes, "there is a very beautiful fortress of earth and stone that has its own large windows that look out toward the city . . . Inside of it are many housing quarters and a main tower in the middle." It was built, he claims, "when the city was founded . . . by a big-ear lord [*orejón*] who came from the region of Condesuyu, toward the sea." The lord's successors, he reports, improved and expanded it: "this way, it was always becoming more magnificent and growing." Effusive in his praise for this structure, Sancho lauds its polished and expertly joined stonework, its strength, and, above all, its size. "It has so many rooms and towers," he notes, "that one person would not be able to see all of it in one day." Its walls, he observes, "are of rocks so large that whoever sees them will say that they have not been placed there by human hands, for they are as large as pieces of mountains."[1]

Sancho was not the only early chronicler to reflect with wonder on Sacsahuaman. Betanzos, too, notes its size, writing that 10,000 workers were needed to transport the stones for its walls from the nearby quarries of Oma, Salu, and Guairanga. "Most of these stones are so big that 500 men carried one of them," he writes, "and others, 1000."[2] Their massive scale continues to impress today's visitors to the site, who may be tempted to agree with Sancho's suggestion that they were not placed there by human hands (fig. 5.1). The most remarkable of Sacsahuaman's surviving structures is a trio of gargantuan stepped walls some 400 m (1,300 ft.) in length that zigzag across the site on an east–west axis (fig. 5.2). Similarly shaped terraces appear at a number of other sites in the region, but the scale of those at Sacsahuaman sets them apart. "Each one [is] taller than the other," observes Sancho, "and the last inside of the others, the tallest of them." They were, he says, "the most beautiful thing[s] one can see among the buildings in that land."[3]

In light of the events that would unfold in the years after the Act of Foundation, Sancho's characterization of Sacsahuaman as a fortress was prescient. In 1536, the Spaniards of Cuzco would be besieged by native forces determined to drive them out of the city. When Sancho's

(facing page) Detail of figure 5.7.

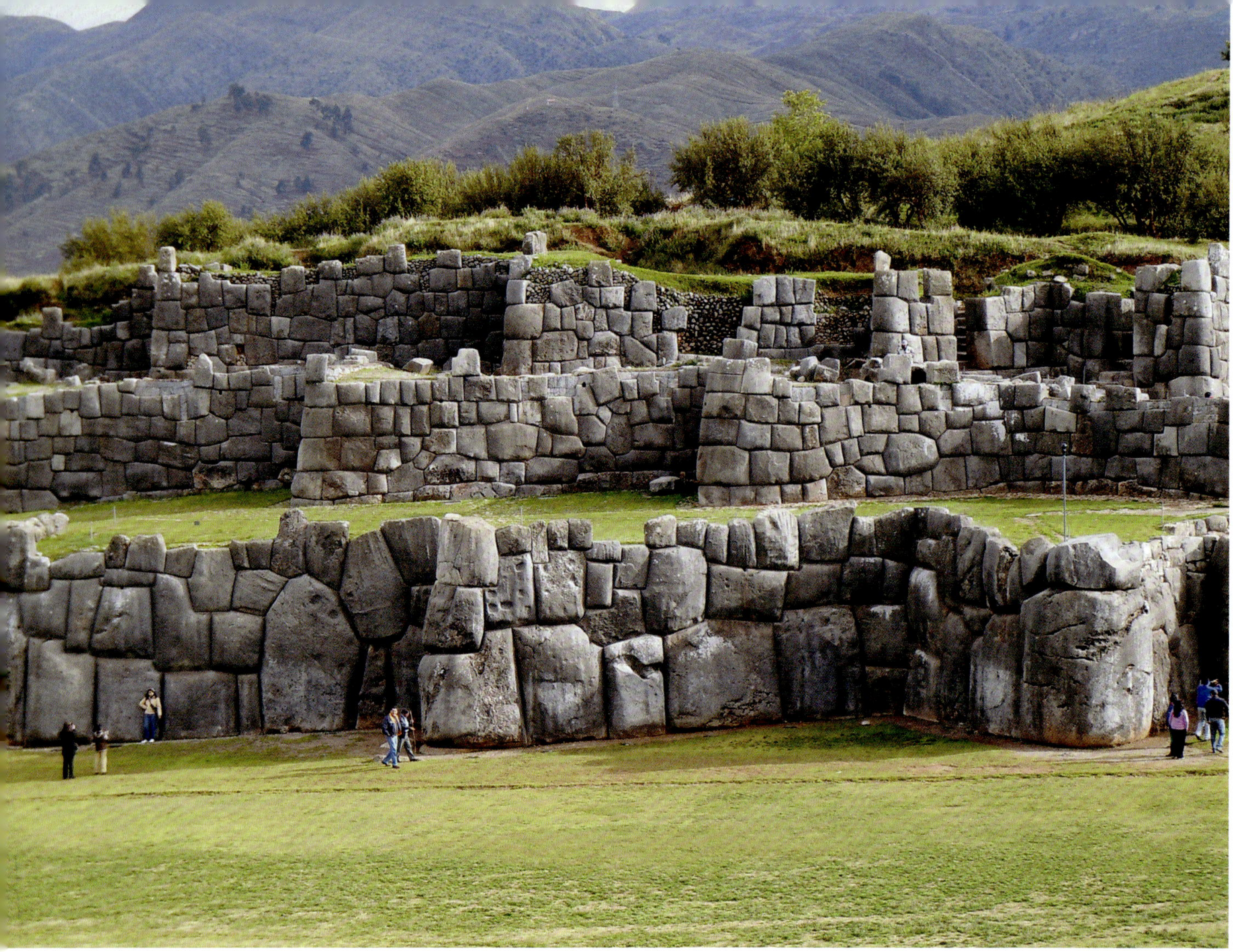

FIG. 5.1 Megaliths at Sacsahuaman, Cuzco. Early Spanish chroniclers were amazed by the size of the blocks at this massive complex, which they interpreted as a fortress.

contemporary Diego de Silva y Guzmán composed his account of that campaign, which quickly came to be known as the Siege of Cuzco, he presented Sacsahuaman as a principal setting for battle. Subsequent tellings of the story by both Spaniards and Andeans would describe the complex similarly, embedding it in new narratives, suffusing it with new values, and, in so doing, contributing to the transformation of Inca Cuzco into Spanish Cuzco.

In Sancho's view, Sacsahuaman was a massive stronghold for use in the city's defense. "Five thousand Spaniards can stay within it," he supposed, adding that "it cannot be attacked, nor can it be mined, because it is set on top of a rock."[4] It may, indeed, have struck many of those who saw it as an exemplary fortress, but it was not the only one the men in Francisco Pizarro's company encountered as they made their way through the Andes. Francisco de Xerez notes the presence of buildings he called "fortresses" in nearly every Inca settlement in which he and his compatriots lodged. In Tumbes, he recalls, they stayed in "two strong houses, one of them built like a fortress." In describing Cajamarca, he writes of a stone fortress with a staircase on the city's plaza—perhaps an *ushnu*—and, on an adjacent hilltop, another one "set on a massive outcropping, and most of it

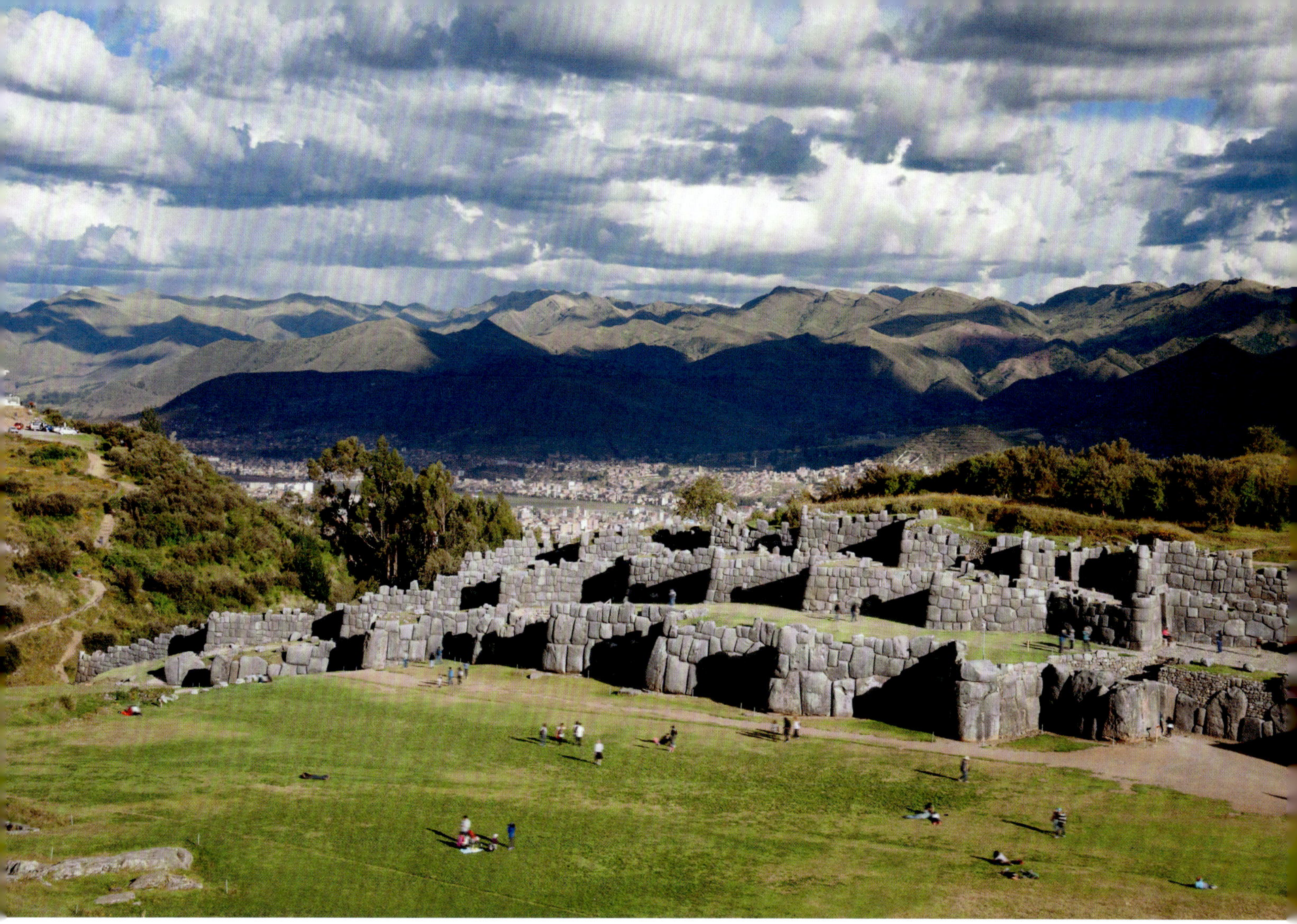

FIG. 5.2 Zigzag terrace walls at Sacsahuaman, Cuzco. The fortified site, which today survives only in ruins, would become an important battleground in the struggle for Cuzco of 1536–37.

cut out of the rock." Just a year or so later, Sancho would follow suit, praising the beauty of a fortress at Vilcashuamán and later observing that, on the road from Xauxa to Cuzco, skirmishes with native enemies involved the Spanish "driving them from their fortresses."[5]

For both Xerez and Sancho, the construction of buildings on elevated sites, the use of stone as a building material, and the presence of imposing perimeter walls were among the characteristics that led to the identification of certain structures as fortresses. Their perceptions were conditioned by their recognition of similarities between some of the buildings they saw in Peru and those they remembered from the other side of the Atlantic. For example, in Trujillo, where Pizarro and his brothers had lived, a hilltop fortress whose foundations were set under Muslim rule looms over the town's church and plaza (fig. 5.3). This widespread settlement type had emerged in the Iberian and Italian peninsulas by the eleventh century, as dispersed settlements were reorganized into villages formed beneath defensive hilltop castles. In Spain, some of those imposing structures had been built under Muslim rule and were later converted into castles for Christian feudal lords.[6] Perhaps the most renowned example is the Alhambra, the magnificent Nasrid fortress-palace taken by Ferdinand and Isabella at the conquest of Granada in 1492 and modified for their use and, later, for that of their grandson Charles V (fig. 5.4).[7]

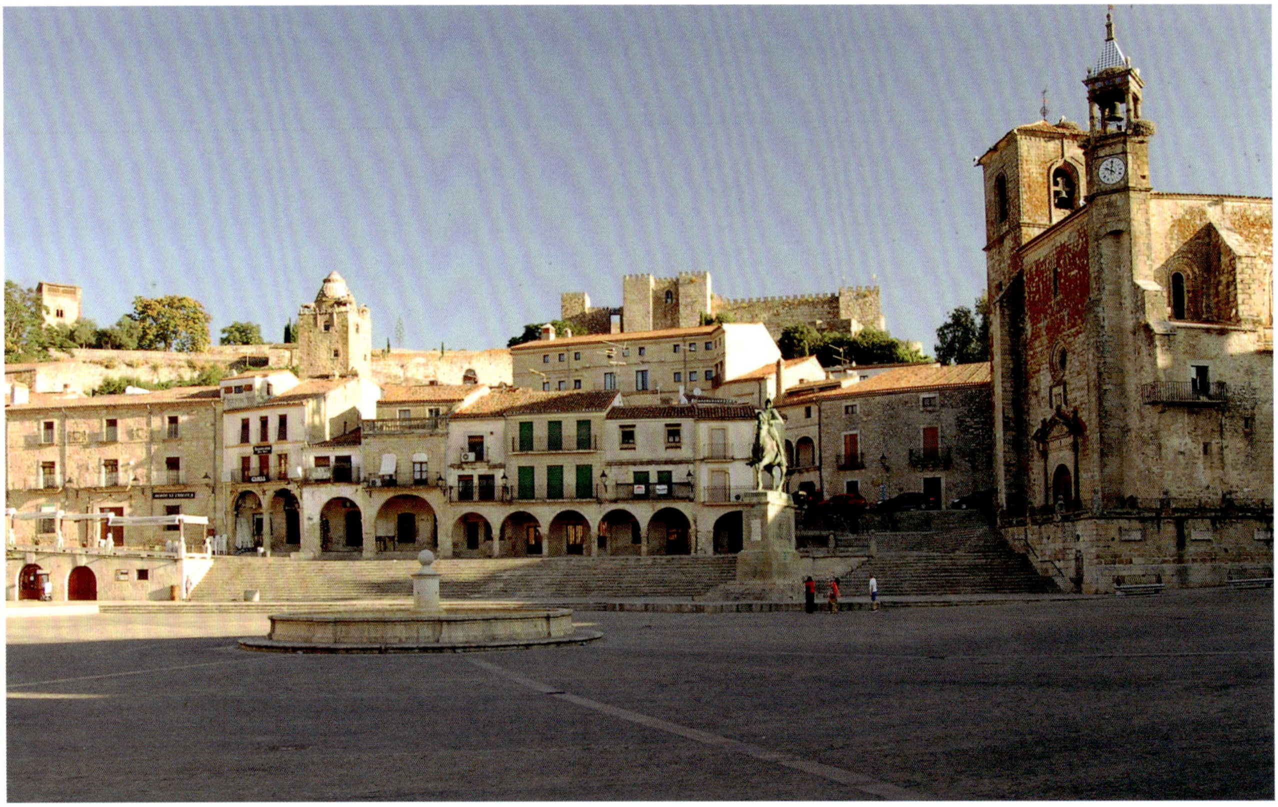

FIG. 5.3 (*above*) The main plaza in the Pizarros' hometown of Trujillo, Extremadura, Spain, with a hilltop fortress beyond. Familiarity with such structures in Spain no doubt influenced settlers' reactions to Sacsahuaman.

FIG. 5.4 (*facing page*) The Alhambra in Granada, Spain. Built under Muslim rule, this fortress-palace was captured by Christian forces in 1492. In the 1530s it was a royal residence of the Holy Roman Emperor Charles V and the Empress Isabel.

If the form of Sacsahuaman evoked Iberian counterparts for Sancho, so too did its construction. Of the tower, he observes, "the stone of which it is made is beautifully worked and joined, one [stone] with the other such that there is no mortar, and the stones are so polished so that they are like flat slabs, with the joins in order with the custom of Spain." The stonework of the massive zigzag walls, he writes, calls to mind Roman architecture on the Iberian Peninsula, in particular the aqueduct of Segovia (fig. 5.5) and the city walls of Tarragona (fig. 5.6). These references emphasize the fame of certain Roman period structures among sixteenth-century Spaniards, a renown derived not only from their antiquity but also from their massive scale and skillfully cut and set stones, the features Sancho so admired at Sacsahuaman.[8] His emphasis on the similarities between Inca architecture and Roman architecture—voiced in multiple passages—contrasts sharply with the reactions of many who visit the site today and find the stonework incomparable and the techniques used by its makers nearly incomprehensible.[9]

Further contributing to this tendency among Sancho and his contemporaries to identify structures in the Inca Empire as fortresses were terms used in the licenses issued to the leaders of expeditions to the Americas in the early sixteenth century. These texts were largely void of references to architecture, but they almost always provided stipulations about the construction of fortresses. The license granted to Pizarro in 1529, for example, includes the following passage:

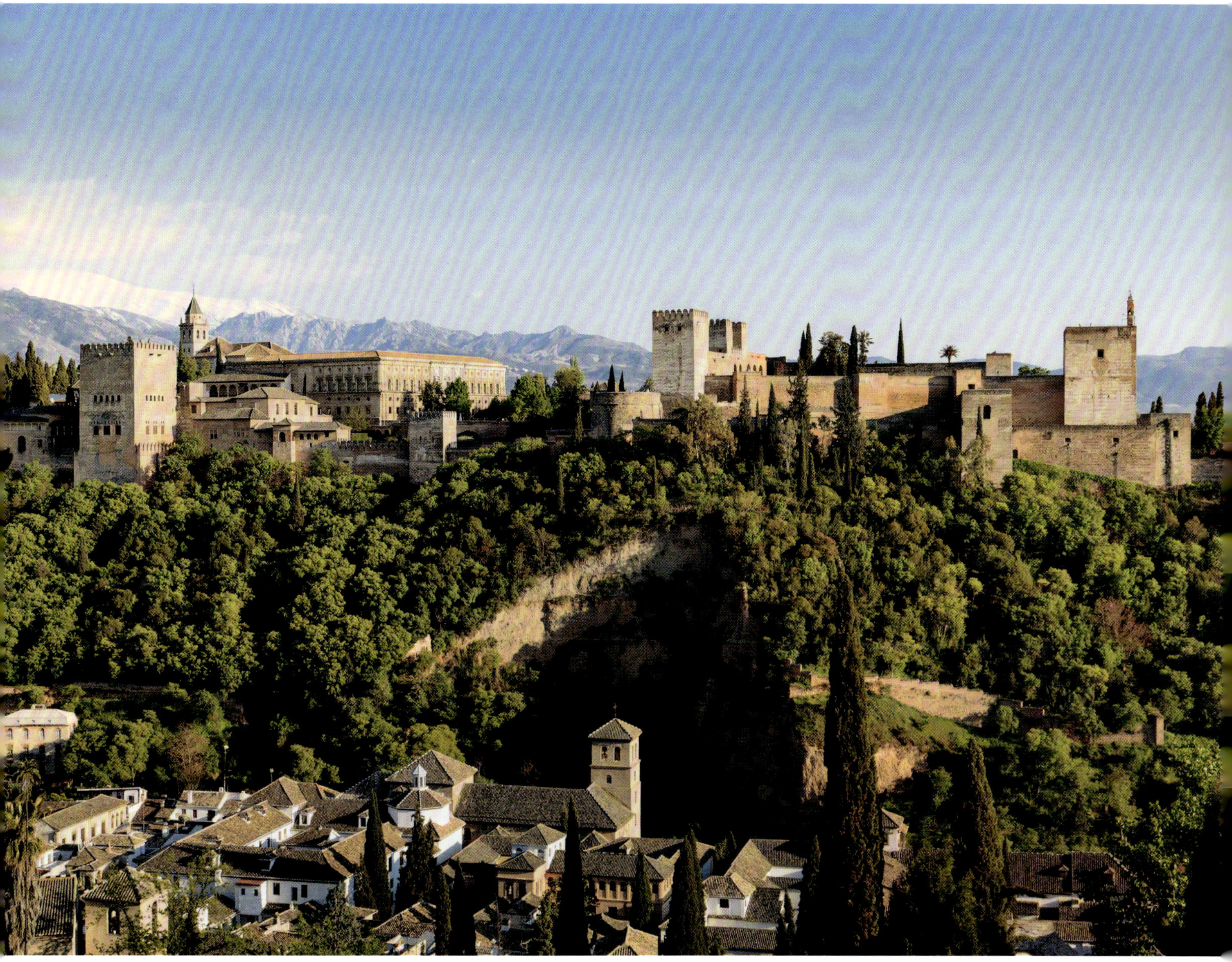

> You can make in the said lands and provinces of Peru up to four fortresses in the most appropriate regions and places that seem to you and to our said officials necessary to guard and pacify the said lands . . . [and] you will make them at your own cost.[10]

Other early sixteenth-century conquest licenses provide even greater detail about these structures and their function. The license issued in Medina del Campo on September 30, 1504, to Alonso de Ojeda for the exploration and settlement of Coquibacoa—in the northwest of present-day Venezuela—obligates the governor to build a fortress for defense in case of attacks by native adversaries.[11] A similar stipulation in the license for settlement on the island of San Juan (Puerto Rico), advises Vicente Yáñez Pinzón to make a fortress "so that the Christians can defend themselves well against the Indians and other people who come to the said island."[12] The fear of native rebellions that pervades the *cabildo*'s Acts

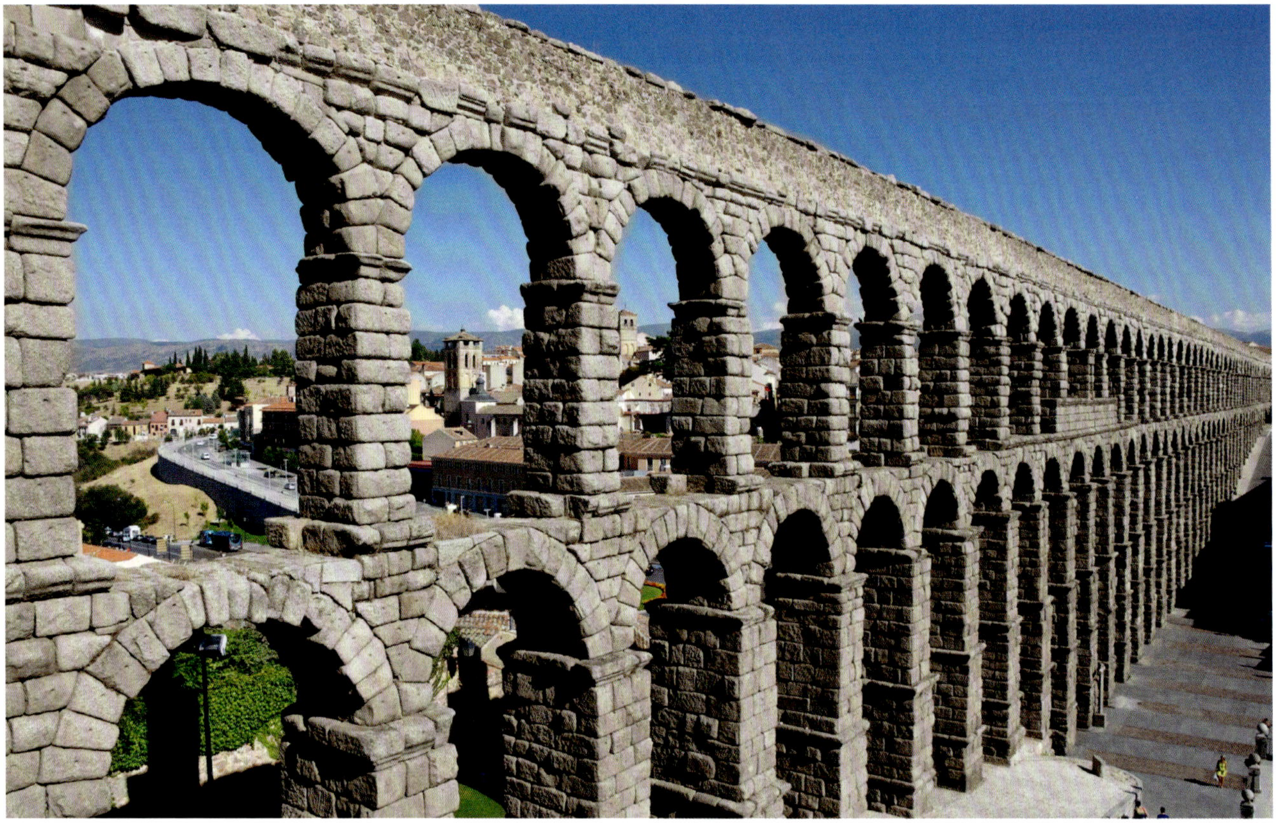

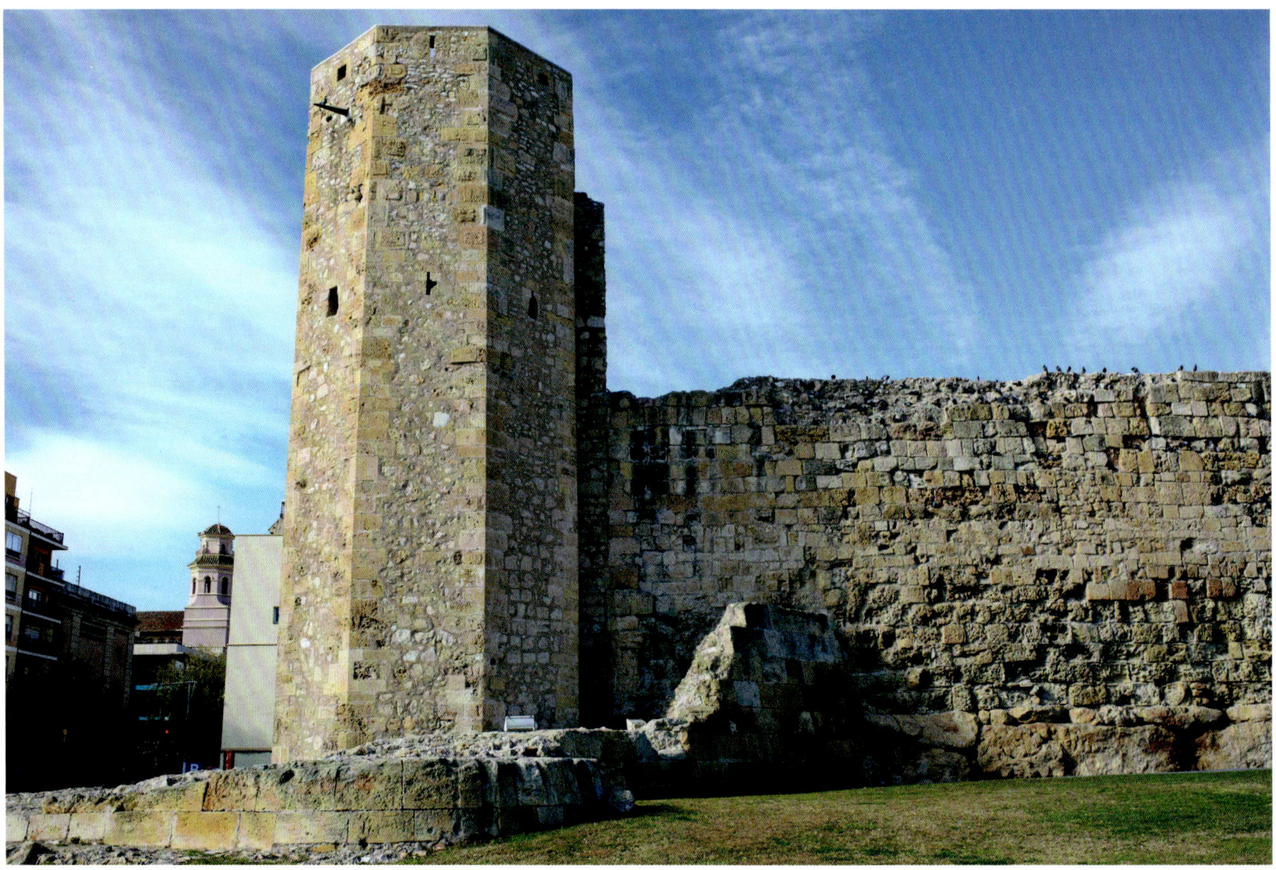

and civic ordinances in Cuzco—with their proscriptions against the destruction of Inca buildings and the eviction of their longtime residents—provides additional context for Sancho's composition of the description in his *Relatione*. If such a rebellion occurred, he must have thought, then the fortress would house and protect the Spanish.

Sancho's textual emphasis on Sacsahuaman is informed by his experiences and expectations, but at the same time it validates Pizarro's decision to establish a Spanish city in Inca Cuzco. Not only was that city already equipped with a plaza and a stock of houses for lords and settlers; it also had a fortress the likes of which had never before been seen. And in light of the stipulation in the Crown's license to Pizarro that he would have to pay for the construction of fortresses in Peru, the structure takes on an economic value, too, just as the gilded House of the Sun does in the reports of Mena and Xerez. In Cuzco, Pizarro would not have to finance the construction of a fortress; he could simply take charge of an existing one.

Among the features of Sacsahuaman most admired by Sancho was its tower. He writes that it was built with "four or five curving walls," a reference to its plan based on concentric circles.[13] The footings of those walls remain visible at the site today, but they suggest that the tower consisted of three concentric circular walls rather than four or five (fig. 5.7). Sancho also notes that the walls of the tower were stepped, like the three zigzag walls to the north, and that its interior chambers were relatively small. The surrounding complex of storehouses, however, was vast, its rooms filled with items including weapons and clothes for warriors, collected, he says, from all the provinces of the empire. Supporting his description, the stone remains around the footings of the tower today take the shape of a grid of small rectangular rooms, a form used elsewhere in the empire for storehouses, and are likely the part of the complex to which Sancho was referring (fig. 5.8). It began to be dismantled in the 1550s, and its stones were used to build the churches, monasteries, convents, and houses of Spanish colonial Cuzco.[14]

Modern excavations in this sector of Sacsahuaman—called Muyuqmarka (Round Tower) by archaeologists—have uncovered a variety of objects including metal tools, animal bones and teeth, human and llama figurines in silver, gold, and *Spondylus* shell, and pottery. Some of these objects were found in association with the eighty human burials scattered throughout the site, many of them in the zigzag terraces. The buried assemblages, archaeologists suggest, may have been offerings made as part of the dedication of these structures, a practice noted elsewhere in Cuzco as well as at other Inca sites.[15]

Architectural remains still visible at Muyuqmarka, together with archaeological findings and data provided in colonial-period sources, have led some researchers to identify this complex as a vast ceremonial center boasting a sophisticated hydraulic system, structures built around sacred natural rock outcrops, and spaces with highly restricted access, perhaps including residential spaces for the Sapa Inca and his retainers. This part of Sacsahuaman, some have argued, was a House of the Sun conceived as an upper-Cuzco counterpart to the one built near the confluence of the streams in lower Cuzco, on the site Angelina Yupanqui and her contemporaries believed to have been the place Manco Capac and Mama Ocllo planted corn and built a house.[16]

Sancho's experiences and his description of Sacsahuaman enact a transformation of the site, whatever its function may have been among the Inca of the late fifteenth and early sixteenth centuries. For him, its architectural form and function are clear: it is a fortress rising above the residential sector of Cuzco. A similar transformation takes place on the title pages of the *relaciones* of Xerez and Mena, in which the maker of the woodcut image set the scene of Friar Valverde's encounter with Atahualpa at Cajamarca in a space dominated by a walled castle on a hill in the distance (see fig. 2.6).

FIG. 5.5 (*facing page, top*) Roman aqueduct of Segovia, Spain. Pedro Sancho saw similarities between Inca stonework and that of Roman structures he knew in his homeland.

FIG. 5.6 (*facing page, bottom*) Roman city wall at Tarragona, Spain. Sancho was reminded of Tarragona's ancient city wall as he contemplated the stonework at Sacsahuaman.

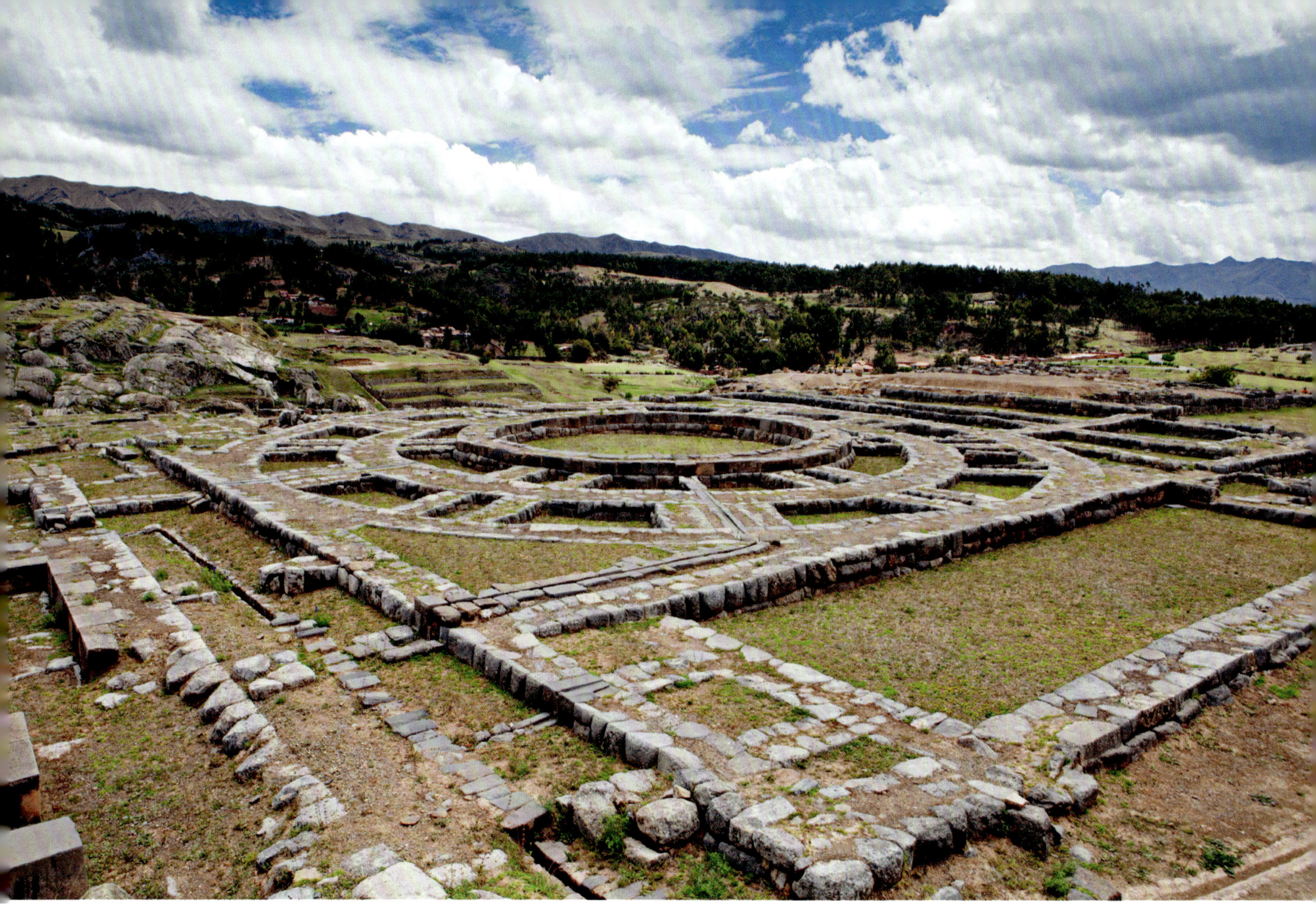

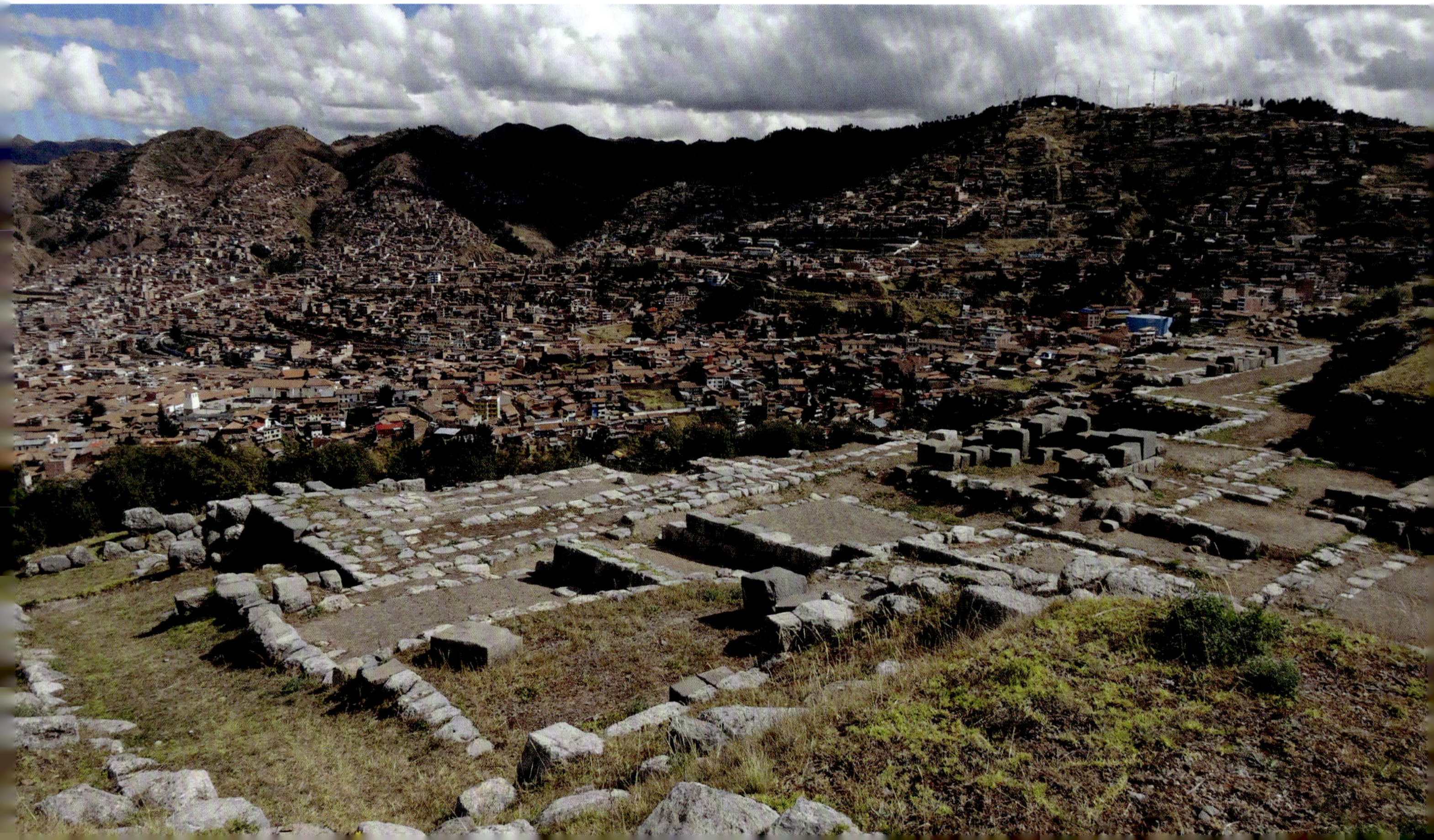

If Sancho's writings cast Sacsahuaman as a fortress, they simultaneously position it within a transatlantic network of such structures, among them sites where the forces of the kings of Spain and the Holy Roman Emperor had won victories over their foes. "Many Spaniards who have seen it, and who went to Lombardy and other foreign kingdoms," he writes, "say they have not seen another building like this fortress nor a stronger castle."[17] This comparison between the fortress of Cuzco and its counterparts elsewhere in the Spanish world, however, would come to be rooted in more than just similarities in design and materials. In the months after Sancho's composition of his *Relatione*, unrest in Cuzco would lead to armed conflict, and Sancho's vision of Sacsahuaman as a fortress would become a reality.

Sometime in March or April 1536, large numbers of native warriors amassed by Manco and his allies mounted a series of relentless and destructive attacks on Cuzco and its environs. These episodes would not subside until a year later, in April 1537. They are documented in a number of sixteenth-century sources, including the *Suma y narración* by Betanzos and a later text based on the account of Titu Cusi Yupanqui, one of Manco's sons. The sources coincide in their recounting of certain narrative details, but diverge in others. Taken as a group of texts reporting on the same series of events in Cuzco, they reveal multiple perspectives on the city at a critical moment in its history, as factions of Spaniards and native Andeans fought to define and control it.[18]

Of all the sixteenth-century accounts of the siege, the one composed closest in time to the events it records is a report in manuscript form held today in the collection of the Biblioteca Nacional de España in Madrid and known as the *Relación del sitio* (*Report on the Siege*).[19] The text opens with a prologue addressed to Charles V and concludes with the phrase "from this city of Cuzco, 2 April 1539."[20] The name of its author does not appear anywhere in the manuscript, but its contents and use of the first person suggest he was a Spanish participant in the conflict who wrote about it from Cuzco. On the basis of evidence both internal and external to the manuscript, Porras Barrenechea attributed it to Diego de Silva y Guzmán, a man who was not among the first Spanish settlers of Cuzco but who had arrived there in 1535.[21] He hailed from Ciudad Rodrigo, southwest of Salamanca, near Spain's modern border with Portugal, and made the voyage to the Americas in 1535 with Hernando Pizarro, who had returned to Seville to deliver the Crown's share of the gold and silver from Cajamarca.

Porras Barrenechea's attribution is not universally accepted, but it is convincing in many ways. The text is strongly supportive of Hernando Pizarro, presenting him as an exceptional man whose bravery, selflessness, and loyalty led the Spanish through great challenges and, ultimately, to resounding victories. It is the kind of account one might expect to have been written by one of his allies. Its florid style provides even stronger evidence of Silva's authorship. His father was Feliciano de Silva, the writer of a number of early sixteenth-century chivalric romances, whose son would have had significant exposure to such literature. Diego de Silva himself had penned a poetic account of the conquest of Peru, entitled *La conquista de la Nueva Castilla*, in 1538, the year before the composition of the *Relación del sitio*.[22]

Silva's account opens sometime in the first half of 1536. Hernando Pizarro, having returned to Peru from Spain, was then in Lima, a city founded by his brother Francisco in January 1535 and known in these early years of Spanish colonial rule as Ciudad de los Reyes (City of the Kings). As the text begins, Hernando departs for Cuzco, prompted by his brother's appointing him to replace Soto as his lieutenant there. The situation in Cuzco at this time was tense; Silva writes that Juan Pizarro had recently taken Manco prisoner on the suspicion that he was organizing a rebellion. Arriving in Cuzco in February or March 1536, however, Hernando found that Manco had been freed from his imprisonment. Silva describes his reaction:

FIG. 5.7 ***(facing page, top)*** Concentric foundations of the circular tower at Sacsahuaman, Cuzco. The tower and its surrounding structures have been dismantled, and the stone used for colonial buildings in Cuzco.

FIG. 5.8 ***(facing page, bottom)*** Foundations of rectangular rooms at Sacsahuaman, Cuzco. These rooms were probably storehouses.

> He praised [Manco] greatly for his service to Your Majesty, for one of the main things that was ordered on this expedition was to see to his [Manco's] good treatment . . . so that the Inca was shown that [You] favored and were pleased by him, and did not suspect him of any ill will or intention.[23]

A rebellion, Silva suggests, was not on Hernando Pizarro's mind. Of greater interest to him was the acquisition of gold, a subject he raised in a meeting with his brothers Juan and Gonzalo in the *cabildo* hall, presumably the structure in the vicinity of the church that Soto had designated as such. He spoke to them, Silva says, "about how it was appropriate that the Spanish residents [of Cuzco] make some offering to His Majesty, for they had so benefitted from the land, and the Royal Treasury was so depleted with the wars of the Turk and the French."[24] The wars to which he referred were the battles of the Holy Roman Emperor's forces against those of Suleiman I and the Ottoman Empire, which had recently entered into an alliance with Francis I of France. In July 1535, less than a year before Hernando Pizarro is said to have made this statement, the emperor's troops had recaptured the city of Tunis and its port, La Goleta, in North Africa, which had previously been taken by the Ottomans. Silva's reference to battles in the Mediterranean joins Sancho's earlier reference to Lombardy in emphasizing the transatlantic political geography within which the Spaniards in sixteenth-century Peru conceived of Cuzco, and which would take shape on *mappae mundi* such as those produced in the Agnese workshops (see fig. 2.11).

As the Pizarro brothers were discussing the collection of gold, news arrived that some native peoples in the lands south of Cuzco had risen in rebellion and had killed a group of Spaniards. Silva writes that Hernando Pizarro came to suspect the revolt had been launched by an Andean leader called Vilaoma, who had accompanied Diego de Almagro on his expedition into that part of the Inca Empire. Betanzos, too, would refer to Vilaoma, comparing him to the pope, and noting that he was elderly and the caretaker of the sacred golden figure in the House of the Sun. While Vilaoma sometimes spoke for himself, Betanzos claims, at other times he spoke for the Sun, "as if the Sun were a man and spoke with other men."[25] Upon his return to Cuzco, Silva writes, Vilaoma met with Manco in the House of the Sun and advised him to incite a rebellion and kill the Spaniards in Cuzco as well as those in Lima.[26]

Silva's portrayal of these events may or may not be accurate, but he sharpens the distinctions between the two sides—Spaniards and Andeans—who would ultimately engage in battle in and around Cuzco for more than a year. He contrasts the loyalty of Hernando Pizarro, who planned to provide financial support for the wars of Charles V, with the treachery of Manco, who conspires with Vilaoma to plan a rebellion. He provides an architectural dimension to this opposition, contrasting the *cabildo* house—the seat of city governance and the location of the foundry where gold would be melted before being sent to support the wars of the Holy Roman Emperor—with the House of the Sun, which had already been stripped of its gold, and which, for Silva, retained its association with unorthodox religiosity and seditious politics. In effect, the text severs the relationship of complementarity between the House of the Sun and the plaza of Cuzco that had long been in place among the Inca.

According to Silva, Manco and Vilaoma initiated their plot in April 1536. They departed Cuzco for Yucay, in the Urubamba River valley not far to the northwest, where they assembled an army; in the weeks that followed, they launched a series of attacks on Cuzco and its environs. Betanzos reports that there were relatively few Spaniards in Cuzco at this time: "250 Christians, including priests, monks, children, and the sick. There were no more than one hundred men of war among them, and these and the rest barely made a battle corps."[27] The first series of attacks and counterattacks took place at Sacsahuaman, which Silva, like Sancho, calls a fortress. The Spaniards' native allies were guarding the complex, he writes, when it was besieged by Manco's troops. After engaging in battle for some time and realizing they were greatly outnumbered, the guards retreated, running down the steep hillside into the heart of Cuzco to the protection of the Pizarros and their confederates.

Not long thereafter, Hernando Pizarro and his men resolved to retake Sacsahuaman. They climbed uphill on horseback and charged their foes *en masse*, a maneuver designed to disperse dense formations of warriors. They scaled the stone walls of Sacsahuaman—perhaps the zigzag terraces that survive today—and engaged in combat, wielding lances, swords, and daggers, while protected by

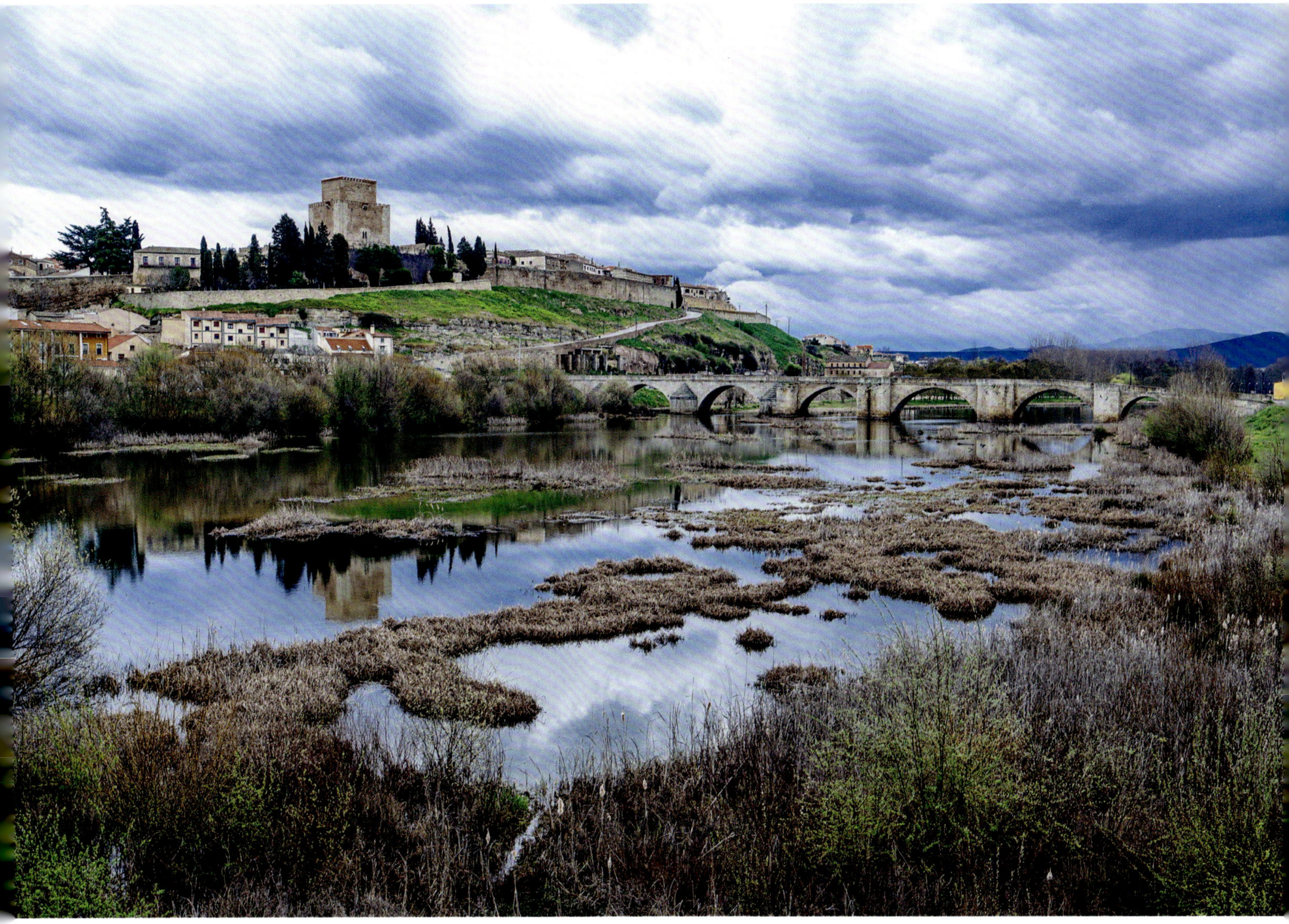

FIG. 5.9 Ciudad Rodrigo, Salamanca, Spain; the birthplace of Diego de Silva y Guzmán. The town's layout, with a castle overlooking the settlement below, informed Silva's understanding of Cuzco's geography.

metal helmets and padded cloth armor. Manco's men fought with stones, which they dropped on their enemies from above and hurled with slingshots, as well as with bows and arrows. The Spanish were aided, Silva writes, by divine intervention: "God was fighting with them, for without a single death [to the Spanish], all of the [enemy] Indians died, leaving none alive."[28]

Sacsahuaman was besieged again the following day by a new wave of Manco's men, described by Silva as amounting to 100,000 warriors (*indios de guerra*) and 80,000 retainers (*indios de servicio*). They employed a new strategy, shooting flaming arrows onto the roofs of the buildings on the steep hillside that descended onto the plaza of Cuzco. The wind aided their efforts, helping to spread the blaze from one thatched roof to another. "At one point," Silva writes, "it seemed that no less than the entire city was aflame, and the cries of the Indians so loud, and the smoke so dense that no one could see or hear anyone else."[29] Weeks of intense fighting in and around Cuzco followed, with the Spanish and their allies suffering setbacks, injuries, and deaths. "On this day and those that followed," says the author, "the city was always burning, and the [enemy] warriors were full of pride since it seemed to them that the Spanish were not able to defend themselves."[30]

With the city in ruins, and Manco's men in control of much of it, Hernando Pizarro turned his attention once more to Sacsahuaman. He presented his disheartened followers with a choice, reported by Silva with high drama: "We neither have nor hold anything more than the plaza, and so either we all lose our lives or we win back the fortress, for winning it back secures the town, and any other way would be to lose it."[31] His men agreed to attack their foes once again and formed three brigades, each led by one of the Pizarro brothers. Silva focuses particularly on the actions of Juan Pizarro, writing that he and his men charged the entrance to Sacsahuaman, which is described as a fortified portal: "From the doorway in the wall, two thick walls projected outward on either side, making another doorway in front of it, and these projecting walls were roofed on top."[32] The location of this fortified portal remains unclear, but it may have been part of the tower and its adjoining rooms and storehouses. From atop it, Manco's warriors threw stones onto the Spanish, and among those they struck was Juan Pizarro. "They injured him," writes Silva, "by hitting him in the head with a stone thrown by hand from above with great force since, as I already said, he came without a helmet."[33] Juan would never recover from the injury. He died in Cuzco about two weeks later.

The Spanish retreated that day, but the battle would continue for some time. The men of Cuzco, led by Hernando Pizarro, eventually prevailed by the end of May, breaking into the tower at Sacsahuaman when their foes ran out of stones, arrows, and determination, and killing more than 1,500 enemy warriors. As Silva describes it,

> The victory was so remarkable, that Hernando Pizarro ordered that a flag be placed above [Sacsahuaman] so that all of the Indians who came would recognize it . . . and the enemies were struck with such fear and helplessness that right away they left the encampments they had near the town and retreated to their fortified bases.[34]

Silva presents the early stages of the year-long battle as a sequence of victories and losses accompanied by movement back and forth between Sacsahuaman and the heart of the Spanish colonial city. In structuring the narrative in this way, he follows Sancho in presenting Cuzco as a fortress town comparable to Trujillo, Granada, or his native Ciudad Rodrigo, where the fourteenth-century fortified castle of Enrique II loomed over its surroundings (fig. 5.9). His textual imagery also resonates with early sixteenth-century visual images of warfare, for example *The Battle of Pavia*, in which the forces of the Holy Roman Emperor, on the right, attack those of Francis I, on the left (fig. 5.10).[35] Like this painting, Silva's account, too, records the weapons and techniques of combat and sets the conflict against the backdrop of a fortification, a territorial prize marked with the fluttering standard of the Holy Roman Emperor. Visual and textual representations of the Battle of Pavia circulated widely, and for Silva and the other Spaniards of Cuzco—some of whom had fought in earlier battles in Europe—a rich stock of images both physical and metaphysical must have informed their perceptions of the Siege of Cuzco and, indeed, the city itself.[36]

Hernando Pizarro may have raised the standard at Sacsahuaman as a sign of victory in May 1536, but fierce

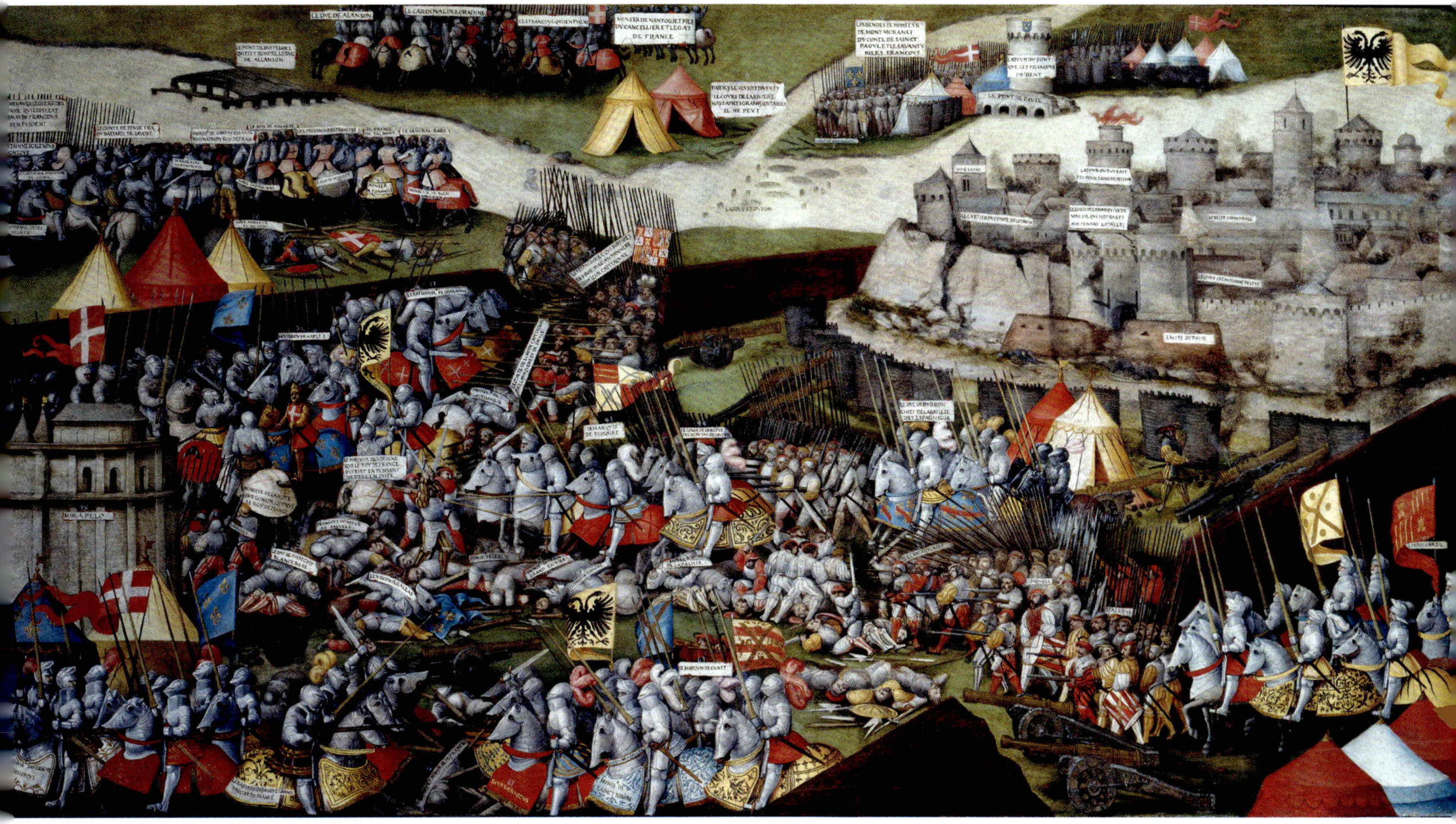

FIG. 5.10 Artist unknown, *The Battle of Pavia*, *c.* 1525–28. Oil on panel, 117 × 220 cm. Ashmolean Museum, University of Oxford. Conflict imagery such as this may have provided a reference point for Silva's account of the Siege of Cuzco.

attacks on Cuzco continued during the following weeks and months. Strategies used by Manco's forces included the weaponization of the city's infrastructure by redirecting water channels to cause flooding, erecting barricades, and digging ditches in the streets to impede passage on horseback. Manco's men did not rely on horses, and they devised new ways to move about in the city under siege. "Since the houses were all burned," notes Silva, "the Indians could walk on top of the walls."[37]

Having endured months of attacks, Hernando Pizarro adopted a new strategy in January 1537. He had learned that Manco had fled to Ollantaytambo, about 70 km (44 mi.) to the northwest of Cuzco. A mountainside complex of terraces built with the signature stonework of royal Inca architecture, Ollantaytambo—like Machu Picchu—is believed to have been a royal estate built in the fifteenth century for Pachacuti, and additional construction may have taken place in the early sixteenth century (fig. 5.11).[38] The Spaniards' new strategy, Silva writes, was to lay siege to Ollantaytambo and to capture Manco. Seventy horsemen, thirty footmen, and their native allies set out from Cuzco preceded by an advance company of twenty horsemen led by Gonzalo Pizarro. They arrived at an open field Silva describes as being bordered by eleven rising terraces populated by a multitude of Manco's men armed with bows and arrows. The Pizarros and their forces did battle with those of Manco, who shot arrows at them and diverted water from a nearby river onto the field of battle, flooding

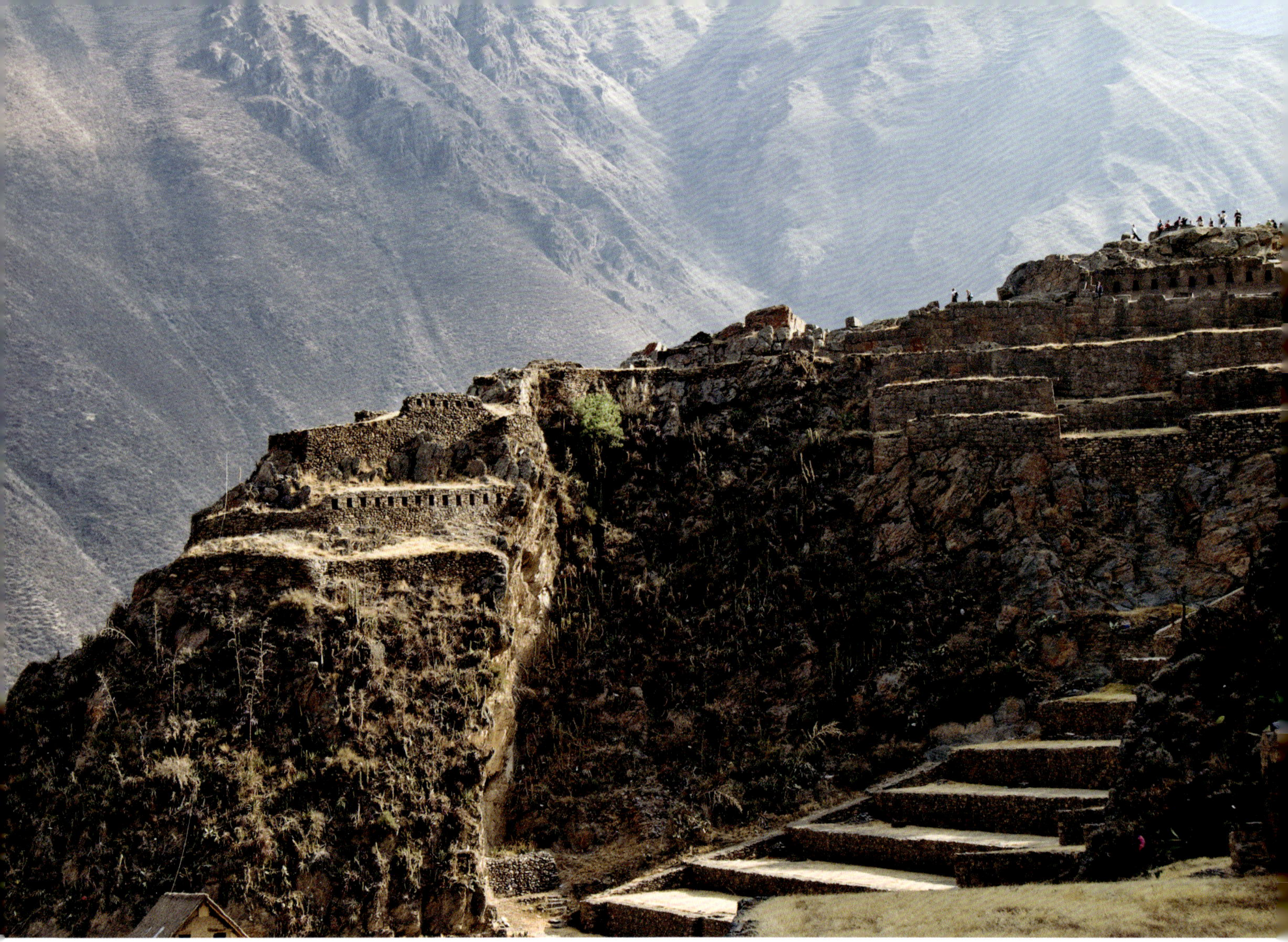

FIG. 5.11 The Inca royal complex at Ollantaytambo, northwest of Cuzco. Manco Inca fled to this site after the Siege of Cuzco, and defeated the Spanish in a battle fought nearby in 1537.

it and hindering the Spaniards' ability to move swiftly on horseback. That maneuver, together with the overwhelming numbers of Manco's warriors, left the Spaniards with few options. They retreated.[39]

Silva describes the situation in Cuzco at this time as dismal. Few able-bodied men remained to defend the city, the food supply was dwindling, and there was widespread fear among the citizenry. Demoralizing the Spanish even further was the arrival of a macabre offering from Manco: a bundle containing six severed heads and a stash of torn documents, among them a letter from the Empress Isabel with news of the Holy Roman Emperor's victories against the Ottomans in Tunis. The message was clear: Manco's men had captured and killed Spaniards in a brutal way, and they had succesfully disrupted not only their enemies' mobility but also their lines of communication.[40] The severed heads and torn documents, together with the burned roofs, crumbling walls, and impassable streets, hint at the ways in which the grand vision of Spanish Cuzco conceived by Francisco Pizarro and recorded by Pedro Sancho had begun to disintegrate just two years after its inception.

Silva stresses the ingenuity of Hernando Pizarro at this moment of crisis, quoting the words he allegedly spoke to his brother Gonzalo:

> The city is in more danger than it ever was, because if we are besieged again, we do not have horses to fight one more day, and even if we could, we could not protect the maize we have planted, which would be a great loss, and would put us in much more need.[41]

He proposed an eleventh-hour strategy: the Spanish would launch a night-time attack on a council of Manco's principal military leaders taking place outside Cuzco, believing—Silva writes—that "with this council disrupted . . . all of the others will lose their pride."[42] Gonzalo Pizarro assembled a group of twenty-six horsemen, twenty of whom would accompany him on the raid, while the remaining six would accompany his brother Hernando. Silva describes the surprise attack on Manco's council in hyperbolic terms, writing that it was "one of the most beautiful skirmishes that has ever been seen, because as it was clear at that moment that they would either lose the land or win it, they did things so remarkable that they cannot be believed."[43] In Silva's account, this attack on Manco's council of chiefs was a decisive moment in the year-long fight over the possession of Cuzco. To mark their victory, he writes, the Pizarros returned to Cuzco and, in the plaza, they cut off the right hands of 400 enemy captives. This was not the first time the Spanish had practiced this form of punishment: as Silva notes, Gonzalo Pizarro had cut off the right hands of 200 captives in a campaign leading up to the battle at Ollantaytambo.[44] In the aftermath of the attack on the chief's council, however, the Pizarros sent the 400 severed hands to Manco, a grisly counter-gift to the severed heads and torn documents he had earlier sent to them.

One wonders if Manco ever received the severed hands, or, indeed, if the Spanish even knew his whereabouts at this point. Sometime after the victory at Ollantaytambo, Manco set off for Vitcos, a settlement some 200 km (124 mi.) to the northwest of Cuzco in the remote region known as Vilcabamba (fig. 5.12).[45] He would never return. The story of his departure for Vitcos and his stay in the region is told in the account composed by Titu Cusi Yupanqui (*c.* 1530–71) decades later, around 1570.[46] The author describes himself in the text as the grandson of Huayna Capac and the son of Manco and states that he was born in Cuzco around the time Francisco Pizarro and his men arrived. He was probably in the city during the Act of Foundation and the Distribution of Lots, though he would have been in his infancy. He spent most of his life, however, in the Vilcabamba region, having been recognized as the ruler of the Inca polity centered there sometime after his father's death in 1544, and it is from the Inca city that shares its name with the region that he dictated a historical narrative to the Augustinian friar Marcos García and a scribe, Martín de Pando. Entitled the "Relacion de como los españoles entraron en el piru," it is known today through a copy held in the library of the Royal Monastery of San Lorenzo at El Escorial, where it is bound with a number of other texts on the Americas, including one of the sixteenth-century copies of Betanzos's *Suma y narración*.[47]

In addition to telling the story of his own experiences in Vilcabamba and those of his father, Titu Cusi Yupanqui provides a detailed account of the Siege of Cuzco that squares with that of Silva in some ways and departs from it in others. Both present Manco's imprisonment as the event that sparked the conflict and provide details of his plotting to take the city, the attack on Sacsahuaman, the retreat to Ollantaytambo by Manco and his cohort, and the Spaniards' attack on them there. Other similarities relate to form rather than content; for example, both sources rely extensively on reported speech to convey their story. Silva most frequently quotes Hernando Pizarro and his pronouncements to his men, but Titu Cusi Yupanqui centers on speeches delivered by Manco. Silva's use of direct discourse aligns his account with coeval *relaciones* and forms of official correspondence, among them the reports of Hernán Cortés to Charles V on the conquest of Mexico, which similarly purport to record the speech of conquistadors and that of Moctezuma II, the Aztec emperor. In the case of Titu Cusi Yupanqui, however, the convention may stem from a different tradition and mode of production involving the recitation of an oral history that privileged dialogue.

Titu Cusi Yupanqui's account also differs from that of Silva in its conceptualization of Cuzco and the places and buildings in which the events of 1536–37 occurred. For example, he presents Manco's house in Cuzco as a prominent setting in the narrative. It is there, he says, that a group of Spaniards confronted Manco and shackled his ankles, putting him under house arrest on suspicion of planning a revolt.[48] This telling of the story echoes the tale of Atahualpa's capture in Cajamarca, asserting that in order to gain his freedom, Manco, too, ordered his subjects to fill a large room with gold and silver as a ransom. They did so, says the author, and when Manco was freed, he dined with his captors in one of the rooms of his house.[49]

The plaza and the church, too, are prominent settings for the events of 1536–37 in Titu Cusi Yupanqui's *relación*. The author's recounting of the initial campaign of the siege describes Manco's forces—400,000 men, he says—encircling Cuzco as the Spanish and the "black men" (*negros*) with them gathered in the plaza. Manco's warriors attacked the city, burning the Spaniards' houses and setting fire to the church. He writes that it was the "black men" of Cuzco, perhaps African slaves, who extinguished the fire. The church sheltered the Spaniards that night; Titu Cusi Yupanqui says they remained there praying for divine intervention, "kneeling with their hands at their mouths."[50]

The starkest difference between the story of the Siege of Cuzco told by Titu Cusi Yupanqui and the one penned by Silva, though, is in the respective authors' understanding of Cuzco's place in a larger spatial order. For Silva, Cuzco is a node in a transatlantic network of towns whose allegiance was to the Holy Roman Emperor, and the Siege of Cuzco was one of a number of skirmishes occurring in the Americas, Europe, and Africa over territories the Spaniards sought to claim for their sovereign. For Titu Cusi Yupanqui, however, Cuzco was something else:

> The extent of [the lands of the Inca] is more than 1,200 leagues in length and about another 300 in width divided in the following way. In describing the world, it is good to know about east and west and north and south. In our tradition, we call them Andesuyu, Chinchaysuyu, Condesuyu, [and] Collasuyu, surrounding a center in this way: Andesuyu to the east, Chinchaysuyu to the north, Condesuyu to the west, [and] Collasuyu to the south. This is how we regard them from Cuzco, which is the center and head of all of the land, and since it is in the middle, my ancestors who were there called their lineage "lords of Tahuantinsuyo," which means lords of the four parts of the world, for they thought it certain that there was no more world than this.[51]

This conceptualization of Cuzco as the "center and head of all the land" structures Titu Cusi Yupanqui's account of his father's initial attack. As Manco's forces approached the city, they made their presence known to the Spanish through sound: "whistling and horns and trumpets and a great shouting of voices that frightened everyone."[52] The warriors, he explains, had come from the four parts of Tahuantinsuyu. Those from Chinchaysuyu formed a blockade at the place called Carmenca, where Pizarro had entered the city from the north three years earlier. Those from Condesuyu arranged themselves at Cayocache, a settlement on a hill to the southeast of Cuzco that was, according to Betanzos, the place Pachacuti had designated home to the lineage of Alcavicça. Those from Collasuyu were the most numerous; Titu Cusi Yupanqui does not say where they were stationed, but it is likely they gathered in the terrain beyond (or to the northeast of) the House of the Sun. Those from Andesuyu completed the ring of combatants surrounding the city, situating themselves on or beyond the steep mountainside that rises to the northeast of the plaza.

The description traces a diagram of Tahuantinsuyu in which warriors from its four constituent parts approach the center, surround it, and attempt to retake it. This view of Cuzco is not that of Sancho and Silva, who see it instead as a fortress town like those they knew in Spain. Rather, it is one that sees Cuzco as the magnetic center of the vast lands of the Inca ruler, drawing Manco's loyalists from far and wide. Titu Cusi Yupanqui's portrayal of Cuzco in this way is retrospective, having been recorded around 1570, but his father and other native elites in the 1530s likely held the same view, or a similar one, during the period of the Spanish occupation.

In recounting the events that led to the Siege of Cuzco, Titu Cusi Yupanqui gives voice to his father's objections to the Spaniards' actions in multiple passages. One of them appears as part of the story of Manco's imprisonment in the House of the Sun. According to Titu Cusi Yupanqui, his father rebuked his captors directly, saying:

> What have I done to you to make you want to treat me this way and tie me up like a dog? This is the way you repay the good work I have done in bringing you into my land and giving you what I had with such affection and devotion?[53]

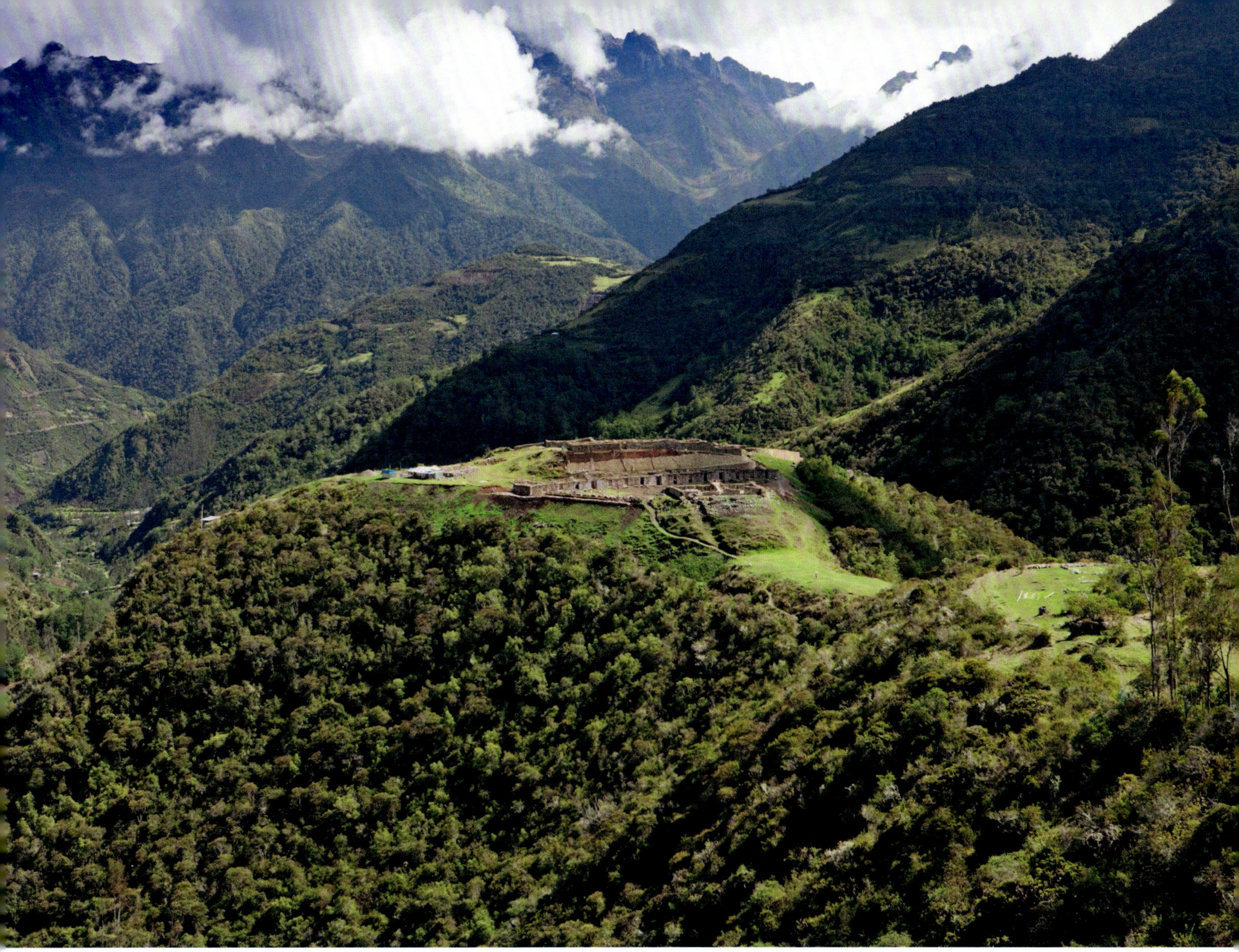

FIG. 5.12 Vitcos, a high-status Inca center in the Vilcabamba region. Manco Inca established himself at Vitcos in 1537, and remained there until his death.

This story of the Siege of Cuzco ends with the battle at Ollantaytambo and the report that Manco resolved to build a fortress (*fortaleza*) there "because some day we could make use of it."[54] That day did, indeed, come. Silva characterizes the Spaniards' attack on Manco's men there as a failure, writing that the Pizarros and their allies were forced to retreat and return to Cuzco. Titu Cusi Yupanqui describes it differently, noting that Manco's warriors killed one Spaniard and three men of African descent, but that "in the end, neither party was given the victory."[55] He does not address the dire situation Silva describes in Cuzco following the retreat from Ollantaytambo, and, in fact, the events documented in the remainder of the manuscript are all set in Vitcos and Vilcabamba.

As the events of the Siege of Cuzco were unfolding, Francisco Pizarro was in Lima, presumably accompanied by Angelina Yupanqui. It was there that he received word of

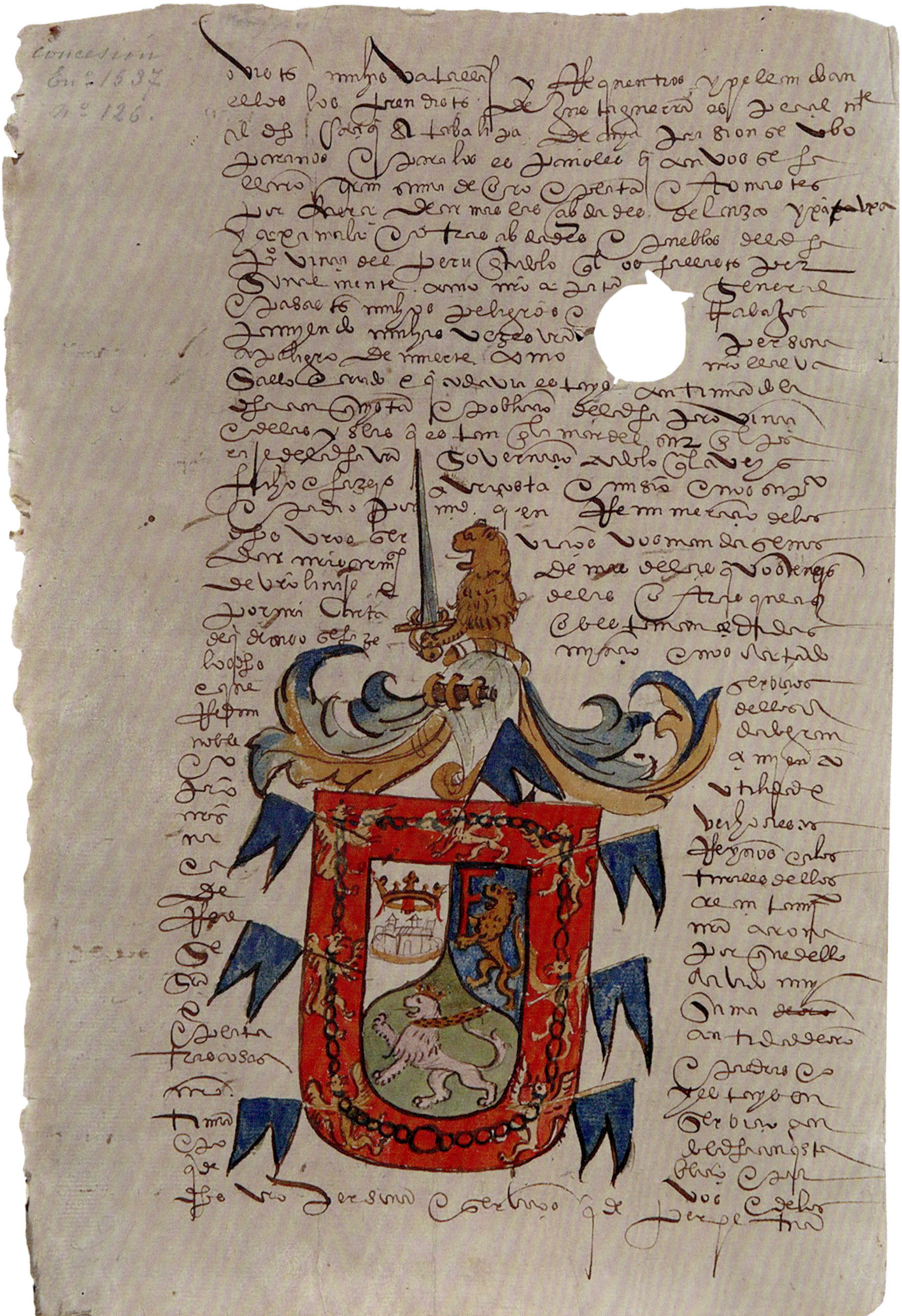
concesion
1537
126.

the new coat of arms the Crown had granted him in 1537. A document issued in Valladolid and signed by the king describes it in this way:

> A coat of arms, with the said city of Cuzco in the first part at the top, in memory of your having settled and conquered it, with a crown of the King, in gold, and attached to it a red tassel that the said *cacique* Atahualpa wore . . . and in the other quarter at the top on the left-hand side a rampant gold lion with a red "F" in its paws, and in the third quarter at the bottom, the principal one on this coat of arms, a gray-brown lion with a gold crown of the King, restrained with a gold chain, in memory of the imprisonment of the said *cacique*.[56]

Depicted colorfully in documents produced in connection with the grant, the escutcheon includes an image of Cuzco imagined—like Tumbes on Pizarro's earlier coat of arms—as a fortified city (fig. 5.13). It bears no resemblance to the city as it appeared in the 1530s, but operates instead as something like a hieroglyph, a symbol designed to call to mind a particular place. The shield also includes an image of the *mascaypacha*, the symbol of Inca rulership described in the text as a "red tassel," which is shown as an attachment to the golden crown. The accompanying text describes it as an ornament worn by Atahualpa, but in 1537 it would have been worn by Manco, to whom the document does not refer.

The fusion of that symbol of Inca rulership with one of European rulership introduces the iconographic appropriation and transformation that would continue in Spanish colonial Peru for nearly three centuries. However, what is remarkable about this early example of the phenomenon is that it was produced not in the Americas but, rather, in Valladolid, and in a document signed by the king of Spain. Coats of arms like this one—some of them for Spaniards, and others for Andeans—would serve as the vehicles for visual juxtapositions and syntheses throughout the 1540s as the struggle to shape Cuzco's form and history continued amid ongoing violence and unrest.

FIG. 5.13 ***(facing page)*** The coat of arms granted to Francisco Pizarro in 1537. Ink and pigment on paper. Casa de Alba, Madrid. The arms combine traditional heraldic imagery with the *mascaypacha* (*top left*), the red tassel that denotes kingship among the Inca.

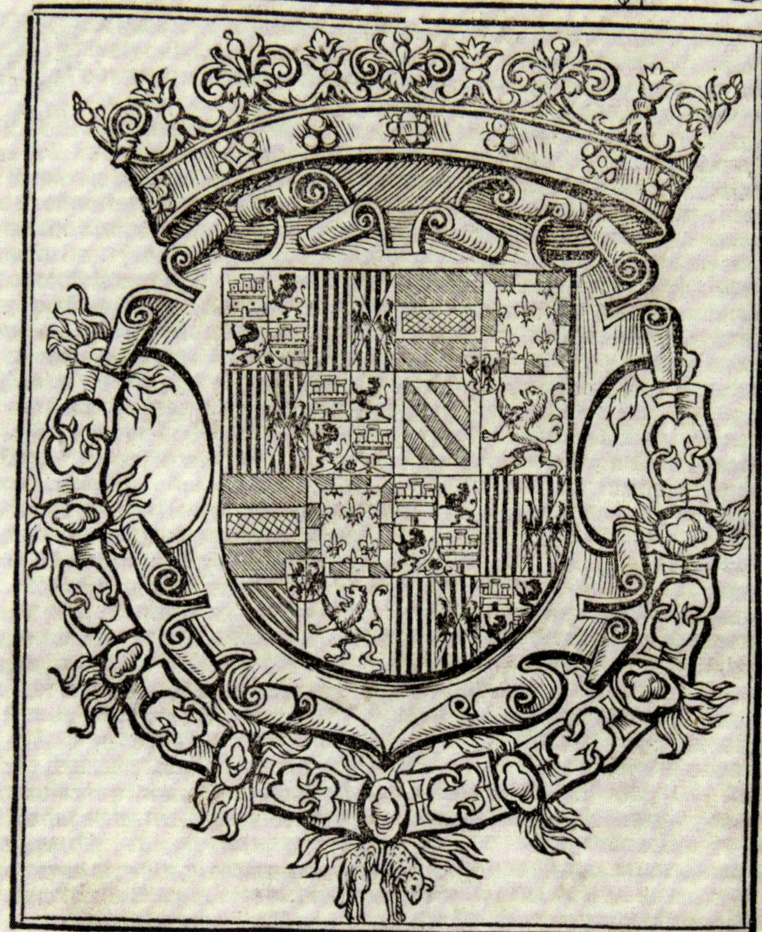

PARTE PRIMERA

Dela chronica del Peru. Que tracta la demarcacion de sus prouincias: la descripcion dellas. Las fundaciones de las nueuas ciudades. Los ritos y costumbres de los indios. Y otras cosas estrañas dignas de ser sabidas. Fecha por Pedro d Cieça de Leon vezino de Seuilla.

1553.

Con priuillegio Real.

CHAPTER 6

Recouping Spanish Cuzco

Cieza de León and the Civil Wars of Spanish Peru

While Hernando and Gonzalo Pizarro were defending Cuzco against Manco and his allies, a young Spaniard who had recently arrived in the Americas was wending his way through the natural and political landscapes of Castilla del Oro, the region extending from Panama eastward along the southern rim of the Caribbean through the northernmost territories of modern Colombia and Venezuela. Pedro de Cieza de León, from Llerena, in southeastern Extremadura, had arrived in the Americas in 1535. His interest in Peru had been sparked by a remarkable scene he witnessed in Seville, when Hernando Pizarro arrived there with a flotilla of ships laden with gold and silver from the Andes. Like many of his contemporaries, he imagined he would find his own treasure in Peru, and so he crossed the Atlantic, eventually arriving at the Caribbean port of Santo Domingo and continuing onward to Cartagena, on the northern coast of what is today Colombia.

FIG. 6.1 (*facing page*) Title page of Pedro de Cieza de León, *Parte primera de la Crónica del Perú* (Seville: Martín de Montesdoca, 1553). Woodcut, ink on paper. Newberry Library, Chicago. The image shows the arms of Charles V, Holy Roman Emperor, thereby setting the chronicle within a global and imperial context.

In the years that followed, Cieza de León took part in a number of expeditions in Castilla del Oro. He attached himself to powerful Spaniards, including Pedro de Heredía (d. 1555) and Jorge Robledo (d. 1546), the founders of several towns in the region. He was present at some of those foundations, and for his service he was later awarded a sizable and profitable *encomienda*—a grant of native labor—near the town of Arma, south of Medellín.[1] He also connected with Sebastián de Benalcázar (d. 1551), a longtime associate of Francisco Pizarro who had received a sizable share of gold and silver at Cajamarca before heading northward to stake claims to territory and treasure in the vicinity of Quito. In the mid-1540s, Cieza de León joined Benalcázar as he and his cohort turned south to engage in the conflicts that have come to be known as the "civil wars" of Spanish Peru, a series of bloody clashes among the splintered factions of Pizarro's men.[2]

Historians have seen the civil wars as watersheds in Peru's early colonial history—events signaling the end of the era of the Pizarros and the beginning of a new political order among the Spanish.[3] Cieza de León wrote at length about the conflicts in his *Crónica del Perú* (*Chronicle of Peru*; hereafter, *Crónica*), a grand literary work on the history of the Inca and the first decades of Spanish colonial rule in the Andes. He conceived of it in four parts, completing the first by 1550 and publishing it three years later in Seville as *Parte primera de la Crónica del Perú* (*First Part of the Chronicle of Peru*; hereafter, *Parte primera*). Dominating the title page is a woodcut print of the Holy Roman Emperor's coat of arms, its central shield composed of the heraldic symbols of his territorial possessions, including Castile and Leon, Aragon, Granada, Austria, Burgundy, Brabant, and Flanders (fig. 6.1). The imagery provides a sweeping geographic context for the book's contents, which recount the story of how the author and his contemporaries claimed even more territories for the Crown in the Americas. Beneath the coat of arms, several lines of text provide the volume's title and survey its main themes: "Which deals with the limits of its [Peru's] provinces, the description of them, the foundation of new cities, the rites and customs of the Indians, and other unfamiliar things worthy of being known."[4]

The *Parte primera* differs from other parts of the *Crónica* in that it was the only section to be published during its author's life. Two manuscript versions of the second volume are known: one of them, thought to be in the author's own hand, is in the Vatican Library, and an incomplete copy is in the library of the Escorial. The second volume would not appear in print until the late nineteenth century, when Marcos Jiménez de la Espada—who first published the Escorial manuscript of Betanzos's *Suma y narración*—brought it to light.[5] The third part of the *Crónica*, too, remained unpublished during Cieza's lifetime. The subject of the text—the actions of Francisco Pizarro and the events of the 1520s and 1530s in Peru—was known through the author's reference to it in the *Parte primera*, but no manuscript version was found until the 1970s, when the historian Francesca Cantù came upon a copy of it in the Vatican Library and published its first edition.[6]

The fourth part of the *Crónica* focused on the civil wars in Peru. Cieza de León conceived of it as consisting of five books, each one focusing on a particular and, in his mind, definitive battle. By the time of his death in 1554, however, he had completed only three of those books. The fourth part of the *Crónica*, like the second, did not appear in print until the nineteenth century, when it was published as three separate volumes dealing with the battles the author dubbed the "War of Las Salinas," the "War of Chupas," and the "War of Quito."[7] Manuscript versions of these texts are held in the library of the Palacio Real in Madrid as well as in those of the Hispanic Society of America and the New York Public Library.[8]

The civil wars took place in and around multiple towns in the Andes, and Cieza de León's account provides insight into those sites and the buildings and spaces where rival factions of Spaniards encountered one another. His descriptions of events taking place in Cuzco in this period are particularly revealing in that they provide a window onto the city and its infrastructure in the years after Manco's siege, when shifting alliances gave rise to shifting perspectives on its most symbolic structures. Cieza de León would not visit Cuzco until the battles had ceased, but his vivid accounts of the city and its inhabitants in this period are informed by contemporaneous documents and the reports of eyewitnesses. What becomes clear on the pages of this part of the *Crónica* is that the Spaniards in the 1540s continued to regard Cuzco as a coveted prize even as its primacy in the Kingdom of Peru was challenged by the rising status of Lima, the new seat of Spanish colonial governance.

The first of the civil wars Cieza de León chronicles is the War of Las Salinas, so called because the skirmish he saw as the key episode in this early phase of hostilities occurred on the salt flats (*salinas*) to the southeast of Cuzco's center. He did not participate in this battle, and he composed his account of it more than a decade after it had occurred. He explains, however, that he drew from the reports of informed Spaniards and native Andeans:

> In that which concerns the Spanish, I always looked for wise men, friends who speak the truth, to inform me and to receive reports on things that I myself did not see. And I took the same diligence and care with that which happened among the Indians, receiving reports from the wisest among them who have seen with their own eyes the things about which I ask them. And in much of what happened since the persistent war and siege of Cuzco, and that which I am now telling, I was fully informed by a captain of Huayna Capac named Pisca, who always personally followed Manco Inca in the siege of Cuzco, and for the rest, I was informed by a young man from the "big ear" elites who had been raised by Manco himself.[9]

Cieza de Leon's method paralleled that of Betanzos, who similarly drew upon the reports of native informants who had seen and participated in the events about which he wrote. Eyewitness reports, however, were not his only sources, for he notes that he also relied upon written records:

> In all of these things now being addressed, this history is most true, and it happened in this way. These are official statements taken from the proceedings of the scribes Domingo de la Presa and Alonso de Silva, which they recorded in that time, and they are from the original documents, which through great effort, persistence, and personal cost I have looked for and found.[10]

The author's inclusion of these two men's names is noteworthy, for it points to his efforts at accuracy and impartiality. Domingo de la Presa had been appointed as scribe to the *cabildo* of Lima at the time of its foundation, and he worked closely with Francisco Pizarro during the period about which Cieza de León writes. Alonso de Silva, who is described in the text as "escribano de Su Magestad" (scribe of His Majesty), was the notary of Diego de Almagro. The patrons of these two scribes, Pizarro and Almagro, are the central characters in Cieza de León's recounting of the War of Las Salinas.

Cieza de León sets the stage for his account with a broad claim about the unstable situation in which the Spaniards in Peru found themselves in 1537:

> The Indians still were not completely pacified, nor had the Spanish brought them entirely into their friendship, having not even laid aside those clothes, swords, and shields they used in discovering the provinces. The cities they had founded with such good fortune had neither the importance nor the adornment or the sumptuousness of buildings befitting towns made by the Spanish. The cords with which the plans of those cities had been measured were still at hand, but the plans themselves had no more importance than any other ordinary things that are the foundations for making something magnificent.[11]

The author's reference to the "plans of those cities" as material objects indicates his familiarity with the annotated grids drawn up as part of the foundation of Spanish colonial towns. He may have witnessed the production of such documents in connection with Robledo's foundation of towns in Castilla del Oro earlier in the 1530s. In this passage, the well-planned but not yet adorned city is a metaphor for what the author saw as the still incomplete project of the Spanish conquest of Peru, an undertaking complicated by the actions of the Spanish themselves, who were—he writes—"turning their arms against themselves with great cruelty and insolence."[12]

The event that ultimately led to the confrontation at Las Salinas, Cieza de León says, was the return of Almagro to Cuzco in 1537. In this, he is in agreement with Diego de Silva y Guzmán, whose report of about a decade earlier presents Almagro's return from Chile and its aftermath as a turning point in the narrative. Almagro had been close to Pizarro since the 1520s, when they both were in Panama, and more than a decade later, as we saw in Chapter 3, his name appeared at the top of the list of settlers of Cuzco at the time of its foundation. In the Distribution of Lots in Cuzco, Hernando de Soto had awarded him three prime plots just off of the plaza—more than any other resident apart from Pizarro himself. Sometime in 1535, after his expedition into the northern reaches of the Andes, Almagro headed southward for Chile, believing that he and his men would establish towns and attain great riches in those lands just as Pizarro had done in Cajamarca and Cuzco. In the end, however, his gamble paid no returns. Weary and disappointed, he and his men returned to Cuzco, insisting that he—not Francisco Pizarro—was the rightful governor of the city, and expecting to retake it. His claim was rooted in his assertion that the Crown had awarded him the governorship of Nueva Toledo, a territory south of the lands awarded to Pizarro but whose precise boundaries remained the subject of debate.

Cieza de León writes that Almagro arrived on the outskirts of Cuzco with a group of 450 men on horse and foot, a number that is close to the 500 Silva gives. Among them were many Andeans, including an Inca nobleman named Paullu who was, like Manco, one of the many sons of Huayna Capac. The Cuzco that awaited these men was in poor shape, its infrastructure damaged in the sieges of the previous year, and its political order undermined by the shifting loyalties of its citizens. Some of the city's residents, Cieza de León notes, regarded Pizarro's governance as ruinous and welcomed a change in leadership, believing "that with a new government by Almagro, their estates would be secured." "This pecuniary interest," the author adds, "is what moves the men of this land to take sides with the parties that there are in it."[13] Others, he claims, sided with Pizarro, worrying that Almagro would redistribute *encomienda* grants in Cuzco unfairly among the many Spaniards who had been with him in Chile, thus decreasing the status and income of their current holders.

By April 18, 1537, Almagro and his men had set up camp just outside the city. Francisco Pizarro likely would have obstructed Almagro's approach, but in April 1537 he was in Lima and thus could not confront his adversary directly. Continuing to act as his lieutenant in Cuzco was his brother Hernando, whom Cieza de León—like Silva—presents in a favorable light. Hernando Pizarro, the author notes, invited Almagro to enter the city and take shelter in the houses that Hernando de Soto had awarded him two years earlier. Almagro's response, as reported by Silva, attests to the symbolism the Spanish had projected onto the buildings surrounding Cuzco's plaza: "I will not enter the city," he said, "unless it is my own decision, and I will only stay in the houses where [Hernando Pizarro] is staying."[14] Hernando Pizarro, who had returned to Spain with the treasure of Cajamarca at the time of the foundation of Cuzco, was not among the recipients of lots in the distribution of October 1534, but upon his return he took possession of the lots in Amarucancha that Soto had occupied before he left Cuzco. The passage provides an example of how the buildings of Inca Cuzco had come to be associated with new ideas and values under Spanish colonial rule; the "Compound of Snakes" had become the site of the residence of the highest-ranking official in the city.

The stand-off between the two claimants to the governorship continued. Eventually, believing no other reasonable course of action was open to them, Almagro and his men entered the city. They arrived, Cieza de León notes, under cover of darkness:

> It was raining heavily, and upon arriving at the hour of two o'clock in the morning, Almagro and some of the leaders of his forces went to the church. Captain Rodrigo Orgóñez went straight to those houses where Hernando and Gonzalo Pizarro were staying with about twenty Spaniards who were allies of theirs. Captain Juan de Sayavedra, with a company of men, guarded the main street of the city, which led to the church. Captain Vasco de Guevara guarded another street that led to the Houses [*sic*] of the Sun. And 280 Spaniards, some on foot, and some on horseback, took the streets of the city.[15]

In addition to referring to the house where Hernando Pizarro was staying, Cieza de León mentions other structures in this passage: the church and the House of the Sun. He associates these buildings with streets, and in doing so reveals something of the layout of early colonial Cuzco and the way in which movement through the city occurred. The two streets referenced in the text were perpendicular, one fronting the plaza on the side where Hernando Pizarro's new houses were (labeled 7 on map 4, p. 93), and the other running from the plaza to the House of the Sun. The accounts of Cieza de León and Silva, however, do not elaborate on the events that took place on those streets or in their buildings. Rather, they focus on a scene that unfolded in Amarucancha. Hernando Pizarro, they write, had been asleep in one of its chambers when Almagro and his men entered the city. On waking, he, his brother Gonzalo, and their allies armed themselves and guarded the doors to the compound. Cieza de León describes the structure in general terms: "it was large, and with very strong walls made of stone." Silva, however, provides a more thorough description:

> The lodgings where Hernando Pizarro was were large like a church, and built in the way of the Indians, and in that wall that led into the patio it had two large portals without doors, in which Hernando Pizarro and his brother were defending themselves . . . there must have been fifteen paces between one door and the other.[16]

In this passage the phrase "built in the way of the Indians" reveals a kind of architectural connoisseurship at work, in which the author makes distinctions between different styles and construction techniques. The implication of the passage is that, for Silva, structures "built in the way of the Indians" were distinguishable from other kinds of buildings with which he was familiar.

Almagro's captain, Rodrigo Orgóñez (1490–1538), ordered Hernando Pizarro to surrender; when he did not comply, Orgóñez and his men set fire to the straw roof of the house, emulating a strategy previously employed by Manco's forces. Cieza de León describes what happened next: "The big pieces of wood that supported the house began to fall, the fire having burned all of the straw . . . [and] with a great force, the entire house came down, and all of the beams and old supports fell to the ground."[17] One cannot help but see the house's falling beams in this passage as symbolizing the besieged Hernando Pizarro's fall from power as Almagro and his men assumed control of the city.

As daylight broke, Hernando and Gonzalo Pizarro were taken prisoner and confined in the House of the Sun, where Manco had been imprisoned a year earlier. It is not clear precisely where in the House of the Sun the prisoners would have been kept, nor is it apparent whether anyone else occupied the complex at this time. Relegated to the periphery of Spanish Cuzco, the structure that had served as a temple to the Inca's supreme deity was now being used to house men regarded by at least some in the city as criminals.

As he assumed the governorship of Cuzco, Almagro called a meeting of the *cabildo*. Silva writes that the city council met with him in the church, possibly because the building originally designated for use as the city hall had been damaged in the conflicts of the previous two years. The *alcaldes* and *regidores* received Almagro as governor, though some did so, Silva notes, against their will. Almagro's rule of Cuzco was then announced by the town crier to the citizens who had gathered in the plaza. The governor appointed Paullu as principal lord, a position previously held by his brother Manco in the Cuzco of the Pizarros. "He convened many *caciques* and people both notable and common from all of the land," Silva writes, "who received him and swore an oath to him as was customary among them."[18] Neither Betanzos nor Titu Cusi Yupanqui include this episode in their account, and the question of how many native Andeans were present in Cuzco at this time is difficult to answer. It is reasonable, though, to suppose that in addition to Paullu and other native elites, there was a sizable population of other Andeans who provided labor of various sorts to the Spanish.

It was not long before Francisco Pizarro, who was still in Lima, received word of his brothers' imprisonment. Hoping to gain their freedom, he sent three emissaries to visit Almagro in Cuzco and come to an agreement over the limits of their respective jurisdictions and the governance of the city. The emissaries, Cieza de León notes, arrived there on August 8, 1537; they met with Almagro and visited the imprisoned Pizarro brothers in the House of the Sun, but they could not reach an agreement on matters of jurisdiction and governance, and they left by the end of the month. A few weeks later, Almagro took it upon himself to address the dispute, traveling to Lima to negotiate with Francisco Pizarro in person. He took Hernando Pizarro with him, leaving Gonzalo and some of his allies in prison, and named Gabriel de Rojas, a former Pizarro ally, as his lieutenant.

The Almagro party plodded through the Andes to the coast, where they founded a town in the Chincha Valley, some 200 km (124 mi.) to the south of Lima near the present-day town of Chincha. Cieza de León notes that the town was named for Almagro, who fulfilled his role as founder by appointing *alcaldes* and *regidores*, and ordering the erection of a *picota* in the town square. Over the next few weeks, negotiations between Almagro and Pizarro proceeded, and eventually both men agreed that their dispute should be mediated by a third party: Friar Francisco de Bobadilla, the provincial head of the Order of Our Lady of Mercy.

Bobadilla's order, the Mercedarians, were newcomers to Peru, but they had a long and illustrious history in medieval Spain. Founded in the thirteenth century, they took as their mission the ransoming of Christians held captive by Muslims on the Iberian Peninsula. Three centuries later, a small number of Mercedarian friars participated in campaigns of exploration and the conquest of territory in the Americas. The order's involvement in those projects demonstrates ways in which piety and the quest for treasure interrelated: in theory, the riches of the New World would provide the Mercedarians with funds to be used in ransoming Christians. The order established a monastery in Santo Domingo very early in the 1500s, and among the first friars in residence there was Bartolomé de Olmedo, who would accompany Hernán Cortés into Aztec Mexico in 1519.

For his part, Friar Bobadilla had been in the Americas for perhaps two decades by the time he was asked to mediate in the dispute between Pizarro and Almagro. He had founded a number of monasteries in the region, including one in the city of Panama, and had returned to Spain twice in the 1520s and 1530s, promoting his order's interests to the Crown and recruiting friars to fill new monasteries in the Americas. Pizarro must have known him in his early years in Castilla del Oro with Pedrarias Dávila, with whom Bobadilla, too, was closely allied, and his willingness to accept the friar as the mediator in the dispute with Almagro may have stemmed from this long-standing association. In light of this, Almagro's acceptance of Bobadilla as the mediator seems foolish, but his decision may relate to his own relationship with the order, which was also close. When he undertook his campaign of exploration into Chile, two Mercedarian friars accompanied him as chaplains: Antonio de Almansa and Antonio de Solís.[19]

As he began his investigation into the dispute between Pizarro and Almagro, Bobadilla interviewed six expert navigators in order to determine into whose jurisdiction Cuzco truly fell. Cieza de León records their testimonies, which presented evidence based upon their own calculations. The witnesses were not unanimous, but on November 15, 1537, Bobadilla ruled in favor of Pizarro. Almagro, however, did not accept Bobadilla's judgment. Refusing to turn over either the city of Cuzco or the captive Hernando Pizarro, he instead sought to continue negotiations with Francisco Pizarro on his own. Pizarro agreed to this, presumably in the hope of gaining his brother's freedom. Discussions between the two men progressed, and eventually they reached a surprising agreement: Almagro would retain control of Cuzco without any opposition and, in exchange, he would release Hernando Pizarro to his brother in Lima.

Francisco Pizarro signed off on this arrangement, but, as Cieza de León observes, he did so purely in the interest of expediency, and had no intention of abiding by its terms. With the new pact and the related documents approved by both parties, Almagro released Hernando Pizarro as promised. In the meantime, Gonzalo Pizarro and his allies had escaped from their imprisonment in Cuzco and had made their way to the coast; shortly thereafter, the three reunited Pizarro brothers devised a plot to defeat Almagro and retake Cuzco. As an early salvo in this conflict, they sent word to their adversary that, in spite of the agreement that had been signed, they expected him to recognize Pizarro as the governor of Cuzco, as Bobadilla had determined. Pizarro's message to Almagro was not well received, and the two sides, Cieza de León writes, prepared to fight:

> War was now declared in a way that everyone understood it, and with such cruelty and fervor between the two sides . . . and each of the two factions was working to overtake and vanquish the other, the perpetrators of these seditions claiming to rule and govern these kingdoms themselves, and doing it with little fear of God, ordering that war be proclaimed in public, forming camps and displaying banners, and waging war with such severity as if one side were Venetians and the others Genoese, or if they were Turks and Spaniards.[20]

It is not clear which side Cieza de León was equating with Turks and which with Spaniards, but the passage follows in the tradition of Pedro Sancho and Silva in situating the fight for Cuzco in the broader context of battles for control around the Mediterranean.

Ready for battle, both the Pizarro camp and the Almagro camp left the coast for Cuzco, the latter arriving first, though their leader—Cieza de León writes—was gravely ill. In Cuzco, the Almagrists imprisoned many of the Pizarros' supporters, presumably in the House of the Sun. Silva notes that Almagro's allies also offered payments in gold and silver to those who would side with them, and he provides a fascinating detail about the men's use of those precious metals in preparing for battle: "They all occupied themselves with making corselets of silver and helmets and armbands and all of the rest, so well and no less strong than if they were from Milan . . . In this way the people looked as splendid as soldiers raised in Lombardy."[21] These references to Lombardy, like those to the Venetians and Genoese, and to the Turks and Spaniards, show just how deeply the story of events in sixteenth-century Peru had come to be embedded in a broader set of narratives for Cieza de León and some of his contemporaries. At the same time, those tales of warfare and conquest were mapping an expansionist image of the world that extended the storied empire of Charles V into the Americas.

Hearing of Hernando Pizarro's approach to Cuzco, Almagro's men resolved to meet him and his troops outside the city. They set out to engage their adversaries at Las Salinas, in the vicinity of the present-day parish and church of San Sebastián, just to the east of the city center. The location was important to the Inca as it was the site of Cachipuquiu, a salt spring regarded as a *huaca*.[22] Cieza de León, however, presents the site in functional rather than symbolic terms, the plains near the spring constituting

FIG. 6.2 Artist unknown, *Cuzco during the Earthquake of 1650*, after 1650. Oil on canvas, 33.4 × 46.2 cm (detail). Church of El Triunfo, Cuzco. This is the earliest known image of the church of La Merced, where Diego de Almagro's body was buried after his execution.

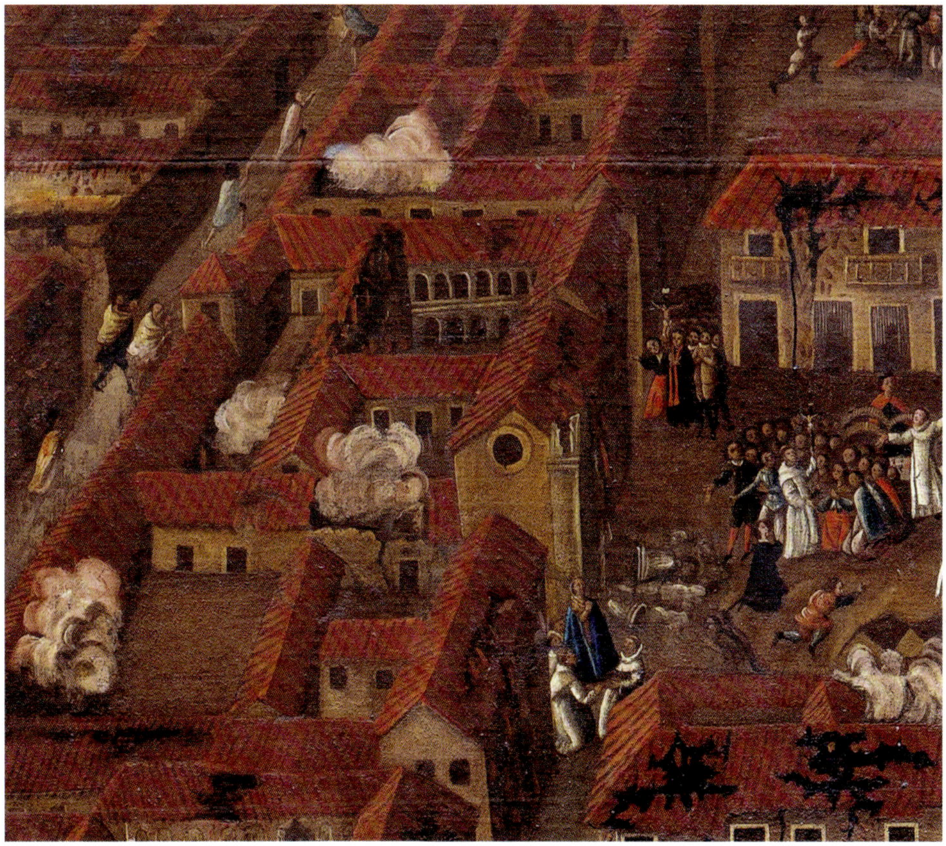

little more than an open field for battle. The War of Las Salinas, he writes, occurred on the Saturday of St. Lazarus, 1538, a few days before Easter, when the Gospel text on Jesus Christ's raising of Lazarus from the grave would have been read at Mass. In 1538, that date fell in early April. Hernando Pizarro led his troops, which Cieza de León claims consisted of 700 Spaniards and their native porters. Surveying the battle from the surrounding hills, he says, were many native Andeans, including the wives of the chiefs and other women who were servants of the Spaniards.[23] For those spectators, and, indeed, for some of the participants in the battle, the site's importance in the sacred landscape of the Inca would not have gone unnoticed.

Cieza de León's account of the battle is vivid, relating in detail the deaths of notable men and their horses, and highlighting the dominance of Pizarro's forces. In a decisive act, one of Pizarro's men beheaded Orgóñez on the battlefield as Almagro—watching from a nearby hilltop and realizing his troops had been defeated—retreated to a tower at Sacsahuaman. The entire conflict at Las Salinas, Cieza de León writes, lasted little more than two hours, after which time the victorious Pizarrists entered Cuzco. Hernando Pizarro ordered that the decapitated head of Orgóñez be brought from the battlefield into the city and placed on the *picota*, perhaps the same one his brother Francisco had set up four years earlier. Almagro, too, was captured and brought into the city. He was imprisoned and condemned to death for his unlawful seizure of Cuzco, and, in early July, he was killed by garrote, the same method of execution used on Atahualpa. His corpse was taken to the plaza and the town crier announced his death; on arriving at the *picota*, the author notes, the bearers cut off his head, which was then displayed with that of Orgóñez. His body was shrouded, and later it was taken to the monastery of Our Lady of Mercy (La Merced), where it was buried.[24]

Silva's account of Almagro's burial in the monastery of the Mercedarian Order is an early reference to that institution in the sixteenth-century sources. Founded in 1537 by

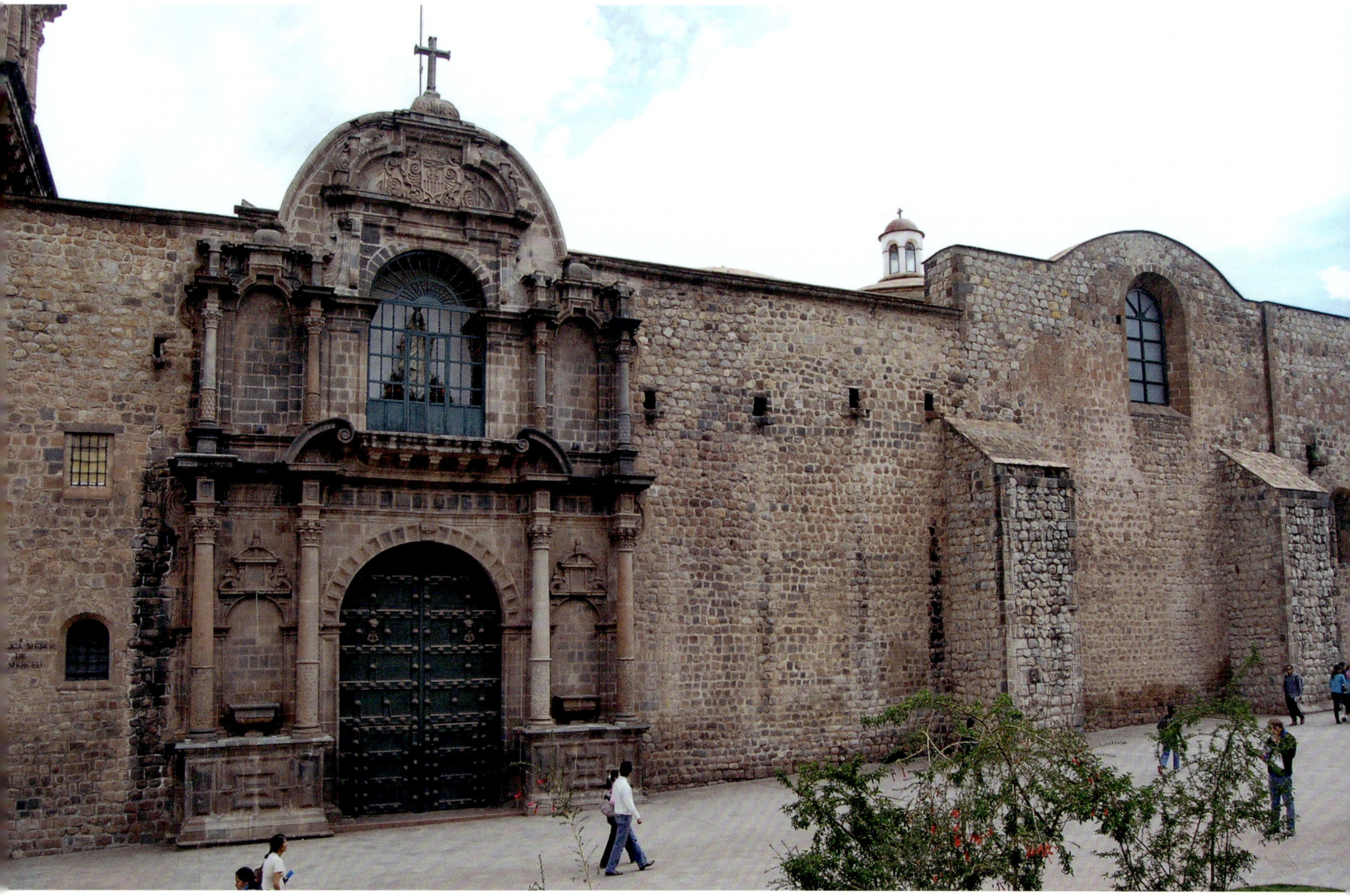

FIG. 6.3 The entrance to the monastery of La Merced, Cuzco, after 1650. The monastery was rebuilt after the 1650 earthquake, its portal employing classical architectural forms and resembling an altarpiece.

a small group of friars, it occupied a structure just south of the main plaza. The appearance of that early complex, however, remains the subject of speculation. The earliest known surviving visual image of it appears in the painting of Cuzco at the time of the earthquake of 1650, where it is shown as a single-nave church with a crumbling bell tower flanking two courtyards (fig. 6.2). That configuration echoes that of the building standing on the site today (fig. 6.3). Rebuilt in the second half of the seventeenth century, the Mercedarian portal resembles a *retablo* with two stories, its ground level dominated by an arched passage into the nave of the church. Like the cathedral's portal, that of the church of La Merced is flanked by columns with Corinthian capitals and niches and is topped by a heavy cornice. On the upper level, columns and other ornamental forms frame a deep balcony, a space used for the ritual of the Mass when it was performed for those gathered in the plaza in front of it.[25]

With the victory at Las Salinas, control of Cuzco was once again in the hands of Francisco Pizarro, who had remained in Lima. When he received word of his brothers' victory, he left for the highlands, arriving in Cuzco several months later. Also arriving in Cuzco around this time was Vicente de Valverde, who had returned to Peru after spending several years in Spain, during which time he had been appointed bishop of Cuzco. In a letter to Charles V dated 1539, he vividly recounts his impressions of the city:

> I attest to Your Majesty that if I did not remember the site of this city, I would not recognize it, at least by its buildings and surrounding villages. Because when Governor Francisco Pizarro entered here, and I entered with him, this valley was so beautiful in its buildings and the settlements it had in its surroundings that it was an amazing thing to see. Because although the city in itself had no more than three or four thousand buildings, it had in its surroundings fifteen or twenty thousand of them almost in sight. The fortress that was above the city seemed from one side to be a very grand fortress like those in Spain. Now, the better part of the city is completely demolished and burned. The fortress has almost nothing standing. All of the towns in the surrounding area have nothing but walls. It is a wonder to find a building still standing. The thing that gave me the most contentment in this city was the church, which, for the Indies, is a very good one. Although for the riches had in this land it could be more like the temple of Solomon than what it is now.[26]

Valverde's lament on the state of Cuzco when he arrived there in 1538 is noteworthy for its references to the city's "demolished and burned" buildings and to Sacsahuaman as one of the city's defining features, a sentiment he shared with Sancho and Silva. His admiration for the church, however, signals the letter's subtext: an appeal for resources to improve the places of worship he was to administer as bishop. He notes that there were seven such churches, placing that of Cuzco first in his list, and referring to it as "the holy church cathedral of Our Lady of the Rosary."[27] This is the church's third Marian dedication in the early sources, the other two being Our Lady of the Annunciation (Pizarro's identification at the Act of Foundation) and Our Lady of the Immaculate Conception (Soto's identification in the Distribution of Lots); it is also significant that Valverde refers to the building as a "cathedral," a designation it has retained right up to the present. Valverde's revision underscores his identification with the Dominican Order, whose friars were especially devoted to Our Lady of the Rosary; it also suggests that changes in the church's size and ecclesiastical status were understood to mark new episodes in its history, turning points significant enough to call for the building's rededication.

It was two years later that Charles V, who had been kept apprised of affairs in Peru through reports sent by colonial officials, issued a decree from Madrid declaring Cuzco the most important (*más principal*) of the cities in New Castile and granting it the first vote in matters concerning the Kingdom of Peru. With that, Cuzco's status as a city of rank was solidified, and its value as a trophy in the civil wars increased in spite of the sad state of its infrastructure as described by Valverde. In recognition of Cuzco's status, the king awarded it a coat of arms whose imagery referenced its recent history. The arms displayed a golden castle on a red field "in remembering that the said city and its castle were conquered by force of arms in Our service." The image of the castle was bordered, the text of the award continues,

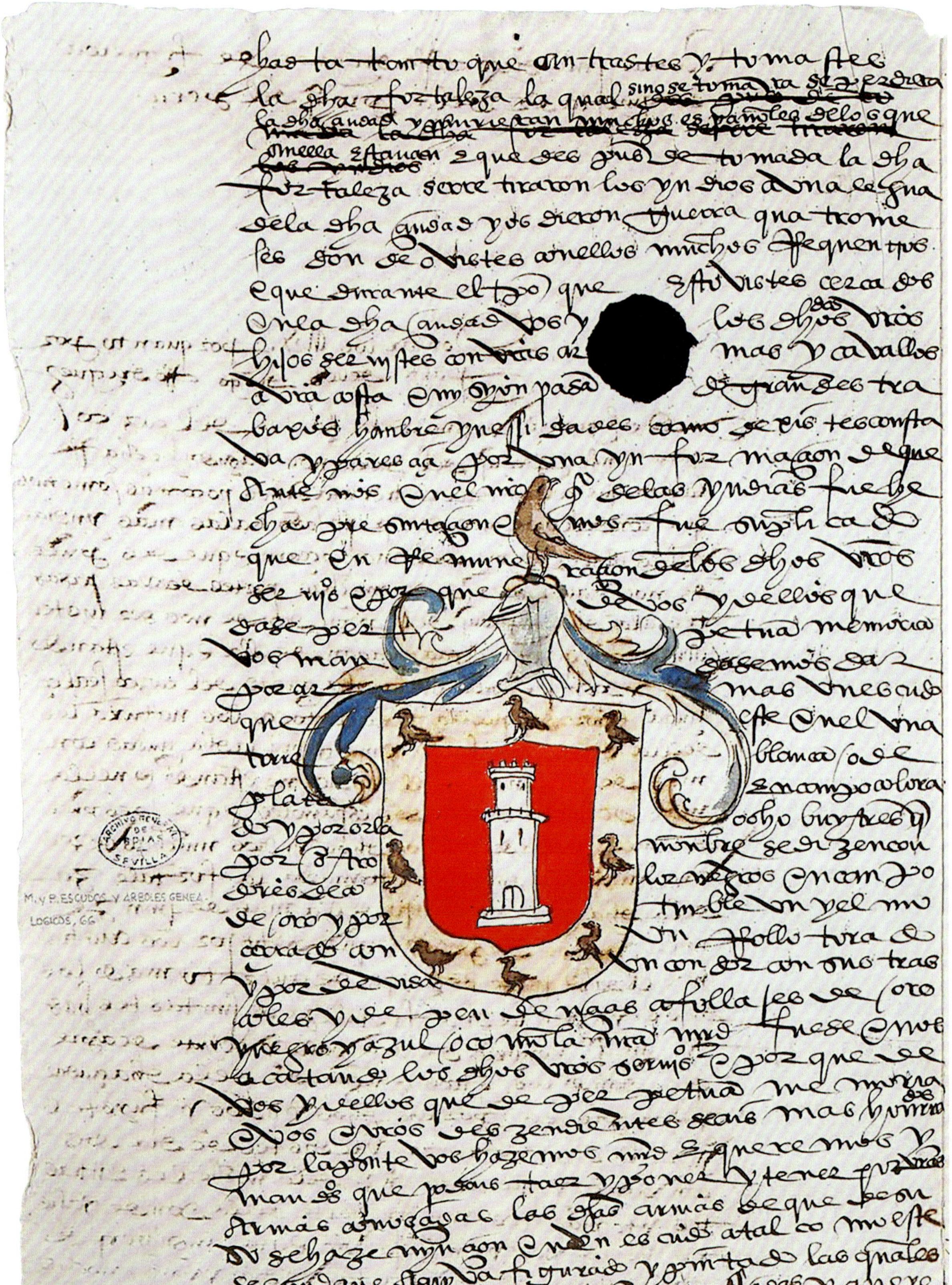
ARCHIVO GENERAL DE INDIAS SEVILLA
M. y P. ESCUDOS Y ARBOLES GENEALOGICOS, 66

with "eight condors that are great birds, resembling vultures, that they have in the province of Peru, as a reminder that at the time this city was won, these birds descended to eat the dead that died there."[28] The golden castle mentioned in the grant calls to mind the tower at Sacsahuaman as well as the gilded House of the Sun in the earliest descriptions of Cuzco. No contemporary image of this coat of arms has yet been found, but the description suggests it resembled the one awarded to Diego Rodríguez de Figueroa, a citizen and defender of Cuzco in the siege of 1536–37 (fig. 6.4).[29]

Among the first actions Pizarro undertook in Cuzco as he reclaimed his governorship was to order his brother Hernando to return to Spain once more with the king's fifth of gold and a set of documents to be presented as evidence against Almagro. He did so, arriving in Seville and presenting his case to the Royal Council of the Indies, the administrative body that managed affairs in the Americas. His case may have been compelling, but his timing was imperfect. Some of Almagro's partisans had arrived in Seville before him and had convinced the council and Crown that the Pizarro brothers' treatment of their patron had been unjust. An unsympathetic Council of the Indies ordered that Hernando be sent to Medina del Campo and imprisoned at La Mota, an imposing hilltop castle whose crenellated walls and tall tower must have called to mind the fortress of Sacsahuaman (fig. 6.5).[30] He would remain imprisoned there for twenty years—outliving all his brothers—before, on his release in 1561, retiring to his hometown of Trujillo.

Meanwhile, Francisco Pizarro had slowly made his way from Cuzco back to Lima. His journey, too, would come to an unfortunate end. Almagro's allies in Lima had been plotting to overthrow him, and in Lima on June 26, 1541 a group of them forced their way into his house and killed him. Of the four Pizarro brothers who came to Peru, only Gonzalo remained there in the final months of 1541. It was around this time that Almagro's loyalists decided their slain leader's son, also named Diego, should be recognized as the new governor of Peru. The young Almagro, however, would have a serious challenger in a distinguished recent arrival to Peru: Cristóbal Vaca de Castro (*c.* 1492–1571). A well-connected man of considerable means and reputation, Vaca de Castro had served as a judge on the royal *audiencia* (court) in Valladolid, a key center of power in Charles V's Spain. In the wake of reports of unrest in Peru, the Council of the Indies charged him with investigating and arbitrating the disputes between the factions respectively aligned with Pizarro and Almagro.[31] Vaca de Castro accepted the post, departing from the Spanish port of Sanlúcar de Barrameda in August 1540 and arriving some months later on the island of Hispaniola. From there he made his way to Panama and, eventually, to Quito. He carried a royal decree stipulating that if Pizarro should die, he himself was authorized to assume the governorship of Peru. With Pizarro's murder, he had a legitimate claim to that office. Pizarro's allies recognized this, and some of them quickly sided with him.[32]

Vaca de Castro arrived in Lima in 1542 and met with the city councilors, who were plotting against the young Almagro. It was in this period that he became acquainted with Juan de Betanzos, who would serve as his interpreter.[33] He left Lima, taking Betanzos with him, and made his way into the Andes to confront Almagro, who had been gathering men and arms in Cuzco. In mid-September 1542, the adversaries confronted each other on the outskirts of Huamanga, about halfway between the coast and Cuzco, at a place Cieza de León calls "Chupas." The native peoples of the region, he writes, "were delighted at seeing the spectacle of Spaniards fighting against each other without having any reasonable quarrel and gave thanks to the Sun for the glorious revenge about to be taken for the ills that had been inflicted on their elders."[34] His account emphasizes the death of notable participants on both sides, among them Pedro de Candía, and tells how, in the end, the supporters of Vaca de Castro succesfully defeated the Almagro party.

Many of Almagro's men were slain in the battle, but Almagro himself survived and returned to Cuzco. His intention, writes Cieza de León, was to gain protection from Manco, who was still in Vitcos but whom Almagro viewed as a potential ally. Vaca de Castro, too, made his way to Cuzco, arriving there with great fanfare. "A solemn

FIG. 6.4 (*facing page*) The coat of arms granted to Diego Rodríguez de Figueroa, citizen of Cuzco, in 1540. Ink and pigment on paper. Archivo General de Indias, Seville. The arms resemble those granted to the City of Cuzco in 1540 to mark its status as the principal city in the Kingdom of Peru.

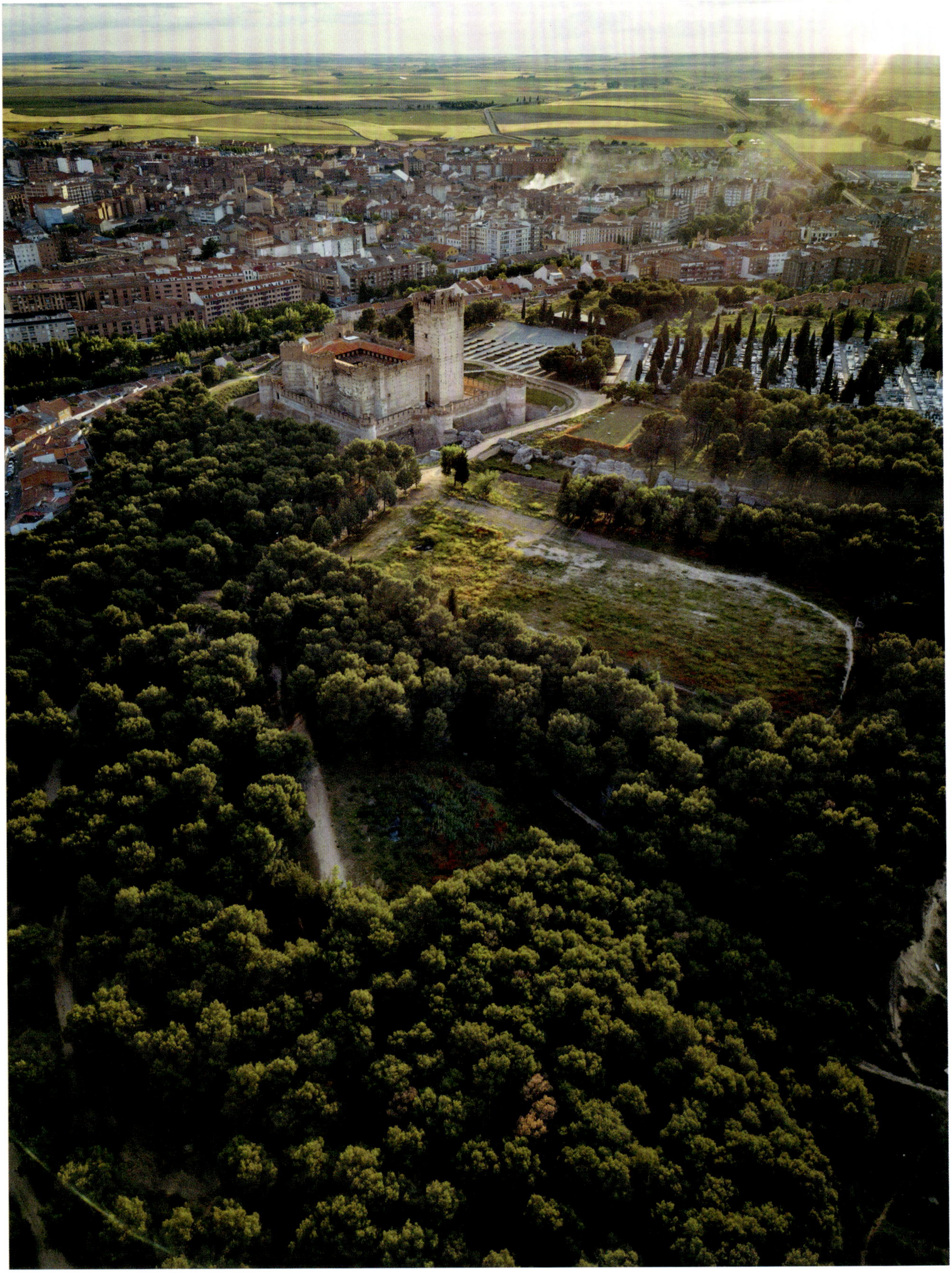

reception was accorded him," notes Cieza de León, "and he was welcomed by all the people with great joy."[35] The text offers little more commentary on the new governor's ceremonial entrance into the city, but it is described more fully in a *relación* penned by an unidentified author in Cuzco sometime in the 1540s and held today in the Archivo del Abadía del Sacromonte de Granada.[36] That text indicates that Vaca de Castro entered the city on November 11, 1542, passing through triumphal arches decorated with flowers, and finally arriving at the ceremony's showpiece: a temporary construction in the form of a castle, in reference to the symbol on Cuzco's coat of arms. There, a child dressed as an angel presented him with the keys to the city. The ceremony continued with the governor's procession into the plaza and, finally, his arrival at the monastery of La Merced, where a celebratory banquet ensued.[37]

Vaca de Castro's ceremonial entry into Cuzco is the earliest documented event of its type in Spanish colonial Peru. Formal entries of rulers into their cities have a long history extending into classical antiquity, and Holy Roman Emperor Charles V himself was the central participant in a number of them. In later years, similarly choreographed entries would take place in Lima, but the fanfare with which Vaca de Castro entered Cuzco points to the primacy of that city at the time. The splendor of the event also set the tone for his subsequent behavior as the new governor. Cieza de León is sharply critical of his conduct in Cuzco, writing that "he became inflated with vanity to a degree quite unsuitable to his station. He ordered there be many gentlemen in his house to attend him as courtiers, and with them he spent money splendidly, having grand sideboards with fine silver and tall candlesticks."[38] He made public displays of his power in other ways, too. Among his first official acts in Cuzco was to condemn the young Almagro—who had never gained Manco's support, and had instead been imprisoned—to death. Cieza de León describes the execution:

> Being taken from the prison, the crier walked in front, saying "this is the judgment his Majesty the Emperor, our Lord, and the Governor Vaca de Castro in his name, orders for this man as a usurper of royal justice, and for having tyrannically rebelled and given battle to the royal standard," and other things about what had been done by him and his followers. And going toward the pillory, next to which stood together an attendant and an executioner ready to kill him, he begged to die in the place where his father had been killed and to be buried in the tomb where his [father's] body was, and that they put him underneath and then put his father's bones above him.[39]

Close to the time of Vaca de Castro's ceremonial entrance and the execution of young Almagro, Charles V issued a set of ordinances for governance in the Americas that would upturn the political order in Peru once more. Issued in Barcelona on November 20, 1542, and known as the *Leyes nuevas* (*New Laws*), they stipulated that the Kingdom of Peru would be ruled not by a governor on the model of Pizarro or Vaca de Castro, but instead by a viceroy, a man appointed by the Crown to serve as the king's personal representative in distant parts of his empire. This system of governance had been operative on the Iberian Peninsula for centuries and in New Spain since 1535, when Charles V appointed Antonio de Mendoza to that office, designating Mexico City as the seat of governance. The viceroyalties of Peru and New Spain thus joined those of Naples, Sicily, Sardinia, Valencia, Catalonia, Navarre, and Aragon in a composite empire whose far-flung provinces were overseen by men drawn from the ranks of the Spanish nobility. The *Leyes nuevas* further stipulated that in Peru, as in the other viceroyalties, justice was to be administered by the *audiencia*, a high court of royally appointed judges overseen by the viceroy. The actions of the *audiencia* of Peru were to be modeled on those of the peninsular *audiencias* of Granada and Valladolid, and the body would be one of four such courts in the Americas, the others being those of New Spain, Guatemala, and Hispaniola. In effect, the *Leyes nuevas* not only situated the Americas within the broader political geography of Charles V's kingdoms, but also divided the American provinces into legal jurisdictions with

FIG. 6.5 (*facing page*) La Mota, Medina del Campo, Spain. Hernando Pizarro was imprisoned in this hilltop castle for twenty years as a result of bitter Spanish factionalism in Peru and disagreements over who should rule Cuzco.

territorial limits. It is with the issue of these laws that the entity known as the Viceroyalty of Peru came into being.[40]

Cieza de León transcribes the *Leyes nuevas* in his volume on the War of Chupas, and a reading of them reveals the profound impact they would have on Cuzco, its governance, and its residents.[41] They stipulated, for example, that the *audiencia* of Peru was to be physically based in the City of the Kings—that is, Lima—rather than in the ancient capital of the Inca. This declaration effectively demoted Cuzco from its position as the principal city in the Kingdom of Peru. Other passages addressed the rights of native peoples in ways that impinged upon the practices and incomes of Spaniards in America. The Crown decreed, for example, that no native person may be made a slave, that they must not be ordered to carry heavy loads, that their lives must not be endangered through the practices of pearl fishing, and, perhaps most significantly for Spaniards in Cuzco, that *encomiendas* (grants of native labor) were to revert to the control of the Crown at the death of the holder, rather than being transferred to his heirs.

Following his proclamation of the *Leyes nuevas*, Charles V appointed Blasco Núñez Vela (*c.* 1490–1546) to serve as the first viceroy of Peru and president of its *audiencia*. Núñez Vela, who was born to a titled aristocratic family in Ávila, had previously served as a royal appointee in Malaga, where he held the position of *corregidor*, a royal administrator representing the Crown's legal interests at the local level.[42] Together with the four newly appointed judges of the *audiencia* he set sail from Sanlúcar de Barrameda on November 3, 1543, arriving at the Caribbean port of Nombre de Dios about two months later. From there, he and his retinue continued to Panama, then to Tumbes and San Miguel, retracing the route taken by Pizarro two decades earlier, and illustrating how the Inca system of roads and way stations facilitated movement through the landscape of sixteenth-century Peru.

As Núñez Vela was traversing the lands over which he would rule, the ordinances he was charged with enforcing were being disseminated in print throughout the Americas. The text was first published in Alcalá de Henares in 1543, its title page bearing an elaborate coat of arms of Charles V, surpassing in detail that which would appear on the title page of Cieza de León's *Crónica del Perú* a decade later (fig. 6.6). The ordinances eventually arrived in Cuzco, where Vaca de Castro ordered the *cabildo* to review them. In his recounting of this episode, Cieza de León indicates that the *alcaldes* and *regidores* did not react positively to the *Leyes nuevas*, insisting that Cuzco rather than Lima should be the principal city of Peru and the place from which the other towns were governed. The *cabildo* also rejected the decree that *encomienda* could revert to the Crown. In an attempt to halt the enforcement of the laws, Vaca de Castro left Cuzco and, accompanied by a well-armed party of citizens, set out for Lima, where he intended to confer with the viceroy.[43]

When word of the promulgation of the *Leyes nuevas* reached Gonzalo Pizarro, who was now in Chaqui, just east of the newly discovered silver mines at Potosí, he, too, took action. "He was much agitated," Cieza de León writes, reporting that Pizarro immediately began gathering men and financial resources with which to resist the viceroy. He traveled north to Cuzco and then west to Lima, arriving in late October 1544. There, he found a principal city without a leader. Núñez Vela had imprisoned Vaca de Castro, appointed new military officers, and ordered the death of some of his most vocal detractors. In response, the *audiencia* had arrested the viceroy, taken him prisoner, and expelled him from the city. They appointed Gonzalo Pizarro as governor and captain general of the Kingdom, and thus, ten years after the foundation of Cuzco, a member of the Pizarro family was once again the political leader of Peru.[44]

From his post in Vitcos, Manco had been following the turbulent state of affairs in Cuzco and Lima through notices brought to him by messengers. By 1544, the young Titu

FIG. 6.6 (*facing page*) Title page of *Leyes y ordenanças nuevamente hechas* . . . (Alcalá de Henares: Joan de Brocar, 1543). Woodcut, ink on paper. John Carter Brown Library, Providence, RI. These ordinances, promulgated by Charles V (whose arms appear on the title page) in 1542, formally instituted the Viceroyalty of Peru and promoted Lima above Cuzco as the principal city.

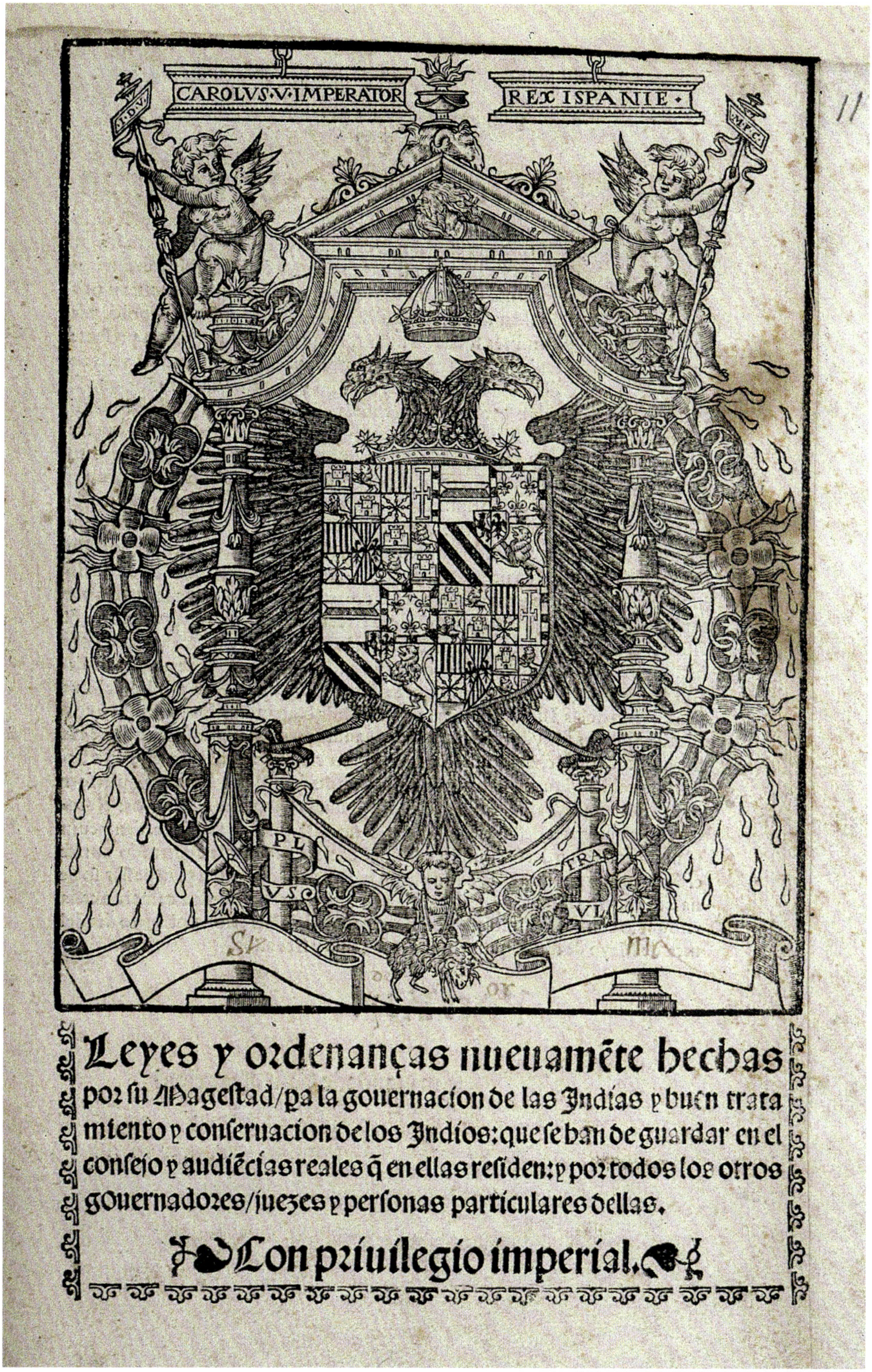

Leyes y ordenanças nueuamẽte hechas por su Magestad/ pa la gouernacion de las Indias y buen tratamiento y conseruacion delos Indios: que se han de guardar en el consejo y audiẽcias reales q̃ en ellas residen: y por todos los otros gouernadores/ juezes y personas particulares dellas.

Con priuilegio imperial.

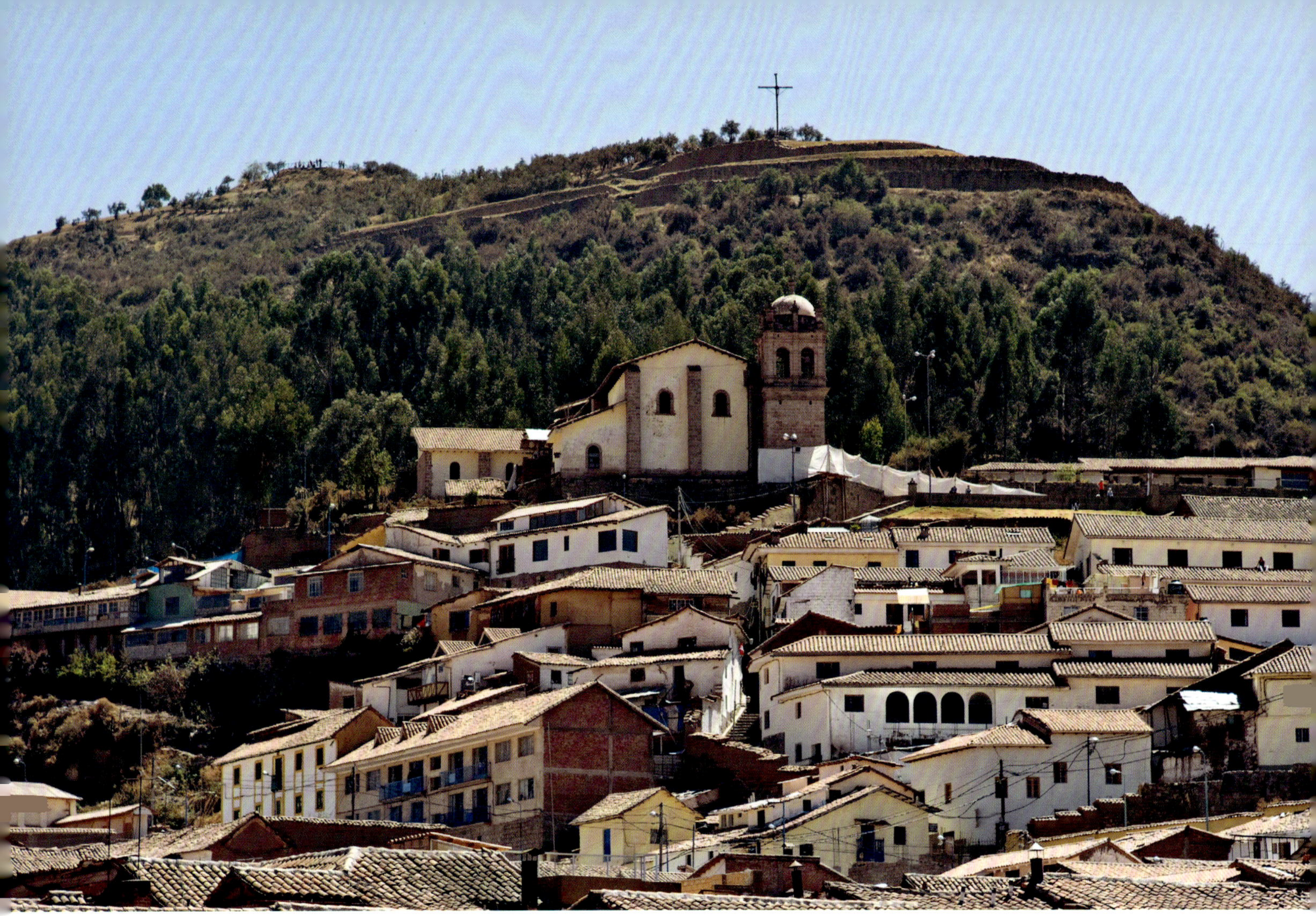

FIG. 6.7 The church of San Cristóbal, Cuzco (*center*). The church stands on the likely site of a residential complex belonging to Cristóbal Paullu, an Inca nobleman who adopted Spanish modes of living and enjoyed high status in early colonial Cuzco.

Cusi Yupanqui was there with his father, and in recounting that period he describes his father's camaraderie with a group of Almagro's allies who had fled to Vitcos, saying that Manco treated them "as if they had been his own brothers." Eventually, however, that relationship took a tragic turn:

> One day, [the Spaniards] were delighting greatly in playing a game of quoits [*herrón*] with just my father and me, when I was a boy . . . and in this game, as I said, as my father was going to pick up the quoit to play, they charged on him with daggers and knives and some swords, and my father, as he felt himself wounded, tried with deadly fury to defend himself on one side and the other, and since he was alone and they were seven, and my father had no weapon, they finally threw him to the ground with many wounds. They left him for dead.[45]

Betanzos, too, recounts the story of Manco's murder during the fateful game of quoits, adding that a group of his native allies eventually killed the Spaniards who had conspired against him and named one of his sons, Saire Topa Yupanqui, as his successor.[46] Titu Cusi Yupanqui, however, tells a different story, omitting any reference to Saire Topa Yupanqui and maintaining that, as his father was dying, he had ordered the native peoples of Vitcos to respect and honor him, Titu Cusi Yupanqui, as their lord since he was Manco's firstborn son and, thus, heir to his kingdom. Titu Cusi Yupanqui soon left Vitcos and settled nearby in the city of Vilcabamba, where he would preside over a community of native Andeans who resisted and sought refuge from Spanish colonial rule for decades.[47]

Paullu, who had entered Cuzco with Almagro the elder in 1537, pursued a very different strategy in his dealings with the Spanish. He fought in the Battle of Chupas, siding with the Pizarros, and in March 1543 he was baptized in Cuzco's main church, taking the name Cristóbal to honor his sponsor, Vaca de Castro. Cuzco's church was also the setting for his marriage to his wife, a descendant of the ruler Inca Roca, who had taken the Christian name Catalina. Like the elite Spanish men in Cuzco, he lived with his wife, dressed in fine velvet clothing, and rode on horseback. He also had a private chapel built as part of his residential complex, which was at or near the site on which the parish church of San Cristóbal would be built, on the hillside to the northwest of the plaza (fig. 6.7).[48] In his public actions and appearance, he aligned himself as much with royal appointees and Cuzco's *alcaldes* and *regidores* as he did with other native elites.

The newly converted and outfitted Cristóbal Paullu was one of a number of native Andeans who would adopt Spanish customs as means of engaging with Spanish colonial administrators and reaping the benefits available to them. One of those benefits was his enduring status as a native lord; another was an *encomienda*, which Vaca de Castro awarded him shortly after his baptism. Paullu's religious conversion and his adoption of a new name and new clothing occurred in concert with changes in the city: the festival plaza of the Inca had been recovered by the Spanish and was now the setting for the proclamation of laws, the assemblage of armed men, and the display of decapitated heads; an Inca festival hall overlooking the plaza was being used as a church, the setting for baptisms and marriages of native Andeans and Spaniards alike; the Caxana and Amarucancha compounds had become the houses of Spanish governors and their lieutenants; and the House of the Sun was used as a prison. Ten years after the foundation of Spanish Cuzco, such appropriation of the buildings and spaces of the Inca city paved the way for more intrusive interventions in the urban fabric as the last of the Pizarro brothers in Peru fought to retain control of Cuzco and the other towns in the region.

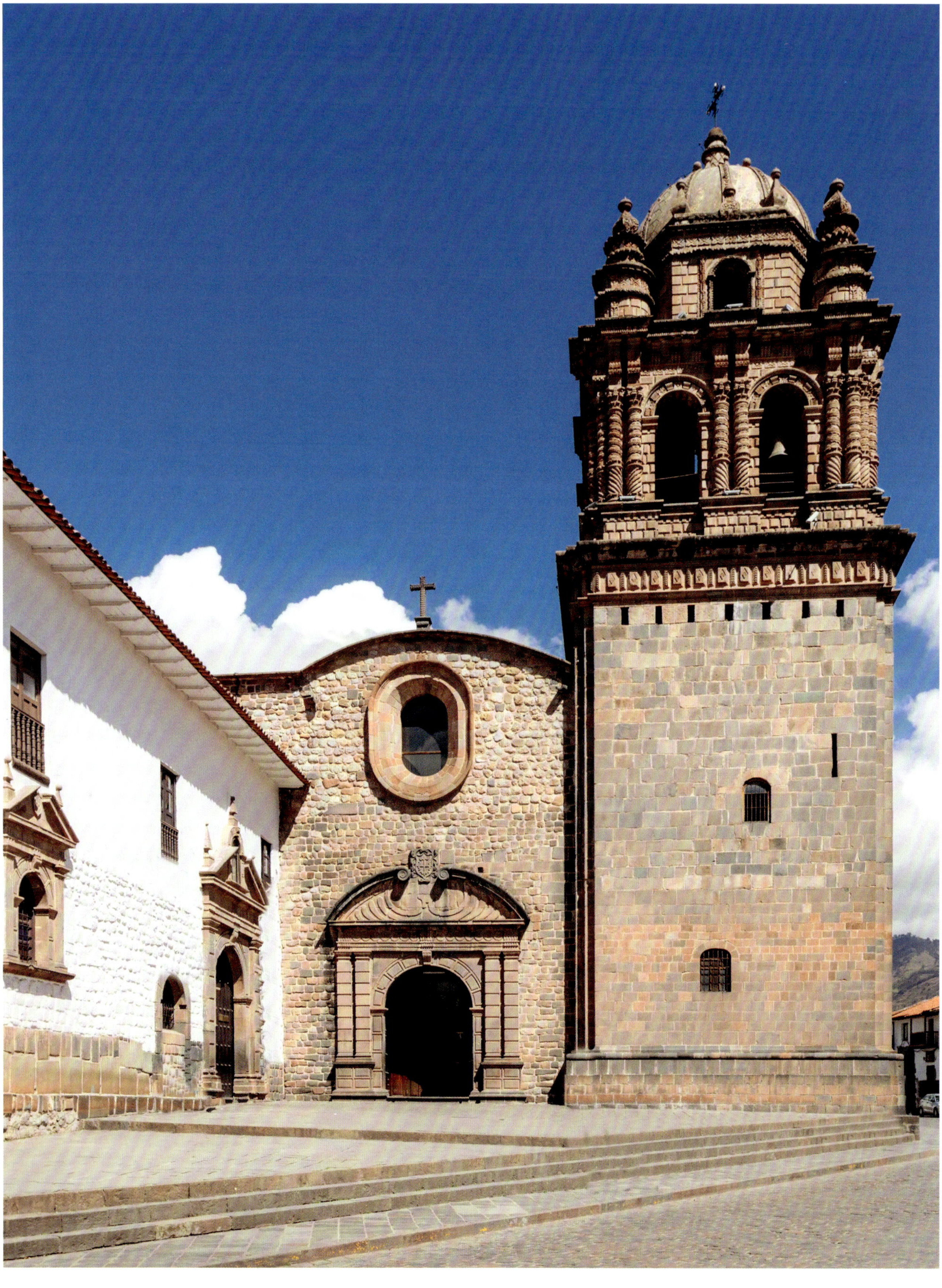

CHAPTER 7

Remembering Inca Cuzco, Remaking Spanish Cuzco

Garcilaso de la Vega and the City Council

In 1539, Isabel Chimpu Ocllo (b. *c.* 1523) gave birth to a son in Cuzco. Like Angelina Yupanqui, Isabel was an Inca princess who traced her lineage to Huayna Capac and his predecessors, and who had taken a Christian name at the time of her baptism. Her son was given the name Gómez Suárez de Figueroa, a nod to his distinguished paternal relatives in Spain, but he is better known today as Inca Garcilaso de la Vega, a variation on the name his father had adopted. The son of a native Andean mother and a Spanish father allied with the Pizarros, he belonged to the first generation of *mestizos* in colonial Peru (individuals with parents from different ethnic backgrounds, whose blood was thus considered "mixed").

Garcilaso would spend the first twenty-one years of his life in his birthplace, before traveling to Spain in 1560 with the inheritance he received at his father's death.[1] For much of his adult life, he lived in the southern Spanish city of Córdoba, and it was there that he composed the *Comentarios Reales de los Incas* (*Royal Commentaries of the Incas*), a history of the Inca and the first decades of Spanish governance in Peru.[2] Some of his writings are based on oral histories related to him by his mother and her relatives; others derive from printed texts and manuscripts to which he had access; and still others record his memories of his early life in Cuzco in the 1540s and 1550s, at the time of the Spaniards' civil wars.

In 1546, when Garcilaso was just seven years old, his father was far away on a battlefield outside Quito, where he fought alongside Gonzalo Pizarro in the conflict that led to the death of Viceroy Núñez Vela. In that same year, Charles V appointed Pedro de la Gasca (1485–1567)—a high-ranking cleric at the cathedrals of Salamanca and Toledo and a member of the Council of the Supreme Inquisition—president of the *audiencia* of Lima.[3] When Núñez Vela was killed, Gasca became the interim viceroy of Peru and a formidable challenger to Gonzalo Pizarro's claim to the governorship. News of these momentous events arrived in Cuzco through written reports and verbal communication, among them an order from Pizarro advising his lieutenant there, Alonso de Hinojosa, to assemble forces to prevent Gasca from entering the city.[4]

In November 1547, Pizarro himself arrived at Cuzco amidst great fanfare. Among his entourage were Garcilaso's father and Garcilaso himself, who says he had left Cuzco the day before to greet the Pizarro party three leagues outside of the city, walking part of the way and then being carried on the backs of native porters. Of their ceremonial entry into the city, he writes that he was led by an older man as he rode on horseback, and that they passed through many triumphal arches decorated with flowers as church bells rang and trumpets blared. "I saw everything I described,"

(*facing page*) Detail of figure 7.13.

he notes, "and could still say in which houses each captain lodged, for I knew all of them and I remember the houses."[5]

Garcilaso's childhood memories of the captains' houses are part of a much larger stock of recollections in the *Comentarios Reales*, and among the most vivid of the images he evokes are those of his birthplace, which is introduced in a chapter entitled "La descripción de la Imperial ciudad del Cozco" ("Description of the Imperial City of Cuzco"). He begins with an explanation of his motive:

> Provoked by the desire to preserve the relics of my homeland—those few that have remained—so that all are not lost, I set out on this task . . . to write about the ancient republic [of the Inca] until its end. And so that the city of Cuzco, her mother and wife, be not forgotten, I decided to sketch out in this chapter a description of her taken from the same tradition that as a native child filled me, of that which I saw with my own eyes.[6]

Garcilaso penned these reflections on preservation and loss in 1602, more than forty years after the time when he roamed the streets of Cuzco and became acquainted with its citizens and buildings. Unlike Pedro Sancho, who recorded his impressions of the city while he was still in Peru and inserted them into a narrative of Francisco Pizarro's movement through the Andes, Garcilaso's retrospective description of Cuzco is part of his comprehensive history of the Inca. He constructs it as an imaginary stroll through the city's streets, in which he identifies the owners of the houses he passes and the religious orders occupying the convents and monasteries, all the while relating the histories of those buildings extending back to the time of the Inca.

Garcilaso's rich treatment of Cuzco's urban plan, its buildings, and its public spaces stands in stark contrast to the detailed but dispassionate vision presented in the Acts of the Cabildo of the 1540s and 1550s. Bound in a volume held at the Archivo Regional in Cuzco, these constitute the archive's earliest records of the city council's deliberations. They provide insight into the wide range of issues taken up by the *cabildo* in this period, including deliberations over property ownership, taxes, and the maintenance of bridges and roads; directives on the smelting of precious metals; appointments of lower civic officials such as procurators and scribes; stipulations on fines and punishments for those who break laws; regulations on the practices of butchers and millers; and the setting of prices for coca, flour, corn, oil, and wine.

Read in relation to each other, Garcilaso's recollections of the Cuzco of his childhood and the *cabildo*'s Acts from the same period construct an image of a city that is at once beholden to its past and resolute in its commitment to change, a setting for cultural conflations and conflicts as the generation of the conquistadors and elderly city councilors gave way to that of Garcilaso de la Vega and his contemporaries. Indeed, the 1540s saw the establishment in Cuzco of a new visual and spatial culture in which images, buildings, and the changing urban plan gave shape to authority, governance, and commerce in a city where few participants in the events of the 1530s remained.

Garcilaso begins his imagined stroll through Cuzco in a sector of the city he calls Collcampata, the area to the northwest of the plaza, where Paullu built his house on the terraces climbing to Sacsahuaman. It was there, he writes, that Cuzco's mythical founder, Manco Capac, had built a palace, and he recalls having seen a building there he took to be its remains: "a grand and very spacious hall [*galpón*] which served as a plaza on rainy days to celebrate in it the major festivals." "Only this building remained standing when I left Cuzco," he writes, "for other similar ones of which we spoke were all left in ruins."[7]

Descending from there along the street he calls "San Agustín," named for the monastery of the Augustinian Order founded there in the late 1550s, Garcilaso identifies the houses of twenty of the city's prominent Spanish residents, among them that of Juan de Salas Valdés, whose lineage would be so prominently displayed on the carved portal to his residence (fig. 7.1; see also fig. 0.7). Stepping into the main plaza, Garcilaso turns to the cathedral, noting that "in the time of the Inca it was a most beautiful hall . . . [within] the houses of the Inca Viracocha, eighth king." "I knew it when it was roofed in straw," he says, "and I saw it covered in tile."[8]

This short passage on the appearance of the cathedral hints at its transformation over time: Garcilaso believed it to have been part of the palace of an Inca king before being

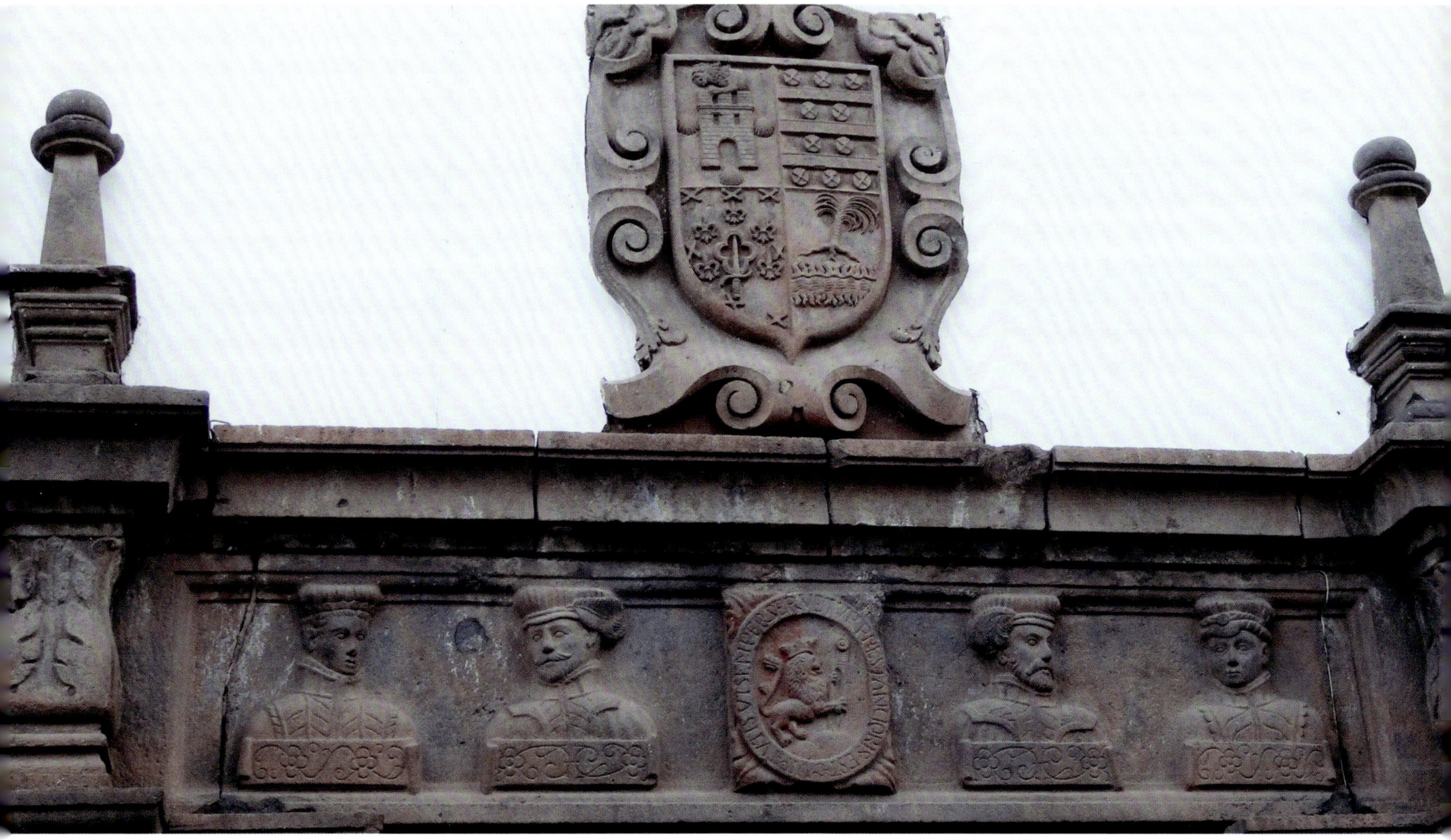

FIG. 7.1 Detail of the entrance to San Agustin 400, house of the Salas Valdés family, Cuzco, late 16th century. The carvings show the lineage of Juan de Salas Valdés, one of twenty prominent citizens whose houses are noted in Inca Garcilaso de la Vega's *Comentarios Reales de los Incas*.

used by the Spaniards as a church, and he notes that he personally saw its roof under construction. A fuller picture of the building in the 1540s and 1550s can be pieced together using information from other documents, among them the Acts of the Cabildo. Indeed, in the *cabildo*'s records from the 1540s and 1550s, the cathedral is the building mentioned most frequently. An early reference to it appears in the entry for January 20, 1545, when the scribe writes that it served as a meeting place when the city councilors convened a joint session with their counterparts in the ecclesiastical *cabildo*, the administrative body charged with overseeing matters under the church's jurisdiction.[9] The Acts note that the men met in the choir (*coro*), an indication that the Inca period hall that had served as the church since the foundation of Spanish Cuzco had been modified with the addition of a choir akin to those of medieval and early modern churches in western Europe, in which two facing rows of seats were positioned perpendicular to the main altar. A choir of this type would have been a suitable place of assembly in that it provided seating for the two distinct groups of officials. A document from the Archivo de la Catedral de Cuzco makes further reference to this part of the nave, noting that 216 pesos were paid to a certain Francisco de Torres sometime in 1545 for unspecified work on the choir chairs, or stalls ("sillas de coro").[10]

Other information about the furnishing of the cathedral in this period comes from an inventory taken on May 8, 1546. It records the presence of a number of

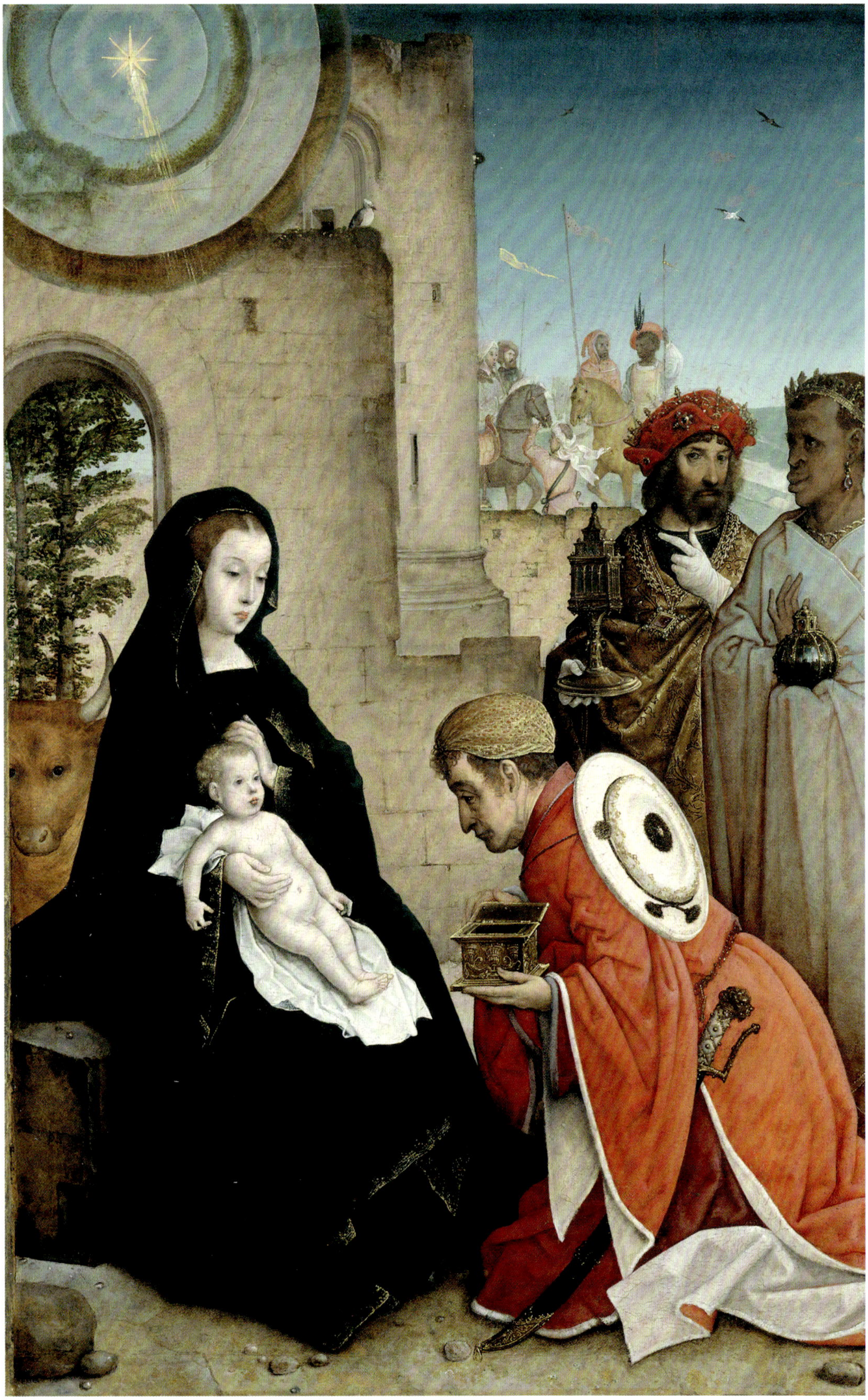

visual images, including a "*retablo* of the Kings" positioned "above the choir," perhaps an indication that it adorned an elevated altar at the northeast end of the nave. The cataloger's description of the image as a *retablo* suggests that it was a painting on wood panel. It may have been brought to Cuzco from elsewhere, in which case it would have resembled panel paintings on the same theme from the early sixteenth century, such as one by Juan de Flandes (*c.* 1460–*c.* 1519), a Flemish painter who produced works in the late fifteenth and early sixteenth centuries for his most important patron, Queen Isabella of Castile (fig. 7.2). Held today in the collection of the National Gallery of Art in Washington, DC, the panel was part of an altarpiece in the church of San Lázaro in Palencia, Spain, in the early sixteenth century. A later register of paintings in the cathedral at Cuzco, taken on February 21, 1553, lists a "wood *retablo* with its doors [*puertas*] in which is [painted] the Adoration of the Kings," probably a reference to the same image.[11]

The inventory of 1546 lists a number of other visual images adorning the church at that time:

> Three cloths [*paños*] from Flanders, on one of them the Salutation, on another the Fifth Sorrow, and another small one of religious images; two other cloths [*paños de lienzo*], each one painted with the Last Supper of the Lord, and on another small *retablo*, the Resurrection of Our Lord; an image [*imagen*] of Ecce Homo and another of Our Lady.[12]

If these visual representations of religious figures and narratives still survive, their whereabouts remain unknown. Dating to this era, however, are two paintings of the Virgin and Child attributed to the Antwerp workshop of Joos van Cleve (*c.* 1485–1541), one found in Cuzco and the other in Lima.[13] Perhaps the earliest surviving European paintings in Peru, they are testaments to the trade in Netherlandish art and its impact on the decoration of Cuzco cathedral in the mid-sixteenth century.

The inventory attests to the presence of new kinds of objects and new sacred iconographies in sixteenth-century Cuzco, even as it also demonstrates the continuing prominence of cloth, a material much used among the Inca to convey information through symbolic patterns and colors. The cataloger of 1546 refers to cloth in two ways: *paños de Flandes* and *paños de lienzo*, the latter described further as "painted" (*pintados*). The distinction suggests that different kinds of objects made of cloth decorated the church's interior. Insight into the nuances of this terminology is provided by a later source, a dictionary of 1611 by the Spanish lexicographer Sebastián de Covarrubias, which glosses *paño* as "woven wool cloth with which we dress ourselves" and *paños de pared* as "tapestry" (*tapicería*).[14] *Lienzo*, on the other hand, is woven linen cloth, and Covarrubias adds that the term is often used to refer to pictures painted on that type of backing.

Given this distinction in terminology, the images of the Salutation, more commonly known as the Annunciation, and the Fifth Sorrow—the Crucifixion—may have been tapestries from Flanders, or perhaps paintings on cloth from Flanders; in either case, the way in which they are described suggests their origins were in Europe. They may have been among the ornaments Vicente de Valverde said he distributed among the churches of Peru in his letter to the king of 1539; alternatively, they could have arrived with the new bishop of Cuzco, Juan de Solano (*c.* 1505–80), who replaced Valverde after his death in 1541.[15] The presence of an image of the Annunciation in Cuzco's place of Christian worship may have been seen as especially fitting in light of Pizarro's dedication of the church to the Virgin of the Annunciation in the Act of Foundation in 1534.

The two paintings on *paños de lienzo*—evidently both on the theme of the Last Supper—may have been brought to Cuzco from afar, but they could also have been commissioned and painted in the Andes. Painting on linen, the material indicated by the cataloger, was a widespread practice in the Netherlands in the fifteenth and early sixteenth centuries, and the first immigrant painters in Cuzco may have produced works using this technique, since wooden

FIG. 7.2 (*facing page*) Juan de Flandes, *The Adoration of the Magi* (panel from the altarpiece in the church of San Lázaro, Palencia, Spain), *c.* 1508–19. Oil on panel, 124.7 × 79 cm. National Gallery of Art, Washington, DC. An altarpiece on the same subject was displayed in the cathedral of Cuzco in the mid-16th century.

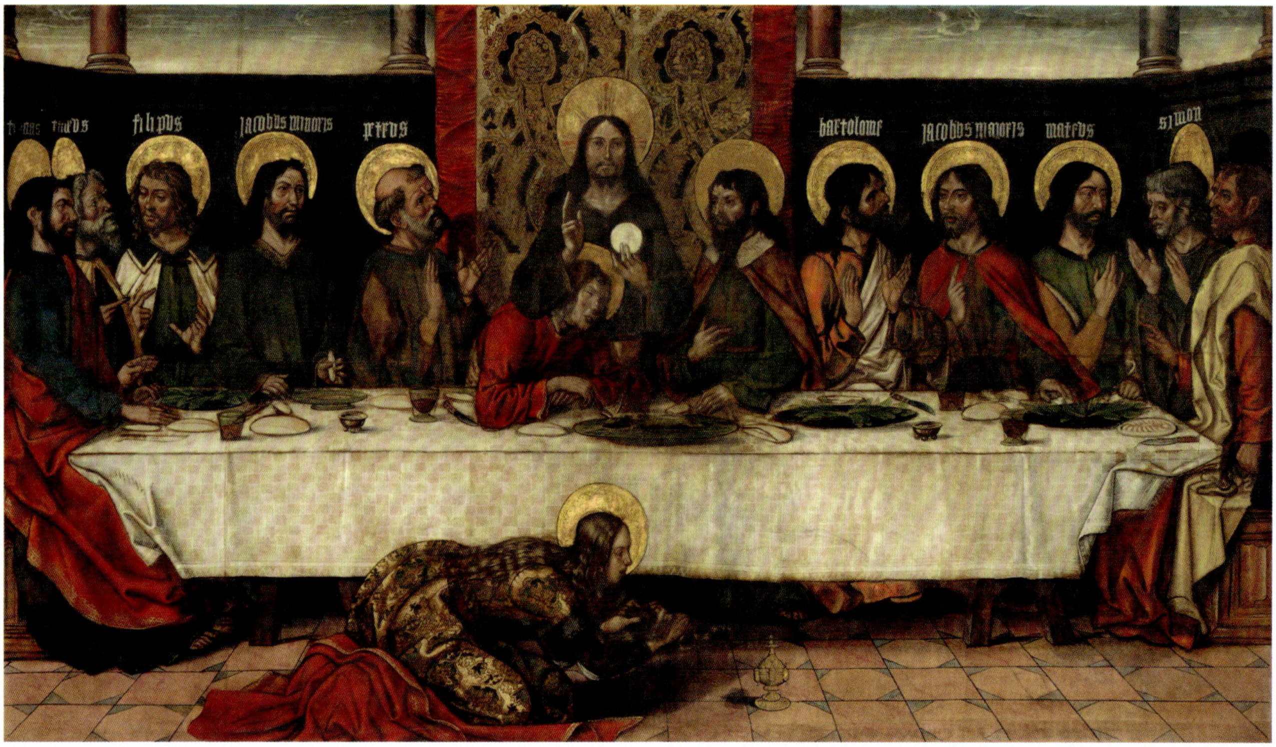

FIG. 7.3 Workshop of Pedro Berruguete, *The Last Supper*, *c.* 1495–1500. Distemper on linen, 189.6 × 330.8 cm. Los Angeles County Museum of Art. Cuzco's cathedral owned two such paintings of the Last Supper.

backings would have been scarce.[16] Few paintings on linen from this era survive, due in part to the fragility of the materials, but a well-preserved example depicting the Last Supper by Pedro Berruguete (*c.* 1450–1504) and his workshop demonstrates the kind of composition that may have hung on the stone walls of Cuzco's first church (fig. 7.3).[17]

One wonders how native Andeans such as Paullu and his wife Catalina, who had been baptized and married in the cathedral, would have responded to these images on cloth. As textiles, they were made using materials and techniques similar to those required for the tunics, dresses, sashes, and mantles worn by high-ranking Andeans in Inca and colonial Peru. Writing in the 1570s, however, Titu Cusi Yupanqui would emphasize disjunction rather than continuity in this field of artistic production as he records his father's address to his followers before their departure for Vitcos. Among Manco's warnings about the treachery of the Spaniards was this:

> What you really have to know is that, if by chance these men tell you to worship what they worship, which are painted cloths [*paños pintados*] which they say is Viracocha and that you must worship it as you would a *huaca*, it is nothing but a cloth [*paño*].[18]

Joining the two-dimensional images on wood and cloth in Cuzco's church in 1546 were two three-dimensional ones: a sculpture (*imágen*) of Christ and another of his mother, Mary. Again, it is unclear if these were works brought to Cuzco from elsewhere or if they were made there. In either case, it is likely that the sculptures would have been made of wood and polychromed, the technique and materials used in fifteenth- and sixteenth-century Spain. The cataloger refers to the image of Christ as *Ecce Homo*, indicating that it represented its subject as he appeared when Pontius Pilate presented him to onlookers after being beaten and crowned with thorns. It may have resembled the work by Pedro's son Alonso Berruguete (*c.* 1488–1561),

FIG. 7.4 Alonso Berruguete, *Ecce Homo*, *c.* 1525. Pigment and wood, h. 146 cm (excl. base). Museo Nacional de Escultura, Valladolid. The *Ecce Homo* figure displayed in Cuzco's cathedral may have resembled this one, which uses techniques and materials characteristic of Spanish sculpture from the 15th and 16th centuries.

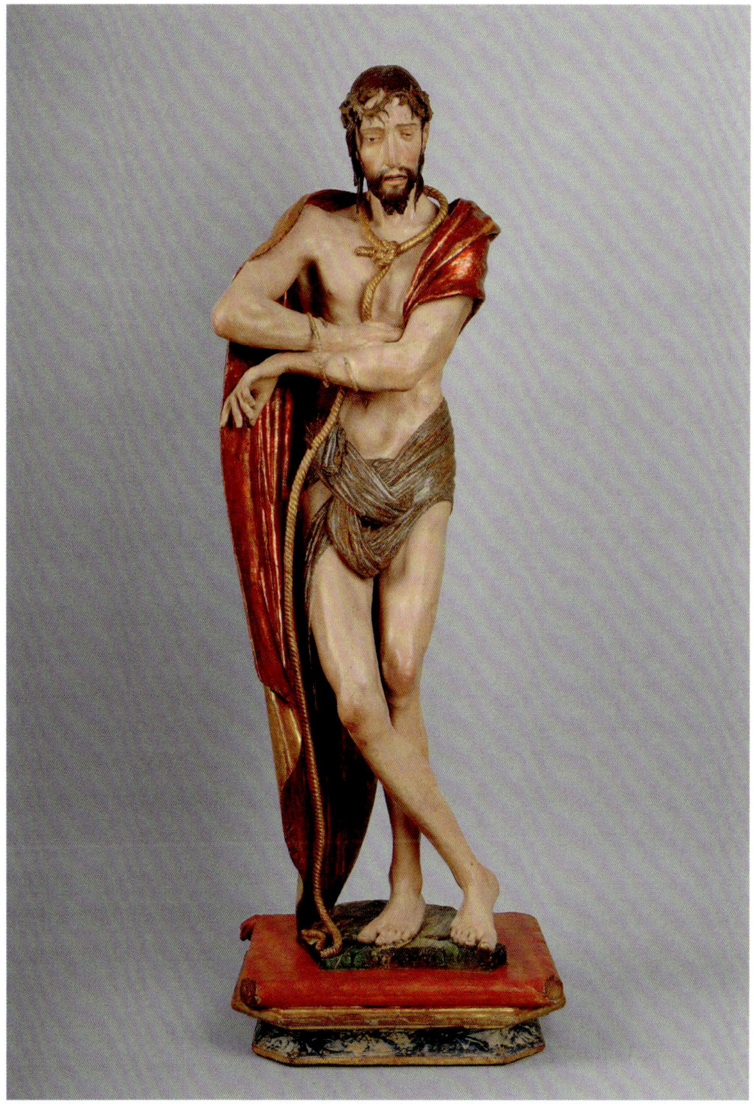

now in the collection of the Museo Nacional de Escultura in Valladolid, Spain (fig. 7.4).

The choir stalls and these visual images were installed in a hall constructed by the Inca and adapted for use as a single-nave church. Its interior must have resembled that of the church of San Juan Bautista in Huaytará, more than 750 km (466 mi.) west of Cuzco, where Christian paintings and sculptures adorn a building adapted from an Inca period structure even today (figs 7.5, 7.6). As these new kinds of images were introduced into the built environment of Spanish Cuzco, so, too, were their subjects. Indeed, the narrative interchanges occurring in Cuzco in this period are striking: while Paullu, Isabel Chimpu Ocllo, and other Andeans were becoming acquainted with the stories of the lives of Christ and the Virgin through visual imagery, Pedro de Cieza de León and Juan de Betanzos were becoming acquainted with a different tale—the history of the Inca as told to them by Andean elders and the readers of *quipus*.

It is perhaps not surprising, then, that Garcilaso de la Vega—whose experiences were unlike those of most of the other residents of Cuzco at mid-century—describes the exterior ornamentation of Cuzco's church in a way that reveals his knowledge of Christian iconography while simultaneously linking it to local history:

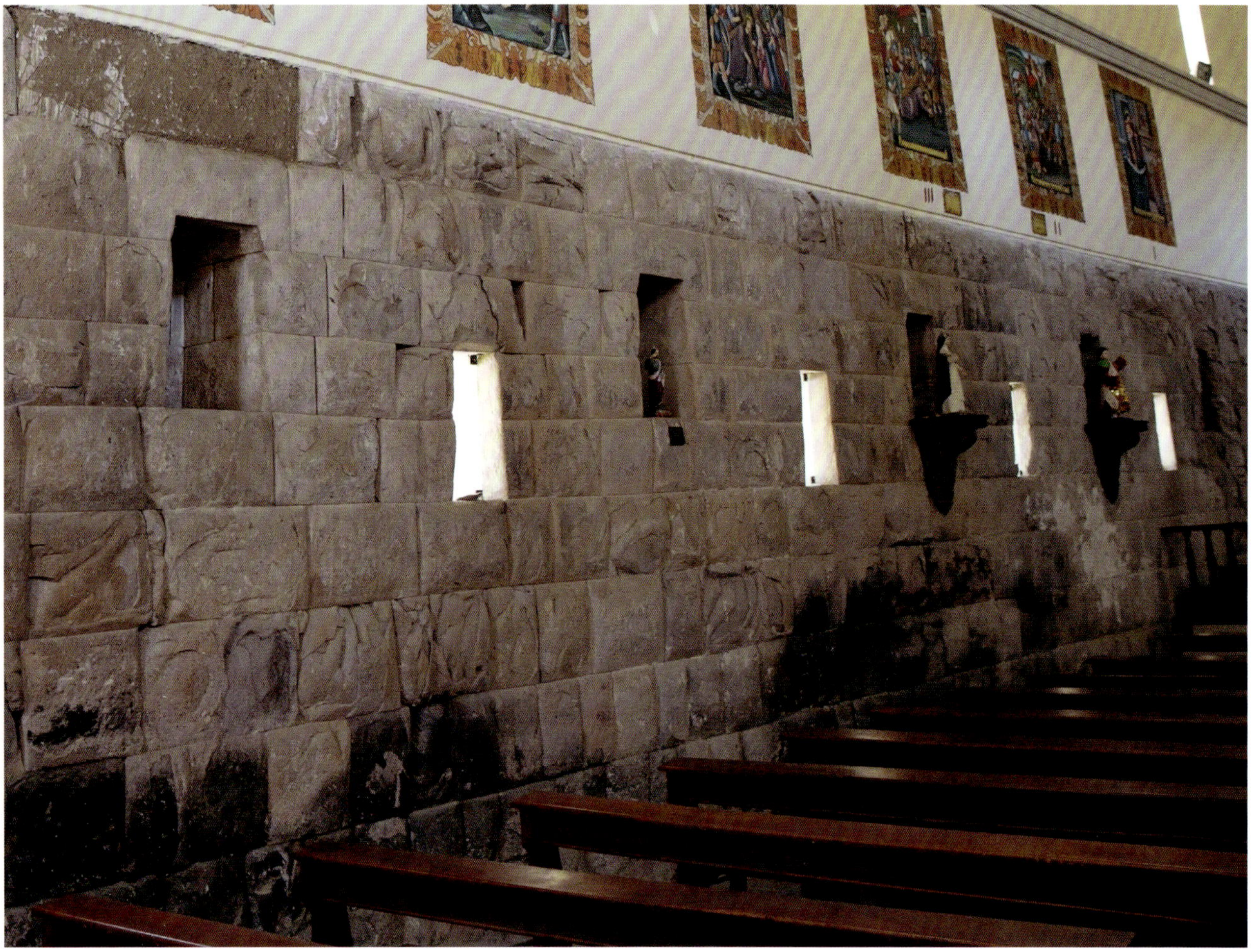

FIG. 7.5 The south wall of the nave at the church of San Juan Bautista, Huaytará, Peru. Bearing Christian iconography atop an Inca wall, the church juxtaposes visual imagery, materials, and styles just as the early cathedral in Cuzco must have done.

> On the gable end of the church they painted the Lord Santiago atop a white horse, clasping his shield, and a sword in his hand, and the sword was curved like a serpent. He had many Indians thrown down at his feet, dead and injured. Seeing the painting, the Indians said a Viracocha like this was the one who destroyed us in this plaza. The painting was still bright in 1560, when I came to Spain.[19]

The image he describes is an early reference to the Spanish colonial iconography known as *Santiago Mataindios* (Saint James the Indian Killer), a variation on images of Saint James as a killer of Muslims (*Santiago Matamoros*) that emerged on the Iberian Peninsula in connection with Christian conquest of Islamic kingdoms in the eighth through the end of the fifteenth centuries.[20] A fifteenth-century print attributed to the German engraver Martin Schongauer (*c.* 1445/50–1491) presents a scene similar to the one described by Garcilaso: at the center of the composition the saint, on horseback and with his sword raised, tramples Muslim combatants at the legendary Battle of Clavijo (fig. 7.7). The imagery would later be adapted by artists in colonial Peru to depict the saint and his horse treading on defeated Incas rather than Turks (fig. 7.8). The painting Garcilaso describes is the earliest recorded appearance of this new iconography, a scene generated by

FIG. 7.6 A statue of Jesus Christ occupies a trapezoidal Inca niche at the church of San Juan Bautista, Huaytará, Peru.

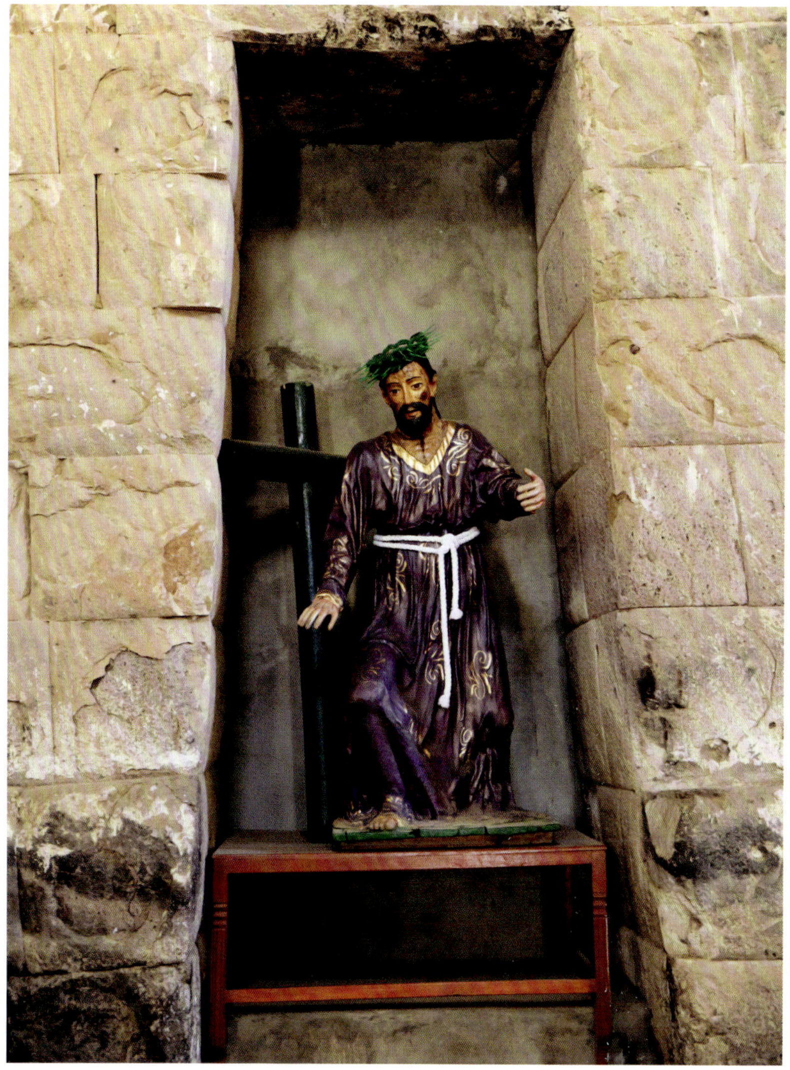

the experience of Spanish colonialism in Peru and perhaps rooted in a legend recorded by Juan de Betanzos. During the Siege of Cuzco, he writes, the Christians were led by an armed and bearded man on a white horse. On his chest, the man wore "a red cross, like the insignia of Santiago that the Marquis [Francisco Pizarro] had on his chest."[21]

Other images circulating in the Cuzco of the 1540s and 1550s would similarly bring the iconography of these two cultures together on a single pictorial field. In 1545, the Crown recognized Paullu's descent from the Inca royal family with a coat of arms. Its imagery, like that on the escutcheon granted to Francisco Pizarro in 1537 (see fig. 5.13), juxtaposed the heraldic iconography of the European nobility with the *mascaypacha*. It is described in a document issued in Valladolid:

> A shield divided in two sections. In the first, on a field of gold, a black eagle, rampant, flanked by two green palms. In the second, on a field of blue, a tiger crowned with a sable tassel, the tassel that only Atahualpa, his brother, had as a crown, accompanied by two serpents with gold crowns, bordered in sable with text that says "Ave María," and between its letters, eight Jerusalem crosses in gold.[22]

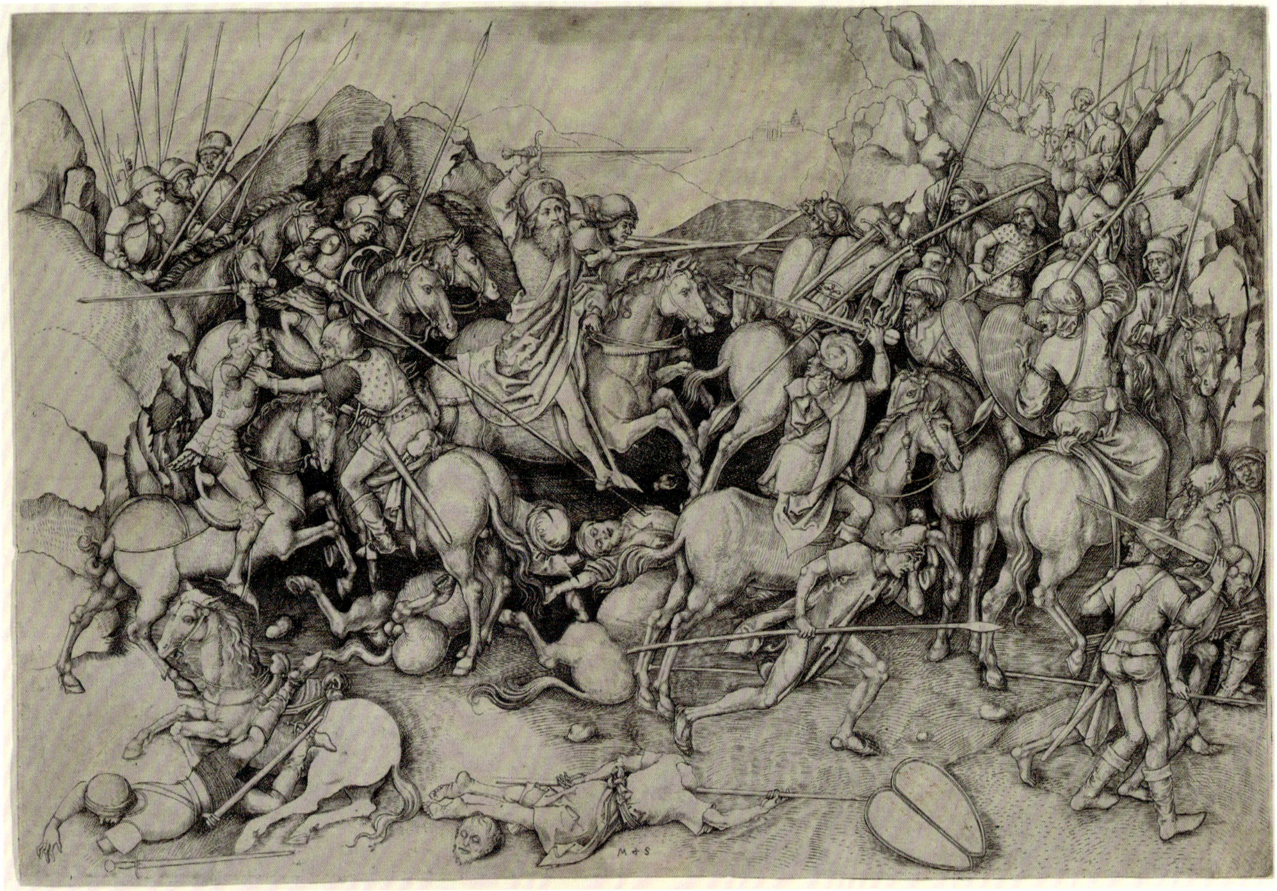

FIG. 7.7 Attributed to Martin Schongauer, *St. James Major at the Battle of Clavijo*, *c.* 1435–91. Ink on paper, 29.2 × 43.3 cm. Metropolitan Museum of Art, New York. In this engraving, Saint James (*center*) triumphantly rides down his Muslim opponents; the trope was later adapted for an Andean context.

No contemporary image of this coat of arms is known today, but some of its elements appear in escutcheons also granted in 1545 to other Andean elites and known through seventeenth-century copies. The one awarded to Luis Clemente Topa in recognition of his descent from Pachacuti includes the *mascaypacha* positioned over the doorway to a tower, probably a reference to the arms of Cuzco (fig. 7.9). The one given to Gonzalo Uchu Hualpa and Felipe Tupa Inca Yupanqui, sons of Huayna Capac, includes a rampant eagle and the *mascaypacha* flanked by crowned serpents (fig. 7.10).[23] Part of the privilege granted to the holders of these coats of arms was the right to display them on the façades of their houses, and thus this kind of heraldic imagery must have pervaded the streets of early colonial Cuzco, serving as a visual language legible to Spaniards and elite Andeans alike, and juxtaposing iconographies that had previously operated in isolation.[24]

Garcilaso continues his imagined tour of Cuzco, turning from the cathedral to the northwest side of the plaza, where he notes the presence of a number of houses with arcades (*portales*). These, he notes, were the main shops of the craftsmen (*oficiales*). Facing them on the other side of the plaza, he recalls, were the shops of the wealthiest merchants. The construction of shops and arcades around

FIG. 7.8 Artist unknown, *Santiago Mataindios*, 17th–18th century. Oil on canvas, 39.37 × 29.85 cm. Collection of Carl and Marilynn Thoma. A similar image was painted on the gable end of the cathedral in Cuzco.

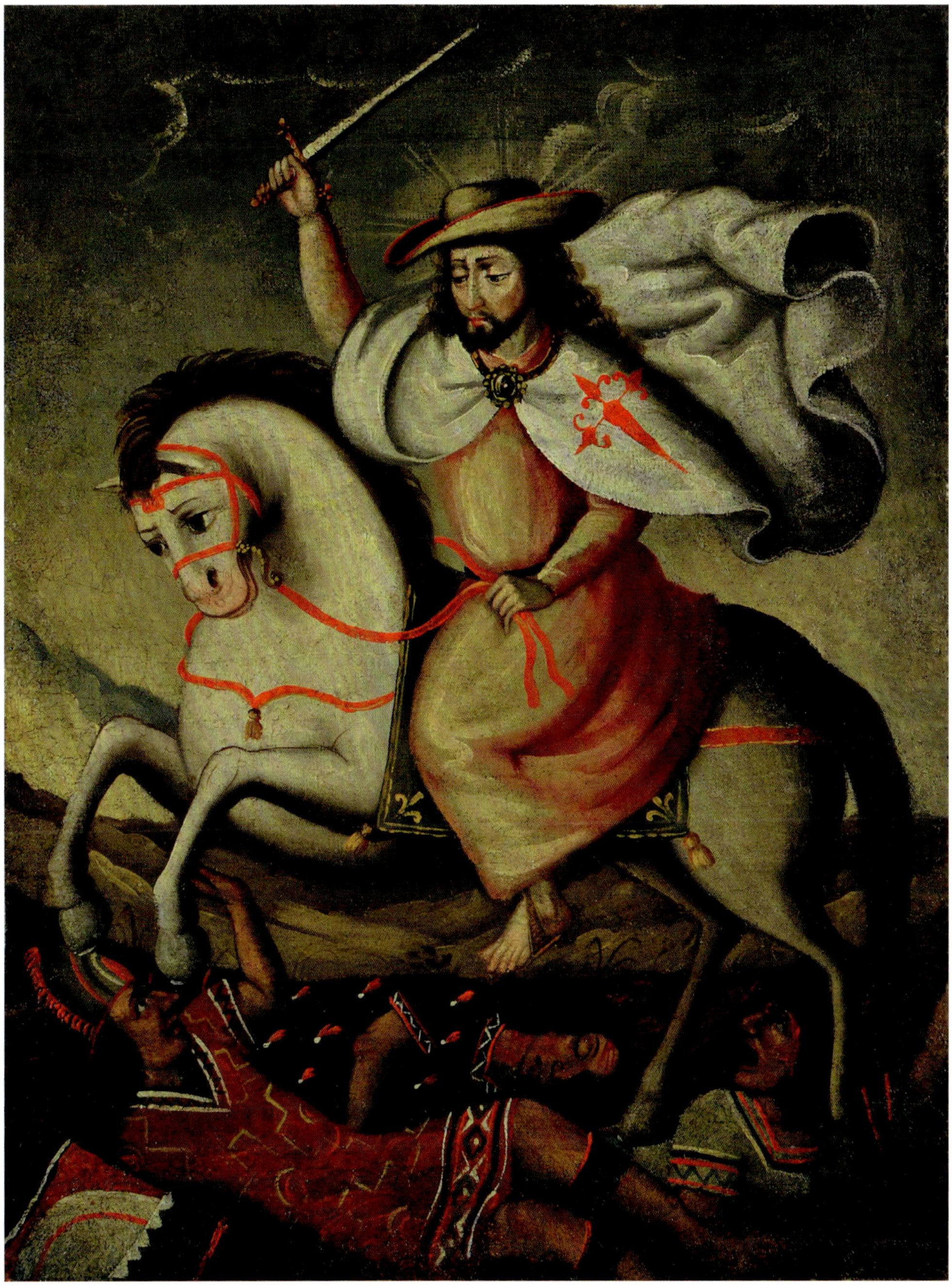

the plaza began by the later 1540s, and information about this project—arguably the first major modification of the plan of Inca Cuzco under Spanish rule—appears in the *cabildo*'s Acts in an entry from 1548:

> Talking about the adornment of the city, because it is one of the principle things in the interest of the city, and which gives contentment to those who live in it, it seemed for the city to be in conformity, that from the bridge that is next to the house of Licenciado Carbajal to the other bridge of Our Lady of Mercy, the building of shops that the city has begun should be continued toward the said bridge of Our Lady.[25]

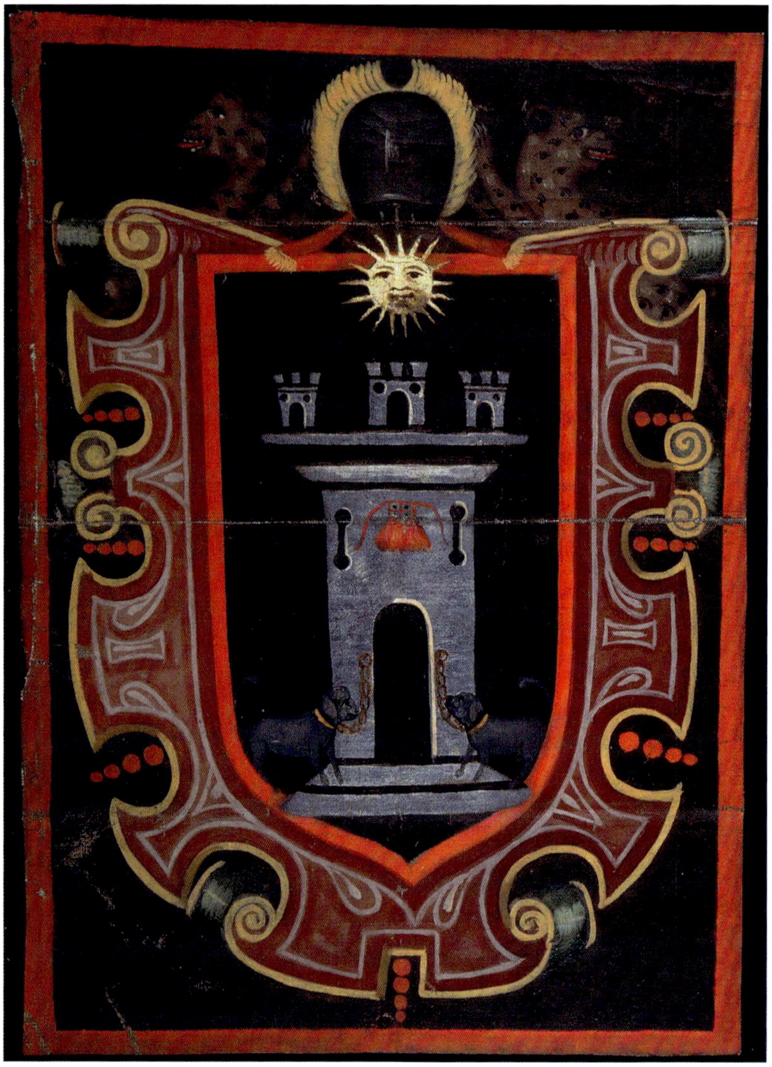

FIG. 7.9 (*left*) The coat of arms granted to Luis Clemente Topa in 1545, 17th-century copy. Ink and pigment on paper. Archivo General de Indias, Seville. A member of the Andean elite in colonial Cuzco, Luis Clemente Topa's arms include both heraldic and Inca imagery, and probably reference those of the city itself.

FIG. 7.10 (*facing page*) The coat of arms granted to Gonzalo Uchu Hualpa and Felipe Tupa Inca Yupanqui in 1545 (right), and a portrait of their ancestor, identified in gold lettering as "the great Topa Inca Yupanqui," flanked by the grantees (left), 17th-century copy. Pigment and gilt on parchment. Archivo General de Indias, Seville. The incipit "A[v]e Maria" in the center of the shield proclaims the Christian faith of its bearers.

The construction under discussion was of a row of buildings following the course of—or perhaps spanning—the canalized Saphi, and running through this part of the city all the way to the monastery of the Mercedarian Order. A detail from the painting of Cuzco at the time of the earthquake of 1650 shows those buildings in later years, their upper stories furnished with windows and balconies, and their tiled roofs collapsing as the earth shook (fig. 7.11).

To justify this major intervention into the town plan, the councilors claimed they were acting in the interest of "conformity." Their use of this term suggests they wanted Cuzco's main plaza to fit with the norms of other plazas, perhaps the rectilinear plazas drawn on the idealized gridiron plans of Spanish colonial cities, where the space was enclosed by buildings on four sides. The councilors mandated that the shops in this new row of buildings be operated and maintained not by the *cabildo*, but by individual citizens:

> Be it known that if any person wants to take the said place and plot in a long-term lease [*censo perpetuo*], that person should appear before the city to ask for the lot that he wants, and fair terms being set, the city will give it to that person, and will give space to build porticos [*portales*] on the front parts.[26]

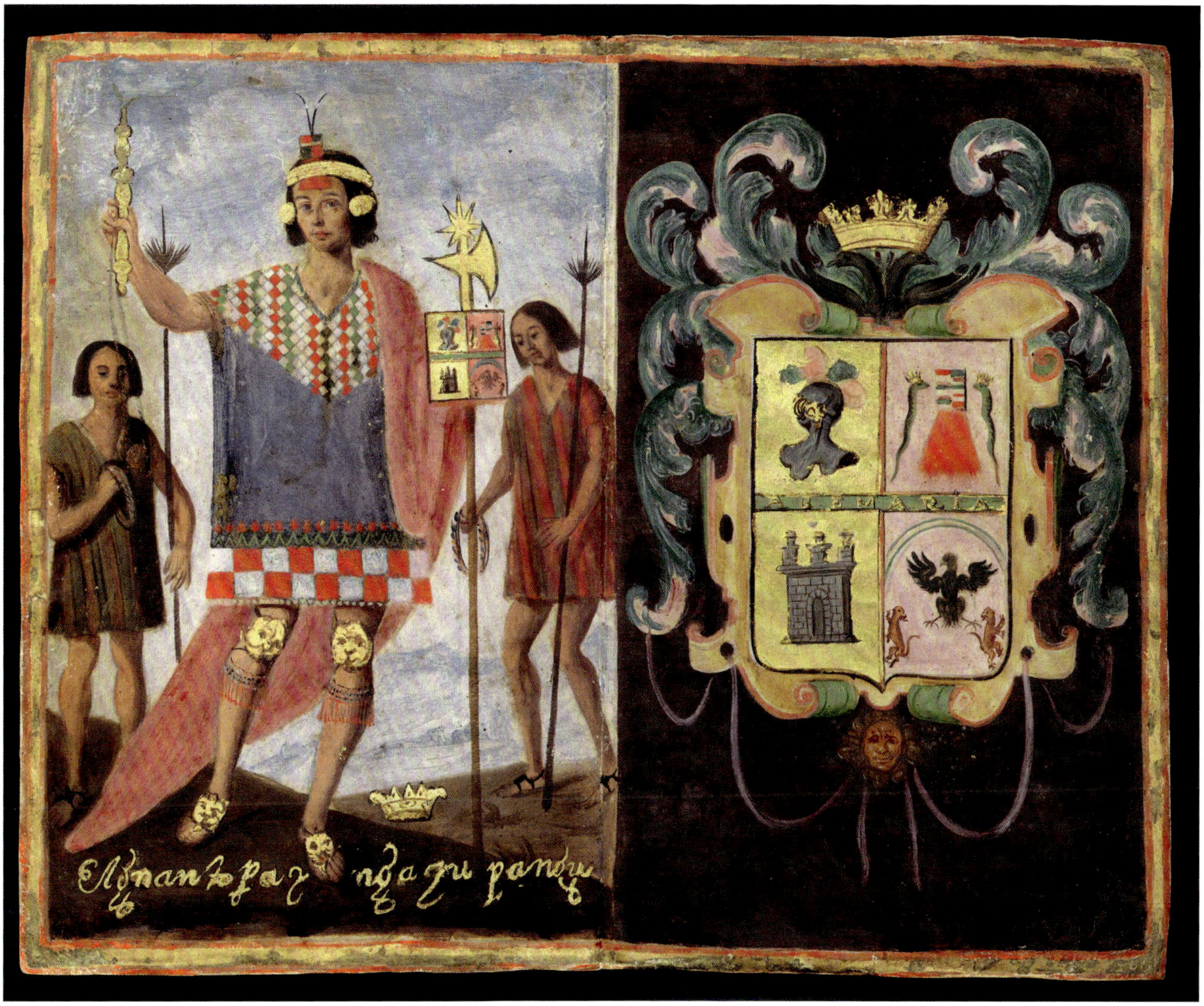

The arrangement through which citizens would pay the city in perpetuity for the right to operate businesses in these spaces suggests that the *cabildo* had motivations beyond just bringing Cuzco's plaza into conformity with other plazas: the shops would also be a new source of income. The passage indicates that the proprietors of the shops would build porticos on the buildings, an expectation aligning this project formally with the design of other plazas in the sixteenth-century Spanish world. Indeed, the construction of such spaces was not limited to the new row of buildings but, rather, could be undertaken by anyone who had a house facing onto the plaza. Those who wished to do so, the councilors stipulated, would have to request a license. There was, moreover, one additional requirement for the construction of porticos onto the plaza: "the pillars have to be of carved brick or of stone, and all of common measurement."[27]

The appearance of the *portales* around the Plaza de Armas in Cuzco today has its origins in this initiative of 1548. The relative uniformity of the arcades, with stone columns topped by simplified and splayed Ionic capitals, follows the *cabildo*'s stipulation on materials and measurements (fig. 7.12). The names by which the porticos are known today—Portal de Carnes (meats), Portal de Harinas (flour), Portal de Panes (breads)—do not date to the sixteenth century but nonetheless attest to the commercial function of these spaces as noted by Garcilaso.

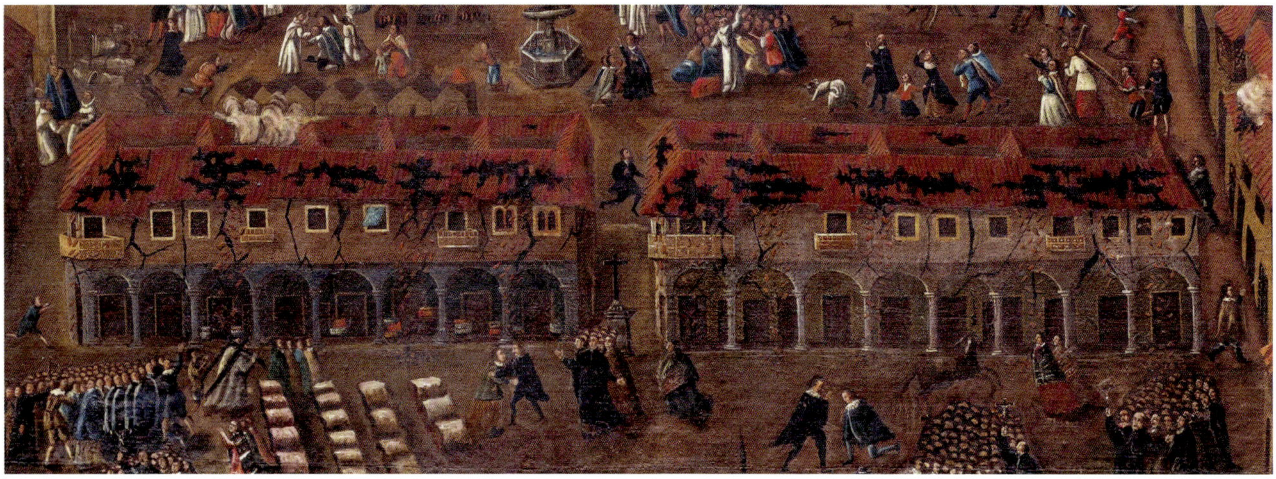

FIG. 7.11 Artist unknown, *Cuzco during the Earthquake of* 1650, after 1650. Oil on canvas, 33.4 × 46.2 cm (detail). Church of El Triunfo, Cuzco. These arcaded buildings were mandated in the 1540s as part of a plan to bring unity and order to the central plaza.

To ensure fair practice in the sale of flour, wheat, wax, and other commodities in the *portales*, the councilors provided an official scale to be housed in the plaza and to be used by an appointed weigher, a certain Juan Alonso de Villa Rubia.[28]

Following his reference to the shops on the plaza, Garcilaso moves beyond the arcades to the buildings behind them, noting the identities of their occupants in Spanish Cuzco and their histories in the time of the Inca. He identifies the structures on the southeastern side of the plaza as Hatun Cancha (see map 1, p. 12), adding that they were the houses of Inca Yupanqui.[29] The district behind it, he says, was called Pucamarca and was the site of the palace of Topa Inca Yupanqui. Adjacent to Hatun Cancha was Amarucancha; it had been the palace of Huayna Capac, he recalls, before being divided into lots and distributed among the Spaniards. At the time he was composing the *Comentarios Reales*, however, it was the site of the church of the Jesuits, who arrived in Cuzco later in the 1500s.[30]

On the northwest side of the plaza, Garcilaso points to the site of Caxana, saying he saw some of its walls as well as an Inca festival hall that later housed the monastery of the Franciscan Order. He believed it to be the palace of Pachacuti. The adjacent site of Coracora, he writes, was the palace of Inca Roca. "Of the Coracora," he recalls, "I did not see anything, because already in my time it was leveled to the ground."[31] He does not elaborate on this intriguing reference to the destruction of Coracora, but other sources reveal that it occurred in the aftermath of a significant series of events in the civil wars of Spanish Peru. In April 1548, Gasca confronted Gonzalo Pizarro somewhere in the valley of Xaquixahuana, just west of Cuzco in what is today the province known as Anta. Accounts of the skirmish report that many—perhaps even most—of Gonzalo Pizarro's men deserted him there, among them Sebastián Garcilaso de la Vega, father of the author of the *Comentarios Reales*. Gasca had prevailed, and the last remaining Pizarro brother in Peru was accused of *laesae maiestatis*, treason against the Crown, and was sentenced to death. He was decapitated, and his head was taken to Lima and displayed in the plaza at the pillar of justice. His body was taken to Cuzco to be buried in the church of La Merced, and Gasca ordered that Coracora, his house on the plaza, be demolished and sown with salt, a ritual of conquest and punishment with roots in ancient history.[32] It was these ruins that Garcilaso remembered having seen as a child.

Following his victory at Xaquixahuana, Gasca went to Cuzco. His name does not appear in the records of the city council until early June 1548, when the documents authorizing his governance were announced by the town crier, Juan Enríquez. Those documents empowered Gasca to administer justice, grant pardons, impose ordinances,

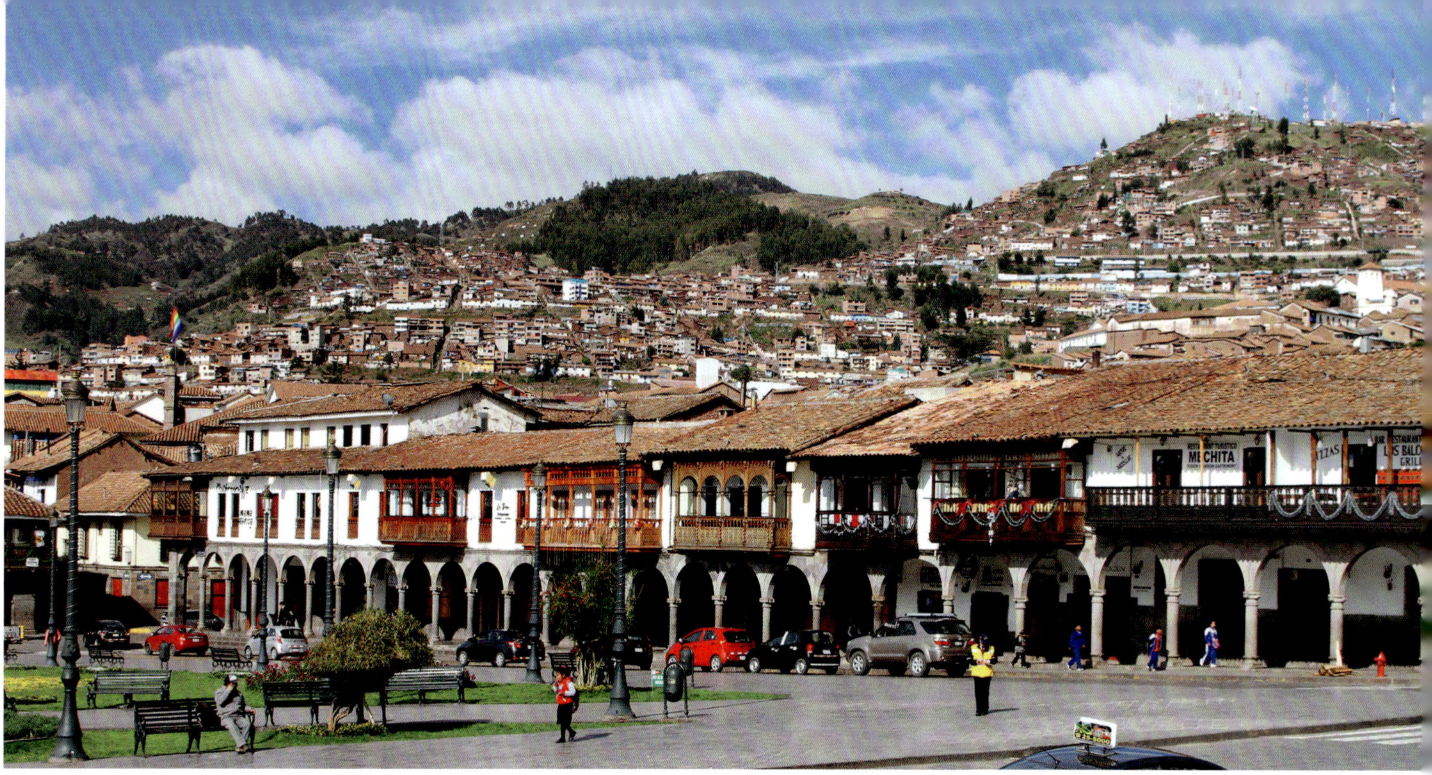

FIG. 7.12 Arcades and balconies on the Plaza de Armas, Cuzco. The appearance of the modern plaza derives from building regulations imposed by the *cabildo* (city council) in the 1540s.

establish and distribute certain kinds of *encomiendas*, and appoint governors of newly settled provinces. Gasca promptly exercised his powers, distributing grants of native labor to some of those who had been loyal to him. But perhaps the measure that would have the most significant effect on governance in Cuzco was Gasca's appointment of Benito Xuárez de Carbajal as the city's first *corregidor*.

The institution of the *corregidor* had been mandated by the *Leyes nuevas* of 1542, and was an extension into the Americas of an office with a long history on the Iberian Peninsula, going back to the fourteenth century in Castile.[33] Carbajal's appointment was authorized by a document specifying his duties, which included acting as the city's highest-ranking judge in civil and criminal lawsuits, ensuring the just treatment of native peoples, and imposing punishment on those who had conspired with Gonzalo Pizarro against the Crown.[34] Not long after he took office, the *cabildo* transferred the *caja de cabildo* (*cabildo* chest) from the house of Diego Maldonado—a longtime city councilor, a recipient of treasure at Cajamarca, one of the first settlers in Cuzco, and one of the city's richest men—to that of the *corregidor*. The chest, the entry notes, contained books and papers—perhaps the very Acts of the Cabildo in which the move was recorded.[35] The idea that these materials now belonged in the house of the *corregidor* attests to the new political order in Cuzco, as the records and tools of governance now resided with an authority more closely linked to the *audiencia* of Lima and, ultimately, the Crown.

Continuing his imaginary stroll through the Cuzco of his childhood, Garcilaso leaves the plaza heading southeast to Intipampa, the "plaza of the sun," and, next to it, the House of the Sun, which he calls Coricancha, "district of gold, silver, and precious stones."[36] His more thorough treatment of that compound appears in an earlier chapter of the *Comentarios Reales*, where he notes that the church of Santo Domingo was, in the time of the Inca, the chamber in which the golden image of the Sun was housed. That chamber's size and shape, he claims, had not been altered, and its principal portal faced north "as it is today."[37] Visitors to the church can still see the north-facing portal to which Garcilaso refers, though its ornamentation dates to the seventeenth century (fig. 7.13).[38] Passing through that doorway and traversing the length of

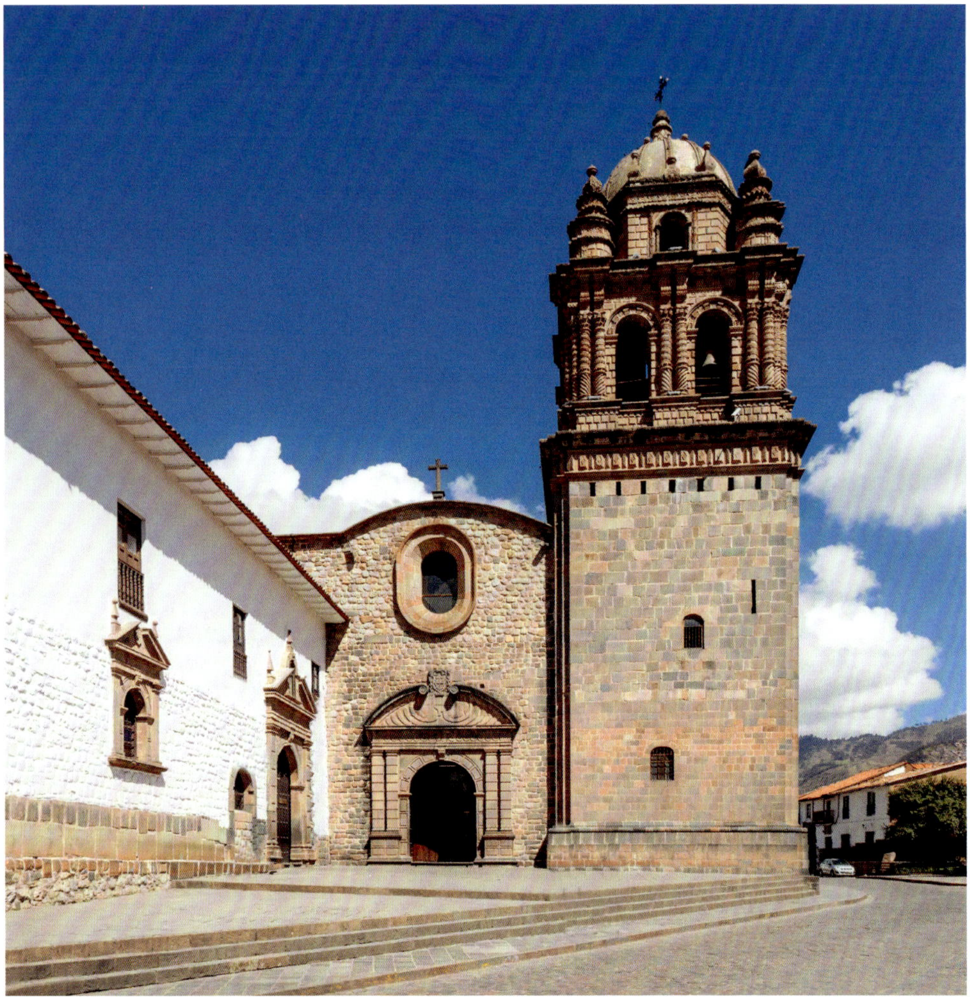

FIG. 7.13 The north portal to the church of Santo Domingo, Cuzco. Now framed with a portal built in the 17th century, the north door has been the main entrance to the church for centuries.

the nave, the visitor approaches the wall at the back of the sanctuary, behind which rests the balcony atop its distinctive Inca period curving wall (see fig. 0.2).

Garcilaso's description of the House of the Sun and its adaptation for use as a church raises questions about precisely when this change occurred. The Dominicans' use of the compound is first referenced in 1539 in a letter from Valverde to Charles V requesting that the king send more Dominican friars to Peru and, specifically, to Cuzco. In the letter, Valverde proposes establishing a new monastery in "a building in this city that the Indians had as the House and Temple of the Sun."[39] Several years seem to have passed before the monastery was established, as Cristóbal Vaca de Castro, in a letter to the king dated 1542, mentions the existence of Dominican monasteries in just four Peruvian cities: Chincha, Huaylas, Xauxa, and Guamanga.[40] A reference to the House of the Sun in a document of 1543, however, notes its location at "the site where at present the monastery of Santo Domingo is established."[41] On November 2, 1548, the city council considered a dispute over the ownership of a fountain housed in the monastery, and thus 1543–48 can be considered a reasonable window for the initial transformation of the space.[42]

Among the modifications made to the Inca temple was the addition of a cloister adjacent to the church, a change facilitated by the formal similarities between that part of the Inca compound and monasteries of the type with which sixteenth-century Dominicans were familiar. Today, that cloister is framed by two stories of galleries, their walls hung with large canvas paintings depicting the life of Saint

Dominic (fig. 7.14). Wethey proposed that the ground-level arcades were constructed in the mid-sixteenth century, and perhaps that space, with its distinct interpretation of the ionic capital and alfiz-framed arches, was under construction in the 1550s, when the young Garcilaso saw Santo Domingo and recalled the former appearance of the building it occupied.[43]

Garcilaso's description of Cuzco, with its multiple references to the functions of buildings in the time of the Inca, demonstrates the persistence of knowledge about the city's ancient plan at mid-century and later. Other sources do not fully corroborate Garcilaso's identification of particular buildings with specific rulers, but what is important is that, for him, certain structures and spaces in Spanish Cuzco were linked to individual Inca kings.[44] Indeed, he presents the Cuzco of his youth as akin to a memory palace, the ancient mnemonic device in which the features of a real or imaginary space—rooms, hallways, portals—serve as prompts for things to be recalled, and in which movement through that space brings to mind a sequence of words, images, and ideas.[45] In the *Comentarios Reales*, it is the Cuzco of the 1550s rather than a single building that structures Garcilaso's recollections, and his imagined tour through the city becomes a spatialized variant of the lists of royal succession that shaped his own account of Inca history as well as those of Betanzos and Cieza de León.[46]

Cuzco in the 1540s and 1550s occupied buildings and districts that, for Garcilaso, were closely linked to particular Inca rulers but also extended beyond them, crossing the Saphi and the commercial structures built on the southwestern side of the main plaza into Cusipata, "place of happiness and rejoicing."[47] In the time of the Inca, Garcilaso writes, that space remained unbuilt and unoccupied, but under Spanish rule the lots around it were distributed to citizens, who built their houses there. The brevity of Garcilaso's treatment of Cusipata in the *Comentarios Reales* stands in contrast to its prominence in the *cabildo*'s Acts. On April 7, 1546, the city councilors met again with the ecclesiastic *cabildo* in the choir of the cathedral to discuss the possibility of enlarging the existing building or, perhaps, constructing an entirely new church on a different site. Among the proposals considered was the purchase of the property adjacent to the cathedral owned by a certain Alonso de Mesa. The cost of doing so, however, proved prohibitive, and so the councilors decided to consider building a new church on the site of the *tianguis*, the open-air marketplace whose name derives from the Nahuatl word *tianquiztli* (market). The term was used by both Nahuatl and Spanish speakers in early colonial Mexico, and would come to be used throughout Spanish America.[48]

The *tianguis* of Cuzco was in Cusipata, the space known today as the Plaza de Regocijo. In early Spanish Cuzco, as today, the Mercedarian monastery dominated its eastern side. The *cabildo*'s Acts provide little other information about the *tianguis* and the activities that took place there, other than to indicate that it was a racially segregated space. In February 1545, the councilors decreed that "no black woman or man enter into the *tianguis* of this city." The punishment for defying this order was severe: "three pesos for each time a black man or woman is seized [in the *tianguis*], and if they don't pay, they shall be given one hundred lashes in public."[49] The reason for establishing this measure is not stated, but it no doubt attests to a belief that good government and civic order were threatened by the presence of people of African descent in a public space also occupied by Andeans and Spaniards.

The councilors proposed a precise site within the *tianguis* for the construction of the new church, describing its boundaries as extending "from the last of the four pillars of the oratory in the said *tianguis* up to the part of the river that passes by the plaza of this said city."[50] The designated plot thus would have extended from somewhere in the market plaza to the edge of the canalized stream separating it from the main plaza. The construction of a new cathedral in Cuzco appears to have been a priority for both the civic and ecclesiastic *cabildos*, but it was perhaps of greatest interest to Bishop Solano, who regarded it as part of his charge from the Crown. In the letter of September 13, 1543, with which Charles V recommended his appointment, the king stipulates that if the churches the bishop finds in Peru are not satisfactory, then he is to provide for their construction.[51] On June 5, 1546, Solano presented that document to the *cabildo*; the scribe read it aloud to them, and the officials held the letter to their heads as they authorized the construction of the new cathedral in the *tianguis*. The project never came to fruition, but if it had, it would have recast the shape and symbolism of the main

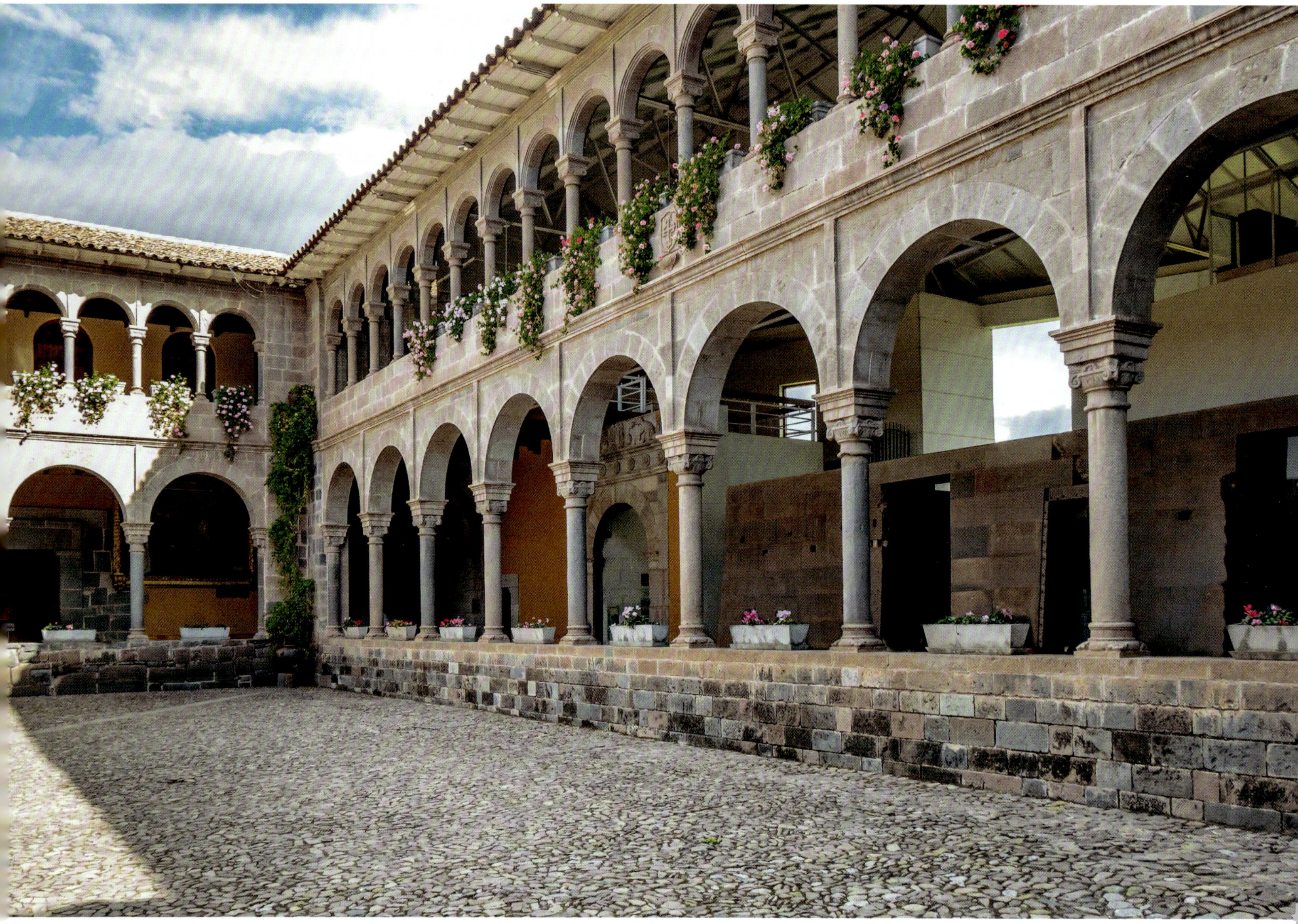

FIG. 7.14 The galleries and arcades in the cloister of the monastery of Santo Domingo, Cuzco, 16th century and later. The young Inca Garcilaso de la Vega may have witnessed the early stages of their construction, which adapted part of an Inca compound for use by Dominican friars.

plaza. Dominating its southwestern side, the cathedral would have effectively enclosed the space, occupying one side of the square as the modified structures of Inca Cuzco occupied the other three. Just two years later, the arcades of new shops would be built there instead, similarly reshaping the plaza of Spanish Cuzco.

To the west of the *tianguis* (or Cusipata) and uphill was a district known as Carmenca. It was from the hilltop in that sector of the city that Francisco Pizarro and his followers caught their first glimpse of Cuzco as they came to the end of the Chinchaysuyu road in November 1533. Garcilaso knew the area well; he writes that among the notable Spaniards living there were Diego de Silva y Guzmán, the author of the *Relación del sitio*, whose house was the closest to the hilltop, and Juan de Betanzos, who lived just downhill from Silva.[52] A map produced in 1643 as evidence in a lawsuit over parish jurisdictions in Carmenca depicts the area in detail, and its rendering of the houses descending from the hilltop provides insight into their design and the materials with which they were built (fig. 7.15). Using line and color to depict adobe walls, wooden doors, and roofs of red tiles and thatch, the artist drew them as rectangular structures surrounding interior patios, a plan with precedents in the history of domestic architecture in both Europe and the Andes.

It is unclear precisely when Betanzos moved into that house in Carmenca, but he was in the city as early as 1543 composing an account of Inca history that would predate the *Suma y narración* by nearly a decade. His collaborators on the project included Francisco de Villacastín, a Spaniard from Segovia who had participated in the Siege of Cuzco as well as the battles of Las Salinas and Chupas, and who, like Betanzos, was proficient in Quechua. Two others—Callapiña and Supno—were from Pacarictambo and were *quipucamayocs*, specialists in recording and reading information on *quipus*. The fifth member of the team was Pedro Escalante, a bilingual native Andean. The document these men produced was a history of the Inca kings beginning with the mythical Manco Capac and ending in the time of Atahualpa and Huascar in the early 1530s. It is known today only through an early seventeenth-century copy held in the Biblioteca Nacional de España, entitled "Discurso sobre la descendencia y gobierno de los ingas" ("Discourse on the Lineage and Government of the Incas"; hereafter, "Discurso").[53]

The "Discurso" is a Spanish translation and transcription of an oral tradition recorded on *quipus* and spoken in Quechua by Callapiña and Supno. Like the *Suma y narración*, it is an early example of cultural production in a Spanish colonial setting in which native Andeans played a central role. Working with Betanzos and Villacastín, they produced a document in Spanish that drew from a Quechua narrative on the foundation and development of Inca Cuzco and the empire more broadly. The task of recording this information, the document intimates, was part of a larger project of information gathering undertaken by Vaca de Castro at a time when Inca history was relatively unknown among the Spanish, and as the appearance of Inca Cuzco was rapidly changing.

When his work with the *quipucamayocs* was complete, Betanzos probably accompanied Vaca de Castro to Lima, where Núñez Vela was being received as the first viceroy of Peru. It was likely there that Betanzos married Angelina Yupanqui, who must have remained in Lima after Francisco Pizarro's death with her only surviving son, also named Francisco. Betanzos and Angelina would return to Cuzco sometime later in the 1540s, and it was perhaps then that they settled in their house in Carmenca.

For Garcilaso, the buildings and spaces of Cuzco at mid-century were an integral part of Inca history, and the remains of its oldest structures—the "relics" of his birthplace—called to mind a sequence of Inca kings including Manco Capac, Inca Viracocha, Topa Inca Yupanqui, and Huayna Capac. For the city councilors, it was the city's future rather than its past that was most important, and the *cabildo*'s Acts show little historical consciousness and no interest in the preservation of royal Inca architecture. The tension between these two positions is further complicated by the projects of historical recuperation being undertaken in the 1540s and 1550s by Betanzos and Cieza de León, who were reconstituting in words on paper that which was being physically dismantled in the city.

The texts from this period provide views of Cuzco from different perspectives, but they also animate that space with a population whose ethnic diversity accords with the inventive iconographies taking shape on coats of arms and on the mural painted on the gable end of the church. The *cabildo*'s Acts document the presence of people of African descent in their references to the town crier Juan Enríquez, the entry about the exclusion of blacks from the *tianguis*, and a later entry—that of October 25, 1548—stipulating that free men and women of African descent in Cuzco were not permitted to have African slaves in their houses, and that those who did would be punished with one hundred lashes and a fine of fifty pesos of gold.[54] An entry of about a month later, November 23, 1548, laments the robberies occurring in the countryside, beyond the limits of the city, and names Diego de Morales as sheriff (*alguacil mayor*) of those regions, authorizing him to arrest and imprison any Spaniards, people of African descent, or Andeans engaging in those unlawful activities. In addition to providing a window onto the social history of early colonial Cuzco, the passage lists the three primary categories of personhood understood to be relevant to the city and its environs at this time. The relatively new category of *mestizo*—the identity embraced by Garcilaso—was still in formation.

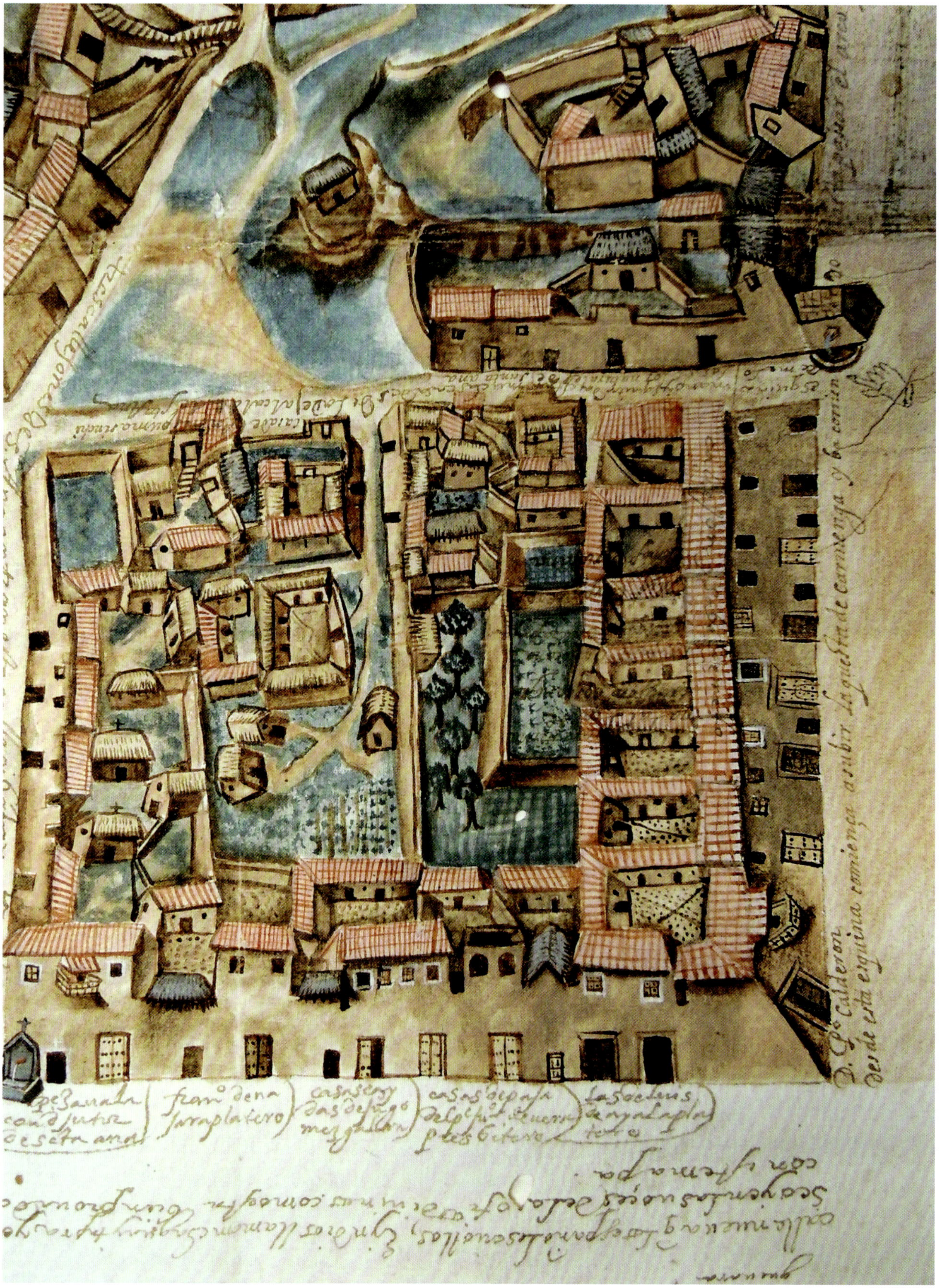

The *cabildo*'s Acts refer to a number of native Andeans in Cuzco, including Paullu, who was known to the Spanish after his baptism as Cristóbal, and Pedro Escalante, the man who had worked with Betanzos, Villacastín, Callapiña, and Supno in composing the "Discurso" in 1543. The council's secretary describes him as a "native Indian of these Kingdoms who is married and has a wife and is Christian and is a Spanish-speaking Indian [*indio ladino*]."[55] The passage speaks of his adoption of the Spanish language and religious practices in the form of marriage, both of which were understood by the councilors as indices of good citizenship. On March 16, 1545 they awarded him half of a housing lot; on June 30, 1548 they awarded him an entire lot; and on December 24, 1548 he was given title to some property where coca was cultivated, a desirable award in that it was a source of income for the title-holder.[56] These entries in the Acts show that Escalante enjoyed the councilors' favor in a way other native Andeans in Cuzco evidently did not, and they demonstrate—as does the case of Paullu, who also converted to Christianity and married—one of the strategies employed by native people in Spanish colonial Peru as they navigated a new social and political landscape. Other Andeans whose names appear in the documents of this period are Angelina Yupanqui, Juana Marca Chimpu (who had married Betanzos's collaborator Villacastín in 1543), and Garcilaso's mother, Isabel Chimpu Ocllo.

Among the Spaniards residing in the Cuzco of the 1540s and 1550s were Betanzos, Villacastín, *corregidor* Carbajal, Sebastián Garcilaso, the city councilors, clerics and members of the religious orders, and, no doubt, some women, though few traces of the latter are left in the documentary record. Spanish and native elites coexisted in the city alongside free and enslaved people of African descent, craft specialists such as Francisco de Torres, who was paid for his work on the cathedral's choir stalls, and the builders—at least some of them native Andeans—who constructed the shops on the south side of the plaza. The unnamed native porters who carried the young Garcilaso out of Cuzco to meet his father and Gonzalo Pizarro on their return from Quito were clearly understood to be different kinds of native Andeans altogether. It was in this multiethnic environment that Cuzco was being remembered and remade in the middle of the sixteenth century.

FIG. 7.15 (*facing page*) Artist unknown, map of Cuzco, 1643. Ink and wash on paper, 113 × 57 cm (detail). Archivo Arzobispal, Lima. This portion of the map shows houses in Carmenca, the area of Cuzco where Diego de Silva y Guzmán, Juan de Betanzos, and Angelina Yupanqui lived in the 16th century.

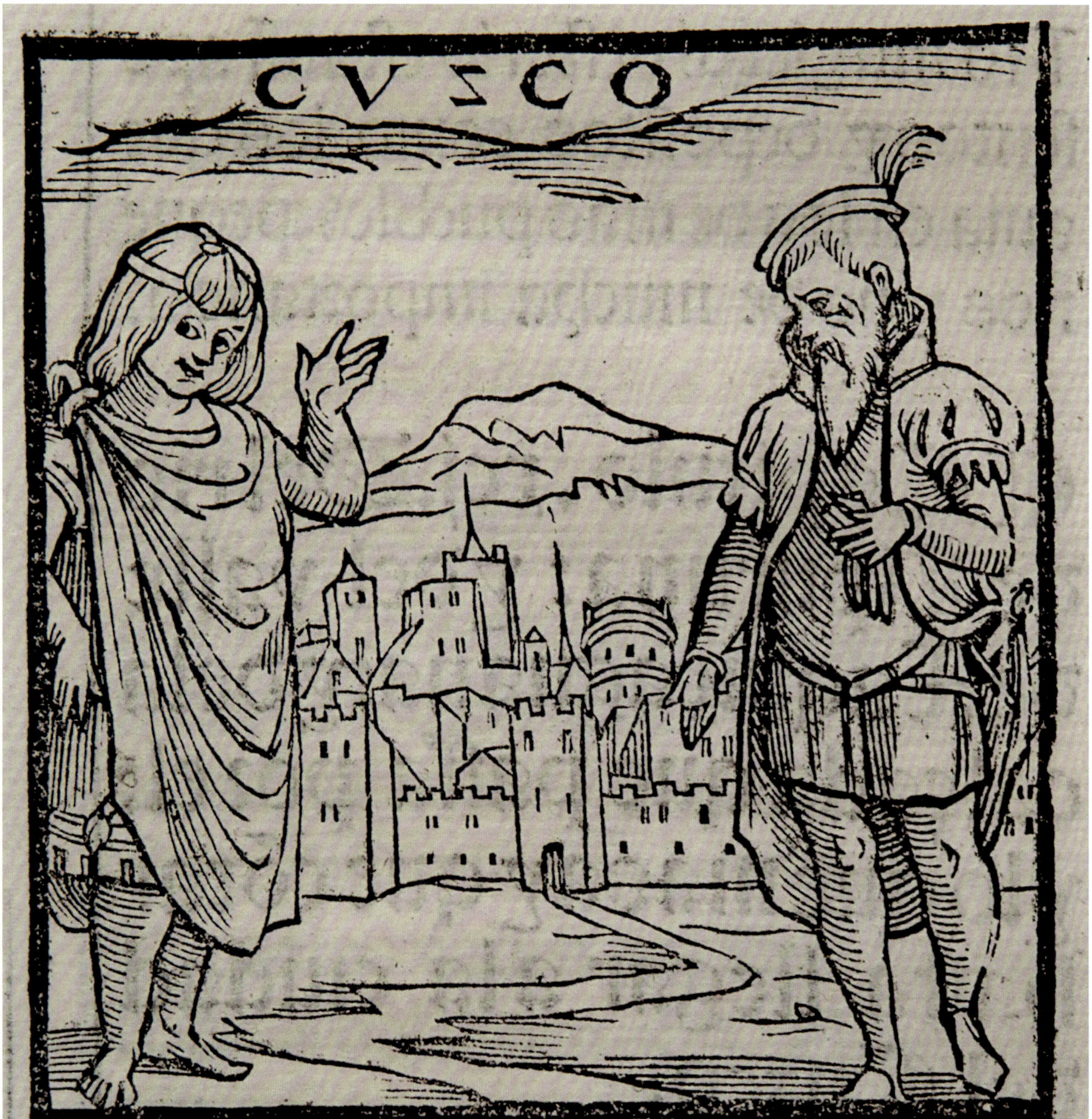
CVSCO

Conclusion

An End and a Beginning

As the young Garcilaso de la Vega was exploring the streets of his birthplace with his childhood friends, and as Juan de Betanzos was composing the *Suma y narración* with the help of Angelina Yupanqui, Pedro de Cieza de León, too, was in Cuzco collecting information for his own history of the Inca, the work that would be published as the *Parte primera de la Crónica del Perú*. His impressions of the city and those of his native collaborators shape the text of a chapter entitled "On the manner and design with which the city of Cuzco is founded, and on the four royal roads that depart from it, and on the great buildings it had, and who its founder was."[1] Unlike Pedro Sancho, who wrote about the city he saw in 1534, Cieza de León presents a vision of Cuzco that is as much about what can no longer be seen as it is about what is visible. Sacsahuaman, he says "was an excellent building, and it is so in these times, although most of it is destroyed."[2] Similarly:

> In many parts of this city there are grand buildings under the ground, and inside of them are found some slabs of stone and water channels and even jewels and pieces of gold which were buried. And certainly, there must be great treasures buried in this city unknown to those who are living there.[3]

The woodcut illustration that accompanied Cieza de León's description of Cuzco when it was printed in Seville in 1553 likewise calls to mind the city's past and its connection with the present (fig. 8.1). Probably designed by an artist associated with the shop of the printer Martín de Montesdoca, it depicts a city whose crenellated walls and barbicans surround an array of buildings with towers, domes, and pitched roofs. It reveals nothing of the particularities of the actual city, instead presenting an image of the city as a concept, an icon like those on the coats of arms of Francisco Pizarro (see figs 2.3 and 5.13) and Battista Agnese's *mappa mundi* (see fig. 2.11).[4] Above the image is the word "Cuzco," and flanking it are two men. On the left, the figure's long hair, headband, and mantle mark him as an Inca, just as the other figure's hat, beard, and tailored clothing identify him as a Spaniard. The references to the city's foundation in the chapter's title and in the text—which names Manco Capac and Francisco Pizarro as Cuzco's two founders—reveal the identities of these figures and suggest that the artist was attempting to reiterate in pictorial terms the chapter's contents. Positioned between Manco Capac and Pizarro, the

FIG. 8.1 ***(facing page)*** Woodcut image of Cuzco, in Pedro de Cieza de León, *Parte primera de la Crónica del Perú* (Seville: Martín de Montesdoca, 1553), fol. 107v. Woodcut, ink on paper. Newberry Library, Chicago. The figures depict the city's founders at two distinct moments in its history: Manco Capac (*left*), and Francisco Pizarro (*right*).

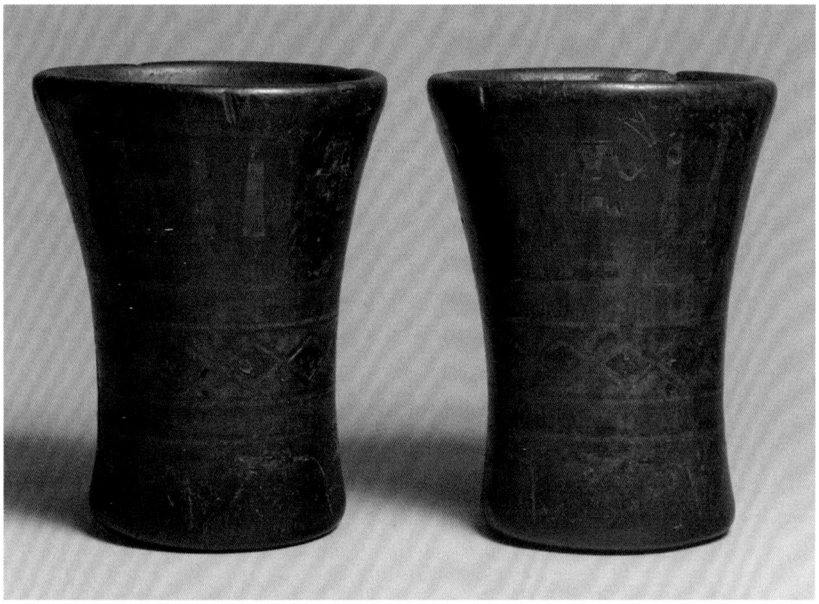

FIG. 8.2 A pair of *queros* (wooden drinking vessels), 16th–17th century. Wood with pigmented resin inlay, h. 17.75 cm. Metropolitan Museum of Art, New York. The pictures at the lips of these *queros* depict a man and woman in traditional Inca garb; the repeating diamond pattern below is a standard design that also appears on Inca tunics.

city is cast as the subject of an imagined dialogue between the two gesturing men, each of whom would have a different story to tell about its history and symbolism.

The nearly contemporary image accompanying the first publication of Pedro Sancho's *Relatione* in Giovanni Battista Ramusio's *Navigationi et viaggi* (1556), too, hints at an encounter, but one of a different sort (see fig. 0.3). Spaniards on horseback approach the city's gates while, inside, the Inca king is held aloft as he and his retinue move toward a stepped platform, perhaps the artist's interpretation of the author's description of the stepped terraces at Sacsahuaman. Unlike the image from the *Parte primera*, which brings together the embodiments of the ancient Inca past and the Spanish colonial present as if they had personally met, the illustration from Ramusio's volume is an image of potentiality, one that sets the stage for an encounter between Incas and Spaniards that has yet to occur. These early images and their associated texts promulgated an image of Cuzco in Europe at mid-century that encouraged readers to imagine the city's past but provided no sense of its appearance in the 1550s, when the plaza was being reshaped and adorned with arcades, and as visual images such as those inside the nave of the church and on its exterior wall were grafting new narratives onto the city's buildings and spaces.

As Cieza de León's reference to the "grand buildings under the ground" suggests, those with knowledge of the city's past experienced it in a way that brought its history to the surface. Betanzos, for example, writes that the site of the *picota* was where the sugarloaf-shaped stone image of the Sun stood in the time of the Inca, and that the monastery of Santo Domingo had been the House of the Sun.[5] For Angelina Yupanqui, Isabel Chimpu Ocllo, and the other elder Andeans of mid-century Cuzco, those places served as what the historian Pierre Nora called "les lieux de mémoire" (sites of memory), and the act of moving through the city's streets and plazas must have brought to mind narratives of the changes they had witnessed.[6] But for *mestizos* such as Garcilaso de la Vega, born in the aftermath of the foundation of Spanish Cuzco, the city had always been a place where the past and present existed in conflict and conversation with one another. It was that conception of the city that would give rise to the inventive visual culture of later colonial Cuzco, where *tocapu* patterns would comfortably coexist with heraldic and figural imagery on tunics and *queros* (fig. 8.2), where Christian ceremonies and festivals would routinely involve participants dressed in Inca garb, and where a distinctive style of painting—the Cuzco School—would emerge to spread throughout the Andes (fig. 8.3). Indeed, the genealogy of religious paintings produced in the native workshops of eighteenth-century Cuzco extends back to the first decades of Spanish colonial rule, when images such as those installed in the cathedral

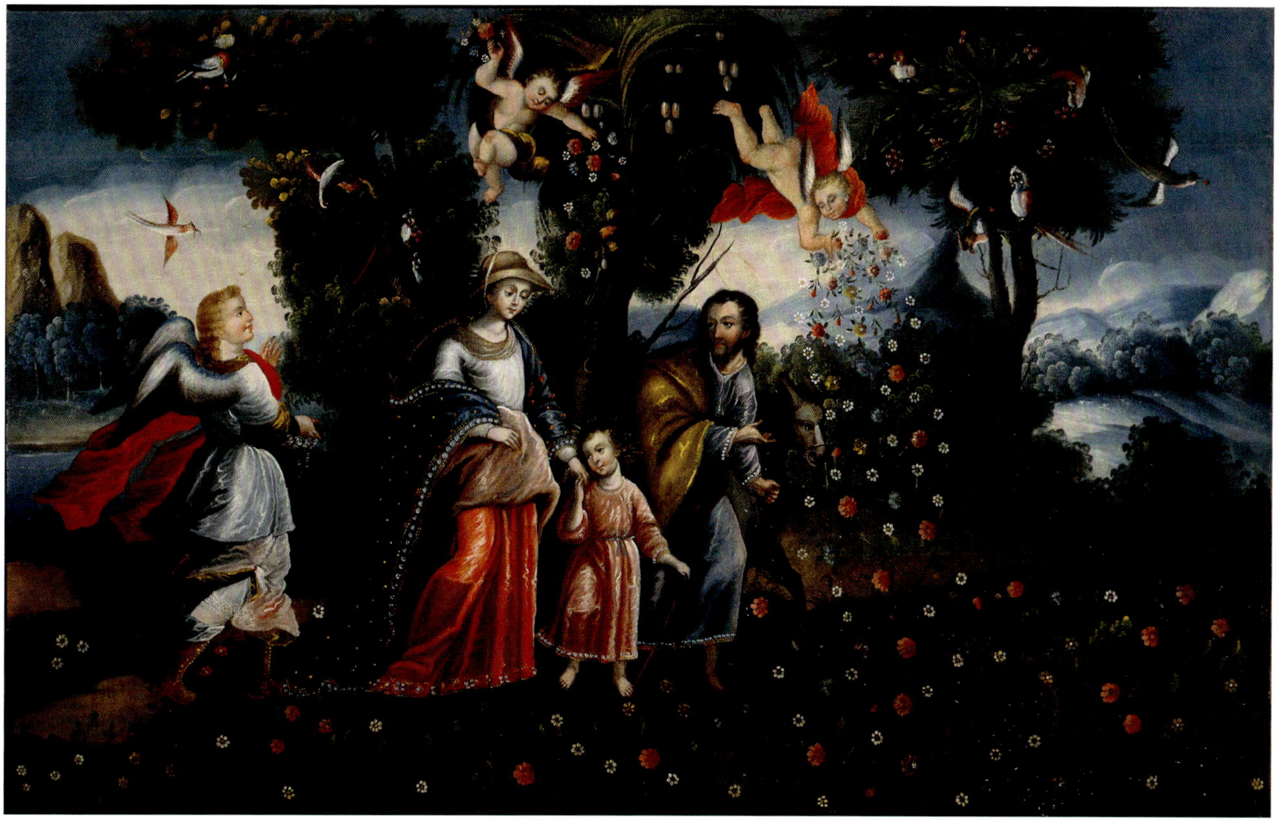

FIG. 8.3 Artist unknown, *Return from Egypt*, 18th century. Oil on canvas, 106.5 × 170 cm. Collection of Carl and Marilynn Thoma. An example of the work of the Cuzco School, the painting derives its composition from a northern European print, but adds a panoramic landscape characteristic of earlier Netherlandish painting, as well as colorful birds and flowers.

of Cuzco introduced a new visual vocabulary to the Andes, the raw materials for iconographic experimentation in the centuries that followed.[7]

The prologue to the *Suma y narración* and its dedication to the Viceroy Antonio de Mendoza attests to its origin in 1551, but its final chapter—appended to the main body of the text—dates to 1557. By that time, Spain had a new king and Peru had a new viceroy. Charles V had abdicated, leaving his American kingdoms to his son, Philip II; Mendoza, who had died in 1552, was succeeded in the office of viceroy by a relative named Andrés Hurtado de Mendoza. By the later 1550s, although Cuzco did not yet resemble the place portrayed in the seventeenth-century painting of the city as it was being struck by an earthquake in 1650 (see fig. 4.6), the descriptive texts of this era attest to significant changes that had taken place there. For the Spanish, the transformation of Inca Cuzco into Spanish Cuzco was, at first, an act of the imagination: a shift in the identities and functions of buildings and spaces brought about by ritual and writing. Later, the largely metaphysical changes of the 1530s gave way to the construction and renovation of buildings, their dressing with roof tiles, and their decoration with painted and sculpted imagery. But the early colonial sources reveal much more than the material conditions of life in mid-century Cuzco. They hint at the experiences of an ethnically diverse citizenry, and at a host of cross-cultural exchanges of knowledge facilitated by literacy, translation, and bilingualism as native elites became familiar with the practices of Spanish colonial governance and the sacred rites and narratives of the Church, as Spaniards learned and wrote about the achievements of Manco Capac, Pachacuti, and Huayna Capac, and as new categories of personhood and a novel visual and spatial culture took shape in the ancient capital of the Inca Empire.

Abbreviations

AASG	Archivo del Abadía del Sacromonte de Granada
ACC	Archivo de la Catedral del Cuzco
AGI	Archivo General de Indias, Seville
AHN	Archivo Histórico Nacional, Madrid
ARC	Archivo Regional del Cuzco
BNE	Biblioteca Nacional de España
fol.	folio
fols.	folios
leg.	legajo
lib.	libro
MP	Mapas y Planos
ms.	manuscript
n.	note
n.p.	no pagination
no.	number
part.	partida
r	recto
RB	Real Biblioteca, Palacio Real, Madrid
tit.	title
v	verso

Notes

INTRODUCTION

1. "Quake in Cuzco" 1950.
2. Kubler 1952, pp. 7–8.
3. Cummins 1996.
4. On the Mexican case, Toussaint et al. 1938; Caso 1956; Calnek 1979; Mundy 2015.
5. Kagan 2000, p. 69; Schreffler 2014.
6. Archaeological studies of the Inca settlement are synthesized in Farrington 2013. Agurto Calvo's (1980) survey centers on the identification of Inca remains in the city, as does that of Paredes García (2001). The studies of Hyslop (1990) and Bauer (2004, pp. 107–57) link those remains in Cuzco to colonial-period texts that refer to them.
7. Agurto Calvo 1980, pp. 122–28.
8. Zuidema 1983.
9. Archaeological studies focused on Spanish colonial Cuzco include Estrada Ibérico et al. 2009; Paredes García 2009.
10. On the Salas Valdés portal, Tord 1978.
11. Surveys and critiques of these sources include MacCormack 1991; Ramírez 1996; Niles 1999; Julien 2000; Adorno 2008; Pease 2008a; Salomon 2015. Porras Barrenechea 1962 is an earlier and influential study of the subject.
12. Hemming 1970, p. 17.
13. Wethey 1949, pp. 16, 39.
14. Viñuales 2004.
15. Fraser 1990.
16. Lockhart 1994; Lamana 2008.
17. On critiques of this approach, see also Lamana 2008, pp. 1–19.
18. Lefebvre 1991.
19. For example, Gell 1998; DeMarrais et al. 2004; Brown 2015.
20. On the productive capacity of texts and images in early colonial Spanish America, Greenblatt 1991; Lefebvre 1991, pp. 151–52; Rama 1996, pp. 1–49; Rappaport and Cummins 2011, pp. 219–50.
21. Bauer and Stanish 1990; Chatfield 2009.
22. The author's full name is Juan Diez de Betanzos. I follow Domínguez Faura 2015a in referring to him as Betanzos throughout this book. To the text of 1551 was appended a brief chapter dating to 1557.
23. Rowe 1967.
24. Cook 1982, pp. 108–14; Verano 1992, p. 16.

CHAPTER 1

1. Santo Tomás 1560, fol. 174v: "tallo de arbol quando echa"; González Holguín 1608, fol. 345r: "Las plumas blandas de las aves xugosas mantecosas lleno el canon de sangre o manteca."
2. Betanzos 1551–57, fol. 95r; Betanzos 2015, pp. 315–16: "habla ventura." On the ceremony of the first hair-cutting more generally, Classen 1993, pp. 61–62; Yaya 2012, pp. 121–22.
3. On his biography, Martín Rubio 1999; Mannheim 2008, pp. 186–89; Domínguez Faura 2015a, pp. 13–27.
4. Betanzos 1551–57, fol. 2r; Betanzos 2015, p. 119: "uno de bocablos y otro de notiçias y oraçiones enteras y coloquios y confisionario."

5. On Angelina Yupanqui, Domínguez Faura 2015a, pp. 19–21; Phipps 2015. On her status and economic power in relation to other elite Andean women, Rostworowski 1989; Vicuña Guengerich 2015; Quispe-Agnoli 2016.

6. Betanzos 1551–57, fol. 2; Betanzos 2015, p. 120. "Porque no la traduje y recopilé siendo ynformado de uno sólo sino de muchos y de los más antiguos y de crédito que hallé entre estos naturales."

7. "Discurso sobre la descendencia" 1543–1608.

8. Betanzos 1551–57, fol. 2; Betanzos 2015, p. 120: "Para ser verdadero y fiel traduçidor tengo de guardar la manera y horden del hablar d[e] estos naturales."

9. Betanzos 1551–57, fol. 95r; Betanzos 2015, pp. 316: "muger ligítima y principal de su hijo."

10. Betanzos 1880. The manuscript is Real Biblioteca del Monasterio de El Escorial, ms. L-I-5.

11. Betanzos 1551–57. The manuscript is Fundación Bartolomé March, Palma de Mallorca, cat. no. 106-VII.

12. Betanzos 1551–57, fol. 3r; Betanzos 2015, p. 123.

13. On Tiahuanaco, Protzen and Nair 2013; Vranich and Stanish 2013.

14. Betanzos 1551–57, fol. 4v; Betanzos 2015, p. 126: "Dios hazedor del mundo."

15. Young-Sánchez 2004, pp. 31–35; Janusek 2005.

16. Dean 2010.

17. Classen 1993, pp. 70–72.

18. Betanzos 1551–57, fol. 5r; Betanzos 2015, p. 129: "Casas pequeñas pagizas y muy ruines."

19. Betanzos 1551–57, fol. 5v; Betanzos 2015, p. 129: "Lo que quiere dezir este nombre Cozco no lo saben declarer más de dezir que ansí se nombrava antiguamente."

20. Cerrón-Palomino 2013, pp. 106–8.

21. Betanzos 1551–57, fol. 5v; Betanzos 2015, p. 129: "Casa de produzimiento."

22. On the various versions of the Inca origin myth and the geographic features associated with it, Urton 1990; Bauer 1991.

23. Pease 1973; Urton 1990; Julien 2000; Yaya 2012, pp. 169–77.

24. Betanzos 1551–57, fol. 5v; Betanzos 2015, pp. 129–30.

25. On *uncus* and their patterns, Rowe and Rowe 1996; Pillsbury 2002; Phipps 2004, pp. 17–25; Hamilton 2018, pp. 208–15.

26. Xerez 1534, fol. 10r: "un esquadron de i[n]dios vestidos de una librea de colores a manera de escaques."

27. Betanzos 1551–57, fol. 5v; Betanzos 2015, p. 130: "Bestidas muy ricamente con unas mantas y faxas que ellos llaman chunbis muy labradas de oro y con los prendederos de oro muy fino los cuales son los unos alfileres largos de dos palmos que ellos llaman topos."

28. On the *chumbi* and other garments worn by Inca women, Phipps 2004, pp. 20–21. Betanzos 1551–57, fols. 39v–40r; Betanzos 2015, p. 197: "Vestida de ropa fina texida de oro y lana fina . . . Llevaba una faxada por la çintura una faxa texida con lana fina e oro, en la qual faxa yban muchas y diversas pinturas."

29. Betanzos 1551–57, fol. 5v; Betanzos 2015, p. 130: "Y ansimismo sacaron estas mugeres el serviçio con que avían de servir y guisar de comer a sus maridos, como son ollas y cantaros pequeños y platos y escudillas y basos para beber todo de oro fino."

30. Cummins 2002.

31. Betanzos 1551–57, fol. 38v; Betanzos 2015, p. 195: "buelta de tienpo."

32. Betanzos 1551–57, fol. 19v; Betanzos 2015, p. 161: "Una casa al sol, en la qual casa pusiesen y fuese puesto un bulto a quien en el lugar del sol reberençiasen y hiziesen sacrifiçio."

33. Betanzos 1551–57, fols. 19v–20r; Betanzos 2015, p. 162. On this episode, see also MacCormack 1991, pp. 285–300.

34. Betanzos 1551–57, fol. 23r; Betanzos 2015, p. 168.

35. On quarries, Protzen 1993, pp. 137–53; Béjar 2003; Ogburn 2013. On Inca techniques for cutting and fitting stone, Protzen 1983; Protzen 1993. On the symbolism attached to this labor and its products, Dean 2010, pp. 76–79, 112–15. On the continued use of these materials and techniques in the colonial period, Nair 2007.

36. Betanzos 1551–57, fol. 70r; Betanzos 2015, p. 260: "sacrifiçio solemne." On the use of blood in this and other cases in Inca ritual, MacCormack 1991, pp. 111–12.

37. Betanzos 1551–57, fol. 21; Betanzos 2015, p. 164. Other sources refer to the idol as *Punchao*. See Duviols 1976; Julien 1999; Julien 2007, Hamilton 2018, pp. 203–5.

38. On archaeological research at Coricancha, Farrington 2013, pp. 163–77. On the *cancha*, Farrington 2013, pp. 42–45; Nair 2015, pp. 21–23.

39. Hamilton 2018, pp. 221–33.

40. Farrington 2013, pp. 170–75, 317–23. On *capacocha* and the ritual assemblage associated with it, Schroedl 2008; Reinhard and Ceruti 2010; Hamilton 2018, pp. 233–40.

41. Betanzos 1551–57, fol. 21v; Betanzos 2015, p. 164: "así como fuera persona que comiera e beviera."

42. Betanzos 1551–57, fol. 88r–v; Betanzos 2015, pp. 299–300: "Y como llegase a la puerta quitóse los çapatos y llevando su cabeça algo baxa hizo su acatamiento al sol; y luego él mismo ensendió delante del bulto del sol, en un brasero de oro, un haze pequeño de leña que allí le llevavan los servidores del sol . . . y ençendiendo la lunbre quemó en ella un cordero sacrificándolo al sol, degollándolo primero bivo y ofreçiendo aquella sangre que del cordero salía al sol. Y esto hecho, saliósse de allí haziendo al sol su acatamiento y entró dentro de la cassa en çierto aposento donde le metió el mayordomo del sol y ansimismo entraron con el Ynga su primo Yamque Yupangue y los dos señores que avían sido governadores y otros ningunos no entraron y delante dellos aquel señor mayordomo del sol dio quenta al Ynga de las cosas y riquezas que a su cargo tenía del sol."

43. González Holguín 1608, p. 149: "La plaza del Cuzco de las fiestas, huelgas, y borracheras." On the etymology of the term, Cerrón-Palomino 2013, pp. 213–14.

44. Betanzos 1551–57, fol. 21v; Betanzos 2015, p. 165: "Una piedra de la hechura de un pan de açúcar, puntiaguda para arriba y enforrada de una hoja de oro."

45. Betanzos 1551–57, fol. 22r; Betanzos 2015, p. 166: "Hasta que los españoles entraron en la çiudad."

46. Meddens et al. 2010.

47. Studies on *ushnus* include Farrington 2013, pp. 37–39, 60–63; Meddens 2015.

48. Farrington 2013, pp. 141–44, 385 n.6.

49. Betanzos 1551–57, fol. 19r; Betanzos 2015, p. 161: "Cómo Ynga Yupanque hizo la casa del sol y el bulto del sol."

50. Betanzos 1551–57, fols. 35v–36r; Betanzos 2015, pp. 189–90: "Que los tres señores, sus amigos, poblasen desde las casas del sol para abaxo hazia la junta de los dos ríos en aquel espaçio de casas que entre los dos ríos se hizieron y desde las casas del sol para abaxo al cual sitio mandó que se llamase Hurin Cuzco que dize lo bajo del Cuzco."

51. Betanzos 1551–57, fols. 35v–36r; Betanzos 2015, pp. 189–90: "E de las casas del sol para arriba, todo lo que tomavan los dos arroyos hasta el çerro do[nde] ahora es la fortaleza, dió e repartió a los señores más propi[n]c[u]os, deudos suyos e deçendientes de su linaje por línea recta."

52. Zuidema 1964; Yaya 2012.

53. Betanzos 1551–57, fol. 4v; Betanzos 2015, p. 126: "adoratorio o ydolo."

54. Zuidema 1964; Bauer 1998.

55. Betanzos 1551–57, fol. 26; Betanzos 2015, pp. 173–74. On walking and the production of space, Lefebvre 1991.

CHAPTER 2

1. On the road system, Hyslop 1984; Matos Mendieta and Barreiro 2015. On the Chinchaysuyu road, Pino Matos 2015.

2. On the architecture of Inca Quito, Salomon 1986, pp. 147–49; Espinosa Apolo 2002–3a; Porras 2002–3; Terán and Pino 2005; Pérez Arteta 2017, pp. 129–325.

3. Betanzos 1551–57, fol. 96v; Betanzos 2015, p. 318: "Le quitó el juizio y entendimiento y diole una sarna y lepra que le puso muy debilitado."

4. On smallpox in Peru and elsewhere in the sixteenth-century Americas, Cook 1998; Alchon 2003, pp. 67–68.

5. Betanzos 1551–57, fol. 97v; Betanzos 2015, p. 319: "Los señores que con él estavan le hizieron abrir y toda su carne sacar, adereçándole porque no se dañase, sin le quebrar gueso ninguno le adereçaron y curaron al sol y al ayre; y después de seco y curado, vistiéronle de ropas preçiadas y pusiéronle en unas andas ricas y bien adereçadas de pluma y oro. Y estando ya el cuerpo ansí, enviáronle al Cuzco."

6. Betanzos 1551–57, fol. 97v; Betanzos 2015, p. 320: "Comiença la ystoria de los dos hijos de Guaina Capac llamados Atagualpa y Guascar y de las guerras y divisiones que entre estos dos hermanos uvo sobre quién sería señor y reynaría de los dos."

7. Betanzos 1551–57, fol. 102r; Betanzos 2015, p. 330.

8. On Caranqui, Bray and Echeverría Almeida 2014.

9. Betanzos 1551–57, fol. 121r; Betanzos 2015, p. 375: "A nuestro pueblo de Tangaralá son llegadas una gentes blancas y barbudas y traen una manera de obejas sobre las cuales vienen y caminan y son muy grandes, más que las nuestras muy mucho: y estas gentes vienen tan vestidas, que no se les paresçe de sus carnes si no las manos y la cara y desta la mitad della porque la otra mitad traen cubierta con las barbas que les naçen en ella; y estas gentes se çiñen çiertas çeñiduras ençima de sus vestidos y destas çiñiduras traen colgado çierta pieça de plata que pareçe a estos palos que las mujeres meter en sus urdienbres para apretar lo que ansí tejen." On Huamachuco, Topic 2009; Topic and Topic 1993.

10. On the comparison, see also Cummins 1996.

11. Mena 1534, fol. 2r: "Año de mil y quinientos y treynta y uno en el mes de febrero nos embarcamos en el puerto de Panama que es en tierra firme dozientos y cincuenta hombres los ochenta de caballo

y [l]levamos por capitan al muy magnifico y esforçado cavallero francisco piçarro." On Mena, Pease 2008a; Porras Barrenechea 1986, pp. 85–89. On Bartolomé Pérez, Álvarez Márquez 2009, vol. 1, pp. 178–80; Domínguez Guzmán 1975, pp. 41–42.

12. AGI, Lima, 565, leg. 1, fol. 16; *Colección de documentos inéditos* 1873, p. 6: "tierra y provincias del Perú."

13. AGI, MP, Escudos, 7: "Caroli caesaris auspicio et labore ingenio ac impensa Ducis Pizarro inventa pacata." See also Estenssoro 2010.

14. Kagan 2000.

15. *Colección de documentos inéditos* 1873, pp. 10–11: "En los seis años primeros . . . que el oro que se cogiere en las minas nos paguen el diezmo; e complidos los dichos seis años paguen el noveno, e así, descendiendo en cada un año, hasta llegar al quinto. Pero del oro y otras cosas que se ovieren de rescate o cabalgadas o en otra qualquier manera, desde luego no han de pagar el quinto de todo ello." On the search for gold in the Americas more generally, Hoopes 2011.

16. Weckmann 1992, pp. 80–85.

17. Scott 2011.

18. On the Ribeiro map, Davies 2003; Brotton 2014, pp. 186–216.

19. Mena 1534, fol. 2r: "Tuvimos noticia de un gran señor llamado Atabalipa: el cual tenía guerra con su hermano mayor llamado el Cozco."

20. Ramírez 2005, pp. 13–56.

21. Mena 1534, fol. 4r: "el libro de nuestra santa ley."

22. Lockhart 1972, p. 202.

23. Leitch 2010, p. 175; Cummins 2011, pp. 211–20.

24. Mena 1534, fol. 4r: "pensando que lo quería besar."

25. On this episode, MacCormack 1989; Seed 1991; Lamana 2008, pp. 27–64; Cornejo Polar 2013, pp. 13–58; Herring 2015.

26. On the *relación* as a literary genre in the early modern Spanish world, Mignolo 1982; Portuondo 2009, pp. 63–66.

27. Mena 1534, fol. 5r: "que desguarnecerian ciertas casas que estanan [*sic*] chapadas con oro."

28. On Zárate, Bueno, and Moguer, Lockhart 1972, pp. 285–86, 401–4.

29. Mena 1534, fol. 5r: "y llevaron mucha gente que los llevavan en hamacas: y eran muy bien servidos."

30. On the translation of the name, Mena 1534, fol. 5v: "que en su lengua quiere decir barbero"; cf. González Holguín 1608, p. 309: "un pajarito."

31. Mena 1534, fol. 5r–v: "Estos bohíos estaban de la parte que sale el sol chapados de oro de unas planchas grandes: y quanto mas les venia dando la sombra del sol mas bajo oro en ellos." On the use of the term *bohío* in sixteenth-century Spanish American texts, Fraser 1990, pp. 26, 71–72. Fraser, citing a seventeenth-century text, suggests that "it is the material [mud and straw], not the shape or size, which is the identifying feature of a *bohío*." Mena's reference to the "bohíos del sol" in Cuzco, whose walls were plated with gold, is at odds with this interpretation. I would suggest instead that Mena uses the term *bohío* to refer to a single-room structure regardless of its construction materials.

32. Mena 1534, fol. 5v: "Una silla . . . [que] era tan grande que pesaba diez y nueve mil pesos . . . una fuente muy grande de oro muy fino . . . pesaba esta pieza mas de doce mil pesos."

33. On weight, Stielau 2014. Betanzos 1551–57, fols. 39v–40r; Betanzos 2015, p. 197: "cada uno los cuales suelen pesar dos libras de oro."

34. On Xerez, Pease 2008b.

35. Xerez 1534, fol. 13r: "hay otras veinte casas las paredes chapadas de una hoja delgada de oro por de dentro y por de fuera."

36. Xerez 1534, fol. 20v: "Y dijo que la ciudad del Cuzco es tan grande como se ha dicho, y que está sentada en una ladera cerca del llano. Las calles muy bien concertadas y empedradas, y en ocho días que allí estuvieron no pudieron ver todo lo que allí había; y que una casa del Cuzco tenía chapería de oro."

37. Mena 1534, fol. 5v: "En todas aquellas casas del pueblo dizen que havia tanto oro que era cosa de maravilla."

38. Betanzos 1551–57, fol. 21v; Betanzos 2015, p. 165: "al tienpo que la edificavan, estando asentando, çierta piedra quebróse de la juntura de la tal piedra un pedaço como tres dedos de ancho e largo, y mandó Ynga Yupangue que luego fuese allí derretida çierta plata y baziada de tal manera en la piedra."

39. Betanzos 1551–57, fol. 67v; Betanzos 2015, p. 254: "Que de aquel oro que ansí se avía traydo se hiziese una çinta ancha de dos palmos y medio y que fuese delgada y del gordor que es agora un plato de estaño pequeño . . . Siendo puesta por la parte de afuera desde donde dize la paja de la cobertura hasta do[nde] la cantería es de la cassa."

40. Bauer 2004, p. 147.

41. Polo 1986, p. 245: "Il palagio del signore dell'isola è molto grande, ed è coperto d'oro, come si cuoprono di qua le chiese di piombo. E tutto lo spazzo delle camere è coperto d'oro, ed èvvi alto bene due dita; e tutte le finestre e mura e ogni cosa e anche le sale sono coperte d'oro, e non si potrebbe dire la sua valuta."

42. Columbus 1990, p. 46: "por no perder tiempo, quiero ir a ver si puedo topar la isla de Çipango"; ibid., p. 72: "Quisiera oy partir para la isla de Cuba, que creo que deve ser Çipango, según las señas que dan esta gente de la grandeza della y riqueza"; ibid., p. 74: "por señas que me hizieron todos los indios destas islas y aqellos que llevo yo en los navios, porque por lengua no los entiendo, es la isla de Çipango, de que se cuentan cosas maravillosas."

43. Columbus 1990, p. 198: "Entre otros lugares que nombravan donde se cogía el oro, dixeron de Çipango, al qual ellos llaman Çibao, y allí afirmaron que ay gran cantidad de oro."

44. *Colección de documentos inéditos* 1883, pp. 246–49. "Tiene oro en mucha cantidad en su casa . . . de casa de este Cacique Davaive viene todo el oro que sale por este Golfo, y todo lo que tienen estos caciques de estas comarcas . . . este Cacique Davaive tiene gran fundición de oro en su casa: tiene cien hombres a la continua que labran oro."

45. Pérez de Oliva n.d., fols. 12r, 13r; Martyr d'Anghiera 1516, fol. 6r: "quem cacicu caunabóam vocant, id est, dominum domus aureae" (contractions and abbreviations in the original expanded).

46. Transcribed in Serrano y Sanz 1918, p. 279: "e agora la mandamos llama Castilla aurifera."

47. Mena 1534, fol. 5v: "Sin ayuda ninguna de indios (porque ellos no les querían ayudar porque era bohío de sol / diziendo que se morirían) los cristianos determinaron con unas barretas de cobre de desguarnecer estos bohíos."

48. On the symbolism of gold among the Inca, Herring 2015, pp. 118–58.

49. Xerez 1534, fol. 20v: "Quitaron setecientas planchas, que una con otra tenían a quinientos pesos, de otra casa quitaron los indios cuantidad de doscientos mil pesos, y que por ser muy bajo no lo quisieron recebir."

50. Xerez 1534, fol. 20v: "La mayor parte de todo esto eran planchas, a manera de tablas de cajas, de a tres y a cuatro palmos de largo. Esto quitaron de las paredes de los bohíos, y traían agujeros, que parece haber estado clavadas." Mena 1534, fol. 6v: "Le hicieron barras: y esto se repartieron entre la gente."

51. Lockhart 1972, pp. 13, 96–102.

52. Mena 1534, fol. 6v: "y a muchos de los que lo ganaron, dió menos de lo que merecian: y esto digolo porque assi se hizo conmigo."

53. Wagner 1931; Baumgärtner 2017, pp. 10–54.

CHAPTER 3

1. Ramusio 1556. On Venice and publications on the Americas, Caracciolo Aricò 1990; Perocco 1997; Horodowich 2005.

2. For Sancho's biography, Lockhart 1972, pp. 276–83; Arocena 1986, pp. 24–48; Pease 2008b. Arguing for Calahorra rather than Medina de Ríoseco as Sancho's birthplace, González Ochoa 2011, pp. 21–30.

3. Sancho 1556, fol. 398v: "cinquecento & tante verghe d'oro, levate da certe muaglie della casa del Cusco."

4. Betanzos 1551–51, fol. 136v; Betanzos 2015, p. 406.

5. Sancho 1556, fol. 399v: "Quella notte (percioche morì al tardi) su lasciato il suo corpo in piazza, accioche del morir suo fosse dato à tutti notitia."

6. Sancho 1556, fol. 402v: "Niuno di Spagnuoli vi fu che volesse accettar di starvi."

7. Sancho 1556, fol. 403v: "Se il fiume ha le rive fassose da una banda & l'altra, armano sopra d'este un muro grande di pietra alto, et poi mettono quattro stanghe grosse di duo palmi o poco meno che traversano il fiume, & nel mezzo in forma di graticci tessono vimini verdi grossi come dua dita ben tessuti, che non sia piu lento l'uno che l'altro, ligati in buona forma, & sopra di questi mettono delle rame attraversate, in modo che non si vede l'acqua, & in questo modo e il pavimento del ponte, & nel medesimo modo tessono un muro alle sponde del ponte, con questi medesimi vimini, accioche niuno possa cadere nell'acque di che non ci è poi niun pericolo, benche a'chi non è pratico par cosa picolosa il passarlo, p[er]che essendo il tratto et lo spacio grande, piega il ponte quando l'huomo vi passa, che sempre va abbassando sin al mezzo, & doppo va montando sin che l'habbia finito di passare all'altra riva, & quando si passa trema molto forte."

8. Ochsendorf 1996, 2004, 2015; Bauer 2006.

9. Sancho 1556, fol. 407r: "senza altro contrasto ne battaglia, i venerdi à hora di messa maggiore, à 15 del mese di Novembre l'anno della nativita del nostro Salvatore, & Redentore Giesu Christo MDXXXIII." Busto Duthurburu (1962–63, p. 173) argues that the entry into Cuzco must have occurred on a Saturday rather than a Friday, as indicated by Sancho.

10. Sancho 1556, fol. 407r: "Fece il Governator allogiar tutti i Christiani negli alloggiamenti ch'erano all'intorno della piazza della città."

11. Betanzos 1551–57, fol. 141r; Betanzos 2015, p. 415.

12. On conceptions of "city," Bonet Correa 1991; Kagan 2000, 2013; Escobar 2013. On the plaza in the

early modern Spanish world, Bonet Correa 1991; Low 2000; Escobar 2003.

13. Sancho 1556, fol. 399v: "Per esser soliti di gran tempo a star sotto l'ubidienza sempre d'un solo Signore, & tributarlo, che se non si forse fatto faria nata gran confusione, percioche ciascuno si faria ribellato con la sua signoria, & per tirargli all'amicitia delli Spagnuoli, & alla obedienza di sua Maestà."

14. Sancho 1556, fol. 407v: "Et ritornato, nella piazza della città, gli huomini di quella terra gli dierono l'obedienza secondo il lor costume, riconoscendolo per lor Signore."

15. Betanzos 1551–57, fol. 141r; Betanzos 2015, p. 415: "Le hicieron sus fiestas y regozijos, çerimonias y ayunos y sacrifiçios."

16. Garcilaso de la Vega 1609, fols. 154v–155r.

17. Sancho 1556, fol. 407v.

18. Serrano y Sanz 1918, pp. 292–95: "Vos ruego y requiero que entendays bien esto que os he dicho, y tomeys para entenderlo y deliberar sobre ello el tiempo que fuere justo, y reconoscays a la Yglesia por señora y superiora del universo mundo, y al Sumo Pontifiçe, llamado Papa, en su nombre, y al Rey y a la Reyna nuestros señores en su lugar, como a superiores e señores y reyes desas yslas y tierra firme . . . Vos dexaran vuestras mugeres, hijos, y haziendas libres sin servidumbre, para que dellas y de vosotros hagays libremente todo lo que quisieres e por bien tuvieres . . . Si no lo hicieres . . . certifico que con la ayuda de Dios y entraré poderosamente contra vosotros y vos haré guerra por todas las partes y maneras que yo pudiere, y vos subjetaré al yugo y obediençia de la Yglesia y de Sus Altezas, y tomaré vuestras personas y de vuestras mugeres e hijos y los haré esclavos, y como tales los venderé y dispondré dellos como Su Alteza mandare, y vos tomaré vuestros bienes, y vos haré todos los males e daños que pudiere . . . y protesto que las muertes y daños que dellos se recrecieren, sean a vuestra culpa, y no de Su Alteza, ni mia, ni destos cavalleros que conmigo vinieron."

19. Seed 1995, pp. 72–81.

20. Sancho 1556, fol. 407v: "facendosi altre solennitá che per fuggir[e] prolissità non si scrive . . . se levò in piede il Cacique, & con un vaso d'oro diede à bere di sua mano al Governatore & Spagnuoli."

21. The reading of the *Requerimiento* is not recorded by Betanzos. Lamana (2008, pp. 100–3) questions its occurrence as described by Sancho. On the episode, see also Cummins 2002, pp. 118–20.

22. Xerez 1534, n.p.: "Vista aquella comarca y ribera por el reverendo padre fray Vicente de Valverde, religioso de la orden de señor Santo Domingo, y por los oficiales de sus majestades, el Gobernador con acuerdo destas personas, como sus majestades mandan, porque en esta comarca y ribera concurren las causas y cualidades que debe haber en tierra que ha de ser poblada de Españoles, y los naturales della podrán servir sin padescer fatiga demasiada, teniendo principalmente respecto a su conservación como es la voluntad de sus majestades que se tenga."

23. Vela Cossio et al. 2012; Astuamán Gonzáles 2016.

24. AGI, Indiferente, 418, leg.1, fols. 39r–42r; *Colección de documentos inéditos* 1879, p. 13.

25. AGI, Patronato, 26, ramo 5; *Colección de documentos inéditos* 1883, pp. 280–98.

26. AGI, Panama, 32, no. 54; Castillero Calvo 1971, pp. 186–9.

27. On Acts of Foundation, Morales Padrón 1955; Domínguez Compañy 1984; Fraser 1990, pp. 51–63.

28. Sancho 1556, fol. 409r: "Ordinò il Governatore che si congregassero in quella città la maggior parte di spagnuoli che con seco haveva, & fece un'atto di fondatione, & formatione del popolo, dicendo che lo fermava & fondava nel medesimo esser suo, & esto prese la possessione nel mezzo della piazza, & in segno di fondare, & cominciare a edificare il popolo, & Colonia, fece certe cerimonie come si contiene nel atto che fu fatto, delquale io Scrivano in voce alta lessi al cospetto di tutti."

29. RB, 2/1960, fol. 5r: "sacado del original por mi, Simon de Alzate, escribano de su Magestad." Alzate's authorization to work as a scribe and public notary, dated March 14, 1531, is documented in AGI, Panama, 235, leg. 7, fol. 189r–v. He was named *escribano de numero* on May 26, 1546, in AGI, Lima, 566, leg. 5, fols. 247r–250r. He is described as "natural de Motrico [Guipúzkoa]" in a lawsuit initated on May 18, 1547, in AGI, Justicia 396, no. 1.

30. RB, 2/1960, fol. 1r: "hizieron casas y moradas donde se alvergasen e biviesen; buscaron la tierra mas aparejada para bivir que pudieron hallar que produciese fruto y les diese mantenimiento . . . y hizieron leyes con que la repubica se rrigiese y fuese bien governada."

31. Vitoria 2008.

32. Castillero Calvo 1971, p. 186: "se funde y haga pueblo de cristianos."

33. RB, 2/1960, fol. 2r: "asentada en valle fertile de mantenimientos en medio de dos rrios cerca de fuentes de buenas aguas y monte de leña sierras y pastos para criar ganados y rrios y lagunas de pesquerias."

34. Castillero Calvo 1971, p. 187: "se hallan las calidades y bastimientos y cosas necesarias para poblar y hacer pueblo y poderse mantener y sustentar."

35. RB, 2/1960, fol. 2r: "Cassas de depositos y de senores y hedeficios viejos de canteria despoblados sin dueño ny señor de donde los espanoles que aqui poblaren podian a poca costa y sin muncho trabajo sacar madera y piedra para los edeficios del pueblo asi cassas como yglezia y muro de piedra."

36. RB, 2/1960, fol. 2r: "Que la plaça deste pueblo que hago sea esta que estava hecha de los naturales y los solares donde an de hedificar sus cassas los vezinos sean traçados y dados al de rredor della en lo mejor ya donde yo senalaré."

37. RB, 2/1960, fol. 2r: "Oy lunes veynte y tres dias del mes de março año del nacimiento de n[uest]ro salvador ihu xpo de mill e quinientos e treynta e quatro años en esta picota que pocos dias ha mande hazer y poner en medio desta plaça en las gradas de piedra que tiene que no estan acabadas de labrar con este punal que en my cinta trayo yo labro algo dellas y corto y labro un ñudo del madero de la d[ic]ha picota como a todos los que sois presentes lo es bien visto y hago todos los otros actos de posesion e diligencias de fundacion destas obras que soy obligado e debia hazer."

38. Zuidema 1989; Meddens 2015.

39. Rykwert 1976, pp. 37–40; Fraser 1990, pp. 59–61.

40. *Siete Partidas*, part. 7, tit. 31, ley 4: "Cuando condenan a alguno a que sea azotado o herido públicamente por yerro que hizo o lo ponen por deshonra de él en la picota."

41. On the *picota* in peninsular Spain, Ferrer González 1980; González Blanco 1984. On the *picota* in the Americas, Bernaldo de Quirós 1948; Fraser 1990, pp. 57–61.

42. Tena Fernández 1968, p. 40; Busto Duthurburu 1983, pp. 30, 40 n.10; González Montero 2016.

43. On precedents, Rykwert 1976, pp. 65–66, 132–35; Morales Padrón 1955, pp. 329–30. On the ritual in Frontera de Cáceres, Vega Bolañes 1954, pp. 133–38: "Cortando de los árboles ramas e arrancando de las yervas e cavando con sus manos de la tierra." On Trujillo and Santiago, Domínguez Compañy 1984, pp. 93–94, 99–100.

44. RB, 2/1960, fol. 2v: "Senaló por solar a la yglezia q[ue] se hedificare en esta d[ic]ha ciudad una cassa questaba las paredes della hecha de los naturales y que sale de la delantera della a la plaça, deesta d[ic]ha ciudad y por ambas partes dos calles puestas al reglas d[ic]ha yglezia. Puso por nombre e vocacion n[uest]ra senora de la anunciacion."

45. Wethey 1949, pp. 64–65; Escobar Medrano et al. 1999; Viñuales 2004, pp. 78–81.

46. Mignolo 2003, pp. 219–58.

CHAPTER 4

1. RB, 2/1960, fols. 3v–4r.

2. Kagan 2000, pp. 1–18.

3. On Beltrán de Castro in Bruselas, Esgueva Gómez 2007, pp. 40–41. On Pedro de Candía in Tumbes, AGI, Lima 565, leg. 1, fol. 51r. On Pedro del Barco, AGI, Lima 204, no. 12. On Valdivieso, Lockhart 1972, pp. 246–48. On Gonzalo de los Nidos, AGI, Lima 204, no. 2.

4. Emphasis mine. RB 2/1960, fol. 4r–v: "Les daba e dio todo poder cumplido para que puedan usar y exercer los dichos oficios de alcaldes e regidores en esta dicha ciudad e sus terminos ellos cada uno dellos segun y de la manera que lo deben e pueden usar e segun que los usan y exercen los otros alcaldes e regidores en las villas y lugares de estos reinos y de los otros sus comarcanos que en nombre de sus magestades estan pobladas."

5. On town councils and their makeup in Spanish America, Bayle 1952; Gibson 1966, p. 97; Domínguez Compañy 1981, pp. 201–81; Guillamón Alvarez 1991. On the *cabildo* in the Viceroyalty of Peru, Moore 1954. On the *cabildo* in Cuzco, Decoster 2001. On the appointment of officials in Frontera de Cáceres, Vega Bolañes 1954, pp. 136–37. For Natá, Castillero Calvo 1971, p. 193.

6. Rama 1996.

7. Sancho 1556, fol. 413r: "La Città del Cusco per esser la principale di tutte dove facevano la residentia i Signori è si grande & cosi bella, & con tanti edificij, che saria stata degna da veder in Spagna."

8. Sancho 1556, fol. 413r: "Fatte le strade in croci molto dritte, tutto immattonate, & in mezzo di ciascuna va vn condotto d'acqua murato di pietra . . . la piazza è fatta in quadro, & sta per il piu piano, è immattonata di pietre minute."

9. Sancho 1556: fol. 413r: "Tutta piensa di casamenti di Signori p[er]che in essa non vivono genti povere, & ogni Signori vi fabricava la sua casa, & tutti i Caciqui medesimamente, perche non risedevao i Caciqui in essa continouamente & la maggior parte di queste case sono di pietra, & l'altre hanno la meta della facciata di pietra: vi sono molte case di terra, & sono fatte con bell'ordine."

10. Sancho 1556, fol. 413r: "marmo bianco & rosso."

11. On the use of color, Niles 1999, pp. 234, 246, 289; Nair and Protzen 2015, pp. 222–23.

12. On Caxana, Hyslop 1990, pp. 41–42; Niles 1999, pp. 232–36; Dean 2001, p. 172; Bauer 2004, pp. 117–21, 212 n.23; Farrington 2013, pp. 146–49.

13. On Amarucancha, Hyslop 1990, pp. 43, 313 n.5; Bauer 2004, pp. 126–27, 214 n.47; Farrington 2013, pp. 149–53.

14. On the *mamacona*, *acllacona*, and *acllahuasi*, Rostworowski 1999, p. 176; Graubart 2000; Farrington 2013, pp. 186–87.

15. On Hatun Cancha, Farrington 2013, pp. 186–98.

16. On Ochullo, Farrington 2013, pp. 153–54. On the palace of Huascar, Farrington 2010; Farrington 2013, pp. 154–56.

17. Sancho, 1556, fol. 413v: "Ciascun Signore passato ha qui la sua casa di queste robbe di tributi che gli furono dati in vita loro, p[er]che niun[o] Signore che succede (cosi è legge tra loro) puo doppo la morte del passato arrivar[e] à esso in la heredità."

18. Rivera Serna 1965, p. 14.

19. Lockhart 1972, pp. 271–72. For Narváez's request for royal recognition in 1539, AGI, Lima, 204, no. 8.

20. In 1965, Raul Rivera Serna published a transcription of the volume working from a microfilm. As he notes (1965, pp. 5–6), portions of it had previously been transcribed and published by Horacio Urteaga, Carlos Romero, and Jesús Covarrubias.

21. Rivera Serna 1965, pp. 16–19. Manuscript copies of the royal provisions dated November 1, 1529, are AGI, Lima 565, leg. 1, fol. 21v ("Governación"); AGI, Lima 565, leg. 1, fol. 25r. ("Adelantamiento"); and AGI, Lima 565, leg. 1, fol. 24r ("Capitan General"). On the ceremony, Rappaport and Cummins 2011, pp. 196–98.

22. Rivera Serna 1965, p. 23: "en la casa e posada del Hernando de Soto en un galpon grande."

23. Rivera Serna 1965, p. 25: "Para el bien de la tierra e naturales della e desta ciudad d[e] espanoles que en ella han de quedar e residir." On town council ordinances in Spanish America more broadly, Domínguez Compañy 1981, pp. 151–200.

24. Rivera Serna 1965, p. 25: "Por cuanto esta ciudad se fundo en el mismo asiento e pueblo que los naturales tenian hecho . . . estan edificadas y asentadas muchas casas de los señores que han sido en esta ciudad los cuales por [ser] ricos edificios e de grandes señores los naturales e hombres principales e caciques de la tierra que al presente ay las tienen en gran estima y veneracion e se rehedificasen or removiesen por los españoles que en esta ciudad y en las dichas casas ay dar y posar podria ser que los naturales se rebelasen."

25. Rivera Serna 1965, pp. 25–26.

26. On García, Lockhart 1972, pp. 380–84.

27. Rivera Serna 1965, p. 27: "Ninguno de los dichos vecinos ni otras personas ningunas no sean osados de entrar ni entren en ningunas casas ni buhios de caciques e principales desta dicha ciudad del Cuzco . . . ni consenter que sus indios yanaconas entren en los tales buhios . . . Que ninguno mande a sus indios trae leña y paja de ningun buio ni casa desta dicha ciudad ni de otro pueblo dellos comarcanos."

28. Rivera Serna 1965, p. 24.

29. On funding the purchase of ornaments for churches in Spanish America, AGI, Lima 565, leg. 2, fol. 99r; AGI, Lima 565, leg. 1, fols. 76v–77r; AGI, Lima 565, leg. 2, fol. 141v. On Hernán Gómez, AGI, Lima 566, leg. 4, fols. 273r–281v.

30. Rivera Serna 1965, p. 24: "No paresçia haber otra casa mas aparejada ny en major sityo desta dicha cibdad ques una Casa que esta en esta plaça al esquyna de la Calle Real que va a las casas del Sol e a por linderos de una parte Amaro Cancha e de la otra parte la Plaça e de la otra parte la dicha Calle Real."

31. Wethey 1949, pp. 57–58.

32. Rivera Serna 1965, p. 32.

33. AGI, Lima 565, leg. 1, fol. 16r; *Colección de documentos inéditos* 1873, p. 11: "Conçedemos a los dichos vecinos e pobladores que le sean dados por vos los solares e tierras conbenientes a sus personas, conforme a lo que se a fecho e haçe en la dicha Ysla Española."

34. Palm 1955, vol. 1, pp. 75–79; Veloz Maggiolo and Ortega 1992. On the assignment of lots in Spanish America more generally, Domínguez Compañy 1981, pp. 241–81.

35. *Colección de documentos inéditos* 1883, pp. 39, 285: "Habeis de repartir los solares del lugar para facer las casas, y estos han de ser repartidos segun las calidades de las personas, é sean de comienzo dados por órden; por manera que hechos los solares, e pubelo parezca ordenado, así en e lugar que se dejare para plaza, como el lugar en que hobiere la iglesia, como en la órden que tovieren las calles, porque en los lugares que de nuevo se hacen dando la órden en el comienzo sin ningun trabajo ni costa quedan ordenados é los otros jamas se ordenan."

36. On the idea of orderliness in official instructions and other urban literature of the period, Fraser 1990, pp. 21–50.

37. Rivera Serna 1965, p. 33.

38. Rivera Serna 1965, p. 33: "Señalose por casa del cabildo e fundición el galpon grande questa en el anden encima de la Plaza."

39. Castillero Calvo 1971, p. 188: "Segun y por la orden y manera que por la traza que yo hice de la dicha ciudad y pueblo parecen señalados y trazados."

40. Castillero Calvo 1971, p. 188: "Que por las calles y plazas del dicho pueblo salgan derechas y por orden y concierto hice y funde el dicho pueblo haciendo cada hilera de las que en esta dicha plaza parecen de cuatro solares j[u]ntos y confines y la dicha isleta toda cercada de calles públicas y cada solar de todos los susodichos que así van señalados le señale y por la present[e] le señalo cien pasos que son doscientos y un pies de marca así de delantera como de traviesa y para la iglesia y casa del cabildo señale dos solares los susodichos de los cuales a de quedar para la iglesia la mayor parte de ellos y para la casa del cabildo el resto y entre la iglesia y la dicha casa del cabildo una calle en medio lo cual queda a disposición del teniente que ahora es en mi lugar en esta ciudad para que los señale según que en esta traza parece y así mismo para la plaza pública señale una isleta entera que sera cuatro solares."

41. Rivera Serna 1965, p. 33.

42. Rivera Serna 1965, pp. 33–34: "En las carnicerías a la casa del Sol."

43. Rivera Serna 1965, p. 34: "Dos solares en el corral donde agora [está] en la parte del que quisiere dentro del . . . En el corral do[nde] agora está."

44. Rivera Serna 1965, p. 25: "Por cuanto la mayor parte de los solares que sean repartido en esta ciudad a sido en lo edificado que los indios naturales thenian antes de agora en lo cual ay muchas cuadras o corrales que tiene mas de los dichos dozcientos pies que tenemos asignados e señalados por un solar e otras que tienen menos por manera que no se pueden dar los dichos dozcientos pies juntos en algunos solares sin daño e perjuizio de algunos vecinos e sin dañarse otros solares que ya estan por nosotros dados e señalados."

45. Rivera Serna 1965, p. 37: "Por cuanto en muchos de los solares que estan repartidos en los vecinos en esta cibdad al presente biven e avitan indias mamaconas del Sol e de los señores antepasados e podria ser que si luego las echasen de sus casas e moradas sucediese en daño y desasociego de los naturales e se rebelasen del servicio de Su Magestad contra los españoles que en esta ciudad estan ordenamos e mandamus que ningun vecino ni otra persona alguna admueba ni edifique haga ni deshaga buhios ni pueda de las casas donde las dichas mamaconas estan e indios naturales que en su solar estoviesen."

46. Rivera Serna 1965, pp. 22–23.

47. Stanislawski 1946; Kubler 1948, vol. 1, p. 94; Fraser 1990, pp. 36–37; Lefebvre 1991, pp. 151–52; Rama 1996, p. 5; Rappaport and Cummins 2011, pp. 219–50.

CHAPTER 5

1. Sancho 1556, fol. 413r: "Sopra il colle . . . è una Fortezza di terra et di pietra molto bella, che ha le sue finestre grandi che guardano verso la Città . . . dentro di essa sono molti allogiamenti, & una torre principale nel mezzo . . . Ha tante stanze & torre che una persona non le potrebbe veder tutte in un giornno . . . sono di pietre cosi grandi, che chi le vedra, non dirà che vi sieno state poste per mano d'huomini humani che sono cosi grande come pezzi di montagne . . . Fu edificata da un Signor Oregione che venne dalle parti di Condisuio verso il mare . . . & tutti gli altri Signori che gli sono successi doppo, fecero qualche poco di miglioramento in essa fortezza onde sempre si venne magnificando & accrescendo."

2. Betanzos 1551–57, fol. 83v; Betanzos 2015, p. 288: "Que las más destas piedras son tan grandes que quinientos yndios trayan una dellas y otras mil."

3. Sancho 1556, fol. 413r: "vn piu alto dell'altro, & l'ultimo piu à dentro è il piu alto di tutti . . . La piu bella cosa che si possa veder per edificio in quel paese sono questi gironi." On zigzag walls at other Inca sites, Farrington 2013, p. 36. On the scale of Sacsahuaman, Hamilton 2018, pp. 136–41.

4. Sancho 1556, fol. 413r: "Vi potriano star dentro cinque mila Spagnuoli, non se gli puo dar batteria, ne si puo miniare, percioche è posta sopra un sasso."

5. Xerez 1534, n.p.: "Dos casas fuertes, la una a manera de fortaleza"; "Asentada en un pennon, la mayor parte d[e] él tajado." Sancho 1556, fol. 405v: "levatigli da il lor forte."

6. Glick 1995, pp. 92–124.

7. Torres Balbás 1951; Rosenthal 1985; Malpica Cuello 1999; Galera Mendoza 2013.

8. Sancho 1556, fol. 413r: "La pietra di che è fatta è benissimo lavorata, & in modo conguinta l'una con l'altra, che non par che cisia mistura di calce, & le pietre sono cosi liscie chi piaono tavole spianate, con la ligature in ordina all'usanza di Spagna." On the impact of ancient Roman history on the conquest of Peru more generally, MacCormack 2006.

9. Dean 2010, pp. 143–78.

10. Porras Barrenechea 1944, vol. 1, p. 20: "Podais fazer en las dichas tierras e provincias del Perú hasta quatro fortalezas, en las partes e lugares que os convenga, pareciendo a vos e a los dichos nuestros oficiales son nesçesarias para guarda y

pacificación de dicha tierra . . . las quales aveis de fazer a vuestra costa."

11. AGI, Indiferente General 418, leg. 1, fols. 134–37. Transcribed in Vas Mingo 1986, pp. 138–43: "se pueda defender a los yndios" (p. 139).

12. AGI, Indiferente General 418, leg. 1, fols. 164–66. Transcribed in Vas Mingo 1986, p. 149: "que sea tal que los christianos se puedan bien defender de los yndios e de otras personas que a la dicha ysla vinieren."

13. Sancho 1556, fol. 413r: "É di quattro ò cinque gironi."

14. Dean 1998; Dean 2010, pp. 144–52.

15. Barreda and Valencia 1999; Bauer 2004, pp. 98–105; Julien 2004; Farrington 2013, pp. 310–16.

16. Barreda and Valencia 1999; Silva González 2007; Farrington 2013; Mar and Beltrán-Caballero 2014; Mar and Beltrán-Caballero 2015.

17. Xerez 1534, n.p.: "tan ancha la cerca como cualquier fortaleza de España"; Sancho 1556, fol. 413r: "Molti Spagnuoli che l'hanno veduta, & sono andati in Lombardia, & in altri Regni stani, dicono non haver veduto un'altro edificio come questa fortezza ne castello piu forte."

18. Studies of the siege and its primary sources include Flickema 1981; Himmerich and Valencia 1998; Lamana 2008, pp. 125–57.

19. BNE, ms. 3216. Coello 2008; and Manzo 2014 are recent studies of the manuscript.

20. BNE, ms. 3216, fol. 137r; Coello 2008, p. 531.

21. Porras Barrenechea 1951; Coello 2008, pp. 21–32.

22. Coello 2001, pp. 51–136; Coello 2008, pp. 32–36.

23. BNE, ms. 3216, fols. 2v–3r; Coello 2008, pp. 410–11: "A quien encaresçía mucho quanto devía al serviçio de vuestra magestad porque una de las cossas más prinçipales que en esta jornada le mandó fue entender, en su buen tratamiento . . . de que el ynga se mostrava, estar tan favoresçido y contento que no se sospechava d[e] el, ninguna rruin, voluntad ni propósito."

24. BNE, ms. 3216, fol. 3r; Coello 2008, p. 411: "Quánto combenía que los beçinos hiçiesen á vuestra magestad algún serviçio pues estavan tan aprovechados, de la tierra, y la rreal haçienda tan gastada con las guerras del turco y françeses."

25. Betanzos 1551–57, fol. 142r; Betanzos 2015, p. 417: "Como si el sol fuera un hombre y hablara con los hombres."

26. BNE, ms. 3216, fol. 4r; Coello 2008, p. 411.

27. Betanzos 1551–57, fol. 146r; Betanzos 2015, p. 427: "Doçientos y çinquenta cristianos con clérigos y frailes y moços y muchachos y enfermos, entre los quales no avía sin çient hombres de guerra y éstos apenas y los demás hazían cuerpo de gente." Flickema (1981, p. 21 n.3) provides the similar numbers reported by other chroniclers.

28. BNE, ms. 3216, fols. 9v–10r; Coello 2008, p. 417: "Dios peleava por ellos porque sin morir un ombre, todos los indios, murieron sin dejar uno a vida."

29. BNE, ms. 3216, fol. 11r; Coello 2008, p. 418: "No paresçía sino que toda la çiudad era una llama de fuego adonde era tan grande la grita de los indios, y el humo tan espesso que no se veían ni oyan los unos a los otros."

30. BNE, ms. 3216, fol. 12r; Coello 2008, p. 419: "Este día y los otros siguientes, siempre ardía la çiudad y la gente de guerra se ensoberveçía, paresçiéndoles que ya los españoles no eran parte para defenderse."

31. BNE, ms. 3216, fol. 15r; Coello 2008, p. 422: "Es nesçessario perder todas las vidas o ganar la fortaleza porque ganándola se asegura el pueblo y de otra manera sería perderse."

32. BNE, ms. 3216, fols. 17v–18r; Coello 2008, p. 424: "Desde la puerta del muro, salían de una parte y de otra unos paredones, hasta hazer otra puerta adelante y estos cubiertos, por cima."

33. BNE, ms. 3216, fol. 18r; Coello 2008, p. 424. "Le hirieron, de una pedrada a mano, echada de lo alto, en la cabeça, con tanta fuerça que como por lo que ya dije, venía sin çelada."

34. BNE, ms. 3216, fols. 20v–21r; Coello 2008, pp. 427–28: "Havida esta victoria tan señalada mandó Hernando Piçarro poner en lo alto una vandera, para que todos los indios viniesen en conosçimiento della . . . Fué tanto el temor y desmayo que desto rreçibieron, los enemigos que luego, a la ora dexaron las estançias que tenían junto al pueblo y se rretiraron á sus rreales que tenían muy fortalecidos."

35. Wilson 2003.

36. Cuneo 1998, pp. 122–34.

37. BNE, ms. 3216, fol. 12v; Coello 2008, pp. 419–20: "Como las casas fueron del todo quemadas, los indios podían andar por ençima de las paredes."

38. On Ollantaytambo, Protzen 1993.

39. BNE, ms. 3216, fols. 28v–33v; Coello 2008, pp. 435–39.

40. BNE, ms. 3216, fol. 34r–v; Coello 2008, p. 440; Lamana 2008, pp. 136–38; Rappaport and Cummins 2011, pp. 191–218.

41. BNE, ms. 3216, fol. 59r–v; Coello 2008, pp. 462–63. "La ciudad está en peligro más que nunca estuvo, porque si somos cercados otra vez no tenemos caballos para pelear de un dia arriba y ya que pudiésemos, no podemos defender que no nos cojan

el maíz que tenemos sembrado, lo cual sería grandísima falta."

42. BNE, ms. 3216, fol. 59v; Coello 2008, p. 463: "Desbaratada esta junta . . . todos los demás perderán el orgullo que tienen."

43. BNE, ms. 3216, fol. 60r–v; Coello 2008, p. 463: "Una de la más hermosas escaramuças que xamás se vio, porque como veya que en aquella coyuntura estava perderse la tierra o ganalla, hiço cosas tan señaladas que no se puede creer."

44. BNE, ms. 3216, fol. 28v; Coello 2008, p. 435.

45. On Vitcos and Vilcabamba, Bauer et al. 2015; Meseth et al. 2015.

46. Titu Cusi Yupanqui 1570; Titu Cusi Yupanqui 2006, pp. 1–172.

47. On Titu Cusi Yupanqui's biography, Regalado de Hurtado 2008; Julien 2006, pp. ix–xiv; Bauer 2005, pp. 12–17. The manuscript is Real Biblioteca del Monasterio de El Escorial L.I.5 (1570), fols. 132r–196v.

48. Titu Cusi Yupanqui 1570, fol. 14r–v; Titu Cusi Yupanqui 2006, pp. 37–39.

49. Titu Cusi Yupanqui 1570, fol. 22v; Titu Cusi Yupanqui 2006, p. 59.

50. Titu Cusi Yupanqui 1570, fol. 38r; Titu Cusi Yupanqui 2006, p. 101.

51. Titu Cusi Yupanqui 1570, fol. 16r–v; Titu Cusi Yupanqui 2006, pp. 42, 44: "Toda ella mas de mill e dozientas leguas de largo y otras casy trezientas de anchor rrepartida en esta manera, a la discrision del mundo, conbiene a saver, en oriente e poniente y norte y sur en nuestro uso llamamos Andesuyo, Chinchaysuyu, Condesuyo, Collasuyo, rrodeando desta manera: Andesuyo al oriente; Chinchaysuyu al norte; Condesuyo al poniente; Collasuyo al sur; esto haziamos puestos en el Cuzco, que es el çentro y cabeça de toda la tierra, y por esto y por estar en el medio se nonbravan mis antepasados puestos alli, por ser su çepa, señores de tauantinsuyo, que quiere dezir señores de las quarto partidas del mundo, porque pensaban de çierto que no avia mas mundo que este."

52. Titu Cusi Yupanqui 1570, fol. 36v; Titu Cusi Yupanqui 2006, p. 96: "Muchos chifflos y bozinas e tronpetas e gran griteria de bozes que asonbravan a todo el mundo."

53. Titu Cusi Yupanqui 1570, fol. 14r; Titu Cusi Yupanqui 2006, pp. 36, 38: "¿Que os he hecho yo porque me quereis tratar de esa manera y atarme como a perro? ¿desa manera me pagueis la buena obra que os he hecho en meteros en mi tierra y daros en lo que en [e]lla tenia con tanta voluntad y amor?"

54. Titu Cusi Yupanqui 1570, fol. 41r; Titu Cusi Yupanqui 2006, p. 106.

55. Titu Cusi Yupanqui 1570, fol. 42r; Titu Cusi Yupanqui 2006, p. 108.

56. AGI, Gobierno, Lima, leg. 565, lib. 2, fol. 254; Porras Barrenechea 1944, vol. 2, p. 393: "Un escudo, que en la primera parte alta dél estaba la dicha ciudad del Cuzco, en memoria de habella vos poblado y conquistado, con una corona de Rey, de oro, sobre ella, de la cual esté asida una borla colorada que el dicho cacique Atabalipa traia . . . y en el otro quarto alto de la mano izquierda un leon rapante de oro, con una F colorada en las manos, y en el otro tercero cuarto bajo y más principal del dicho escudo, otro leon pardo con corona de Rey, de oro, preso con una cadena de oro, en memoria de la prision del dicho cacique."

CHAPTER 6

1. On the system generally, Zavala 1992; Ruiz Rivera and Pietschmann 1996. On the institution in Peru, Puente Brunke 1992; Lockhart 1994, pp. 11–37.

2. For Cieza de León's biography, Sáenz de Santa María 1985; Porras Barrenechea 1986, pp. 279–305; Pease 2008a.

3. Pérez de Tudela y Bueso 1963; Vargas Ugarte 1966, pp. 118–32; Hemming 1970, pp. 227–72; Del Busto Duthurburu 2000, vol. 2, pp. 295–330.

4. Cieza de León 1553, title page: "Que tracta la demarcación de sus provincias: la descripción dellas, las fundaciones de las nuevas ciudades, los ritos y costumbres de los indios, y otras cosas estrañas dignas de ser sabidas."

5. Cieza de León 1880.

6. Cieza de León 1880, 1979. The manuscripts of the second part are Biblioteca Apostolica Vaticana Reg. Lat. 951 (which also contains the third part of the *Crónica*), and Real Biblioteca del Monasterio de El Escorial, ms. L-I-5.

7. Cieza de León 1877a, 1877b.

8. Sáenz de Santa María 1976. The manuscripts are: Palacio Real, Madrid, Real Biblioteca II/1873; Hispanic Society of America, New York B1481; and New York Public Library, New York, ms. Col 2570, no. 71.

9. Cieza de León 1991, p. 97: "En lo que toca a los españoles, sienpre busqué hombres savios, amigos de dezir verdad, para ser ynformado e tomar las relaçiones que me heran neçesarias de lo que yo no ví, la mesma diligencia e cuydado tengo de lo que pasava entre los yndios, de tomar la relaçión de los más avisados dellos, e que oviesen visto por sus ojos las cosas que yo les pregunto. E mucho de lo que pasó desde la porfiada guerra e çerco del Cuzco y lo que agora boy contando, me dió entera notiçia un capitan de Guaynacapa, llamado Pisca, que por su persona syenpre syguió a Manco

Ynga en el çerco del Cuzco, e de lo demás me informé de un mancebo de los orejones que abía yido criado del mismo Manco Ynga."

10. Cieza de León 1991, p. 102: "En todas estas cosas que agora la ystoria va tratando es verísima, e que pasó asy, e que son palabras formales sacadas de los proçesos de los escrivanos Domingo de la Presa e Alonso de Silba que hizieron en aquel tienpo, e de los originales que con muy travajo y soliçitud mía yo he buscado, e a costa de mis dineros hallado."

11. Cieza de León 1991, p. 6: "Aún no estavan los yndios del todo paçíficos, ny los españoles enteramente los avían traído a su amistad, ni dexavan de tener en sus casas aquellas ropas, espadas y rodelas con que descubrieron las provinçias, ny las ciudades que avían fundado con tanta feliçidad no tenían el ser ni adornamiento de suntuosydad de edefiçios que se requería por ser hechas por los españoles, antes vibían los cordeles con que las traças de las tales çiudades se avían medido, y ellas en sí no tenían más ser que tienen aquellas cosas communes y que las quieren çimentar para las hazer magníficas."

12. Cieza de León 1991, p. 6: "Buelben las armas contra sí con gran crueldad e yntemeridad."

13. Cieza de León 1991, p. 22: "Creyendo que con el nuevo de Almagro sus haziendas serían cunplidas, porque este ynterese pecunial es lo que muebe a los desta tierra a acostarse a los vandos que avido en ella."

14. BNE, ms. 3216, fol. 70v; Coello 2008, p. 472: "Deçi[d] a Hernando Pizarro que yo no tengo de entrar en la ciudad si no por mía, y que no tengo de posar sino en las casas que él posa."

15. Cieza de León 1991, p. 37: "E llobía mucho en gran manera, e llegaron a ora de las dos de la noche, yéndose el Adelantado con algunos prençipales de su real a la yglesia; Rodrigo Orgoñez, capitán, fue derecho a aquellas casas adonde estavan Hernando Piçarro e Gonçalo Piçarro, con hasta veynte españoles amigos suyos que allí estavan. El capitán Juan de Sahabedra, con una compañía, guardó la calle prençipal de la çiudad, que yva a salir a la yglesia. El capitán Vasco de Guevara guardava otra calle que yba a salir en las casas del Sol, e los españoles serían por todos pasados de dozientos e ochenta, así de a pie como de a cavallo, e tomaron las calles de la çiudad."

16. Cieza de León 1991, p. 37: "Grandes e muy fuertes paredes de bibas piedras eran hechas." BNE, ms. 3216, fol. 75r; Coello 2008, p. 476: "El aposento donde estava Hernando Piçarro era grande como una iglesia, y edificado a la manera de yndios, y en aquel lienço que salía al patio tenía dos portadas grandes sin puertas, en las cuales estava defendiéndose Hernando Piçarro y su hermano, el cual andava de una puerta a otra, acudiendo siempre adonde avía la mayor priesa; avría de una puerta a otra quinze pasadas."

17. Cieza de León 1991, p. 40: "Començaron a caer los creçidos maderos sobre que la casa se sostenía, habiendo el ynçendio consumido la paja . . . con gran ímpetu, toda la casa venía avaxo . . . e cayó toda la baraçón e antiguos horcones en el suelo."

18. BNE, ms. 3216, fols. 84v–85r; Coello 2008, p. 485: "Combocó muchos caçiques y gente principal y común de toda la tierra los quales le resçibieron e juraron según entre ellos los usan."

19. Nolasco Pérez 1924, pp. 31–51, 171; Barriga 1933, vol. 2, pp. 141–59; Aparicio Quispe 2001, vol. 1, pp. 14–20.

20. Cieza de León 1991, p. 248: "Ya la guerra estava declarada de tal manera que por todos hera entendida, y con tanta crueldad e ynçendio tratada entre unos y otros . . . y en las dos parçialidades cada uno travajava por superar y vençer al otro, pretendiendo los autores de estas sediçiones mandar y governar estos reynos syn tener ygual y conpañero, y aviéndose en ello con poco temor de Dios, mandando pregonar guerra pública, formando canpos e desplegando vanderas, y tratando la guerra con tanto rigor como sy los unos fueran beneçianos y los otros ginoveses, o como sy fueran turcos y españoles."

21. BNE, ms. 3216, fols. 107v–108r; Coello 2008, p. 506: "Entendieron todos en hazer coseletes de plata y çeladas y braçales y todo lo demás, tan bien hechos y no menos fuertes que si fueran de Milán, porque la flaqueza de la plata la hacían fuerte con echarla doblada. Desta manera se puso la gente tan luçida, como los soldados criados en Lombardía."

22. Bauer 1998, p. 86. On the salt beds, Arancivia 1896, p. xvii.

23. Cieza de León 1991, pp. 283–89.

24. Cieza de León 1991, pp. 310–14. On the battle, see also Stewart 1988.

25. On the building, Wethey 1949, pp. 55–56; Viñuales 2004, pp. 94–115.

26. AGI, Patronato 192, no. 1, ramo 19, fol. 5r: "Certifico a Vuestra Magestad q[ue] si no me acordara del sitio de esta cibdad yo no lo conosciera a lo menos por los edificios y pueblos della porq[ue] quando el gover[nad]or don fran[cis]co picarro entro aqui y entre yo con el estava este valle tan

hermoso en edificios y población q[ue] entorno tenia q[ue] era cosa de admiración vello. Porq[ue] aunq[ue] la cibdad en si no tenia mas de tres or quatro mil casas tenia entorno quasi a vista quince o veinte mil. La fortaleza q[ue] estava sobre la cibdad parescía desde aparte una muy gran fortaleza de las de españa. Agora la mayor parte de la cibdad esta toda derribada y quemada. La fortaleza no tiene quasi nada enhiesto. Todos los pueblos de alrededor no tiene sino paredes q[ue] por maravilla ay casa enhiesta. La cosa que mas contentamiento me dió en esta cibdad fue la ygl[es]ia q[ue] para en indias es harto buena cosa. Aunq[ue] segun la riqueza ha avido en esta t[ie]rra pudiera ser mas semejante al templo de salomon de lo q[ue] es."

27. AGI, Patronato 192, no. 1, ramo 19, fol. 5r: "esta sancta igl[es]ia cathedral de n[uest]ra senora del rosario."

28. AGI, Lima, 565, leg. 3, fol. 209v; AGI, Lima, 566, leg. 4, fol. 59v; Montoto de Sedas 1928, p. 75: "un castillo de oro en campo colorado en memoria que la d[ic]ha ciudad y el castillo della fueron conquistados por fuerza de armas en n[uest]ro servicio e por oral ocho condures que son unas aves grandes a manera de buytres que ay en la provincia del peru en memoria que al tiempo que la d[ic]ha ciudad se gano abaxaron las dichas aves a comer los muertos que en ella murieron los quales esten en campo de oro." On the coat of arms, Ramos Gómez 2004, pp. 163–67.

29. AGI, Patronato Real 169, no. 2, 1540, ramo 1.

30. Cieza de León 1991, pp. 395–97; Cieza de León 1994a, pp. 91–93. On La Mota, Fernández Martín 1991; Cañas Gálvez 2007, pp. 92–94.

31. AGI, Indiferente 415, leg. 2, fols. 365r–378r. On Vaca de Castro, Viforcos Marinas and Paniagua Pérez 1991; Domínguez Faura 2008, pp. 156–57.

32. Cieza de León 1994a, pp. 168–71.

33. Domínguez Faura 1994; 1998.

34. Cieza de León 1994a, pp. 282–85: "Se asonbraban del resonido de sus propias bozes que recudía a toda parte, y tenían gran gozo de ver la magestad de los españoles pelear unos con otros, sin querer tener el feudo natural, dando graçias a su sol porque tan famosa vengança se tomava de los daños que en sus mayores se avian hecho."

35. Cieza de León 1994a, p. 304: "Le fue hecho solemnísimo reçivimiento e de todos fue reçibido con mucha alegría."

36. The document is AASG, 11/4/48.

37. AASG, leg. 1, pt. III, fols. 632–47, cited and summarized in Díaz Gito 2013.

38. Cieza de León 1994a, p. 305: "Hinchióse tanto de vanidades que no conformava con las letras que tenia, e mandó que estuviesen en su casa muchos cavalleros como sus continos, e con ellos gastava vien expléndidamente, arreándose de grandes aparadores de fina plata e creçidos blandones, lo qual fuera vien escusado para su autoridad."

39. Cieza de León 1994a, p. 308: "Sacado de la prisión, el pregonero yva delante diziendo 'Esta es la justicia que manda hazer Su Magestad el Enperador, nuestro señor, y el governador Vaca de Castro en su nonbre, a este hombre, por usurpador de la justiçia real e porque se levantó en el reyno tiránicamente y dio vatalla al estandarte real,' y otras cosas sobre lo que por él e sus valedores avía sido hecho. E yendo hazia la picota junto a la qual estava un repostero y el verdugo aparejado para le matar, dixo que rogava que pues moría en el lugar que avía sydo muerto su padre y le avian de enterrar en la sepultura donde estava su cuerpo, que lo hechasen a él devaxo e luego ençima pusyesen los huesos de su padre."

40. AGI, Patronato, 170, ramo 47; *Leyes y ordenanças* 1543.

41. Cieza de León 1994a, pp. 349–69.

42. AGI, Lima 566, leg. 5, fols. 1r–3r.

43. Cieza de León 1994a, pp. 382–85; Cieza de León 1994b, pp. 21–29.

44. Cieza de León 1994a, pp. 94–95, 108–9.

45. Titu Cusi Yupanqui 1570, fol. 53r–v; Titu Cusi Yupanqui 2006, p. 138: "Estaban un dia con mucho rregoçijo, jugando al herron solos mi padre y ellos y yo, que entonçes hera mochacho . . . yendo el dicho mi padre a levantar el herron para aver de jugar, cargaron todos sobre el con puñales y quchillos y algunas espadas; y mi padre, como se syntio herido, con la rrabia de la muerte procuraba de deffendersse de una parte y de otra, mas como hera solo y ellos heran siete y mi padre no tenia arma ninguna, al fin le derrocaron al suelo con muchas heridas; le dexaron por muerto."

46. Betanzos 1551–57, fols. 146r–152; Betanzos 2015, pp. 427–36.

47. Titu Cusi Yupanqui 1570, fol. 55r–v; Titu Cusi Yupanqui 2006, p. 143.

48. Lamana 2008, pp. 193–225; MacCormack 2004; both drawing from BNE, ms. 20193.

CHAPTER 7

1. On his biography, Miró Quesada 1971; Fernandez 2015; Fuerst 2018, pp. 11–39.

2. The work was published in two parts, the second of which appeared

posthumously: Garcilaso de la Vega 1609, 1617.

3. AGI, Indiferente General, 1963, leg. 9, fol. 317v.

4. ARC, Cabildo, Libro Becerro 3–1, fol. 54v; *Actas del Cabildo* 1958, pp. 149–50.

5. Garcilaso de la Vega 1617, fol. 189v: "Vi todo lo q[ue] he dicho, y pudiera assi mismo dezir en quales casas se aposentaro[n] los capitanes cada uno de por si, q[ue] los conocí todos, y me acuerdo de las casas."

6. Garcilaso de la Vega 1609, fol. 172v: "Yo incitado del desseo de la conservacion de las antiguallas de mi patria, essas pocas que han quedado porque no se pierdan del todo, me dispuse a trabajo . . . el escrivir su antigua republica hasta acabarla, y porque la ciudad del Cozco madre y señora della, no quede olvidada en su particular, determine dibuxar en este capitulo la descripcion della, sacada de la misma tradicion que como a hijo natural me cupo, de lo que yo con proprios ojos vi."

7. Garcilaso de la Vega 1609, fol. 173r: "Yo alcançe della un galpon muy grande y espacioso, que servia de plaça en dias lloviosos para solenizar en el sus fiestas principales, solo aquel galpon quedava en pie quando salí del Cozco, que otros semejantes de que diremos los dexe todos caydos."

8. Garcilaso de la Vega 1609, fol. 17r: "En tiempo de los Incas era un hermoso galpon . . . yo la conosci cubierta de paja, y la vi cubrir de texa."

9. ARC, Cabildo, Libro Becerro 3–1, fol. 7r; *Actas del Cabildo* 1958, pp. 26–27.

10. Mesa and Gisbert 1982, p. 48, citing ACC, Cabildo, Actas Capitulares, lib. 1, "Descargo de cuentas del mayordomo de la iglesia mayor del Cuzco."

11. Mesa and Gisbert 1982, p. 49: "Un retablo de madera con sus puertas en que está la Adoración de los Reyes."

12. Mesa and Gisbert 1982, p. 49: "Tres paños de Flandes en el uno la Salutación, en otro la Quinta Angustia y otro de Imaginería pequeño . . . Otros dos paños de lienzo pintados en cada uno de ellos la Cena del Señor, en otro retablo pequeño de la Resurrección de Nuestro Señor . . . Una imagen de Ecce Homo y otra de Nuestra Señora, sobre el coro un retablo de los Reyes."

13. Wuffarden 2014, pp. 248–49.

14. Covarrubias Orozco 1611, fol. 577r: "La tela texida de lana, de que nos vestimos." See also Julien 1999, p. 28, n.4, 5.

15. AGI, Patronato 192, no. 1, ramo 19, fol. 5r; AGI, Lima 566, leg. 5, fol. 62r–v.

16. Wolfthal 1989; Reynolds 2000.

17. On this era of artistic production in Cuzco and elsewhere in Peru, Wuffarden 2014.

18. Titu Cusi Yupanqui 1570, fol. 45v; Titu Cusi Yupanqui 2006, p. 118: "Lo que mas aveis de hazer es que, por ventura estos os diran que adoreis a lo que ellos adoran que son unos paños pintados, los quales dizen ques Viracochan y que le adoreis como a guaca, el qual no es sino paño."

19. Garcilaso de la Vega 1617, fol. 60r: "En el hastial de aquel templo, que sale à la plaça, pintaron al Señor Sanctiago, encima de un cavallo blanco, con su adarga embraçada, y la espada en la mano y la espada era culebreada; tenia muchos Yndios derribados a sus pies, muertos y heridos. Los Yndios viendo la pintura dezian, un Viracocha como este, era el que nos destruya en esta plaça. La pintura dexé viva el año de mil y quinientos y sesenta, quando me vine a España." On this passage, Cummins 1996, pp. 162–63.

20. Domínguez García 2008; Stanfield-Mazzi 2013, pp. 25–29.

21. Betanzos 1551–57, fol. 146v; Betanzos 2015, p. 428: "Tenía en los pechos una cruz colorada, como el ábito de Sanctiago que tenía el Marqués en los pechos."

22. AGI, Lima 566, leg. 5, fol. 163r: "Escudo partido en dos cuarteles, el 1º, en campo de oro: águila negra rampante flanqueada por dos palmas verdes; 2º, en campo de azur, tigre de su color coronado con borla de sable (borla que solía tener por corona Atabaliba, su hermano) acompañado por dos culebras coronadas de oro; orlado de sable con leyenda que diga 'Ave María' y entre sus letras 8 cruces de Jerusalén de oro." On slight variations in this description in contemporary documents, Dunbar Temple 1940, pp. 65–68.

23. AGI, MP, Escudos 30; AGI, MP, Escudos 78.

24. On Andean coats of arms, Cummins 2002, pp. 274–81; Wuffarden 2005, pp. 201–5; Domínguez Torres 2011.

25. ARC, Cabildo, Libro Becerro 3–1, fol. 83r–v; *Actas del Cabildo* 1958, p. 239: "Platicando sobre el ornato de la ciudad porque es una cosa de las principales y que más conbiene a la ciudad y que dá contentamiento a los que en ella biben, pareció a la ciudad en concordia que desde la puente que está junto a la casa del Licenciado Carbajal hasta la otra puente de Nuestra Señora de la Merced se continua el hedificio de las tiendas que la ciudad tiene enpezadas a hazer hasta la d[ic]ha puente de N.S."

26. ARC, Cabildo, Libro Becerro 3–1, fol. 83r–v; *Actas del Cabildo* 1958,

p. 239: "Se apregone que si alguna persona quisiere tomar el d[ic]ho asiento y suelo a censo perpetuo parezca ante la ciudad a pedir el solar que quisiere, que poniendose en lo justo la ciudad se lo dará y le dará sitio, para que en las delanteras puedan hazer portales."

27. ARC, Cabildo, Libro Becerro 3–1, fol. 83r–v; *Actas del Cabildo* 1958, p. 239: "Ayan de ser de ladrillo labrado o de piedra y todos de un compás y de una corriente."

28. ARC, Cabildo, Libro Becerro 3–1, fol. 89v–90r; *Actas del Cabildo* 1958, pp. 261–62.

29. Garcilaso de la Vega 1609, fol. 175v.

30. Garcilaso de la Vega 1609, fol. 176r–v; Fraser 1992.

31. Garcilaso de la Vega 1609, fol. 176r: "De la casa Coracora no alcançé nada, porque ya en mis tiempos estava toda por el suelo."

32. AGI, Patronato 90B, ramo 39, fols. 17v–18r; Casas Grieve 2003, pp. 310–11 n.1513.

33. Lunenfeld 1987.

34. ARC, Cabildo, Libro Becerro 3–1, fol. 86r–v; *Actas del Cabildo* 1958, pp. 248–50.

35. ARC, Cabildo, Libro Becerro 3–1, fol. 89v; *Actas del Cabildo* 1958, pp. 260–61.

36. Garcilaso de la Vega 1609, fol. 175v: "Barrio de oro, plata, y piedras preciosas."

37. Garcilaso de la Vega 1609, fol. 77r–v: "como oy está."

38. Wethey 1949, pp. 52–53.

39. AGI, Patronato 192, no. 1, ramo 19, fol. 7r: "Para q[ue] se pueblo una casa q[ue] esta en esta cibdad, q[ue] los indios tenían por casa y templo del sol."

40. AHN, Diversos Colecciones 22, no. 38, fol. 22r.

41. "Discurso sobre la descendencia" 1543–1608, p. 12: "el sitio adonde al presente está fundado el convento de Santo Domingo."

42. ARC, Cabildo, Libro Becerro 3–1, fol. 88r; *Actas del Cabildo* 1958, p. 256.

43. Wethey 1949, pp. 50–51.

44. On Inca architecture and its association with mythological and historical narratives, Niles 1999; Dean 2010, pp. 25–64.

45. Yates 2001.

46. On king lists and royal genealogy, Rowe 1945; Julien 2000, pp. 49–165; Covey 2006.

47. Garcilaso de la Vega 1609, fol. 177r.

48. ARC, Cabildo, Libro Becerro 3–1, fol. 33r; *Actas del Cabildo* 1958, p. 88; Molina 1571, fol. 113r.

49. ARC, Cabildo, Libro Becerro 3–1, fol. 9v; *Actas del Cabildo* 1958, p. 33: "Que ningún negra ni negro entren en los tianguiz desta ciudad . . . tres pesos por cada vez que fuere tomado el tal negro o negra, e si no lo diere le sean dados cien azotes públicamente."

50. ARC, Cabildo, Libro Becerro 3–1, fol. 33r–v; *Actas del Cabildo* 1958, p. 88: "Desde el postrero pilar de los quatro que tiene una hermita questá en el d[ic]ho tianguis hacia la parte del río que pasa por la plaza desta d[ic]ha ciudad."

51. AGI, Lima 566, leg. 5, fol. 62r–v.

52. Garcilaso de la Vega 1609, fol. 177v.

53. "Discurso sobre la descendencia" 1543–1608. To the text Betanzos and his collaborators composed, a second part on the period after the death of Huascar was added, probably in the early seventeenth century. On the document and its historiography, Domínguez Faura 2008; Urton 2008.

54. ARC, Cabildo, Libro Becerro 3–1, fol. 86r; *Actas del Cabildo* 1958, pp. 246–47.

55. ARC, Cabildo, Libro Becerro 3–1, fol. 14v; *Actas del Cabildo* 1958, pp. 45–46: "Indio natural destos Reynos, atento que es casado e tiene muger y es xpiano e indio ladino."

56. ARC, Cabildo, Libro Becerro 3–1, fols. 74v, 92v; *Actas del Cabildo* 1958, pp. 213–14, 270.

CONCLUSION

1. Cieza de León 1553, fol. 107v: "De la manera y traça con que esta fundada la ciudad del Cuzco: y de los quatro caminos reales que de ella salen: y de los grandes edificios que tuvo: y quien fue el fundador."

2. Cieza de León 1553, fol. 107v: "Tiene la ciudad a la parte del Norte en el cerro mas alto y mas cercano a ella una fuerça, la qual por su grandeza y fortaleza fue exçellente edificio, y lo es en este tiempo: aunque lo mas della esta deshecha, pero todavia estan en pie los grandes y fuertes cimientos con los cubos principales."

3. Cieza de León 1553, fol. 109r: "En muchas partes desta ciudad ay grandes edificios debaxo la tierra: y en las mismas entrañas della oy dia se hallan algunas losas y caños, y aun joyas y pieças de oro de lo que enterravan: y cierto deve de aver en el circuyto desta ciudad enterrados grandes thesoros, sin saber dellos los que son bivos."

4. Kagan 2000, pp. 67–68.

5. Betanzos 1551–57, fols. 6v, 21v; Betanzos 2015, pp. 132, 165.

6. Nora 2001–10.

7. Kusunoki 2016; Mesa and Gisbert 1982.

dhas ta ... que contrastes y tomastes
la dha fortaleza la qual sin que se tomara ...
la dha ciudad ... muchos españoles ... que
[illegible]
en ella estauan e que despues de tomada la dha
fortaleza se rretraron los yndios a vna legua
dela dha ciudad y os dieron guerra quatro me
ses donde distes en ellos muchos rrecuentros
e que durante el tiempo que estouistes cerca de
en la dha ciudad vos y ... los dhos yndios
hijos desistes con ... mas y caballos
avia esta ... pasa ... de grandes tra
bajos hambre y nescesidades como se vio lo consta
va y parescia por vna ynformacion e que
... en el ... delas yndias fue de
dha ... obligacion ... fue suplicado
que en rremuneracion delos dhos ser
uicios e porque ... de vos y ellos que
dase perpetua memoria
vos mandasemos dar
por ... mas ... escudo
que ... este en el vna
torre ... blanca de
plata ... en campo colora
do y por orla ... ocho buytres y
por ... nombre se dizen con
... negros en campo
de oro y por ... timble vn yelmo
cerrado con ... vn follaje ... de
... con ... con sus tras
y por deuisa ... a follajes de oro
... de aguas a follajes de oro
negro y azul ... como la vra md fuese ...
acatando los dhos seruicios por que de
vos y ellos que de perpetua memoria de
vos ... decendientes seays mas honra
dos por la presente vos hazemos md e queremos y
mandamos que podays traer y poner y tener por vras
armas conocidas las dhas armas de que de suso
se haze mencion en vn escudo atal como este
segund que aqui va figurado y pintado las quales
vos damos por vras armas conoscidas y queremos

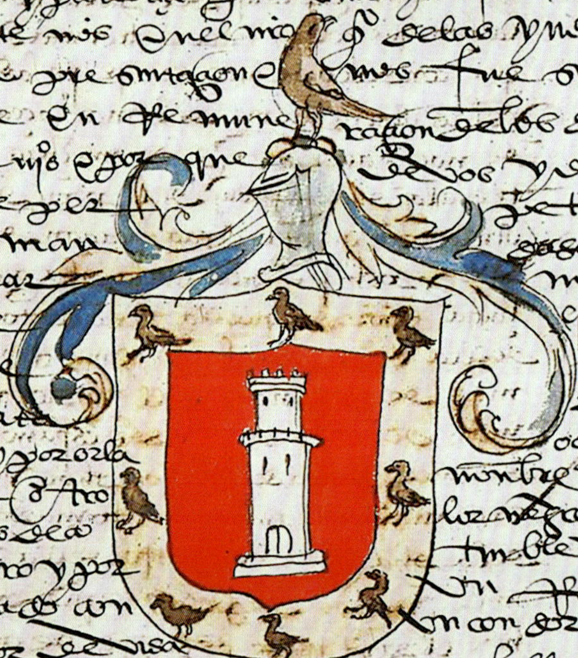

Bibliography

Actas del Cabildo 1958
Actas de los Libros de Cabildos del Cuzco, 1545–1548, transcr. José Pacheco (Cuzco, 1958)

Adorno 2008
Adorno, Rolena, *Polemics of Possession in Spanish American Narrative* (London and New Haven: Yale University Press, 2008)

Agurto Calvo 1980
Agurto Calvo, Santiago, *Cusco, la traza urbana de la ciudad inca* (Cuzco: Instituto Nacional de Cultura, 1980)

Alcalá 1999
Alcalá, Luisa Elena, "Imagen e historia: La representación del milagro en la pintura colonial," in *Los siglos de oro en los virreinatos de América: 1500–1700* (Madrid: Sociedad Estatal para la Conmemoración de los Centenarios de Felipe II y Carlos V, 1999), pp. 107–26

Alchon 2003
Alchon, Suzanne Austin, *A Pest in the Land: New World Epidemics in a Global Perspective* (Albuquerque: University of New Mexico Press, 2003)

Álvarez Márquez 2009
Álvarez Márquez, María del Carmen, *Impresores, libreros y mercaderes de libros en la Sevilla del quinientos*, 2 vols. (Zaragoza: Libros Pórtico, 2009)

Andrien 2008
Andrien, Kenneth J., "Legal and Administrative Texts," in Pillsbury 2008, vol. 1, pp. 107–19

Aparicio Quispe 2001
Aparicio Quispe, Severo, *La Orden de La Merced en el Perú*, 2 vols. (Cuzco: Provincia Mercedaria del Perú, 2001)

Aramburú 1983
Aramburú, Clemencia, *La población del Cuzco colonial (siglos XVI–XVIII)* (Lima: Instituto Andino de Estudios en Población y Desarrollo, 1983)

Arancivia 1896
Arancivia, Felipe, *Estudio técnico de las salinas del Perú*, vol. 1 (Lima: El País, 1896)

Arocena 1986
Arocena, Luis A. (ed.), *La relación de Pero Sancho* (Buenos Aires: Editorial Plus Ultra, 1986)

Astuamán Gonzáles 2016
Astuamán Gonzáles, César W., "La iglesia de San Miguel de Piura (1534–1578), primer templo del Perú virreinal," in Cristina Vargas Pacheco (ed.), *Primeros asentamientos urbanos en Iberoamérica (ss. XVI y XVII)* (Piura: Universidad de Piura, 2016), pp. 13–31

Azevedo 1982
Azevedo, Paulo O. D., *Cusco, ciudad histórica: Continuity and Change* (Lima: Projecto Regional de Patrimonio Cultural PNDU/UNESCO, 1982)

Barreda and Valencia 1999
Barreda, Luis, and Abraham Valencia, "Introducción a la etnología e arqueología de Saqsaywaman," *Revista Universitaria*, vol. 138 (1999), pp. 93–138

Barreiro and Matos Mendieta 2015
Barreiro, José, and Ramiro Matos Mendieta (eds), *The Great Inka Road: Engineering an Empire* (Washington, DC: National Museum of the American Indian, 2015)

Barriga 1933
Barriga, Victor, *Los Mercedarios en el Perú en el siglo XVI*, 4 vols. (Arequipa: Editorial La Colmena, 1933–53)

Bauer 1991
Bauer, Brian S., "Pacariqtambo and the Mythical Origins of the Inca," *Latin American Antiquity*, vol. 2, no. 1 (1991), pp. 7–26

Bauer 1992
Bauer, Brian S., *The Development of the Inca State* (Austin: University of Texas Press, 1992)

Bauer 1998
Bauer, Brian S., *The Sacred Landscape of the Inca: The Cusco Ceque System* (Austin: University of Texas Press, 1998)

Bauer 2004
Bauer, Brian S., *Ancient Cuzco: Heartland of the Inca* (Austin: University of Texas Press, 2004)

Bauer 2006
Bauer, Brian S., "Suspension Bridges in the Inca Empire," in W. H. Isbell and H. Silverman (eds), *Andean Archaeology III: North and South* (Boston: Springer, 2006), pp. 468–93

Bauer and Stanish 1990
Bauer, Brian S., and Charles Stanish, "Killke and Killke-Related Pottery from Cuzco, Peru, in the Field Museum of Natural History," *Fieldiana*, vol. 15 (December 1990), pp. 1–17

Bauer et al. 2015
Bauer, Brian S., Javier Fonseca Santa Cruz, and Miriam Aráoz Silva, *Vilcabamba and the Archaeology of Inca Resistance* (Los Angeles: Cotsen Institute of Archaeology Press, 2015)

Bauer, R., 2005
Bauer, Ralph, "Introduction," in Titu Cusi Yupanqui, *An Inca Account of the Conquest of Peru*, trans. Ralph Bauer (Boulder: University Press of Colorado, 2005), pp. 1–56

Baumgärtner 2017
Baumgärtner, Ingrid, *Der Portulan-Atlas des Battista Agnese: das Kasseler Prachtexemplar von 1542* (Darmstadt: Lambert Schneider, 2017)

Bayle 1952
Bayle, Constantino, *Los Cabildos Seculares en la América Española* (Madrid: Sapientia, 1952)

Béjar 2003
Béjar, Ives S., "La cantera Inca de Rumiqolqa, Cusco," *Boletín de Arqueología PUCP*, vol. 7 (2003), pp. 407–17

Bernaldo de Quirós 1948
Bernaldo de Quirós, Constancio, *La picota en América* (Havana: J. Montero, 1948)

Betanzos 1551–57
Betanzos, Juan de, "Suma y narración de los yngas (1551–57)," Fundación Bartolomé March, Palma de Mallorca, cat. no. 106-V11

Betanzos 1880
Betanzos, Juan de, *Suma y narración de los Incas* (Madrid: Imprenta de Manuel Gines Hernández, 1880)

Betanzos 2015
Betanzos, Juan de, "Suma y narración de los Incas," in Francisco Hernández Astete and Rodolfo Cerrón-Palomino (eds), *Juan de Betanzos y el Tahuantinsuyu* (Lima: Fondo Editorial de la Pontificia Universidad Católica del Perú, 2015), pp. 107–437

Blasco Esquivias 2006
Blasco Esquivias, Beatriz (ed.), *La casa: Evolución del espacio doméstico en España*, vol. 1 (Madrid: El Viso, 2006)

Bonet Correa 1991
Bonet Correa, Antonio, *El urbanismo en España e Hispanoamérica* (Madrid: Cátedra, 1991)

Bray 2015
Bray, Tamara L. (ed.), *The Archaeology of Wak'as* (Boulder: University Press of Colorado, 2015)

Bray and Echeverría Almeida 2014
Bray, Tamara, and José Echeverría Almeida, "The Late Imperial Site of Inca-Caranqui, Northern Highland Ecuador, at the End of Empire," *Ñawpa Pacha*, vol. 34, no. 2 (December 2014), pp. 177–99

Brokaw 2010
Brokaw, Galen, *A History of the Khipu* (Cambridge: Cambridge University Press, 2010)

Brotton 2014
Brotton, Jerry, *A History of the World in Twelve Maps* (New York: Penguin Books, 2014)

Brown 2015
Brown, Bill, *Other Things* (Chicago: University of Chicago Press, 2015)

Buchanan 1996
Buchanan, Dana, "Note on the Translation," in Roland Hamilton and Dana Buchanan (eds), *Narrative of the Incas* (Austin: University of Texas Press, 1996), pp. xv–xviii

Busto Duthurburu 1962–63
Busto Duthurburu, José Antonio, "La marcha de Francisco Pizarro de Cajamarca al Cuzco," *Revista Histórica*, vol. 26 (1962–63), pp. 146–74

Busto Duthurburu 1983
Busto Duthurburu, José Antonio, *Francisco Pizarro y Trujillo del Extremadura* (Lima: Librería Studium, 1983)

Calnek 1979
Calnek, Edward, "Tenochtitlan in the Early Colonial Period," *Acts of the XLII International Congress of Americanists*, vol. 8 (1979), pp. 35–40

Cañas Gálvez 2007
Cañas Gálvez, Francisco de Paula, *El itinerario de la corte de Juan II de Castilla (1418–1454)* (Madrid: Silex, 2007)

Caracciolo Aricò 1990
Caracciolo Aricò, Angela (ed.), *L'impatto della scoperta dell'America nella cultura veneziana* (Rome: Bulzoni, 1990)

Casas Grieve 2003
Casas Grieve, Mercedes de las (ed.), *Relación de las cosas acaecidas en las alteraciones del Perú después que Blasco Núñez Vela entró en él* (Lima: Pontificia Universidad Católica del Perú, 2003)

Caso 1956
Caso, Alfonso, "Los barrios antiguos de Tenochtitlan y Tlatelolco," *Memorias de la Academia Mexicana de la Historia*, vol. 15 (1956), pp. 7–62

Castillero Calvo 1971
Castillero Calvo, Alfredo, *La fundación de la villa de Los Santos y los orígenes historicos de Azuero* (Panama: Dirección Nacional de Cultura, 1971)

Cerrón-Palomino 2004
Cerrón Palomino, Rodolfo, "Las etimologías toponímicas del Inca Garcilaso," *Revista Andina*, vol. 38 (2004), pp. 9–41

Cerrón-Palomino 2013
Cerrón-Palomino, Rodolfo, *Las lenguas de los incas: el puquina, el aimara y el quechua* (Frankfurt am Main: Peter Lang, 2013)

Chatfield 2009
Chatfield, Melissa, "Tracing Firing Technology through Clay Properties in Cuzco, Peru," *Journal of Archaeological Science*, vol. 37 (2010), pp. 727–36

Cieza de León 1553
Cieza de León, Pedro, *Parte primera de la Crónica del Perú* (Seville: Martín de Montesdoca, 1553)

Cieza de León 1877a
Cieza de León, Pedro, *Guerras civiles del Perú*, 2 vols. (Madrid: Librería de la Viuda de Rico, 1877)

Cieza de León 1877b
Cieza de León, Pedro, *Tercero libro de las guerras civiles del Perú, el cual se llama la guerra de Quito*, ed. Marcos Jiménez de la Espada (Madrid: Imprenta de Manuel Ginez Hernández, 1877)

Cieza de León 1880
Cieza de León, Pedro, *Segunda parte de la Crónica del Perú, que trata del Señorio de los Incas . . .*, ed. Marcos Jiménez de la Espada (Madrid: Imprenta de Manuel Gines Hernández, 1880)

Cieza de León 1979
Cieza de León, Pedro, *Pedro de Cieza de León e il "Descubrimiento y conquista del Perú,"* ed. Francesca Cantù (Rome: Istituto Storico Italiano, 1979)

Cieza de León 1991
Cieza de León, Pedro, *Crónica del Perú, Cuarta Parte*, vol. 1, *Guerra de Las Salinas*, ed. Pedro Guibovich Pérez (Lima: Pontificia Universidad Católica del Perú, 1991)

Cieza de León 1994a
Cieza de León, Pedro, *Crónica del Perú, Cuarta Parte*, vol. 2, *Guerra de Chupas*, ed. Gabriela Benavides de Rivero (Lima: Pontificia Universidad Católica del Perú, 1994)

Cieza de León 1994b
Cieza de León, Pedro, *Crónica del Perú, Cuarta Parte*, vol. 3, pt. 1, *Guerra de Quito*, ed. Laura Gutiérrez Arbulú (Lima: Pontificia Universidad Católica del Perú, 1994)

Classen 1993
Classen, Constance, *Inca Cosmology and the Human Body* (Salt Lake City: University of Utah Press, 1993)

Cocking and Murray 1991
Cocking, J. M., and Penelope Murray, *Imagination: A Study in the History of Ideas* (New York: Routledge, 1991)

Coello 2001
Coello, Óscar, *Los inicios de la poesía castellana en el Perú* (Lima: Fondo Editorial de la Pontificia Universidad Católica del Perú, 2001)

Coello 2008
Coello, Óscar, *Los orígenes de la novella castellana en el Perú: La toma del Cuzco (1539)* (Lima: Universidad Nacional Mayor de San Marcos, 2008)

Colección de documentos inéditos **1873**
Colección de documentos inéditos relativos al descubrimiento, conquista, y organización de las antiguas posesiones españolas de América y Oceanía, vol. 19 (Madrid: Imprenta del Hospicio, 1873)

Colección de documentos inéditos **1879**
Colección de documentos inéditos relativos al descubrimiento, conquista, y organización de las antiguas posesiones españolas de América y Oceanía, vol. 31 (Madrid: Imprenta de Manuel Gines Hernández, 1879)

Colección de documentos inéditos **1883**
Colección de documentos inéditos relativos al descubrimiento, conquista, y organización de las antiguas posesiones españolas de América y Oceanía, vol. 39 (Madrid: Bernaldo de Quirós, 1883)

Columbus 1990
Columbus, Christopher, *Primer viaje de Cristóbal Colón*, 2nd edn. (Madrid: Naval, 1990)

Cook 1982
Cook, David Noble, *Demographic Collapse: Indian Peru, 1520–1620* (Cambridge: Cambridge University Press, 1982)

Cook 1998
Cook, David Noble, *Born To Die: Disease and New World Conquest, 1492–1650* (Cambridge: Cambridge University Press, 1998)

Cornejo Polar 2013
Cornejo Polar, Antonio, *Writing in the Air: Heterogeneity and the Persistence of Oral Tradition in Andean Literatures*, trans. Lynda J. Jentsch (Durham, NC: Duke University Press, 2013)

Cortés 1993
Cortés, Hernán, *Cartas de relación*, ed. Ángel Delgado Gómez (Barcelona: Clásicos Castalia, 1993)

Covarrubias Orozco 1611
Covarrubias Orozco, Sebastian de, *Tesoro de la lengua castellana o española* (Madrid: Luis Sánchez, 1611)

Covey 2006
Covey, Alan, "Chronology, Succession, and Sovereignty: The Politics of Inka Historiography and Its Modern Interpretation," *Comparative Studies in Society and History*, vol. 48 (2006), pp. 169–99

Cummins 1996
Cummins, Thomas, "A Tale of Two Cities: Cuzco, Lima, and the Construction of Colonial Representation," in Diana Fane (ed.), *Converging Cultures: Art and Identity in Spanish America* (New York: Brooklyn Museum, 1996), pp. 157–70

Cummins 2002
Cummins, Thomas, *Toasts with the Inca* (Ann Arbor: University of Michigan Press, 2002)

Cummins 2011
Cummins, Thomas, "The Indulgent Image: Prints in the-New World," in Katzew 2011, pp. 203–25

Cuneo 1998
Cuneo, Pia F., *Art and Politics in Early Modern Germany:*

Jörg Breu the Elder and the Fashioning of Political Identity ca. 1475–1536 (Leiden: Brill, 1998)

Davies 2003
Davies, Surekha, "The Navigational Iconography of Diogo Ribeiro's 1529 Vatican Planisphere," *Imago Mundi*, vol. 55 (2003), pp. 103–12

Dean 1998
Dean, Carolyn, "Creating a Ruin in Colonial Cusco: Sacsahuamán and What Was Made of It," *Andean Past*, vol. 5 (1998), pp. 161–83

Dean 2001
Dean, Carolyn, "Andean Androgyny and the Making of Men," in Cecelia Klein (ed.), *Gender in Pre-Hispanic America* (Washington, DC: Dumbarton Oaks Research Library and Collection, 2001), pp. 143–82

Dean 2010
Dean, Carolyn, *A Culture of Stone: Inca Perspectives on Rock* (Durham, NC: Duke University Press, 2010)

Dean 2011
Dean, Carolyn, "Inca Ruins and the Discourse of Mystery," *Third Text*, vol. 25, no. 6 (2011), pp. 737–49

De Certeau 1984
De Certeau, Michel, *The Practice of Everyday Life*, trans. Steven F. Rendall (Berkeley: University of California Press, 1984)

Decoster 2001
Decoster, Jean-Jacques, *Ylustre consejo, justicia y regimiento: Catálogo del fondo Cabildo del Cuzco (causas civiles)* (Cuzco: Centro de Estudios Regionales Andinos "Bartolomé de las Casas," 2001)

Del Busto Duthurburu 2000
Del Busto Duthurburu, José Antonio, *Pizarro*, 2 vols. (Lima: Ediciones Copé, 2000)

DeMarrais et al. 2004
DeMarrais, Elizabeth, Chris Gosden, and Colin Renfrew (eds), *Rethinking Materiality: The Engagement of Mind with the Material World* (Cambridge: McDonald Institute for Archaeological Research, 2004)

Díaz Gito 2013
Díaz Gito, Manuel Antonio, "El recibimiento de Vaca de Castro como Gobernador del Perú en El Cuzco (1542) en la *Vaccaeis* de Calvete de Estrella," *Minerva*, vol. 26 (2013), pp. 181–204

"Discurso sobre la descendencia" 1543–1608
"Discurso sobre la descendencia y gobierno de los Ingas," Biblioteca Nacional de España, ms. 2010 (1543–1608), fols. 122–45

"Documentos relativos a la villa de Bruselas" 1937
"Documentos relativos a la villa de Bruselas y al descubrimiento del golfo de Nicoya," *Revista del Archivo Nacional de Costa Rica*, vol. 1 (1937), pp. 228–31

Domínguez Compañy 1981
Domínguez Compañy, Francisco, *Estudios sobre las instituciones locales hispanoamericanas* (Caracas: Academia Nacional de la Historia, 1981)

Domínguez Compañy 1984
Domínguez Compañy, Francisco, *Política de poblamiento de España en América* (Madrid: Instituto de Estudios de Administración Local, 1984)

Domínguez Faura 1994
Domínguez Faura, Nicanor José, "El cronista Betanzos y las primeras cartillas de evangelización en le lengua general del Ynga," in Gabriela Ramos (ed.), *La venida del reinado* (Cuzco: Centro Bartolomé de las Casas, 1994), pp. 65–74

Domínguez Faura 1998
Domínguez Faura, Nicanor José, "Dos breves notas sobre el cronista Juan Diez de Betanzos," *Revista Andina*, vol. 16 (1998), pp. 211–24

Domínguez Faura 2008
Domínguez Faura, Nicanor José, "Betanzos y los Quipucamayos en la época de Vaca de Castro (Cuzco, 1543)," *Revista Andina*, vol. 46 (2008), pp. 155–92

Domínguez Faura 2015a
Domínguez Faura, Nicanor José, "Juan Diez de Betanzos (1519–76): Vida del author de la *Suma y narración de los Incas* (1551)," in Hernández Astete and Cerrón-Palomino 2015, pp. 13–27

Domínguez Faura 2015b
Domínguez Faura, Nicanor José, "Manuscritos y ediciones de la *Suma y narración de los Incas*," in Hernández Astete and Cerrón-Palomino 2015, pp. 99–105

Domínguez García 2008
Domínguez García, Javier, *De apóstol matamoros a yllapa mataindios: dogmas e ideologías medievales en el (des)cubrimiento de América* (Salamanca: Ediciones Universidad de Salamanca, 2008)

Domínguez Guzmán 1975
Domínguez Guzmán, Aurora, *El libro sevillano durante la primera mitad del siglo XVI* (Seville: Excma. Diputación Provincial de Sevilla, 1975)

Domínguez Torres 2011
Domínguez Torres, Mónica, "Emblazoning Identity: Indigenous Heraldry in Colonial Mexico and Peru," in Katzew 2011, pp. 97–115

Dunbar Temple 1940
Dunbar Temple, Ella, "La descendencia de Huayna Capac: Conclusión del capitulo 'Paullu Inca,'" *Revista Histórica*, vol. 13 (1940), pp. 31–77

Durston 2007
Durston, Alan, *Pastoral Quechua* (Notre Dame, IN: University of Notre Dame Press, 2007)

Duviols 1976
Duviols, Pierre, "'Punchao': Idolo mayor del Coricancha; Historia y tipología," *Antropología Andina*, vols 1–2 (1976), pp. 156–83

Escobar 2003
Escobar, Jesús, *The Plaza Mayor and the Shaping of Baroque Madrid* (Cambridge: Cambridge University Press, 2003)

Escobar 2013
Escobar, Jesús, "City," in Levy and Mills 2013, pp. 61–68

Escobar Medrano et al. 1999
Escobar Medrano, Jorge, Américo Carrillo Rosell, and Liliana Saldivar Antúnez de Mayolo, *Renacimiento de la Iglesia del Triunfo* (Cuzco: Arzobispado del Cusco, 1999)

Esgueva Gómez 2007
Esgueva Gómez, Antonio, *Las fronteras de Nicaragua y Costa Rica en los documentos históricos* (Managua: Instituto de Historia de Nicaragua y Centroamerica, 2007)

Espinosa Apolo 2002–3a
Espinosa Apolo, Manuel (ed.), *La ciudad inca de Quito* (Quito: Tramasocial Editorial, 2002–3)

Espinosa Apolo 2002–3b
Espinosa Apolo, Manuel, "Templos y otros adoratorios," in Espinosa Apolo 2002–3a, pp. 61–95

Estenssoro 2010
Estenssoro, Juan Carlos, "Autorretrato del conquistador como vencido o la invención del Perú: La aparición del Inca y de sus atributos políticos en las representaciones plásticas, 1526–1548," *Colonial Latin American Review*, vol. 19 (2010), pp. 151–205

Estrada Ibérico et al. 2009
Estrada Ibérico, Enrique, Luis Nieto Degregori, and Yisela Ochoa Lind, "De la cancha incaica a la casa colonial: Apuntes para un estudio de la evolución de la casa cuzqueña," in Nieto Degregori 2009, pp. 49–72

Farrington 2010
Farrington, Ian, "The Houses and Fortress of Waskar: Archaeological Perspectives on a Forgotten Building Complex in Inka Cusco," *Journal of Iberian and Latin American Research*, vol. 16 (2010), pp. 87–99

Farrington 2013
Farrington, Ian, *Cusco: Urbanism and Archaeology in the Inka World* (Gainesville: University Press of Florida, 2013)

Fernández 2016
Fernández, Cristián, "Inca Garcilaso's Biography," in Sara Castro-Klarén and Christian Fernández (eds), *Inca Garcilaso and Contemporary World-Making* (Pittsburgh, PA: University of Pittsburgh Press, 2016), pp. 20–32

Fernández Martín 1991
Fernández Martín, Luis, *Hernando Pizarro en el Castillo de la Mota* (Valladolid: Junta de Castilla y León, 1991)

Ferrer González 1980
Ferrer González, José María, "Rollos y picotas en la provincial de Guadalajara," *Wad-al-Hayara, Revista de Estudios de Guadalajara*, vol. 7 (1980), pp. 103–40

Flickema 1981
Flickema, Thomas, "The Siege of Cuzco," *Revista de Historia de América*, vol. 92 (1981), pp. 17–47

Fraser 1990
Fraser, Valerie, *The Architecture of Conquest: Building in the Viceroyalty of Peru 1535–1635* (Cambridge: Cambridge University Press, 1990)

Fraser 1992
Fraser, Valerie, "Architecture and Ambition: The Case of the Jesuits in the Viceroyalty of Peru," *History Workshop*, vol. 34 (1992), pp. 16–32

Fuerst 2018
Fuerst, James W., *New World Postcolonial: The Political Thought of Inca Garcilaso de la Vega* (Pittsburgh, PA: University of Pittsburgh Press, 2018)

Galera Mendoza 2013
Galera Mendoza, Esther, *Estructura urbana y organización productiva en la Alhambra durante el Antiguo Régimen* (Granada: Editorial Universidad de Granada, 2013)

Garcilaso de la Vega 1609
Garcilaso de la Vega, *Primera parte de los comentarios reales* (Lisbon: Pedro Crasbeeck, 1609)

Garcilaso de la Vega 1617
Garcilaso de la Vega, *Historia general del Perú* (Córdoba: Viuda de Andrés Barrera, 1617)

Gasparini and Margolies 1980
Gasparini, Graziano, and Luise Margolies, *Inca Architecture* (Bloomington: Indiana University Press, 1980)

Gell 1998
Gell, Alfred, *Art and Agency: An Anthropological Theory* (New York: Oxford University Press, 1998)

Gibson 1966
Gibson, Charles, *Spain in America* (New York: Harper & Row, 1966)

Glick 1995
Glick, Thomas F., *From Muslim Fortress to Christian Castle: Social and Cultural Change in Medieval Spain* (Manchester: Manchester University Press, 1995)

González Blanco 1984
González Blanco, Antonio, *Horcas y picotas en La Rioja* (Barcelona: Jaimes Libros, 1984)

González Carré et al. 1996
González Carré, Enrique, Jorge Cosmópolis, and Jorge Lévano Peña, *La ciudad inca de Vilcashuamán* (Ayacucho: Universidad Nacional de San Cristóbal de Huamanga, 1996)

González Holguín 1608
González Holguín, Diego, *Vocabulario de la lengua general de todo el Perú llamada lengua Quichua o del Inca* (Lima: Francisco del Canto, 1608)

González Montero 2016
González Montero, Marino, *Rollos y picotas de Extremadura* (Mérida: Editorial De la Luna, 2016)

González Ochoa 2011
González Ochoa, José María, *Cronistas de Indias riojanos* (Logroño: Instituto de Estudios Riojanos, 2011)

Graubart 2000
Graubart, Karen B., "Indecent Living: Indigenous Women and the Politics of Representation in Early Colonial Peru," *Colonial Latin American Review*, vol. 9 (2000), pp. 213–35

Greenblatt 1991
Greenblatt, Stephen, *Marvelous Possessions* (Chicago: University of Chicago Press, 1991)

Greenwich Centeno 2008
Greenwich Centeno, Edwin Raul, *Francisco Pizarro, de Trujillo de Extremadura a la Ciudad de los Reyes* (Lima: Universidad Alas Peruanas, 2008)

Guillamón Alvarez 1991
Guillamón Alvarez, Francisco Javier, "Algunos reflexiones sobre el cabildo colonial como institución," *Anales de Historia Contemporánea*, vol. 8 (1991), pp. 151–61

Hamilton 2018
Hamilton, Andrew J., *Scale and the Incas* (Princeton, NJ: Princeton University Press, 2018)

Hemming 1970
Hemming, John, *The Conquest of the Incas* (New York: Harcourt Brace Jovanovich, 1970)

Hernández Astete and Cerrón-Palomino 2015
Hernández Astete, Francisco, and Rodolfo Cerrón-Palomino (eds), *Juan de Betanzos y el Tahuantinsuyo* (Lima: Pontifícia Universidad Católica del Perú, 2015)

Herring 2015
Herring, Adam, *Art and Vision in the Inca Empire* (Cambridge: Cambridge University Press, 2015)

Himmerich and Valencia 1998
Himmerich y Valencia, Robert, "The 1536 Siege of Cuzco: An Analysis of Inca and Spanish Warfare," *Colonial Latin American Historical Review*, vol. 7 (1998), pp. 387–418

Hocquenghem 1998
Hocquenghem, Anne-Marie, *Para vencer la muerte* (Lima: INCAH, 1998)

Hoopes 2011
Hoopes, John W., "Conquest, Imagination, and the Dawn of the Modern Age," in Carol Haralson (ed.), *To Capture the Sun* (Tulsa: Gilcrease Museum, 2011), pp. 10–43

Horodowich 2005
Horodowich, Liz, "Armchair Travelers and the Venetian Discovery of the New World," *Sixteenth Century Journal*, vol. 36 (2005), pp. 1039–62

Hyslop 1984
Hyslop, John, *The Inka Road System* (Orlando, FL: Academic Press, 1984)

Hyslop 1990
Hyslop, John, *Inca Settlement Planning* (Austin: University of Texas Press, 1990)

Janer 1857
Janer, Florencio, *Condición social de los moriscos de España* (Madrid: Real Academia de la Historia, 1857)

Janusek 2005
Janusek, John W., "Patios hundidos, encuentros rituales, y el auge de Tiwanaku como centro religioso panregional," *Boletín de Arqueología PUCP*, vol. 9 (2005), pp. 161–84

Julien 1999
Julien, Catherine, "History and Art in Translation: The Paños and Other Objects Collected by Francisco de Toledo," *Colonial Latin American Review*, vol. 8 (1999), pp. 61–89

Julien 2000
Julien, Catherine, *Reading Inca History* (Iowa City: University of Iowa Press, 2000)

Julien 2004
Julien, Catherine, "Las tumbas de Sacsahuaman y el estilo Cuzco-Inca," *Ñawpa Pacha*, vols 25–27 (2004), pp. 1–125

Julien 2006a
Julien, Catherine, "An Inca Information Network," *Ñawpa Pacha*, vol. 28 (2006), pp. 41–61

Julien 2006b
Julien, Catherine, "Introduction," in Titu Cusi Yupanqui 2006, pp. vii–xxxv

Julien 2007
Julien, Catherine, "Francisco Toledo and His Campaign against the Incas," *Colonial Latin American Review*, vol. 16 (2007), pp. 243–72

Kagan 2000
Kagan, Richard, *Urban Images of the Hispanic World, 1493–1793* (London and New Haven: Yale University Press, 2000)

Kagan 2013
Kagan, Richard L., "City (Spanish America)," in Levy and Mills 2013, pp. 65–68

Katzew 2011
Katzew, Ilona (ed.), *Contested Visions in the Spanish Colonial World* (Los Angeles: Los Angeles County Museum, 2011)

Kavey 2010
Kavey, Allison B. (ed.), *World-Building and the Early Modern Imagination* (New York: Palgrave Macmillan, 2010)

Kubler 1948
Kubler, George, *Mexican Architecture of the Sixteenth Century*, 2 vols. (New Haven: Yale University Press, 1948)

Kubler 1952
Kubler, George, *Cuzco: Reconstruction of the Town and Restoration of Its Monuments* (Paris: UNESCO, 1952)

Kunny 2016
Kunny, Clare, "In His Own Image: A Humanist Portrait of Antonio de Mendoza, First Viceroy of New Spain," in Donna Pierce (ed.), *New England/New Spain: Portraiture in the Colonial Americas, 1492–1850* (Denver: Denver Art Museum, 2016), pp. 25–36

Kusunoki 2016
Kusunoki, Ricardo, "Esplendor y ocaso de los maestros cuzqueños (1700–1850)," in Ricardo Kusunoki and Luis Edwardo Wuffarden (eds), *Pintura cuzqueña* (Lima: Asociación Museo de Arte de Lima, 2016), pp. 39–57

Lamana 2008
Lamana, Gonzalo, *Domination Without Dominance: Inca–Spanish Encounters in Early Colonial Peru* (Durham, NC: Duke University Press, 2008)

Lampérez y Romea 1922
Lampérez y Romea, Vicente, *Arquitectura civil española de los siglos I al XVIII* (Madrid: Saturnino Calleja, 1922)

Lefebvre 1991
Lefebvre, Henri, *The Production of Space*, trans. Donald Nicholson-Smith (Oxford: Blackwell, 1991)

Leitch 2010
Leitch, Stephanie, *Mapping Ethnography in Early Modern Germany: New Worlds in Print Culture* (Basingstoke and New York: Palgrave Macmillan, 2010)

Levy and Mills 2013
Levy, Evonne, and Kenneth Mills (eds), *Lexikon of the Hispanic Baroque: Transatlantic Exchange and Transformation* (Austin: University of Texas Press, 2013)

Leyes y ordenanças 1543
Leyes y ordenanças nuevamente hechas por Su Magestad (Alcalá de Henares: Casa de Joan de Brocar, 1543)

Lockhart 1972
Lockhart, James, *The Men of Cajamarca: A Social and Biographical Study of the First Conquerors of Peru* (Austin: University of Texas Press, 1972)

Lockhart 1994
Lockhart, James, *Spanish Peru, 1532–1560: A Social History*, 2nd edn. (Madison: University of Wisconsin Press, 1994)

Low 2000
Low, Setha, *On the Plaza: The Politics of Public Space and Culture* (Austin: University of Texas Press, 2000)

Lunenfeld 1987
Lunenfeld, Marvin, *Keepers of the City: The* Corregidores *of Isabella I of Castile, 1474–1504* (Cambridge: Cambridge University Press, 1987)

Lüthy et al. 2018
Lüthy, Christoph, Claudia Swann, Paul Bakker, and Claus Zittel (eds), *Image, Imagination, and Cognition: Medieval and Early Modern Theory and Practice* (Leiden: Brill, 2018)

MacCormack 1989
MacCormack, Sabine, "Atahualpa and the Book," *Dispositio*, vol. 14 (1989), pp. 141–68

MacCormack 1991
MacCormack, Sabine, *Religion in the Andes: Vision and Imagination in Early Colonial Peru* (Princeton, NJ: Princeton University Press, 1991)

MacCormack 2004
MacCormack, Sabine, "¿Inca o Español? Las identidades de Paullu Topa Inca," *Boletín de Arqueología PUCP*, vol. 8 (2004), pp. 99–109

MacCormack 2006
MacCormack, Sabine, *On the Wings of Time: Rome, the Incas, Spain, and Peru* (Princeton, NJ: Princeton University Press, 2006)

Malpica Cuello 1999
Malpica Cuello, Antonio, "La Alhambra de los Reyes Católicos: Nuevos materiales para su estudio," *Aragón en la Edad Media*, vol. 14 (1999), pp. 955–76

Mannheim 2008
Mannheim, Bruce, "Diez de Betanzos, Juan (?–1576)," in Pillsbury 2008, vol. 2, pp. 186–90

Manzo 2014
Manzo, Ángel Amilcar Alberto, *En busca de una epopeya: Relación del sitio del Cuzco* (La Plata: Editorial Yáhuar, 2014)

Mar and Beltrán-Caballero 2014
Mar, Ricardo, and J. Alejandro Beltrán-Caballero, "El conjunto arqueológico de Saqsaywaman (Cusco): Una aproximación a su arquitectura," *Revista Española de Antropología Americana*, vol. 44 (2014), pp. 9–38

Mar and Beltrán-Caballero 2015
Mar, Ricardo, and José Alejandro Beltrán-Caballero, "Inka City Planning in Cuzco," in Matos Mendieta and Marreiro 2015, pp. 25–33

Martín Rubio 1999
Martín Rubio, María del Carmen, "Juan de Betanzos: El gran cronista del Imperio Inca," *Anales del Museo de América*, vol. 7 (1999), pp. 111–24

Martyr d'Anghiera 1516
Martyr d'Anghiera, Peter, *De orbe novo* (Alcalá de Henares: Arnaldi Guillelmi, 1516)

Matos Mendieta and Barreiro 2015
Matos Mendieta, Ramiro, and José Barreiro (eds), *The Great Inka Road: Engineering and Empire* (Washington, DC: National Museum of the American Indian, 2015)

Mazzotti 2008
Mazzotti, José Antonio, *Incan Insights: El Inca Garcilaso's Hints to Andean Readers* (Madrid: Iberoamericana, 2008)

Meddens 2015
Meddens, Frank M., "The Importance of Being Inka: Ushnu Platforms and Their Place in the Andean Landscape," in Bray 2015, pp. 239–63

Meddens et al. 2010
Meddens, Frank M., Colin McEwan, and Cirilo Vivanco Pomacanchari, "Inca 'Stone Ancestors' in Context at a High Altitude Ushnu Platform," *Latin American Antiquity*, vol. 21 (2010), pp. 173–94

Mena 1534
Mena, Cristóbal de, *La conquista del Perú* (Seville: Bartolomé Pérez, 1534)

Mesa and Gisbert 1982
Mesa, José de, and Teresa Gisbert, *Historia de la pintura cuzqueña* (Lima: Fundación Augusto N. Wiese, 1982)

Meseth et al. 2015
Meseth, Enrique, Liang-Chi Wang, Su-Hwa Chen, Jason C. S. Yu, and Michael Buzinny, "Reconstructing Agriculture in Vitcos Inca Settlement, Peru," *Irrigation and Drainage*, vol. 64 (2015), pp. 340–52

Mignolo 1982
Mignolo, Walter, "Cartas, crónicas y relaciones del descubrimiento y de la conquista," in Luis Iñigo Madrigal (ed.), *Historia de la literature hispanoamericana, época colonial*, vol. 1 (Madrid: Cátedra, 1982), pp. 57–116

Mignolo 2003
Mignolo, Walter, *The Darker Side of the Renaissance*, 2nd edn. (Ann Arbor: University of Michigan Press, 2003)

Miró Quesada 1971
Miró Quesada, Aurelio, *El Inca Garcilaso y otros estudios garcilasistas* (Madrid: Ediciones de Cultura Hispánica, 1971)

Molina 1571
Molina, Alonso de, *Vocabulario en lengua castellana y mexicana* (Mexico City: Antonio de Spinosa, 1571)

Montoto de Sedas 1928
Montoto de Sedas, Santiago, *Nobiliario de reinos, ciudades, y villas de la América Española* (Madrid: Compañía Iberoamericana de Publicaciones, 1928)

Moore 1954
Moore, John Preston, *The Cabildo in Peru under the Hapsburgs* (Durham, NC: Duke University Press, 1954)

Morales Padrón 1955
Morales Padrón, Francisco, "Descubrimiento y toma de posesión," *Anuario de Estudios Americanos*, vol. 12 (1955), pp. 321–81

Mundy 2015
Mundy, Barbara, *The Death of Aztec Tenochtitlan, The Life of Mexico City* (Austin: University of Texas Press, 2015)

Murra 1982
Murra, John V., "The *mit'a* Obligations of Ethnic Groups to the Inka State," in George A. Collier et al. (eds), *The Inca and Aztec States, 1400–1800: Anthropology and History* (New York: Academic Press, 1982), pp. 237–62

Nair 2007
Nair, Stella, "Witnessing the Invisibility of Inca Architecture in Colonial Peru," *Buildings and Landscapes*, vol. 14 (2007), pp. 50–65

Nair 2015
Nair, Stella, *At Home with the Sapa Inca: Architecture, Space, and Legacy at Chinchero* (Austin: University of Texas Press, 2015)

Nair and Protzen 2015
Nair, Stella, and Jean-Pierre Protzen, "The Inka Built Environment," in Shimada 2015, pp. 215–31

Nieto Degregori 2009
Nieto Degregori, Luis (ed.), *El ombligo se pone piercing: identidad, patrimonio y cambios en el Cuzco* (Cuzco: Centro Guaman Poma de Ayala, 2009)

Niles 1999
Niles, Susan, *The Shape of Inca History: Narrative and Architecture in an Andean Empire* (Iowa City: University of Iowa Press, 1999)

Nolasco Pérez 1924
Nolasco Pérez, Pedro, *Religiosos de la Merced que pasaron a la América Española (1514–1777)* (Seville: Tip. Zarzuela, 1924)

Nora 2001–10
Nora, Pierre, *Rethinking France: Les Lieux de mémoire*, 4 vols. (Chicago: University of Chicago Press, 2001–10)

Ochsendorf 1996
Ochsendorf, John, "An Engineering Study of the Last Inca Suspension Bridge," in *Proceedings of the 13th Annual International Bridge Conference* (Pittsburgh: Engineers' Society of Western Pennsylvania, 1996), pp. 398–404

Ochsendorf 2004
Ochsendorf, John, "Sustainable Structural Design: Lessons from History," *Structural Engineering International*, vol. 14 (2004), pp. 192–94

Ochsendorf 2015
Ochsendorf, John, "Spanning the Andes: History and Technology of Inka Suspension Bridges," in Barreiro and Matos Mendieta 2015, pp. 51–60

Ogburn 2013
Ogburn, Dennis, "Variations in Inca Building: Stone Quarry Operations in Peru and Ecuador," in Nicholas Tripcevich and Kevin J. Vaughn (eds), *Mining and Quarrying in the Ancient Andes* (New York: Springer, 2013), pp. 45–64

Palm 1955
Palm, Erwin Walter, *Los monumentos arquitectónicos de la Española*, 2 vols. (Ciudad Trujillo: Universidad de Santo Domingo, 1955)

Paredes García 2001
Paredes García, Mónica, *El Cusco incaico: Análisis e interpretación de un registro de restos prehispánicos* (Lima: Ediciones El Santo Oficio Gráficos, 2001)

Paredes García 2009
Paredes García, Mónica, "La exploración arqueológica como herramienta para el estudio de la casona colonial cuzqueña," in Nieto Degregori 2009, pp. 73–94

Pease 1973
Pease, Franklin, *El diós creador andino* (Lima: Mosca Azul Editores, 1973)

Pease 2008a
Pease, Franklin, "Chronicles of the Andes in the Sixteenth and Seventeenth Centuries," in Pillsbury 2008, vol. 1, pp. 11–22

Pease 2008b
Pease, Franklin, "Cieza de León, Pedro de (ca. 1518–1554)," in Pillsbury 2008, vol. 2, pp. 143–51

Pease 2008c
Pease, Franklin, "Mena, Cristóbal de (Sixteenth Century)," in Pillsbury 2008, vol. 3, pp. 407–9

Pease 2008d
Pease, Franklin, "Sancho, Pedro (1514?–1547)," in Pillsbury 2008, vol. 3, pp. 630–32

Pease 2008e
Pease, Franklin, "Xerez, Francisco de (1497–?)," in Pillsbury 2008, vol. 3, pp. 752–56

Pérez Arteta 2017
Pérez Arteta, Juan Fernando, *Quito en el tiempo: Quito mítico, Quito Cara, Quito Inca, Quito hispano, Quito republicano* (Quito: Trama Ediciones, 2017)

Pérez de Oliva n.d.
Pérez de Oliva, Fernán, "Historia de la invención de las Yndias" (n.d.), Yale University, Beinecke Rare Book and Manuscript Library, ms. 128

Pérez de Tudela y Bueso 1963
Pérez de Tudela y Bueso, Juan, "Observaciones generales sobre las guerras civiles del Perú," in Juan Pérez de Tudela y Bueso (ed.), *Crónicas del Perú*, vol. 164 (Madrid: Ediciones Atlas, 1963), pp. ix–cxxi

Perocco 1997
Perocco, Daria, *Viaggiare e raccontare: Narrazione di viaggio ed esperienze di racconto tra Cinque e Seicento* (Turin: Edizioni dell'Orso, 1997)

Phipps 2004
Phipps, Elena, "Garments and Identity in the Colonial Andes," in Phipps et al. 2004, pp. 17–39

Phipps 2015
Phipps, Elena, "Cusi Rimay Ocllo: Les Femmes de la noblesse inca à l'epreuve de la conquête," in Paz Núñez-Regueiro (ed.), *L'Inca et le conquistador* (Paris: Actes Sud, 2015), pp. 179–88

Phipps et al. 2004
Phipps, Elena, Johanna Hecht, and Cristina Esteras Martín (eds), *The Colonial Andes: Tapestries and Silverwork, 1530–1830* (New York: Metropolitan Museum of Art, 2004)

Pillsbury 2002
Pillsbury, Joanne, "Inka *unku*: Strategy and Design in Colonial Peru," *Cleveland Studies in the History of Art*, vol. 7 (2002), pp. 68–103

Pillsbury 2008
Pillsbury, Joanne (ed.), *Guide to Documentary Sources for Andean Studies, 1530–1900*, 3 vols. (Norman: University of Oklahoma Press, 2008)

Pino Matos 2015
Pino Matos, José Luis, "The Inka Road to the Chinchaysuyu," in Matos Mendieta and Barreiro 2015, pp. 75–83

Pizarro 1986
Pizarro, Pedro, *Relación del descubrimiento y conquista del Perú*, ed. Guillermo Lohmann Villena (Lima: Pontificia Universidad Católica del Perú, 1986)

Polo 1986
Polo, Marco, *Il milione* (Florence: L. S. Olschki, 1986)

Ponce 2002
Ponce, Ernesto, "Mazas prehispánicas de metal: Sur de Perú y extremo norte de Chile," *Chungará: Revista de Antropología Chilena*, vol. 34 (2002), pp. 215–23

Porras 2002–3
Porras, Pedro I., "Palacios de los soberanos," in Espinosa Apolo 2002–3a, pp. 19–60

Porras Barrenechea 1944
Porras Barrenechea, Raúl, *Cedulario del Perú: siglos XVI, XVII y XVIII*, 2 vols. (Lima: Departamento de Relaciones Culturales del Ministerio de Relaciones Exteriores, 1944)

Porras Barrenechea 1951
Porras Barrenechea, Raúl, "Diego de Silva, cronista de la conquista del Perú," *Mar del Sur*, vol. 5 (1951), pp. 14–33

Porras Barrenechea 1962
Porras Barrenechea, Raúl, *Los cronistas del Perú: 1528–1650* (Lima: Sanmartí Impresores, 1962)

Porras Barrenechea 1986
Porras Barrenechea, Raúl, *Los cronistas del Perú (1528–1650) y otros ensayos* (Lima: Banco de Crédito del Perú, 1986)

Portuondo 2009
Portuondo, María M., *Secret Science: Spanish Cosmography and the New World* (Chicago: University of Chicago Press, 2009)

Protzen 1983
Protzen, Jean-Pierre, "Inca Quarrying and Stonecutting," *Ñawpa Pacha*, vol. 21 (1983), pp. 183–214

Protzen 1993
Protzen, Jean-Pierre, *Inca Architecture and Construction at Ollantaytambo* (New York: Oxford University Press, 1993)

Protzen and Nair 2013
Protzen, Jean-Pierre, and Stella Nair, *The Stones of Tiahuanaco: A Study of Architecture and Construction* (Los Angeles: Cotsen Institute of Archaeology Press, 2013)

Puente Brunke 1992
Puente Brunke, José de la, *Encomienda y encomenderos en el Perú* (Seville: Publicaciones de la Excma. Diputación Provincial de Sevilla, 1992)

"Quake in Cuzco" 1950
"Quake in Cuzco," *Life*, June 12, 1950, p. 40

Quispe-Agnoli 2016
Quispe-Agnoli, Rocío, "Mulieres Litterarum: Oral, Visual, and Written Narratives of Indigenous Elite Women," in Ileana Rodríguez and Mónica Szurmuk (eds), *The Cambridge History of Latin American Women's Literature* (Cambridge: Cambridge University Press, 2016), pp. 38–51

Rama 1996
Rama, Ángel, *The Lettered City*, trans. John Charles Chasteen (Durham, NC: Duke University Press, 1996)

Ramírez 1996
Ramírez, Susan, *The World Upside Down: Cross-Cultural Contact and Conflict in Sixteenth-Century Peru* (Stanford, CA: Stanford University Press, 1996)

Ramírez 2005
Ramírez, Susan, *To Feed and Be Fed: The Cosmological Bases of Authority and Identity in the Andes* (Stanford, CA: Stanford University Press, 2005)

Ramos Gómez 2004
Ramos Gómez, Luis, "El motivo 'torre' en el escudo de Cuzco y en los queros y otras vasijas andinas de madera de época colonial, del Museo de América," *Revista Española de Antropología Americana*, vol. 34 (2004), pp. 163–86

Ramusio 1556
Ramusio, Giovanni Battista, *Terzo volume delle navigationi et viaggi* (Venice: Giunti, 1556)

Rappaport and Cummins 2011
Rappaport, Joanne, and Thomas Cummins, *Beyond the Lettered City: Indigenous Literacies in the Andes* (Duham, NC: Duke University Press, 2011)

Regalado de Hurtado 2008
Regalado de Hurtado, Liliana, "Titu Cusi Yupanqui, Diego de Castro (ca. 1535–1571)," in Pillsbury 2008, vol. 3, pp. 662–64

Reinhard and Ceruti 2010
Reinhard, Johan, and María Constanza Ceruti, *Inca Rituals and Sacred Mountains: A Study of the World's Highest Archaeological Sites* (Los Angeles: Cotsen Institute of Archaeology Press, 2010)

"Relación de las cosas" 1548
"Relación de las cosas acaecidas en las alteraciones del Perú después que Blasco Núñez Vela entró en él" (1548), Biblioteca del Palacio Real de Madrid, ms. II/1960 bis., doc. 1

Reynolds 2000
Reynolds, Catherine, "The Function and Display of Netherlandish Cloth Paintings," in Caroline Villers (ed.), *The Fabric of Images* (London: Archetype Publications, 2000), pp. 89–98

Rivera Serna 1965
Rivera Serna, Raúl (ed.), *Libro primero de cabildos de la ciudad del Cuzco* (Lima: Universidad Nacional Mayor de San Marcos, 1965)

Rosenthal 1985
Rosenthal, Earl, *The Palace of Charles V in Granada* (Princeton, NJ: Princeton University Press, 1985)

Rostworowski 1989
Rostworowski de Diez Canseco, María, *Doña Francisca Pizarro: Una ilustre mestiza, 1534–1598* (Lima: Instituto de Estudios Peruanos, 1989)

Rostworowski 1999
Rostworowski de Diez Canseco, María, *History of the Inca Realm*, trans. Harry B. Iceland (Cambridge: Cambridge University Press, 1999)

Rowe 1945
Rowe, John H., "Absolute Chronology in the Andean Area," *American Antiquity*, vol. 10 (1945), pp. 265–84

Rowe 1967
Rowe, John H., "What Kind of Settlement Was Inca Cuzco?" *Ñawpa Pacha*, vol. 5 (1967), pp. 59–76

Rowe and Rowe 1996
Rowe, Ann Pollard, and John H. Rowe, "Inca Tunics," in Elizabeth Hill Boone (ed.), *Andean Art at Dumbarton Oaks*, vol. 2 (Washington, DC: Dumbarton Oaks Research Library and Collection, 1996), pp. 453–65

Ruiz de Arce 2002
Ruiz de Arce, Juan, "Memoria," in Stoll 2002, pp. 57–123

Ruiz Medrano 1991
Ruiz Medrano, Ethelia, *Gobierno y sociedad en Nueva España: segunda audiencia y Antonio de Mendoza* (Zamora: Colegio de Michoacan, 1991)

Ruiz Rivera and Pietschmann 1996
Ruiz Rivera, Julián B., and Horst Pietschmann (eds), *Encomiendas, indios y españoles* (Münster: Asociación de Historiadores Latinoamericanistas Europeos, 1996)

Rykwert 1976
Rykwert, Joseph, *The Idea of a Town: The Anthropology of Urban Form in Rome, Italy, and the Ancient World* (Princeton, NJ: Princeton University Press, 1976)

Sáenz de Santa María 1976
Sáenz de Santa María, Carmelo, "Los manuscritos de Pedro Cieza de León," *Revista de Indias*, vol. 36 (1976), pp. 181–215

Sáenz de Santa María 1985
Sáenz de Santa María, Carmelo, *Pedro de Cieza de León: Obras completas*, vol. 3 (Madrid: Consejo Superior de Investigaciones Científicas, 1985)

Salomon 1986
Salomon, Frank, *Native Lords of Quito in the Age of the Inca* (Cambridge: Cambridge University Press, 1986)

Salomon 2015
Salomon, Frank, "Inkas through Texts: The Primary Sources," in Shimada 2015, pp. 23–38

Sancho 1556
Sancho, Pedro, "Relatione per sua maestà," in Giovanni Battista Ramusio (ed.), *Terzo volume delle navigationi et viaggi* (Venice: Giunti, 1556), fols. 398v–414v

Santo Tomás 1560
Santo Tomás, Domingo de, *Vocabulario de la lengua general de los Indios del Perú, llamada Quichua* (Valladolid: Casa de Francisco Fernández de Córdoba, 1560)

Schreffler 2014
Schreffler, Michael J., "Inca Architecture from the Andes to the Adriatic: Pedro Sancho's Description of Cuzco" *Renaissance Quarterly*, vol. 67, no. 4 (2014), pp. 1191–223

Schroedl 2008
Schroedl, Annette, "La capacocha como ritual político: Negociaciones en torno al poder entre Cuzco y los curacas," *Bulletin de l'Institut Français d'Études Andines*, vol. 37, no. 1 (2008), pp. 19–27

Scott 2011
Scott, David A., "The La Tolita-Tumaco Culture: Master Metalsmiths in Gold and Platinum," *Latin American Antiquity*, vol. 22 (2011), pp. 65–95

Seed 1991
Seed, Patricia, "'Failing to Marvel': Atahualpa's Encounter with the Word," *Latin American Research Review*, vol. 26 (1991), pp. 7–32

Seed 1995
Seed, Patricia, *Ceremonies of Possession in Europe's Conquest of the New World, 1492–1640* (Cambridge: Cambridge University Press, 1995)

Serrano y Sanz 1918
Serrano y Sanz, Manuel, *Orígenes de la dominación Española en América* (Madrid: Bailly-Bailliere, 1918)

Shimada 2015
Shimada, Izumi (ed.), *The Inka Empire: A Multidisciplinary Approach* (Austin: University of Texas Press, 2015)

Silva González 2007
Silva González, José Carlos, "Saqsayhuaman, Casa del Sol de los Incas," in *Saqsayhuaman: Estudios fundamentales* (Cuzco: Instituto Nacional de Cultura, 2007), pp. 153–80

Stanfield-Mazzi 2007
Stanfield-Mazzi, Maya, "Shifting Ground: Elite Sponsorship of the Cult of Christ of the Earthquakes in Eighteenth-Century Cusco," *Hispanic Research Journal*, vol. 8 (2007), pp. 445–65

Stanfield-Mazzi 2013
Stanfield-Mazzi, Maya, *Object and Apparition: Envisioning the Christian Divine in the Colonial Andes* (Tucson: University of Arizona Press, 2013)

Stanislawski 1946
Stanislawski, Dan, "The Origin and Spread of the Grid-Pattern Town," *Geographical Review*, vol. 36 (1946), pp. 105–20

Stewart 1988
Stewart, Paul, "The Battle of Las Salinas, Peru, and Its Historians," *Sixteenth Century Journal*, vol. 19 (1988), pp. 407–34

Stielau 2014
Stielau, Allison, "The Weight of Plate in Early Modern Inventories and Secularization Lists," *Journal of Art Historiography*, vol. 11 (2014), pp. 1–29

Stoll 2002
Stoll, Eva, *La memoria de Juan Ruiz de Arce (1543)* (Madrid: Iberoamericana, 2002)

Tena Fernández 1968
Tena Fernández, Juan, *Trujillo histórico y monumental* (Alicante: Gráficas Alicante, 1968)

Terán and Pino 2005
Terán, Marín de, and Inés del Pino, *Algunas reflexiones sobre el Ecuador prehispánico y la ciudad inca del Quito* (Seville: Junta de Andalucía, 2005)

Titu Cusi Yupanqui 1570
Titu Cusi Yupanqui, Diego, "Relacion de como los españoles entraron en el piru," Real Biblioteca del Monasterio de El Escorial L.I.5 (1570), fols. 132r–196v

Titu Cusi Yupanqui 2006
Titu Cusi Yupanqui, Diego, *History of How the Spaniards Arrived in Peru*, trans. Catherine Julien (Indianapolis, IN: Hackett Publishing, 2006)

Topic 2009
Topic, Theresa Lange, "The Meaning of Monuments at Marcahuamachuco," in Joyce Marcus and Patrick Ryan Williams (eds), *Andean Civilization: A Tribute to Michael E. Moseley* (Los Angeles: Cotsen Institute of Archaeology Press, 2009), pp. 241–56

Topic and Topic 1993
Topic, John R., and Theresa Lange Topic, "A Summary of the Inca Occupation of Huamachuco," in Michael A. Malpass (ed.), *Provincial Inca: Archaeological and Ethno-historical Assessment of the Impact of the Inca State* (Iowa City: University of Iowa Press, 1993), pp. 17–43.

Tord 1978
Tord, Luis Enrique, "La casa de los cuatro bustos del Cuzco: Identificación de su blasón y altorelieves," *Boletín del Centro de Investigaciones Histórica y Estéticas*, vol. 23 (1978), pp. 9–33

Torres Balbás 1951
Torres Balbás, Leopoldo, "Los reyes católicos en la Alhambra," *Al Andalus*, vol. 16 (1951), pp. 185–205

Toussaint et al. 1938
Toussaint, Manuel, Federico Gómez de Orozco, and Justino Fernández, *Planos de la Ciudad de México* (Mexico City: Universidad Nacional Autónoma de México, 1938)

Urton 1990
Urton, Gary, *The History of a Myth* (Austin: University of Texas Press, 1990)

Urton 2008
Urton, Gary, "Discurso sobre la descendencia y gobierno de los Incas (sixteenth–early seventeenth century)," in Pillsbury 2008, vol. 2, pp. 191–92

Urton 2015
Urton, Gary, "The State of Strings: Khipu Administration in the Inka Empire," in Shimada 2015, pp. 149–64

Vargas Ugarte 1966
Vargas Ugarte, Rúben, *Historia general del Perú*, vol. 1 (Lima: Milla Batres, 1966)

Varón Gabai 2008
Varón Gabai, Rafael, "Pizarro, Pedro (ca. 1513–1587)," in Pillsbury 2008, vol. 3, pp. 524–28

Vas Mingo 1986
Vas Mingo, Milagros, *Las capitulaciones de Indias en el siglo XVI* (Madrid: Instituto de Cooperación Iberoamericana, 1986)

Vega Bolañes 1954
Vega Bolañes, Andrés (ed.), *Documentos para la historia de Nicaragua* (Madrid: Imprenta Viuda de Gala Sáez, 1954)

Vela Cossio et al. 2012
Vela Cossio, F., L. F. Abril Urmente, and A. Garcia Hermida, "Earth Architecture and Construction in the Colonial Archaeological Site of Piura la Vieja, La Matanza (Piura, Peru)," in C. Mileto, F. Vegas, and V. Cristini (eds), *Rammed Earth Conservation* (Boca Raton, FL: CRC Press, 2012), pp. 593–98

Veloz Maggiolo and Ortega 1992
Veloz Maggiolo, Marcio, and Elpidio Ortega, *La fundación de la Villa de Santo Domingo: un estudio arqueo-histórico* (Santo Domingo: Comisión Dominicana Permanente para la Celebración del Quinto Centenario del Descubrimiento y Evangelización de América, 1992)

Verano 1992
Verano, John W., "Prehistoric Disease and Demography in the Andes," in John W. Verano and Douglas H. Ubelaker (eds), *Disease and Demography in the Americas* (Washington, DC: Smithsonian Institution Press, 1992), pp. 15–24

Vicuña Guengerich 2015
Vicuña Guengerich, Sara, "Capac Women and the Politics of Marriage in Early Colonial Peru," *Colonial Latin American Review*, vol. 24 (2015), pp. 147–67

Viforcos Marinas and Paniagua Pérez 1991
Viforcos Marinas, Isabel, and Jesús Paniagua Pérez, *El leonés don Cristóbal Vaca de Castro, gobernador y organizador del Perú* (Madrid: Hullera Vasco-Leonesa, 1991)

Viñuales 2004
Viñuales, Graciela María, *El espacio urbano en el Cusco colonial: uso y organización de las estructuras simbólicas* (Lima: Epígrafe Editores, 2004)

Vitoria 2008
Vitoria, Francisco de, *Reflectio de potestate civili*, ed. Jesús Cordero Pando (Madrid: Consejo Superior de Investigaciones Científicas, 2008)

Vranich and Stanish 2013
Vranich, Alexei, and Charles Stanish (eds), *Visions of Tiwanaku* (Los Angeles: Cotsen Institute of Archaeology Press, 2013)

Wagner 1931
Wagner, Henry R., "The Manuscript Atlases of Battista Agnese," *Papers of the Bibliographical Society of America*, vol. 25 (1931), pp. 1–110

Weckmann 1992
Weckmann, Luis, *The Medieval Heritage of Mexico*, vol. 1, trans. Frances M. López-Morillas (New York: Fordham University Press, 1992)

Wethey 1949
Wethey, Harold, *Colonial Architecture and Sculpture in Peru* (Cambridge, MA: Harvard University Press, 1949)

Wilson 2003
Wilson, Timothy (ed.), *The Battle of Pavia* (Oxford: Ashmolean Museum, 2003)

Wolfthal 1989
Wolfthal, Diane, *The Beginnings of Netherlandish Canvas Painting, 1400–1530* (Cambridge: Cambridge University Press, 1989)

Wuffarden 2005
Wuffarden, Luis Eduardo, "La descendencia real y el 'renacimiento inca' en e virreinato," in *Los Incas, reyes del Perú* (Lima: Banco de Crédito, 2005), pp. 175–251

Wuffarden 2014
Wuffarden, Luis Eduardo, "Origins, 1532–75," in Luisa Elena Alcalá and Jonathan Brown (eds), *Painting in Latin America, 1550–1820: From Conquest to Independence* (London and New Haven: Yale University Press, 2014), pp. 245–73

Xerez 1534
Xerez, Francisco de, *Verdadera relación de la conquista del Peru* (Seville: Casa de Bartolomé Pérez, 1534)

Yates 2001
Yates, Frances A., *The Art of Memory* (Chicago: University of Chicago Press, 2001)

Yaya 2012
Yaya, Isabel, *The Two Faces of Inca History: Dualism in the Narratives and Cosmology of Ancient Cuzco* (Leiden: Brill, 2012)

Young-Sánchez 2004
Young-Sánchez, Margaret, "The Art of Tiwanaku," in *Tiwanaku: Ancestors of the Inca* (Denver, CO: Denver Art Museum, 2004), pp. 24–40

Zavala 1992
Zavala, Silvio, *La encomienda indiana*, 3rd edn. (Mexico City: Editorial Porrúa, 1992)

Zuidema 1964
Zuidema, R. Tom, *The Ceque System of Cuzco: The Social Organization of the Capital of the Inca* (Leiden: Brill, 1964)

Zuidema 1983
Zuidema, R. Tom, "The Lion in the City: Royal Symbols of Transition in Cuzco," *Journal of Latin American Lore*, vol. 9 (1983), pp. 39–100

Zuidema 1989
Zuidema, R. Tom, "El ushnu," in R. Tom Zuidema and M. Burga (eds), *Reyes y guerreros: Ensayos de Cultura Andina* (Lima: Fomciencias, 1989), pp. 402–54

Index

Page numbers in *italics* indicate illustrations. Places are in Peru unless otherwise stated; buildings and locations in Cuzco are indexed under 'Cuzco buildings and locations'

Picture Credits

Album/Alamy Stock Photo: fig. 3.4

Alex Robinson, Getty Images: figs 5.7, 5.12

Andrés García, iStock.com/AndresGarciaM: fig. 6.5

Andrey X, iStock.com/saiko3p: fig. 7.13

Andy Krakovski, iStock.com/Andy Krakovski: fig. 4.3

The Art Institute of Chicago/Art Resource, New York: fig. 1.8

©Ashmolean Museum, University of Oxford: fig. 5.10

©Biblioteca Apostolica Vaticana, Rome: figs 2.4, 2.5

Birger Niss, iStock.com/BirgerNiss: figs 7.5, 7.6

British Museum, London, ©Trustees of the British Museum: fig. 0.8

Cleveland Museum of Art: fig. 1.6

Collection of Carl and Marilynn Thoma: figs 7.8, 8.3

DC Colombia, iStock.com/DC Colombia: fig. 2.7

DHuss, iStock.com/Dhuss: fig. 5.11

Diego Grandi, iStock.com/diegograndi: figs 1.2, 7.14

©Dumbarton Oaks Pre-Columbian Collection, Washington, DC: figs 1.4, 1.15

Eliot Elisofon, Getty Images: fig. 0.1

Field Museum Library, Chicago: fig. 0.3

Fowler Museum at University of California, Los Angeles: fig. 1.7

Fundación Casa de Alba: fig. 5.13

Gannet 77, iStock.com/Gannet77: fig. 3.2

Gary Martin, iStock.com/tirc83: fig. 4.4

Goddard Photography, iStock.com/Goddard Photography: figs 0.5, 4.2

Hayden Yah, iStock.com/haydenyah: fig. 1.1

Heather Tucker: fig. 1.12, maps 1–4

Ifelino, iStock.com/ifelino: fig. 5.5

Ignacio Ruiz Casanellas, iStock.com/Ignacio Ruiz Casanellas: fig. 5.6

J. Millard, iStock.com/jmillard37: fig. 7.12

©Javier Muñoz y Paz Pastor: fig. 7.4

Jesús Escobar: figs 0.7, 1.13, 2.9, 3.3, 3.5, 4.5, 5.1, 5.3, 6.3, 7.15

The John Carter Brown Library at Brown University: figs 2.8, 2.11, 2.12, 6.6

Jordi Busque, Getty Images: fig. 3.1

KarSol, iStock.com/KarSol: fig. 5.9

Kelvin Jay, iStock.com/kelvinjay: fig. 5.4

Mark Tucan, iStock.com/marktucan: fig. 0.4

Metropolitan Museum of Art, New York: figs 1.3, 1.5, 1.10, 1.11, 7.7, 8.2

Ministerio de Cultura y Deporte, Archivo General de Indias, Seville: figs 2.3, 4.8, 6.4, 7.9, 7.10

©Museum Associates/LACMA: fig. 7.3

National Gallery of Art, Washington, DC: fig. 7.2

New York Public Library: figs 2.2, 2.6

Newberry Library, Chicago: figs 6.1, 8.1

Nick Stanzio: fig. 2.1

OG Photo, iStock.com/OGphoto: fig. 1.9

©Patrimonio Nacional: figs 3.6, 4.1

Raúl Montero Quispe: figs 4.6, 4.7, 6.2, 7.11

Scott DuPre Mills: figs 0.2, 0.6, 3.7, 5.8, 7.1

Sisoje, iStock.com/Sisoje: fig. 6.7

T. Bradford, iStock.com/TBradford: fig. 5.2

Werner Forman Archive/Bridgeman Images: fig. 2.10

Werner Forman Archive/Art Resource, New York: fig. 1.14